Working with Computers

SECOND EDITION

THE DRYDEN PRESS

Harcourt Brace College Publishers

Fort Worth   Philadelphia   San Diego   New York   Orlando   Austin
San Antonio   Toronto   Montreal   London   Sydney   Tokyo

Working with Computers

SECOND EDITION

Patrick G. McKeown

University of Georgia

Executive Editor	Richard J. Bonacci
Developmental Editor	Sue A. Lister
Project Editor	Joan Harlan
Production Manager	Marilyn Williams
Art Director	Beverly Baker
Photo Editor	Steve Lunetta
Publisher	Elizabeth Widdicombe
Director of Editorial, Design, and Production	Diane Southworth
Compositor	GTS Graphics
Text Type	10/12 Times Roman
Cover Image	Gregory Arth

Address for Editorial Correspondence
The Dryden Press, 301 Commerce Street, Suite 3700, Fort Worth, TX 76102

Address for Orders
The Dryden Press, 6277 Sea Harbor Drive, Orlando, FL 32887
1-800-782-4479, or 1-800-433-0001 (in Florida)

ISBN: 0-03-098203-0

Library of Congress Catalog Card Number: 93-72076

Many of the products designated in this book are trademarked. Their use has been respected through appropriate capitalization and spelling.

Photo credits appear on page 339, which constitutes a continuation of the copyright page.

Printed in the United States of America

3 4 5 6 7 8 9 0 1 2   048   9 8 7 6 5 4 3 2 1

The Dryden Press
Harcourt Brace College Publishers

v

Working with Computers was created for instructors who want to give their students a brief yet substantive introduction to computers. The second edition continues in this tradition: In two parts, it combines materials from two highly effective sources—*Living with Computers,* Fourth Edition, and a newly revised edition of *Applications Software Tutorials Using DOS, WordPerfect 5.1, Lotus 1-2-3, dBASE III PLUS, and dBASE IV*—to create a resource that focuses on applications and emphasizes the personal computer.

Part One, "An Introduction to Computers," covers their multitude of uses; the hardware, software, and information systems they comprise; and the effects they have on our society. Part Two, "Software Tutorials," provides hands-on instruction in the use of the most popular commercial software packages for today's most frequently used computer applications. Part One is available by itself in a version entitled *Working with Computers,* Second Edition, or combined with Part Two in a version entitled *Working with Computers with Software Tutorials,* Second Edition.

Part One has two primary objectives. The first is to make students understand that the world today is filled with *smart machines*—that is, machines that are controlled by computers—and that to succeed in this environment people must become computer literate. Important in this discussion is the concept of the computer as a *mind tool* to be used to solve problems and perform work. Once students understand the importance of being able to use computers, the second objective is to help them become knowledgeable and competent computers users. In the process they will learn what the computer *can* and *cannot do* and *how* to use it to solve problems and accomplish tasks.

Part Two provides Tutorials for DOS, WordPerfect 5.1, Lotus 1-2-3 Release 2.3 and 2.4, dBASE III PLUS, and dBASE IV, Version 1.5. Each Tutorial is made up of four or five Sessions, each Session focusing on a particular capability of the package. The exercises both link and illustrate the concepts presented in Part One.

Working with Computers, Second Edition, takes an *integrated approach* in presenting its material. For example, when word processing is discussed in Part One, all elements of the package are integrated for presenting this material. First, screen shots from various word processing packages are shown in Part One to demonstrate word processing concepts. Second, the Tutorials in Part Two cover a similar example. Third, transparency acetates and/or transparency masters of the same figures and software screens are also available. Fourth, the *Instructor's Manual* suggests ways of teaching the concepts and the software and also provides answers to questions and exercises from the word processing portion of both Part One and Part Two of the textbook. In addition, the *Instructor's Manual* contains a supplement by Harvey Kaye that includes numerous student exercises designed not only to enhance students' retention of the material covered in the textbook but to reinforce, at the same time, their basic reading, writing, listening, and speaking skills.

Part One: Introduction to Computers

Part One contains ten chapters, plus an essay on purchasing a personal computer, structured as follows: Chapter 1 provides a brief overview of the uses of computers today, introducing students to different types of computers and essential computer terminology. This is followed by introductory Chapter 2 on computer hardware and Chapter 3 on software. Chapter 4 covers the most important element of systems software—operating systems—in more detail. The preliminary discussion (Chapter 3) of the most important types of software for personal computers is then expanded in Chapters 5–8. These chapters cover the underlying concepts for software packages for word processing and graphics, financial analysis (spreadsheets) and accounting (both business and personal), data base management, and telecommunications and networks, respectively. Finally, Chapters 9 and 10 introduce students to information systems and the human aspects of computer use. An essay on purchasing a personal computer completes Part One.

Highlights of Part One

Integration of the Personal Computer Because of its ever-increasing availability to students, the personal computer must play a significant role in any textbook on computer literacy. Rather than treating the personal computer as a special type of computer to be dealt with in a separate chapter, *Working with Computers,* Second Edition, integrates the personal computer and personal computer software throughout the text. Every chapter discusses aspects of both the mainframe and the personal computer for every topic under consideration. Chapters 5–8 explore the wide variety of applications software available specifically for personal computers.

Boxed Inserts Each chapter of *Working with Computers,* Second Edition, begins with a boxed insert carefully selected to pique the reader's interest in the topic to be covered. The chapters contain numerous other boxed inserts that highlight computer use, showcase selected computer applications, or present views on chapter topics as expressed by leaders in the computer industry. In addition to the boxed inserts, published comments by industry leaders have been excerpted in the text as margin quotations, giving the reader a variety of views on all aspects of the industry.

"Bits of History" Boxes All too often, historical material on computers is combined into a single chapter that students may find less attractive than other sections of the text. To help students enjoy a historical perspective, brief discussions on the history of the chapter topics are presented in special boxed inserts entitled "Bits of History," coming at the ends of those chapters where such discussion is most relevant.

A Guide to Buying a Personal Computer To aid the reader who wants to purchase a personal computer, a special "Guide to Buying a Personal Computer" has been included in *Working with Computers,* Second Edition. The *Guide,* which may be read anytime after the first three chapters, takes a logical approach: Rather than simply reviewing the latest hardware or software, it presents a step-by-step procedure to help the reader assess and meet his or her computer needs now and in the future.

Exciting and Innovative Art Program   Hundreds of full-color photographs and drawings highlight the material discussed. The photographs are pertinent to the text material and as current as possible. Similarly, the drawings demonstrate particular points in the text and are keyed to references therein. Without a doubt, the art program is among the best in the industry and is a tremendous pedagogical asset to the book.

Chapter Components   Each chapter in Part One of *Working with Computers,* Second Edition, begins with a set of Study Objectives and ends with a Review of Key Points. The instructor will find both sections useful in preparing lectures, and the student will find them helpful in preparing for examinations. The Key Terms section is a list of all the new terms introduced in the chapter. (A Glossary at the end of the book defines each of these words and gives their chapter location.) Finally, a set of Review Questions completes each chapter. These questions reflect the major points covered and enable students to assess their mastery of the information in the chapter.

Part Two: Software Tutorials

An innovative key element of the integrated *Working with Computers with Software Tutorials,* Second Edition, package is Part Two, containing software tutorials on DOS, WordPerfect 5.1, Lotus 1-2-3 Releases 2.3 and 2.4, dBASE III PLUS, and dBASE IV, Version 1.5. While Part Two is self-contained in its instructions on using the various packages, it is recommended that students first read the appropriate chapter in Part One, whether on operating systems, word processing, spreadsheets, or data base management, before beginning to work with a specific package.

Each Tutorial on a particular software package is made up of four or five Sessions, with each Session designed to teach a specific capability of the package and requiring about one hour to complete. While the Tutorials may be covered in any order after the Tutorial on DOS, the Sessions within a Tutorial should be covered in the order in which they are presented.

Pedagogical Features

Several pedagogical features in the Tutorials ensure that students will learn while doing: The same examples are used throughout, so that students can make an application build on itself. Also, each Session contains in-depth discussions of the features covered, step-by-step, numbered and cross-referenced keystroke instructions for carrying out an activity with the newly learned commands, "Try It Yourself" Exercises throughout to help the student master the material further, and Exercises at the end of each Session that use the full range of material covered in that Session. By following the Sessions of a Tutorial from their beginning, the student will become proficient in the use of that package.

In addition to the pedagogical features discussed above, there is an Appendix covering functions in Lotus 1-2-3 and a Command Summary at the end of each dBASE III PLUS Session.

Pedagogical Features New to the Second Edition

Part One

- New photos illustrate the most recent software and hardware developments and new uses for computers.
- Updated and new boxed inserts demonstrate some of the many current uses of computers.
- Chapter content revised to include current topics, such as multimedia, hypertext, virtual reality, touchscreens, and new windows applications.
- Networks (LANs) covered in greater detail.

Part Two

- Lotus 1-2-3 updated to address releases 2.3 and 2.4 and WYSIWYG and to include additional exercises.
- dBASE III PLUS updated to include critical set commands and additional exercises.
- dBASE IV expanded from a Session in dBASE III PLUS to a stand-alone Tutorial. The content parallels that of dBASE III PLUS and is compatible with versions 1.5 and higher.

Ancillary Components

The *Working with Computers,* Second Edition, package contains a set of ancillary components, including an *Instructor's Manual* and *Testbook,* which has nearly 1,800 questions, and a package of over 50 full-color *Teaching Transparencies.* Taken in its entirety, this package offers an instructor everything needed to teach a course in computer literacy or introductory information processing or a short course on computer essentials.

Instructor's Manual

For each chapter in the textbook, the *Instructor's Manual,* by Patrick G. McKeown and Ashley McKeown, has a corresponding chapter composed of the following teaching aids: a teaching objective, a set of learning objectives, a chapter outline, an annotated list of boxed inserts, a chapter review with suggested uses of transparencies and transparency masters, a list of teaching suggestions, an annotated list of suggested readings, answers to the review questions at the end of each chapter in the text, and a glossary of the key words for the chapter.

The *Instructor's Manual* contains complete solutions for the software Tutorials. Of particular interest to many instructors will be the suggested readings, which list current, pertinent books and articles that can be very helpful in preparing lectures and developing class projects. The *Instructor's Manual* also includes numerous transparency masters from Parts One and Two. In addition, the *Instructor's Manual* contains a supplement by Harvey Kaye that includes numerous student exercises designed not only to enhance students' retention of the material covered in the textbook but to reinforce, at the same time, their basic reading, writing, listening, and speaking skills.

Testbook

The *Testbook* to accompany *Working with Computers,* Second Edition, prepared by Dr. Lorilee Sadler of Indiana University, Dr. Charles R. McCain of Mountain View College of the Dallas Community College District, Dr. Margaret Anderson of the University of Georgia, Dr. Charles Bohlen of Dayton University, and Craig Piercy of the University of Georgia, contains nearly 1,800 multiple-choice, fill-in, matching, and short-answer questions. It covers all of the important concepts and terminology from the textbook and can be used to prepare quizzes and examinations. The *Testbook* is also available as a computerized Test Bank, available in IBM or Macintosh format.

Tutorial Software

An Interactive multimedia software package with user's manual is available for IBM PC-compatible computers on both $5\frac{1}{4}$- and $3\frac{1}{2}$-inch disks to help students review important concepts presented in classroom lectures. Audio clips and animated segments are included to help clarify complex topics and add interest to the learning environment.

Presentation Software

The Dryden Press offers two presentation software packages to adopters of *Working with Computers,* Second Edition:

- A multimedia presentation software package is available for MS-Windows and Macintosh platforms. It includes a user's manual and a laser disk, which features video segments, hundreds of full-color electronic transparencies, and bulleted lecture outlines for display in the classroom. The laser disk is driven by LectureActive, a user-friendly software program that allows the instructor to organize lectures in advance, using electronic notecard prompts to assure a smooth presentation.
- A dramatic, full-color presentation of concepts is also available. Developed by Randy Goldberg of Marist College, this exciting package was created using Asymetrix Toolbook and operates in MS-Windows.

Programming Languages

The Dryden Press offers several supplements to instructors who wish to introduce their students to programming languages:

- *Structured Programming with MS-BASIC,* by Patrick G. McKeown and Robert D. Brown
- *QBASIC: A Short Course in Structured Programming,* by Gary W. Martin
- *Structured Programming Using Turbo Pascal: A Brief Introduction,* Second Edition, by Margaret Anderson

Acknowledgments

Anyone familiar with the writing and production of a package such as this one knows that it is the result of a team effort. For *Working with Computers,* Second Edition, this team included many people who either helped with writing the book or worked on the editorial and production aspects of its publication.

While writing the text, I received help on numerous technical aspects of the computer from Professor Andrew Seila of the University of Georgia. Professor Robert A. Leitch of the University of South Carolina and Professor Dennis Calbos of the University of Georgia aided me extensively in preparing the systems chapter. Professor Charles R. McCain of Mountain View College provided many thought-provoking articles.

Professor Robert D. Brown provided valuable assistance in the revision of the dBASE III PLUS Tutorial and expansion of dBASE IV from a Session to a Tutorial. Professor Ravija Badarinathi of the University of North Carolina at Wilmington contributed significantly to the revision of the DOS and Lotus 1-2-3 Tutorials. Ashley McKeown and Craig Piercy checked the accuracy of the keystroke instructions in the page proof stage of production. In addition, Professors Brown and Badarinathi and Craig Piercy made valuable contributions to the *Instructor's Manual* and the *Testbook to accompany Working with Computers,* Second Edition. Ashley McKeown coordinated the work on the *Instructor's Manual* and *Testbook,* and Professor Harvey Kaye, City College of CUNY, wrote a unique supplement to the *Instructor's Manual.*

Professor Gena Casas of Florida Community College provided an extensive technical review of the Software Tutorials and provided many valuable suggestions for improving Part Two. Significant contributions were also made by Sylvia Unwin and her students at Tacoma Community College, who carefully read and tested the WordPerfect Tutorial. I sincerely appreciate their careful reading of the manuscript and their many comments. The final product reflects many of their ideas.

A large number of people reviewed the manuscript for *Working with Computers,* Second Edition, including Virginia Anderson, University of North Dakota; Donald Henderson, Makato State University; Alan Lorents, Northern Arizona University; Mike Michaelson, Palomar College; and Fay Simmons, State University of New York—Canton. I sincerely appreciate their careful reading of the manuscript and their many comments. The final product reflects many of their ideas.

During the editing and production of the text, many individuals at The Dryden Press were involved and I wish to express my sincere thanks to all of them: Richard Bonacci, executive editor; Sue Lister, developmental editor; Joni Harlan, senior project editor; Beverly Baker, art director; Steve Lunetta, photo permissions editor; and Marilyn Williams, production manager.

Finally, no acknowledgments would be complete without mention of my wife, Carolyn McKeown, who provided a much needed first read of the manuscript. Without her love and support I would not have been able to complete such a project.

Patrick G. McKeown

IN APPRECIATION

Key to the development of the materials for *Living with Computers,* Fourth Edition—and hence for *Working with Computers,* Second Edition—are those who, through all four editions, have class-tested, reviewed, responded to surveys, and assisted in innumerable ways. I thank them all.

Scott Ahrens
Solano Community College

Margaret S. Anderson
University of Georgia, Athens

Virginia Anderson
University of North Dakota

Carol Asplund
College of Lake County

Joe Dane Autry
Collin County Community College

Tim Baird
Harding University

Beth Barks
Southern Union State Junior College

Coleman Barnett
Tarrant County Junior College Northeast

Edward A. Berlin
Queensborough Community College

George A. Bohlen
University of Dayton

W. H. Bortels
University of Connecticut, Groton

Christopher R. Brown
Bemidji State University

Robert D. Brown
University of Georgia

Eileen Brownell
Junior College of Albany

Kenlon H. Burcham
Wallace State College

Dennis P. Calbos
University of Georgia

Nancy Lee Cameron
Corpus Christi State University

Richard Carney
Camden County Junior College

Gina Casas
Florida Community College

Walter Chesbro
Santa Rosa Junior College

Richard K. Cleek
University of Wisconsin Center—Washington County

William R. Cornette
Southwest Missouri State University

David W. Dalton
Florida State University

Christopher L. Danko
Solano Community College

Dean DeFino
Salisbury State College

Donald L. Dershem
Mountain View College of the Dallas Community College District

Branston A. DiBrell
Metropolitan State College

William C. Driskall
Southern Union State Junior College

Nora Duseault
Herkimer County Community College

Grant Eastman
Tulsa Junior College

Michael Ellerson
University of Georgia, Athens

Richard A. Ernest
Sullivan Junior College

Ronald Flaxmeyer
University of Cincinnati

Patricia Fouts
Virginia Polytechnic Institute

Y. H. Freedman
Mount Royal College

Theodore W. Frick
Indiana University

Robert S. Fritz
American River College

Jack Goebel
Montana College of Mineral Science and Technology

Thomas J. Hammell
*University of Connecticut—
East Lyme*

Donald L. Henderson
Mankato State University

Russell Hollingsworth
Tarrant County Junior College Northeast

Peter L. Irwin
*Richland College of the Dallas
Community College District*

Bill Jackson
Metropolitan State College

Jan Karasz
Cameron University

Richard Lee Kerns
East Carolina University

Bob King
Camden County Junior College

Reinhard L. Knieriemen, Jr.
Orange County Community College

M. C. Kolatis
County College of Morris

Diane H. Krebs
Valparaiso University

Catherine Leach
Henderson State University

Robert A. Leitch
University of South Carolina, Columbia

Alan Lorents
Northern Arizona University

Stan Marder
Mesa College

Gary W. Martin
Solano Community College

Charles R. McCain
*Mountain View College of the Dallas
Community College District*

James McCain
State University of New York at Brockport

Mike Michaelson
Palomar College

Francisca O. Norales
Virginia State University

Edward J. O'Connell, Jr.
Syracuse University

Pam Ogaard
Bismarck State College

Debra A. Osz
Dret School

Sheilah Pantaleo
Allegany Community College

Jeanette Parker
Southern Union State Junior College

Michael A. Perl
Brookhaven College

Gerhard Plenert
California State University, Chico

Guy Pollack
*Mountain View College of the Dallas
Community College District*

Ajay Popat
University of Alabama, Birmingham

Judy Preston
Brookhaven College

Bruce Purcell
Santa Rosa Junior College

Cliff Ragsdale
*Virginia Polytechnic Institute and State
University*

David Ribeiro
Solano Community College

Tom Scharnberg
Tarrant County Junior College Northeast

Nancy Schmitt-MacDonald
Barnes Business College

Al Schroeder
*Richland College of the Dallas
Community College District*

Gregory L. Scott
El Camino College

L. W. Simmerson
Solano Community College

Faye Simmons
State University of New York, Canton

Steve Spencer
University of Georgia

Uthai Tanlamai
California State University, Fresno

Richard Terry
Brigham Young University

Glenn N. Thomas
Kent State University

Evan M. Thompson
California State University, Stanislaus

Bill Todd
Williamsburg Technical College

Sylvia Unwin
Tacoma Community College

John Urquhart
Norfolk State University

Louis Voit
McMurray College

Douglas R. Vogel
University of Arizona

Karen Weil-Yates
Hagerstown Junior College

To Carolyn

". . . still the one . . ."

CONTENTS IN BRIEF

CONTENTS

An Introduction to Information Systems   254

9

An Introduction to Computers and Society   286

10

A Guide to Buying a Personal Computer   309

American Standard Code for Information Interchange (ASCII) Ordering Symbols   328

Glossary   330

Index   340

Working with Computers

SECOND EDITION

PART ONE

An Introduction to Computers

Chapter 1 of this textbook provides a brief overview of the work computers do in the world today. In reading it, you will become acquainted with the different types of computers and with some essential computer terminology. Chapter 2 introduces you to computer hardware, while Chapter 3 outlines the various types of utility and applications software that actually control the operation of the computer. Then we'll expand upon this preliminary discussion of operating systems and applications software packages for personal computers as follows: Chapter 4 covers personal computer operating systems in more detail. Chapters 5, 6, 7, and 8 cover packages for word processing and graphics, financial analysis (spreadsheets) and accounting (both business and personal), data base management, and tele-communications and networks, respectively. Finally, we round out our discussion with two chapters on information systems and the human aspects of computer use. A guide to purchasing a personal computer closes Part One.

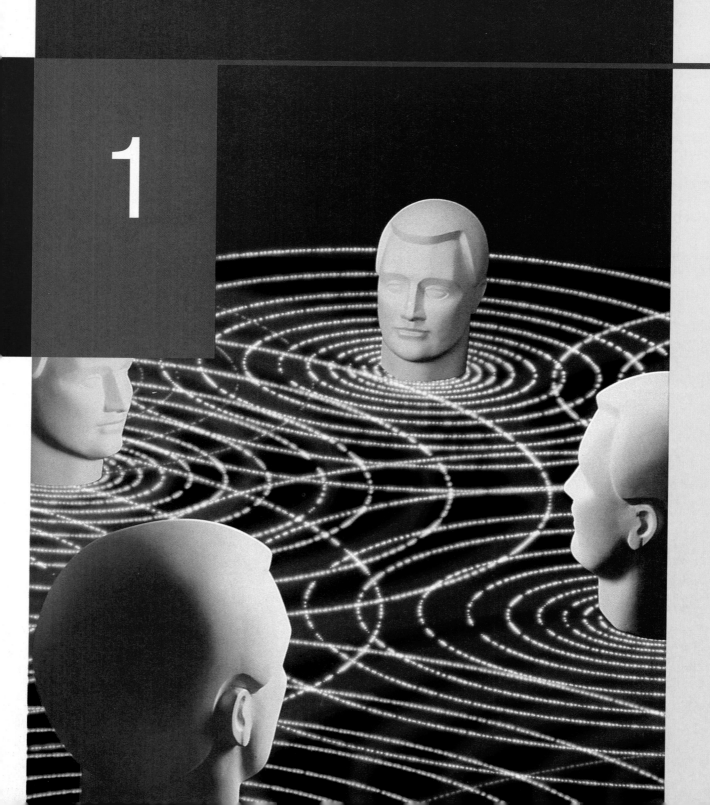

1

The Age of Smart Machines

This chapter provides an overview of the role of computers as smart machines and discusses the concept of the computer as a mind tool—that is, a device that can ease our mental labors while also enabling us to extend our creative abilities. The first section of the chapter describes the prevalence of smart machines in society today, discusses the importance of information to organizations, and relates smart machines to computers. Examples of tools that are being replaced by the computer are listed. Also, the advantages and limitations of the computer are discussed. The second section provides an overview of computer terminology and considers the importance of computer literacy in the world today. The third section discusses the types and sizes of computers. Some of the more important applications of the present-day computer are reviewed in the final section of the chapter. Reading this chapter should give you a good understanding of what a computer can and cannot do, as well as a sound beginning vocabulary of computer terminology.

STUDY OBJECTIVES

After reading this chapter, you should be able to

- point out various smart machines in the world around us and understand the importance of information;
- understand the concept of the computer as a mind tool;
- list various tools being replaced by the computer;
- discuss the difference between data and information;
- differentiate between computer hardware and software and discuss the importance of programming;
- understand the importance of computer literacy in the world today;
- identify the different types and sizes of computers;
- list applications of the computer in the world around us;
- understand the many uses of multimedia;
- recognize the many ways in which the computer affects our lives.

WILL YOU DRIVE A "SMART" CAR?

It is 1996, and you have just arrived at Hartsfield Airport in Atlanta for the Olympic Games. You hop into your "smart" rental car and punch your destination—the swimming venue—into a touchscreen mounted on the dashboard. With this information, an onboard computer, guided by a satellite and sensors in the road, uses a voice synthesizer to guide you to the swimming pool while bypassing the major expressway traffic jams that Atlanta is famous for. The system instructs you in your native language to "take a right at the next intersection. Now, exit at Martin Luther King Jr. Drive."

Does this idea sound like something out of *Star Trek?* Although it might, 25 automobiles with such systems have already actually been tested in Los Angeles. Orlando, currently, is testing 100 cars, and Chicago plans to test 4,000 cars in 1994. In the Los Angeles test, drivers received constantly updated information about accidents, congestion, and construction projects, and the computer suggested alternative routes. In the Orlando test, information on lodging, restaurants, and entertainment will also be available to drivers. In the Chicago test, the test vehicles will send information on traffic conditions back to the traffic center as well as receive it.

In all of these tests, so-called Intelligent Vehicle Highway Systems (IVHS) are being considered. In IVHS, traffic data are relayed from highway sensors by satellite to a central computer and then to in-car computers that display electronic maps. The computer navigates the driver through the least congested route using voice synthesizers or flashing arrows. Such a system is technically possible now, but whether it will be used for the 1996 Olympic Games will depend on the availability of federal funding.

Source: David Beasley, "Automatic Transmission," *The Atlanta Constitution,* May 20, 1991, pp. D1, D3.

"Smart" cars provide directions to drivers.

The "smart" car just discussed is not a vision of the future—it is in large-scale testing at several locations around the country. What differentiates this car from current vehicles is its widespread use of computers to handle guidance and communication tasks. It is an example of a **smart machine,** computer-based machines that can make decisions and provide information. These smart machines have become commonplace in the last few years, and, in fact, it is almost impossible to go through a single day without some contact with one. Examples of smart machines you may use include the following:

- programmable microwave ovens
- programmable videocassette recorders and compact disk players
- digital wristwatches
- checkout scanners
- touchtone, programmable telephones
- fax machines
- automatic teller machines (ATMs)
- personal computers and computer terminals in offices

Automatic teller machines provide both information and cash—any time of the day, any day of the week.

If you look around, you will, no doubt, find many other smart machines in addition to those listed. For example, "smart" weapons were credited with shortening the Gulf War of 1991 and reducing loss of life on both sides of the conflict. Undoubtedly, many more will appear in the near future.

Smart machines have become so widely used at work that business and industry would quickly come to a halt if smart machines suddenly quit working. The scope of **information technology,** as the use of smart machines is often referred to, grows daily as new machines are developed and placed on the market. For example, it is estimated that over 66 percent of all homes in the United States have a VCR and that over 350,000 ATMs are in use. In addition, in 1989, 70 percent of U.S. white-collar workers used a computer, whereas only 25 percent used them in 1983. It is safe to say that, during the last ten years, smart machines have dramatically changed the way we live and that we are, indeed, living in the age of smart machines!

What differentiates smart machines from their predecessors is that these machines not only carry out operations to reduce human labor, but also provide information about those operations. For example, while the obvious use of a checkout scanner is to speed the entry of prices, thereby allowing the customer to spend less time waiting in line, it also provides the store manager with information on sales and inventory levels. Similarly, an ATM can confirm our checking and savings balances, supply us with cash (if the balance is sufficient), accept deposits, and update our accounts for a bank hundreds of miles away.

The capability of smart machines to provide information as well as carry out a user's instructions has made our society increasingly dependent on them. John Naisbitt, a noted authority on the progress of Western society, predicted this outcome in *Megatrends* (1983), *Re-Inventing the Corporation* (1985, with Patricia Aburdene), and *Megatrends 2000* (1990). In these books, Naisbitt discusses the evolution of the United States from an agricultural society 100 years ago to an industrial society in the first two-thirds of this century to what he calls an **information society,** built on the transfer of information. He notes that in

A laser-light bar code reader not only speeds the customer's checkout, but also generates inventory and marketing data.

> **It is not too much to say that we are moving from an economy that rested on the motor car to an economy that rests on the computer.**
>
> *John Naisbitt and Patricia Aburdene*
>
> *Re-Inventing the Corporation* (New York: Warner, 1985), p. 19.

1950, information professionals—teachers, programmers, analysts, clerks, bureaucrats, and accountants—accounted for only 17 percent of the American work force. In 1983, this number had risen to over 65 percent. A second study showed that between 1970 and 1990, *90 percent of all new jobs* were in the information and knowledge areas and predicted that by the year 2000, over 75 percent of all jobs will be in this area.[1]

In 1985, the information industry made up 3.3 percent of the gross national product (GNP). It has been predicted that the information industry will be the largest industry in the world by 1995, making up 6 percent of the GNP. Furthermore, the data processing and communications industry, which was a $300 million industry as recently as 1987, is predicted to account for $1 *trillion* during the 1990s.[2] Figure 1-1 shows how our economy will become more information based over the next few years.

As further evidence of the importance of the smart machine in the business world today, consider that presently all organizations, both public and private,

---

[1] Richard Crawford, *In the Era of Human Capital* (New York: Harper Business, 1991), p. 26.
[2] William R. Synnott, *The Information Weapon* (New York: John Wiley, 1987), p. 3.

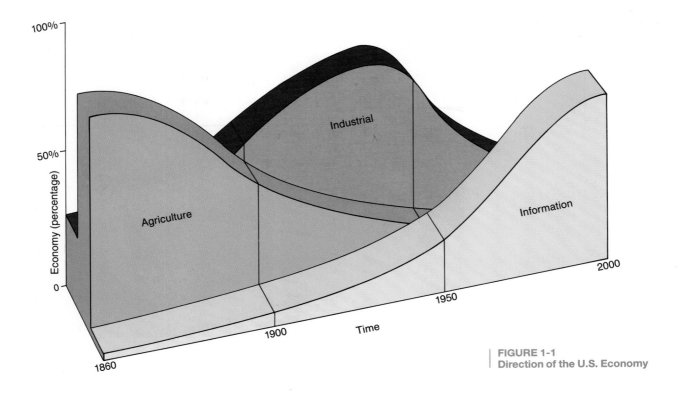

FIGURE 1-1
Direction of the U.S. Economy

profit and nonprofit, have some form of **information system (IS)** that enables an efficient management of information. An IS combines smart machines and human users to transform raw facts into a form that can be used to make decisions. In many situations, the smart machines are tied together to form a **network** that enables them to share information, leading to increased productivity. The most successful organizations are those that have learned to treat information as their most important asset, which they can use to gain a competitive advantage in the marketplace.

Computers and the Smart Machine

The feature common to all smart machines is their use of computer technology to supply "intelligence." A **computer** is *a machine that stores and manipulates symbols using instructions from a human user.* All computers are built around tiny pieces of silicon ($\frac{1}{16}$ to $\frac{1}{2}$ inch square) called **computer chips,** which utilize miniaturized electronic circuitry to carry out instructions from the user. When one of these computer chips is installed in a machine, such as a VCR or a fax machine, and is programmed to direct the machine's operations, the chip is referred to as a **microprocessor.**

We often encounter computers in the form of a terminal linked to a large centralized computer, or sitting on our desk in the form of a personal computer. Regardless of the form in which we find it, remember that the computer is a special type of tool—a very powerful **mind tool** that extends but does not replace the human mind. We have long used tools to ease our physical labors. In fact, the aim of the Industrial Revolution was to enhance production by using

A personal computer brings the power of computing to the desktop.

tools and machines to increase human physical productivity. Now the computer can do the same thing for our mental labors.

Some Tools Being Replaced by the Computer

Like the telephone, the computer has become indispensable to many professionals.

John Scully, president and CEO, Apple Computer

"Professionals and Their Computers," *Personal Computing,* October 1987, p. 228.

As examples of easing mental effort by using the computer, consider five tools commonly used in offices everywhere—the calculator, the typewriter, the file cabinet, the drafting table, and the telephone. All these tools are to some extent being replaced or enhanced by the computer; in the process, the human effort is reduced through the power of the computer.

Like a calculator, the computer can perform calculations. But the real power of the computer is its capability to allow the user to determine the effect of changes in the data or of changes in the assumptions underlying the calculations. Similarly, computers can be used to create and revise documents with far greater ease than the standard typewriter. Computers can actually be used to develop professional-typeset-quality documents ready for publication. While it will be a long time before all storage of information on paper is ended, computers can now store information much more efficiently than filing cabinets, and computers allow the user to retrieve needed items of information without searching through many file folders. Drafting tables are also rapidly being replaced by computers that enable the user to either draw freehand or combine figures from a figure library to create a complete drawing. Finally, fax machines have now made it possible not just to talk over the telephone but also to send text and drawings over telephone lines to distant points.

Advantages and Limitations of the Computer

Two features of the computer strongly contribute to the rapid replacement of many "paper and pencil" tools. These are *speed* and *accuracy*. A computer is limited only by the speed at which electrical signals can be transmitted. This enables even personal computers to execute millions of operations per second in processing raw facts called **data** into a usable form known as **information.** The computer's speed enables it to carry out a desired operation in a fraction of the time needed to do the same thing manually. In terms of accuracy, a computer will do *exactly* what it is instructed to do without error. This enables the computer to repeat the same operations as many times as necessary, without error.

Of course, the computer does have limitations. A computer does not have reasoning capabilities. Rather, it must use instructions from the user to process the data the user inputs. If either the instructions or the data entered are incorrect, the results from the computer will also be incorrect. The fact that a computer can generate erroneous results has led to use of the term **computer error.** However, this term is itself in error since the problem is not with the computer, but with the instructions or data given it by the human user. An acronym even exists to describe this process: GIGO—garbage in, garbage out! So when you receive an incorrect bill or are charged an incorrect amount by a computerized checkout system, remember it's not the computer that has caused the problem; it's the data or instructions input by a human user!

Since computers play such a large role in our lives, it is very useful to have at least a basic understanding of how they work and what they can and cannot do. In this section, we will look at what a computer can do, the parts of the computer, and some ideas on computer use.

As mentioned earlier, a computer processes data into information. Recall that data are the raw facts that are entered into the computer for processing and that information is data that have been processed into a form that is useful to the user. Data can be in the form of numbers, letters of the alphabet, or any other type of symbols. On the other hand, information is the arrangement of data into tables, graphs, and reports. Because of this terminology, the operations that the computer performs are sometimes referred to as **data processing.** Figure 1-2 shows the process of converting data into information.

Parts of the Computer

Processing data into information requires that the two primary elements of the computer—hardware and software—work together to accomplish the desired task. The computer's machinery is referred to as **hardware** and is made up of

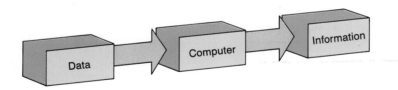

FIGURE 1-2
Conversion of Data into
Information

FINDING MISSING KIDS WITH COMPUTERS

Losing a child is a great fear of every parent. If a child is kidnapped, time may be as great an enemy as the kidnapper, because a child's features change dramatically in only a few months or years. To help the parents and authorities searching for over 7,000 missing children in the United States, the National Center for Missing and Exploited Children (NCMEC) has developed a computer system that "ages" children electronically. This has helped authorities find children who have been missing for several years.

A computer software package called PhotoSketch uses all types of information about a missing child to create a current image of the child. This process uses videotapes, photos, information on identifying marks, and even photographs of parents and siblings to determine genetic effects on physical development. The software package integrates all information about the child into a composite photo that is then modified by simulating the basic structural changes that take place during aging.

Once the "aged" photo has been created, NCMEC disseminates it in various ways, including publishing flyers that reach 55 million households per week. This campaign generates as many as 4,000 to 5,000 leads for each child portrayed on a flyer. Many of these leads come in through the NCMEC hotline: 1-800-THE-LOST.

Sources: "National Center for Missing Children," *Government Technology*, February 1991, p. 17; and Patricia Keefe, "High Tech Helps Speed Location of Missing Children," *Computerworld*, October 21, 1991, p. 63.

An "aging" computer program simulated the aging process in the photo of this child.

CHILD AT AGE 2 WHEN ABDUCTED AGE-PROGRESSION AS 7 YR. OLD

RECOVERY PHOTOGRAPHS AGE 7

electronic devices and circuits. The human-provided logic and instructions to the computer are termed **software.** A common saying that helps to differentiate hardware from software is "If you bump into it, then it's hardware!"

A great deal has been written and said about the marvels of computer hardware, and hardly a week goes by without the introduction of a smaller, faster, or less expensive computer. However, hardware can do *nothing* without software to supply instructions. The software is made up of one or more lists of instructions called **programs.** The process by which programs are developed is called **programming.** Many smart machines in everyday use have instructions already built into a computer chip so that all the user needs to do is press a button. Computer instructions in this form, known as **firmware,** blur the line between hardware and software.

Over the past 20 years, computers have become faster and smaller while also becoming much less expensive. Had the automobile industry undergone the same transformation, a Rolls Royce might cost $2.50 and get over 100 miles to the gallon! A computer that cost over $4,000 a few years ago can now be purchased for less than $1,000. However, while hardware costs have been dropping, software costs have not changed very much. The reason for this dichotomy is that hardware can be mass produced on a factory assembly line, but each piece of software must be created anew by individuals or groups of programmers. Developing software is a creative task similar to writing a novel or painting a portrait; as a result, the cost of software remains high compared to the cost of hardware.

Programming often entails writing sophisticated programs required to handle very complex processing.

Computer Literacy—A Requirement for Living

Computer literacy is a growing social concern. But, what is computer literacy? It has been defined variously as the ability to write programs to solve problems, a detailed understanding of the machinery of the computer, or a knowledge of the many uses of the computer. However, we will define **computer literacy** as *an understanding of what a computer can and cannot do and an ability to make the computer do what the user desires.* This definition emphasizes using the computer as a mind tool to solve problems and accomplish tasks more efficiently.

The importance of computer literacy was once hotly debated, but now most people agree that all students should be exposed to computers at some time during their academic careers. Today, students must be prepared to function in a society in which computers and other smart machines are the rule rather than the exception. This view was well stated by Dr. John Kemeny, past president of Dartmouth College and co-inventor of BASIC (Beginner's All-purpose Symbolic Instruction Code), the most popular computer language for personal computers. According to Kemeny, "In the next three decades, intelligence will be built into most manufactured objects and those who lack even minimal computer literacy will have difficulty functioning in everyday life."[3]

It is important to remember that *it is not necessary to learn programming to be a computer user.* In the past this was not true; every user also had to be

> A computer illiterate can be two things: A person who doesn't know how to utilize a computer or software tool to perform his job; or a person who dramatically underutilizes the features of a software package or computer.
>
> *Elliot Masie, president of the Association of Computer Training & Support (ACTS)*
>
> Quoted in "Defeating Computer Illiteracy," *Computerworld,* December 3, 1990, p. 116.

---

[3] Richard A. Shaffler, "Courses in Computer Literacy Beginning to Draw Bad Marks," *The Wall Street Journal,* September 16, 1983, p. 37.

Engineers often become proficient end users as they take advantage of computer capabilities to help solve problems they encounter in their work.

TYPES OF COMPUTERS

a proficient programmer. Now an enormous amount of software available in retail outlets performs many standard tasks. **Computer packages** that contain commercial software include an explanation of the software as well as instructions for its use. Computer packages make the computer available to everyone, not just to those people who have learned to program.

Note that our definition of computer literacy does not assume either an understanding of the electronics that make up the computer's machinery or the ability to write programs. The definition *does* assume an understanding of a computer's uses and limitations and a knowledge of the software packages needed to accomplish a desired end. However, if the purpose for which you wish to use the computer requires a greater understanding of hardware or programming, then you must increase your knowledge to meet your needs.

Beyond computer literacy, two additional levels of knowledge have been defined. **Computer competence** means that an individual can use the computer to solve sophisticated problems in his or her field of expertise. The computer-competent person is comfortable using the computer and looks for better ways to use it for problem solving. Another term often used to describe the person who reaches this level of computer use is *end user.* **End users** are very involved in using existing software to its fullest extent to do their jobs more effectively. However, end users usually are not information-systems professionals or computer scientists, and they are usually not interested in developing applications for others to use. These tasks are normally handled by individuals who have achieved **computer mastery.** This term refers to information-systems professionals or computer scientists whose jobs center around computing and who have acquired the knowledge necessary for success in this field.

Now that we know what a computer is, we can consider the types of computers used in information systems today. In terms of size (the most common means of classification), computers fit broadly into three types—mainframes, minicomputers, and microcomputers, which are also called personal computers.

A **mainframe** is a very large, expensive computer (usually selling for well over $1 million) that requires a special support staff and a special physical environment (for example, air conditioning). Mainframes are usually housed in a computer center and are generally used in large business, government, or academic institutions where they support multiple users (usually more than 100 at one time) and can handle multiple processing tasks concurrently. This means that a mainframe can, for example, do a statistical analysis for one user, print a report for a second user, and process student grades concurrently.

Users access a mainframe on **computer terminals** that interface with the computer. These terminals are usually composed of a keyboard for entering data and instructions and a display screen for viewing the work and any resulting output. They usually do not have their own computing capabilities.

A subset of mainframes is **supercomputers,** or "monsters," which are the biggest and fastest computers in use today. These very large computers are used almost exclusively for research projects that require extremely high-speed processing and large storage capacities.

At the other extreme in terms of size are **personal computers (PCs),** which are small, one-user computers. These computers are relatively inexpensive

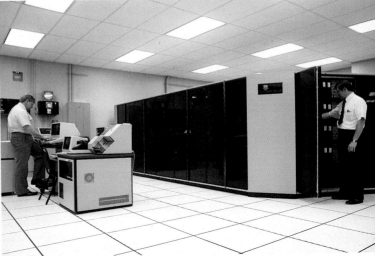

(Left) Supercomputers like the one shown here are the fastest computers in use today. (Right) A mainframe computer can support multiple users and multiple computing activities.

A personal computer like this Macintosh can enhance the life of a handicapped person in many ways.

to purchase ($500 to $5,000) and do not require a special environment or special user knowledge. They fit on a desktop and are sometimes referred to as **desktop computers.** Such personal computers are commonly used by a single user to handle one task at a time. PCs are slower than mainframes and cannot store as much data.

Somewhere between a mainframe and a personal computer is the **mini-computer** (also called a *midrange* or *midsize* computer), which is used by organizations that need more processing power than is available with personal computers, but less than a mainframe offers. A minicomputer can support multiple users and may have some support staff, but not on the same level as a mainframe. Like mainframes, minicomputers can handle multiple users and multiple tasks concurrently through the use of terminals.

A special type of terminal is a **workstation,** a high-performance, single-user device that has characteristics of both a stand-alone PC and a terminal. Like PCs, workstations have built-in computing power. However, they are also connected to a minicomputer or a mainframe and to other workstations to take advantage of the increased computing power of the larger machine and to share information. Workstations also differ from PCs in that they can carry out multiple tasks concurrently. The NeXT computer, developed by Steven Jobs—cofounder of Apple Computers—is considered by many to be a workstation because of the capabilities it offers beyond those available on a PC. Hewlett-Packard and Sun are also well known for their workstations.

Table 1-1 compares the differences between the various computers just discussed. This table lists computers from the smallest—the PC—to the largest—the supercomputer—and compares cost, number of simultaneous users, and the number of tasks that can be carried out concurrently. It also arranges the computers in order of speed from slowest to fastest. The PC is shown to be able to accomplish one or multiple tasks because different sizes and types of PCs have different capabilities.

Like a mainframe, a midrange computer can serve multiple users, but it does not usually require the extensive support that the larger computer does.

Not just a PC on a tabletop, a workstation can often provide high-speed computing and high-quality graphics to the individual user.

Currently the dividing line between personal computers and workstations is hazy as personal computers become more powerful and can support multiple tasks. For simplicity's sake, in the remainder of this text we will include workstations with personal computers since both computers have single-user capability. Similarly, we will include minicomputers and supercomputers whenever we refer to mainframes since each can accommodate multiple users.

From Monsters to Micros

Of the various categories of computers discussed above, the personal computer has received by far the most publicity over the last decade. This is due in part to the phenomenal growth in the use of personal computers since their introduction in 1975. This growth since 1985 is shown in Figure 1-3.

Given the prevalence of PCs in all phases of our lives—business and industry, home and hobby, science and technology, and education—it is surprising that the original IBM PC was introduced as recently as 1981 and the Apple Macintosh in 1984. In the few years since the introduction of these

> **The first decade of [personal] computers has rendered 100 million individuals into more productive analysts and writers.**
>
> *Andrew Grove, CEO of Intel Corporation*
>
> Quoted in "Intel Chief Focuses on Future of the PC," *PC Week,* November 11, 1991, p. S/22.

TABLE 1-1
Comparison of Different Sizes of Computers

Computer	Size	Cost	Number of Users	Number of Tasks
PC	Small	<$5,000	One	One/multiple
Minicomputer	Medium	<$100,000	Multiple	Multiple
Mainframe	Large	>$1,000,000	Multiple	Multiple
Supercomputer	Large	>$2,000,000	Multiple	Multiple

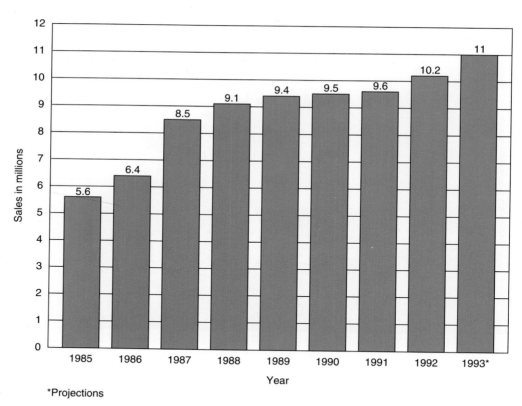

*Projections

FIGURE 1-3
Personal Computer Sales

Source: International Data Corp.

ground-breaking machines, the PC has become commonplace in all facets of our lives. It is estimated that in 1991 about 25 million PCs were being used in U.S. businesses, 17 million homes had a PC, and 46 percent of U.S. children used a PC in school. Figure 1-4 shows 1990 sales of PCs in various fields.

The growth of personal computer use is mainly due to the large amount of software developed that allows the use of this mind tool without the need to learn programming. While larger computers also have software available, it is not always as accessible or easy to use. A second factor in the phenomenal growth of the personal computer is its instant access. To gain access to the larger computers, a user may have to wait until a terminal is available. An account number is usually required as well.

It is important to remember that while the personal computer is often publicized in the national media, it will never replace larger computers. In fact, the growth in use of personal computers has been matched by an equivalent growth in the use of mainframe computers—for several reasons. First is the demand by PC users for information stored on mainframes, since the larger machines offer storage capacity beyond that possible on personal computers. Second is the incredible computing speed available only on mainframes and supercomputers. One study showed that a supercomputer performed in 90 seconds the same operation that one of the faster personal computers required *20 hours* to perform.

As we shall see in later chapters, the difference between the two sizes of computers is really just that—a difference in size. The principles of operation are the same, and once you have become familiar with one, it is very easy to

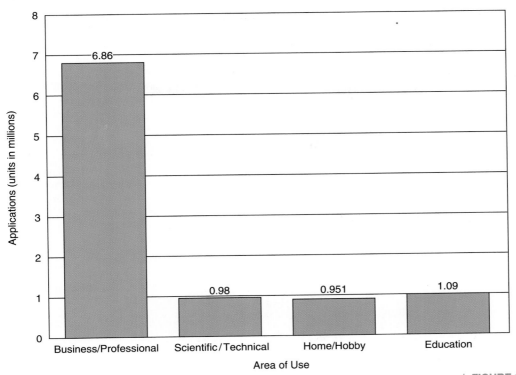

FIGURE 1-4
1990 Sales of PCs

Source: International Data Corp.

learn to use the other. In either case, the computer is a tool of the mind that can make our information processing labors much easier.

Classifying Computers by Logic and Purpose

In addition to classifying computers by size, we may also classify them by their type of logic and their purpose. In terms of type of logic used, a computer can be either a digital computer or an analog computer. A **digital computer** uses numbers and is therefore a *counting machine*. An **analog computer** uses physical relationships and is a *measuring machine*. Analog computers are often used to work with physical measurements. Today almost all computers are digital, so we will consider only this type of computer.

In terms of its purpose, a computer may be classified as a special-purpose computer or a general-purpose computer. A **special-purpose computer** is designed for only one purpose. The microprocessor chips installed in many of the smart machines discussed earlier are actually special-purpose computers that can carry out only a designated purpose. Similarly, the computers used for arcade games or for guiding the National Aeronautics and Space Administration's (NASA's) space shuttles are also examples of special-purpose computers that cannot be used for other purposes. A **general-purpose computer,** on the other hand, can be used for many applications. For example, the same general-purpose computer may be used to play games, to handle payroll computations, to use graphics to design buildings, or to solve complex mathematical problems. In this

> I see PCs as the natural evolution for applications that never belonged on a huge machine that needs its own room to cool.
>
> *James Cannavino, president, Entry Systems Division, IBM*
>
> Quoted in "IBM's Cannavino: Sign of the Times," *PC Week,* February 27, 1989, p. 13.

IT'S GOING TO BE A DIGITAL WORLD

Before the computer chip became widely available, we lived in an analog world. Our watches, telephones, televisions, music systems, and automobile speedometers were all analog machines that monitored conditions such as movement, temperature, and sound and converted them into a continuous analogous representation. However today, many of these same machines are being converted into digital machines that break the relationships into discrete units.

While analog machines can capture the subtle nature of the real world, they cannot make repeated copies of their output without marked signs of deterioration. On the other hand, digital output can be copied repeatedly with no loss of integrity. For example, it is possible to make repeated digital copies of copies of a CD, but copies of a copy of a record or audiotape quickly become useless.

Machines that have already been converted to a digital format include telephones, clocks and watches, and speedometers. Similarly, examples of the latest digital machines are:

■ Interactive compact disks (CD-I), which include video images, as well as audio, and which can be played over a normal TV using a CD-I player;

■ Portable players that play a $2\frac{1}{2}$-inch minidisk (MD) for 74 minutes with no skips due to jolts;
■ Digital audiotape (DAT) that allows individuals to record music of the same quality as is currently available on CDs;
■ 35mm still cameras that allow you to have your pictures placed on a CD with up to 100 photos per disk and a companion player that allows you to display the photos on your television;
■ Musical keyboards that can be coupled with a PC or Nintendo Entertainment System.

In addition, other uses of digital technology may provide us with sources and forms of information that no one can yet imagine.

Sources: Alan Freedman, *The Computer Glossary*, 4th ed. (Point Pleasant, Pa.: The Computer Language Co., 1989), p. 17; and Edmond C. Baig, "Totally Digital," *U.S. News & World Report*, November 25, 1991, pp. 78, 81.

The Phillips Compact Disc Interactive player brings video, pictures and animation to the CD.

text, primary attention is given to the general-purpose digital computer, because it is the most commonly encountered type of computer.

LIVING WITH COMPUTERS

In view of the widespread use of microprocessors in smart machines such as VCRs, telephones, and microwave ovens and the dependence of business and industry on computers, it should be obvious that we are indeed "living with

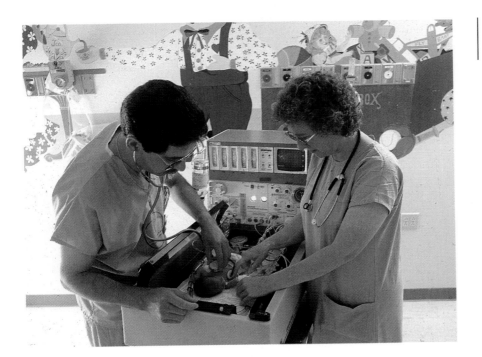

computers." Rarely does a day go by without a report in newspapers or magazines or on television of some new application of the computer. To show you some of the many seen and unseen impacts of the computer, computer applications in various areas of the world around us are summarized in this section. Other applications are discussed in detail in later chapters.

Applications in Business, Industry, and Government

You are undoubtably familiar with many business uses of computers that affect your life everyday—for example, computerized mailing lists and billings—but businesses also use the computer for many "behind-the-scenes" tasks. For example, many companies rely exclusively on the computer for monitoring inventory and ordering, receiving, and paying for goods. Data processing is also important in many companies for computing payrolls applying to many different pay scales and deductions. A not-so-hidden business use of the computer is the point-of-sale (POS) system that is used at retail checkout counters to speed the processing and automate inventory control. Airlines and national hotel chains depend on large mainframe computers to handle reservation systems. Very few offices today are without either a personal computer or a terminal hooked into a mainframe. The PC is often used for various clerical operations, such as word processing, while the terminal allows the office to link into the corporate information center.

On the financial side, banks have for some time been using a computerized check-handling system involving magnetic ink. Now, ATMs and bank-by-telephone services have made the computer even more important in banking. Financial institutions also make heavy use of computers to process and store many transactions each day. The use of computers for **electronic funds transfer**

(**EFT**) means that many people can now transfer money and make purchases from the comfort of home. Another development involves the use of a computer chip in a card that allows the user to make purchases without checks or credit card verification.

Industries of all sizes and types are relying heavily on computers to manage large inventories necessary for manufacturing industries, to help design products and manufacturing processes, and to control machines that build the products. The management of inventories is critical—too much inventory is expensive and too little inventory can shut down the entire manufacturing or supply process. Two areas in which the computer has improved productivity are computer-aided design (CAD) and computer-aided manufacturing (CAM). In CAD, computers replace drafting machines, thereby speeding the design process; in CAM, microprocessors control various manufacturing processes, such as continuous-flow paper making.

Automated machines called **robots** are commonly used to reduce costs and defects while increasing safety in manufacturing tasks that are unsafe or boring. These robots are not the walking, talking variety seen in various science fiction movies, but are primarily microprocessor-controlled "arms" that can perform the same hot, dirty, or dangerous task—such as welding or painting automobile bodies—time after time without loss of concentration or reduction in efficiency.

Governments at the local, state, and national levels have found the computer to be an important tool in efficiently serving their citizenry. For example, computers were an integral part of many weapons used in the 1991 Gulf War. In fact, computers are a crucial element of most U.S. armed forces defense systems in use today. The Internal Revenue Service (IRS) uses computers to compare financial records of businesses and individuals to detect possible tax fraud. Recently, IRS agents have used laptop personal computers for their auditing duties. Similarly, the Bureau of the Census would not be able to complete the U.S. population count without the help of many mainframe computers.

(Top) Today, even sweaters are being designed on computer-aided design (CAD) systems. (Bottom) Robots on automobile assembly lines perform the repetitive, boring, or dangerous jobs.

PCs IN SMALLTOWN AMERICA

There is no doubt that PCs are now commonplace in large organizations, but only about one-half of small businesses are currently using a computer. In an innovative research program to determine consumer preferences for computer products, Apple Computer has given more than $300,000 in hardware and software to small businesses and public organizations in a small town in Oregon. The town, Jacksonville, was chosen because of its size—2,200 residents—and its proximity to Applegate Valley.

In this project, Apple sought two groups of people: those who had been too intimidated by or too busy to invest in PCs and those who had already used a PC. Thirty-one businesses, the elementary school, library, city government, chamber of commerce, and the police and fire departments were all given newer models of the Macintosh computer. Over half of those receiving a computer had never used one before. Apple also provided training and specialized software, and its representatives made regular visits to Jacksonville to monitor progress.

The results of this research project have been very positive, with most recipients reporting high satisfaction with the products and improved efficiency in their jobs. An average of 12 tasks that were previously accomplished by hand were computerized. For example,

- a jeweler uses his PC for word processing and bookkeeping and hopes to start designing jewelry on the computer;
- a tax service owner has automated his tax preparation process;
- a bed and breakfast owner has launched a reservation service and newspaper.

In addition, the experiment brought unexpected benefits to the town, including bringing together people, who did not know each other previously, to use computers. Apple plans to continue monitoring the Jacksonville experiment as well as repeating it in other countries.

Source: Jeff Bernard, "Ripe with Possibilities," *The Atlanta Constitution*, November 5, 1991, p. C-1.

There is high satisfaction with Apples in Jacksonville.

Other national agencies make widespread use of computers to process the ever-increasing backlog of paperwork or to carry out assigned duties. For example, the National Oceanic and Atmospheric Administration (NOAA) uses supercomputers to make long-range weather forecasts and uses PCs to compute the effect of acid rain on the environment. Also, the Environmental Protection Agency (EPA) uses computers to predict the effect of oil spills like the one that damaged the Persian Gulf in 1991.

Computers are used in the various state legislative bodies around the country to speed up the processing of legislative acts. National, state, and local law enforcement agencies use computers to fight crime in many ways. For example, a computer analysis of crime patterns in Seattle enabled the police department to assign more officers to critical areas and reduce the time needed to respond to emergency calls.

Medical, Educational, and Sports Applications

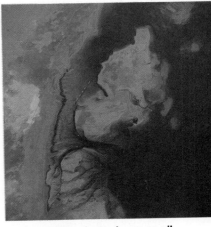

This satellite photo shows an oil spill in the Persian Gulf.

The advances brought about by the use of information technology are very visible in the fields of medicine and education. In the medical field, the computer is being used in every conceivable way to diagnose and treat all types of diseases and conditions. Probably the best known computerized diagnostic tool is the computerized axial tomography (CAT) scan, which allows the doctor to visualize a cross section of the body part through a series of X rays that are combined by the computer. Magnetic resonance imaging (MRI), a relatively new technique that is complementary to computerized axial tomography, relies on computer-visualized images of organs produced through the behavior of the nuclei of atoms in our bodies in a magnetic field. Treatment of diseases is being improved through the use of microprocessor-controlled smart machines that release just the right amount of a medicine into the bloodstream at just the right time.

Doctors may now be assisted in diagnosis and treatment by software packages called **expert systems (ESs).** Each package provides the physician with expert advice to formulate questions for patients and suggest treatment based on the answers. The computer has also been extremely useful in making handicapped individuals more independent and better able to live productive lives. For example, it is now possible for an individual with head injuries and speech loss to carry on a conversation using a personal computer equipped with a speech synthesizer, or for a quadriplegic to gain physical independence in a wheelchair controlled by a microprocessor. Blind people are finding that personal computers can be programmed to verbalize text on the screen, and deaf people are using computers to answer telephone calls by displaying a message on the screen.

In education, the computer is being used at all levels, from kindergarten to college. Colleges have been adding PCs to the mainframe and minicomputer they have used for years, and some institutions require incoming students to purchase a PC for class use.

At the elementary school level, the greatest current uses are in computer-aided instruction (CAI), in which the computer acts as a tutor to the student, and in computer-managed instruction (CMI), which frees teachers from many administrative chores that distract from their main purpose of classroom teaching. Many students find CAI a better way to learn since it is nonjudgmental and self-paced. The software determines the student's level of understanding by the

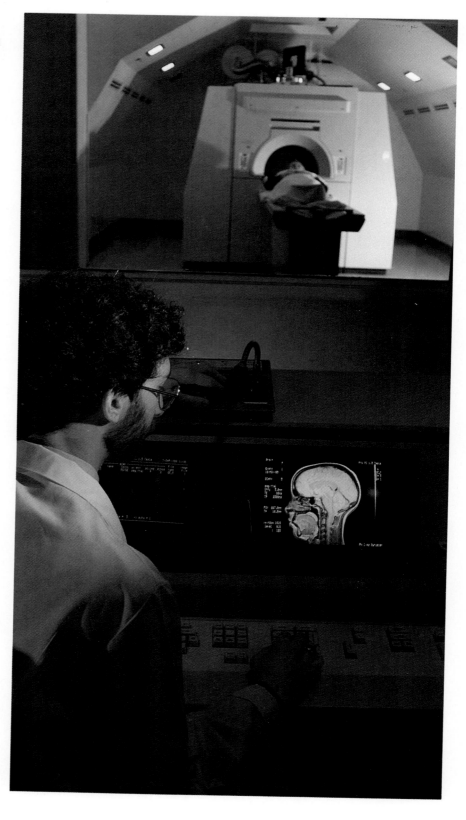

MRI measures the behavior of nuclei in our body in a magnetic field. Then a computer generates a clear image of the data—here, the inside of a patient's skull.

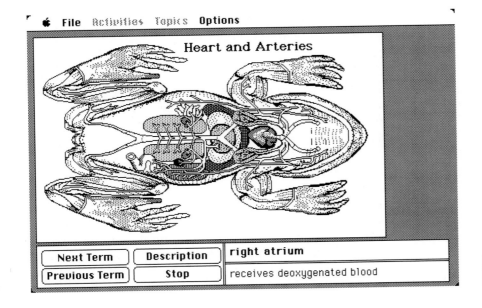

A pointer attached to headgear enables this handicapped student to press keys on the keyboard and do work.

number of correct responses to test questions and adjusts the pace of the lesson to match the level of response. Teachers find that newer software, with its high-quality graphics and animation, can hold the interest of even the easily distracted student far better than many standard teaching methods.

At the secondary school and college levels, personal computers are helping students learn to use software packages and computer programming. At the college level, mainframe computers are also used to teach programming. Further, computers can enhance learning in areas, such as biology or psychology, that are not normally associated with computers. In these courses, the student uses the computer to run simulated experiments to learn the techniques of scientific investigation.

 File   Activities Topics   Options

Heart and Arteries

| Next Term | Description | right atrium |
| Previous Term | Stop | receives deoxygenated blood |

Educational computer software makes learning science concepts easier.

Retarded, learning disabled, and handicapped students have been taught successfully with the computer. For these special students, the computer is never tired and, when combined with appropriate software, can be a very interesting teacher.

In the area of sports, computers analyze large amounts of data to help coaches scout opponents and prospective players. The computer has also helped athletes by graphically breaking up their body movements for closer study to improve technique. Individuals and teams in various sports have improved their performance by using the computer to find weak points to improve upon and strong points to stress.

Multimedia

Fundamentally, multimedia will change people's understanding of what a PC is.

Rob Lippincott, Lotus Development Corporation

Quoted in "Rob Lippincott Speaks on the Future of Multimedia," *Lotus Quarterly*, Fall 1990, p. 12.

The PC revolutionized the computer industry only a decade ago, but it is already becoming more than just a tool for crunching numbers and processing words. It is being used increasingly in combination with audio and video equipment—such as VCRs, laser disks, CDs, and high-fidelity stereo—to produce interactive, full-motion videos, or what is referred to as **multimedia.** It is predicted that the market for multimedia will increase dramatically over the next few years. Recently, for example, a multimedia presentation is credited with helping Atlanta, Georgia, win the bid for the 1996 Summer Olympics.

Multimedia applications greatly enhance the learning process. In business, multimedia already is being used for sales demonstrations and training and is expected to become an important part of the over $4-billion worldwide market for presentations. In education, a multimedia system would have many uses: Geography lessons could include a mix of words, maps, video, and sound. A history film could be paused so the student could "call up" related history videos for viewing. A multimedia French language system has already been developed by Stanford University and Massachusetts Institute of Technology (MIT), in conjunction with Apple Computer, Inc. In this combination of PC, television, sound, and innovative software, a Macintosh computer is loaded with information about Paris, including color pictures, video clips, maps, street sights and sounds, and even a Parisian, who leads the viewer through the city. Using a mouse, a student can explore various popular locales, visit natives, and, along the way, learn French.

Multimedia applications are being developed for various other markets, including, and perhaps most especially, the home. Many industry leaders believe that multimedia may become the system that will make the PC as widespread as the television and VCR are today. Analysts agree, however, that such a development will probably not occur until multimedia systems cost less than $1,000, which may happen by the mid-1990s.

Applications in Our Personal Lives

We have already discussed the importance of the microprocessor in smart machines around us, but there are many other areas in which computers—primarily personal computers—can help us carry out various tasks and can make our lives more enjoyable. While the high level of home use of personal computers that was forecast five years ago has not quite been reached, a large segment of the population has found that they can do their primary jobs more efficiently,

MULTIMEDIA HELPS CONVICT CHILD ABUSERS

A pressing problem in courts all over the United States is obtaining convictions in child abuse cases. The accused assailants often go free because the young witnesses do not want to be in the same room as their abuser or are too traumatized to face them. To solve this problem, the Bexar County District Attorney's office in San Antonio, Texas, has turned to a multimedia system. The Multimedia Information Network Exchange (Minx) system incorporates full-motion and full-color video and voice and data transmission into two desktop workstations, one in the courtroom and one in the room with the youthful witness. The workstations, which look like ordinary television sets, are linked via television cable and computer control unit.

Since children usually feel no fear in talking to the TV look-alike in the "Teddy Bear Room," they can testify freely about their terrifying experiences without feeling the threatening physical presence of the defendant. Through a voice-activated system, the witness can see and hear what is going on in the courtroom while the judge and jury and the prosecuting and defense attorneys have access to the witness through monitors. Since this is a two-way system, it does not appear to violate the defendant's Sixth Amendment rights to confront the accuser, and videotapes of the proceedings are used for the appellate process. In the first five cases in which it was used, the Minx system had a 100-percent conviction rate.

Source: Carol Hilderbrand, "Multimedia Eases Testimony," *Computerworld,* July 1, 1991, p. 35.

Multimedia can include text, stills, animation, video and sound.

provide services to various clubs and organizations, or manage their hobbies better by using a personal computer. For example, if a sports booster club needs a mailing list of members, a personal computer and printer combined with appropriate software can do the job in a fraction of the time required of an individual using a typewriter. Or, if a bird watcher wants to catalog the birds observed by year and location, he or she may do this easily with a computer.

Computer and video games have been providing enjoyment for countless numbers of children of all ages for almost 30 years. Many of today's "computer old-timers" got their start by playing the Star Trek game on mainframe computers. The proliferation of personal computers has simply increased the game playing. In fact, one of the perennial best-selling PC software packages is Flight Simulator, which allows the player to fly a variety of aircraft to various airports across the country. This concept has been incorporated into the MBA program

Management Flight Simulator at MIT provides management students with a realistic application of decision making.

In computer games like the one shown here, players virtually have to learn to fly if they want to compete successfully!

HARBOUR TOWN
SUSAN   E
Hole: 18 Par: 4 Shots: 4
Ball to Pin: 40 FT.

Skip
Grid
Profile

SWING P

Menu   Setup Top Scores Drop

Address   0   P
Draw
Straight   Gimmie   Rotate   CLUB
Fade   Lie
Chip User1
Putt User2   GREEN   WIND

at MIT in a program called Management Flight Simulator, in which new students learn about managing an airline company. Logic games, including chess, popular board games such as Monopoly or Scrabble, and many adventure/detective games that require the player to make decisions in order to score points are also popular types of games for the PC. In addition, the extremely popular Nintendo game systems offer graphics that are much improved over those of the older game systems.

Computers are becoming a fact of life in other areas of recreation. For example, at EPCOT (Experimental Prototype Community of Tomorrow) in Walt

BITS OF HISTORY

Early Attempts at a Mind Tool

Humans have always tried to make the basic operations of writing and counting easier. The first successful counting device was the Chinese abacus, which is very fast in the hands of an experienced operator. After the Renaissance in Europe, individuals concentrated on building machines that could perform arithmetic operations. In 1614, John Napier of Scotland invented logarithms and the slide rule. In 1643, Blaise Pascal of France created a machine that could add and subtract. In 1673, Gottfried Wilhelm von Leibnitz of Germany developed a calculator that could multiply.

The first attempt at anything that approaches our definition of a computer occurred in 1820 when Englishman Charles Babbage built a machine to make arithmetic computations. His Difference Engine was a special-purpose device for calculating the values of polynomials of the form $x^2 + 3x + 20$ to an accuracy of six places. After this success, Babbage tried to develop a more sophisticated device—the **Analytical Engine**—which would be able to perform any type of arithmetic calculation. The crucial conceptual breakthrough in the Analytical Engine was that it would *store* the series of operations to be made. Babbage was aided by Lady Ada Lovelace, the daughter of English poet Lord Byron. Lovelace clearly described Babbage's ideas in written form, supplementing notes on his work with ideas of her own. Unfortunately, the technology of the time was not advanced enough for Babbage to build his machine, which used gears and wheels to carry out the necessary logic. A model that was built later from his plans worked as Babbage claimed it would.

Many of the ideas of Babbage and Lovelace were very advanced. In fact, if the technology had been available to build Babbage's Analytical Engine in 1840, the computer might have been developed 100 years earlier than it was. As an example of their farsighted ideas, consider this quote from Lady Lovelace. Her words may also be applied to modern computers:

The Analytical Engine has no pretension whatever to *originate* anything. It can do whatever *we know how to order it to perform*. It can *follow* analysis; but it has no way of *anticipating* any analytical relations or truths. Its province is to assist us in making *available* what we are already acquainted with.

For her tireless effort on this "grandfather" of the modern computer, Lady Lovelace has been honored by having a computer language named after her; the language is Ada.

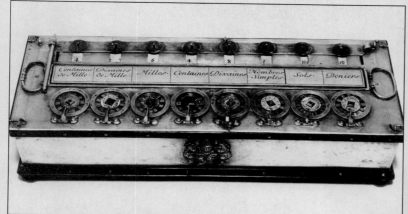

Pascal's adding machine, called the Pascaline, used wheels and gears to add and subtract numbers.

Babbage's Difference Engine was designed to compute mathematical tables.

Disney World near Orlando, Florida, computers run the entire show, including the fountains, the rides, the information service, and the animated figures in the shows. There is even a special presentation on the impact of computers at EPCOT. Similarly, the popular Andrew Lloyd Webber musical *Starlight Express* uses six separate computer systems to run the lights, sound system, and other elements of the scenery.

A LOOK AHEAD

The purpose of this textbook is to provide information and experience to enable you to function in a world rapidly becoming populated with smart machines. In the process you should become computer literate. You will be introduced to hardware, software, information systems, and the effect of the computer on our society—the material necessary for the first half of our definition of computer literacy, that is, knowing what a computer can and cannot do. In later chapters we will expand upon this information with a detailed study of applications software packages. If you combine this material with the software that accompanies this book or is provided by your instructor, you will become fully computer literate by learning how to make the computer do what you want done.

REVIEW OF KEY POINTS

1. The world is rapidly being populated with smart machines that not only carry out tasks, but also make decisions and provide information. Smart machines are, in reality, a type of computer based on the microprocessor computer chip.

2. Because the computer can help ease our mental labors, it is often referred to as a mind tool. Many of today's tools—including calculators, typewriters, file cabinets, drafting tables, and the telephone—are being replaced or enhanced by the computer.

3. A computer is a machine that stores and manipulates symbols quickly and accurately. The two parts of a computer are hardware and software. Hardware is the electronic part, and software is the set of instructions that directs the computer's activities.

4. The process of developing software is called programming, and the resulting software is made up of one or more programs. However, by using commercially available software packages, an individual may be able to use a computer without being a programmer.

5. Computer literacy is an understanding of what a computer can and cannot do and an ability to make the computer do what is desired.

6. Computers can be classified according to size as supercomputers, mainframes, minicomputers, workstations, and personal computers. The use of mainframe computers and personal computers is increasing simultaneously, and both are important tools in the information society.

7. Computers may also be classified by the type of logic they use or by the purpose for which they are designed.

8. The computer has applications in many fields and affects our lives in numerous ways.

9. Multimedia is the combination of the computer and various audio and video devices.

KEY TERMS

analog computer
Analytical Engine
computer
computer chip
computer competence
computer error
computer literacy
computer mastery
computer package
computer terminal
data
data processing
desktop computer
digital computer
electronic funds transfer (EFT)
end user
expert system (ES)
firmware
general-purpose computer
hardware

information
information society
information system
information technology
mainframe
microprocessor
mind tool
minicomputer
multimedia
network
personal computer (PC)
program
programming
robots
smart machines
software
special-purpose computer
supercomputer
terminal
workstation

REVIEW QUESTIONS

1. List those machines in your home that are "smart." Discuss other machines that could be improved if they were made "smart."
2. What differentiates smart machines from other types of machines? What element is at the heart of any smart machine?
3. Discuss why the computer is referred to as a "mind tool." *extends the human mind*
4. Why are information systems important to organizations?
5. List some examples of organizations that are heavily dependent on information as an asset.
6. What are the levels of computer use beyond computer literacy? What is an *end user*?
7. List three current or future situations for which you must become computer literate.
8. Why do we say that computer hardware is useless without software?
9. What are two important advantages of the computer?
10. Discuss why the term *computer error* is a misrepresentation.
11. Discuss the difference between data and information.
12. Explain the term *data processing.* What are the input and output for data processing? Give an example.
13. List the various classifications of computer in the categories of

size, logic, and purpose. In each category, which type is the most prevalent?

14. What are the important differences between a workstation and a personal computer?

15. Discuss three applications of computers that affect you on a daily basis. What is multimedia?

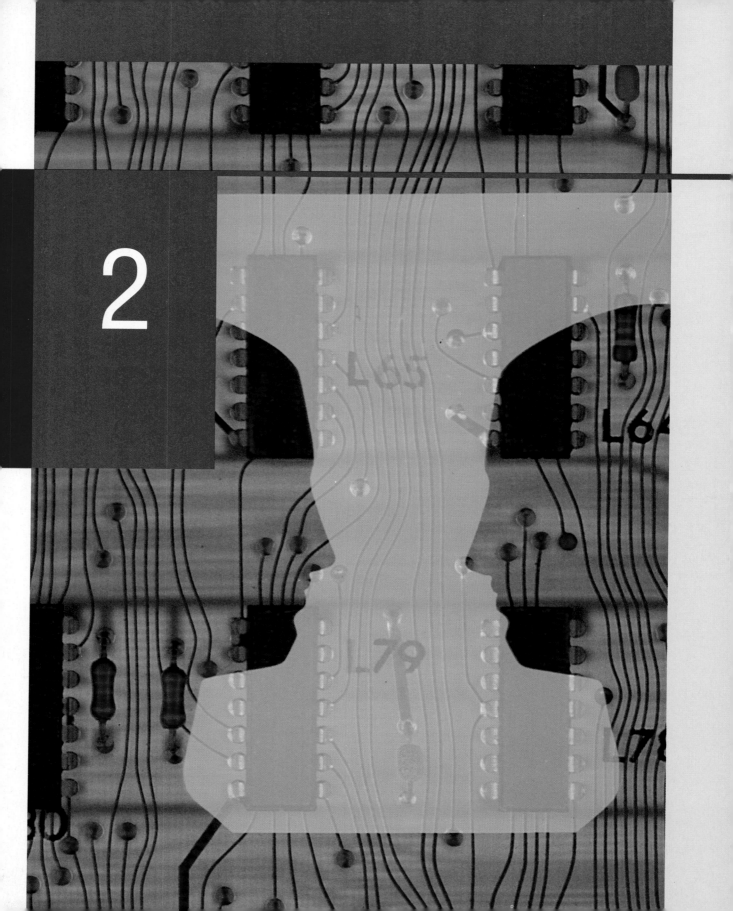

2

An Introduction to Computer Hardware

In Chapter 1 we said that the computer has two parts—hardware and software. Here in Chapter 2 we discuss the computer's hardware components. This chapter introduces the various hardware devices that make up a computer. Coverage of this topic includes a look at the components of a conceptual computer and how it works. We then discuss some hardware elements and how they combine to "build" a computer. We also will discuss briefly the manner in which a computer stores symbols.

STUDY OBJECTIVES

After reading this chapter, you should be able to

- understand conceptually how a computer works;
- recognize the four major hardware components of the computer;
- understand how these four components interact to manipulate and store symbols;
- describe the various units of a mainframe computer;
- put together a personal computer using examples of each of the elements;
- discuss how a computer stores symbols in the processing/internal memory unit;
- include in your vocabulary the most important computer hardware terminology.

MONITORING WEATHER AT PORTLAND GENERAL ELECTRIC

At Portland General Electric (PGE), an electric power utility company in Portland, Oregon, monitoring the weather and smokestack emissions is not just a sidelight, it's a requirement of doing business. Because PGE operates a nuclear power plant, the Nuclear Regulatory Commission (NRC) requires that weather conditions, which might affect the dispersal of routine low levels of radiation released from the plant, be monitored daily. This includes measuring wind speeds and directions and other atmospheric conditions. Similarly, to meet air quality and stack emission requirements of the Oregon state environmental office, PGE must monitor the emissions from its coal plant and two combustion turbine plants.

While keeping accurate environmental records can be expensive, PGE's failure to do so could result in regulatory fines. In 1986, when a PC system was installed, PGE used a monitoring system that involved collecting magnetic tapes from weather and emissions data loggers, mounting the tape on PGE's mainframe, and executing a program to produce the needed reports. This system involved a lag of several days between the collection of data and the meteorologist's being able to check it for possible malfunctions in the data recording device. Thus, any malfunctions would not be discovered for several days. The data logger was backed up by strip charts, but significant additional labor was required to convert the data to a usable form.

To speed up the processing of weather data, in 1989 PGE installed a local area network (LAN) composed of PCs that accept the data from an improved data logger/cassette recorder system. These PCs are used to check the data for reasonableness using a series of BASIC programs written by meteorologist Terry Worrell. After being processed by PCs on the LAN, the data are transferred to PGE's mainframe, where more accuracy checks are run before the data are included in reports that are sent to the NRC. The data are also transferred to a PC-based data base management program that generates reports for the state environmental office.

Source: Interview with Terry Worrell, meteorologist at PGE, November 6, 1991.

Data retrieval devices combined with a PC have enabled Portland Gas and Electric to monitor closely the environmental conditions around its power plant.

As defined in Chapter 1, computer **hardware** is the electronic part of the computer that stores and manipulates symbols under the direction of the computer software. In the preceding box, various types of computer hardware, including a personal computer and a mainframe, are used to monitor the weather at Portland General Electric.

Because the hardware's operations are electronic, the computer is both fast and accurate. The speed of many operations performed within the computer is limited only by the speed of electricity. These operations also obey physical laws that do not change from operation to operation and are therefore accurate. If you will recall, a computer mistake can almost always be traced to a human error, either in the design of the computer or in the software.

To understand how the computer hardware is combined to make a machine that stores and manipulates symbols, we first look at a **conceptual computer,** which can demonstrate the major functions of a computer without involving the operational details of the machine. The conceptual computer shown in Figure 2-1 has four major elements: input, processing/internal memory, secondary storage, and output. The figure also shows the flow of data into the computer and of processed information out of the computer.

A computer must be able to **input,** or receive, the data to be manipulated and the software instructions for manipulating those data. Input to a computer performs the same function as the input humans receive through sight, hearing, touch, taste, and smell. In the PGE example at the beginning of the chapter, input to the PC is from the weather data logger cassette tapes and input to the mainframe is from the PC.

Once the data and instructions are input, the computer must be able to store them internally and then process the data based on the instructions. This storage and processing, which occurs in the **processing/internal memory unit,** can involve many different types of operations, including arithmetic operations

*I would not want to
waste anyone's time
by documenting the
generality that
computing has
changed the world.*

William F. Buckley, Jr.,
author and editor

". . . Makes a Difference Where You
Are," *Personal Computing,* October
1989, p. 23.

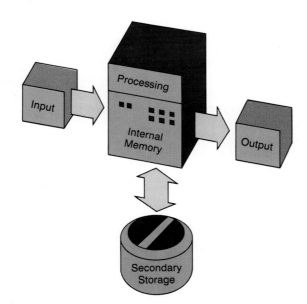

FIGURE 2-1
The Conceptual Computer

(addition, subtraction, and so on) on numbers, operations on letters of the alphabet, and operations that result in pictures (known as graphics). The processing/internal memory unit is comparable to the human brain, which also stores and operates on data. In the PGE example, the PC processes the weather data to check them for reasonableness and to prepare them for further processing by the mainframe.

Because the internal memory of a computer does not have an unlimited capacity, a storage area is needed outside of the computer to hold the data and information, which can be brought back into the internal memory as needed. This external storage unit is called **secondary storage.** Another reason for having secondary storage is that the computer's internal memory is erased when the power to the computer is turned off. Anything in internal memory that must be saved before the power is turned off should be transferred to secondary storage. The file cabinets we use to save large amounts of data and information are analogous to a computer's secondary storage.

Finally, because the processed information is of no use unless it is provided to the user, the computer has a process called **output.** We humans output the results of our brains' operations in the form of speech, writing, pictures, or body movements. In the PGE example, output from the PC is in an electronic form that is sent directly to the mainframe, where it is processed and output as printed reports.

ELEMENTS OF HARDWARE

We have looked at a conceptual computer and have discussed the parts of a computer in general terms. We have also seen how the input of data into the computer, the flow of data and information between the computer and secondary storage, and the output of information from the computer link the components of the conceptual computer together. Before we discuss further how a computer works, we should look at the four major parts of a real computer. After reading this section, you should have a clear idea of the main components of a computer.

Input

The many methods of input to a computer range from grocery checkout bar codes to easy-to-use voice input. Currently, the most popular form of input is the typewriterlike **keyboard,** which sends the appropriate electrical signal to the computer when the user presses a key. The symbol corresponding to this key is stored in the computer's internal memory and usually is shown simultaneously on the screen.

Other common forms of input include the joystick used for games and a device called a **mouse** that communicates with the computer when the user moves it over a flat surface and presses one or more buttons. **Touchscreens** that transmit a signal to the computer based on what part of the screen is touched are used in various situations, as are **light pens** that the user points at a portion of the screen to select it for further investigation. Touch screens provide information to visitors all over EPCOT Center at Walt Disney World in Florida. A visitor merely touches one of several colored areas on the screen to receive a message about a feature of EPCOT. The newest forms of input are **pen-based computing** and **voice recognition.** In the former case, the user writes on the screen; in the latter case, the user speaks to the computer.

(Top left) By touching the stylus to various points on the touchpad, the user can make changes to the map on the screen. (Top right) To select from the menu, the user simply points at a particular place on the screen. (Bottom) With a bar code reader, important price and inventory information can be input easily to the computer.

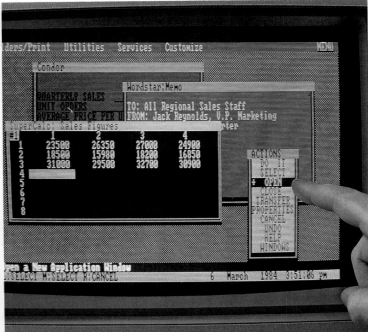

Processing/Internal Memory

To manipulate and store symbols, the computer must have a "brain" that can perform certain predetermined operations and "remember" information. This "brain" is the processing/internal memory unit of the computer and is made up of three parts: (1) the arithmetic–logic unit, where actual processing is carried out; (2) the control unit, which directs all of these operations; and (3) the internal, or main, memory. The control unit and the arithmetic–logic unit together form the **central processing unit (CPU)** of the computer.

All three units use the computer chips discussed in Chapter 1. Recall that a **chip** is a tiny piece of silicon that packs many thousands of electronic elements into a tiny area. These elements, called **transistors,** actually carry on the control and logic operations at over 1 million operations per second! A combination of transistors and circuits on a chip results in an **integrated circuit** that is the key to the power and speed of all computers today. Because the chip is so small, it must be attached to a carrier device with wire prongs. This plugs it into the main circuit board, which contains other chips for the CPU, the main memory, and the control of input, output, and secondary storage devices.

A CPU chip, or **microprocessor,** contains the control unit and the arithmetic–logic unit. The **control unit** manages the processing of data into information and the **arithmetic–logic unit (ALU)** handles the actual processing by performing arithmetic and logic operations on the data. Mainframe computers

A microchip is so small that it and its holder can easily pass through the eye of a needle.

This computer circuit board, consisting of many electronic devices soldered onto a printed circuit, can control various operations of the computer.

will have several CPU chips, but a personal computer will usually have only one. Having multiple CPU chips enables the mainframe to run faster and handle the large volume of processing for which it is responsible.

To help you understand what is going on in the CPU with the control and arithmetic–logic units, think of these units as two clerks working inside the computer: the head clerk (the control unit) and the working clerk (the arithmetic–logic unit). The head clerk's job is to tell the working clerk what calculations and comparisons to do based on instructions from the keyboard. The working clerk can only add, subtract, or compare two data items and must be told by the head clerk specifically what to do. Since the head clerk cannot do these calculations or comparisons and the working clerk cannot understand instructions from the keyboard, the two clerks must work together.

To store the data internally, the head clerk uses a blackboard (the internal memory). While the working clerk can communicate only with the head clerk, the head clerk can communicate with the user through a bulletin board (the screen) on which results are posted. The head clerk also stores data and information in file cabinets (the secondary storage).

To carry out a task, the head clerk receives instructions over the phone (the keyboard) and looks up the meaning of these instructions in a reference manual (the software). After interpreting the instructions, the head clerk retrieves needed data from the blackboard (the internal memory) and sends these data, and instructions as to what should be done with them, to the working clerk for action. After carrying out the instructions, the working clerk returns the result of this operation to the head clerk, who writes it on the blackboard. The head clerk may send results to the filing cabinets or retrieve additional data from there. The head clerk may also post results on the bulletin board or send them out to be printed.

Internal Memory

The third part of processing/internal memory is the **internal memory,** which also is made up of computer chips. Internal memory is divided into two major types—random-access memory and read-only memory. **Random-access memory (RAM)** is the section of memory that is available for storing the instructions to the computer and the symbols that are to be manipulated. It is the internal memory that is accessible to the user; it is called RAM because any area of the memory can be accessed with equal ease regardless of where a piece of information is located. A shortcoming of RAM is that it is **volatile**—the memory exists only while the computer is turned on or is connected to the mainframe. This volatility and the limited availability of internal memory require that secondary storage be used to save information before the computer is turned off or is disconnected from the mainframe.

Read-only memory (ROM) is the section of memory that is placed in the computer during the manufacturing process, and it is nonvolatile. This type of memory gives the CPU instructions during the startup or **booting process,** before the user has given the computer any instructions. When the computer is started up, ROM tells it to go to secondary storage to read instructions into RAM that allow the computer to process data into information. ROM is also useful in managing many of the computer's operations, such as providing the characters on the screen when a key is pressed or results are being displayed.

CPU speed and the typical amount of memory available have both increased by more than a factor of 10 since 1981, and the rate of improvement is likely to continue for another 10 years.

William Gates, founder and CEO, Microsoft Software

Quoted in "The Future of High-Performance Personal Systems," *MIPS Special Supplement,* February 1989, p. 8.

PC Memory

There is often some confusion about the amount of internal memory in IBM compatible PCs that use the MS-DOS operating system. The first 640 Kbytes (640 Kbytes is equivalent to 655,360 characters—see p. 60 and Table 2-3 on p. 64) of RAM is termed **conventional memory,** and it is the only memory that MS-DOS was designed to recognize when it executes a program, including itself. This restriction exists regardless of how much actual RAM the PC contains. The RAM between 640 Kbytes and 1 Mbyte is called **upper memory.** This means that the upper memory of a PC with at least 1 Mbyte (1,024 Kbytes) of RAM is 384 Kbytes. Upper memory is normally reserved for software required by hardware devices, such as monitors or network linkages. However, with MS-DOS 6.0 and other memory manager programs, it is possible to move some types of software to upper memory and thereby free portions of conventional memory for other software.

All RAM between 1 and 32 Mbytes is referred to as **extended memory.** Conventional RAM plus any RAM up to 8 Mbytes is referred to as **expanded memory.** Because expanded memory was developed for MS-DOS, many popular MS-DOS–based software programs have been written for expanded memory. Unfortunately, these programs cannot use extended memory (any RAM above 1 Mbyte) unless they are used in conjunction with a **memory manager,** which is a utility-type software. With a memory manager, extended memory emulates expanded memory. However, PCs using the OS/2 operating system or the Windows operating environment can use extended memory directly. Figure 2-2 shows the relationship among conventional, upper, extended, and expanded memory on an IBM compatible PC that uses MS-DOS.

> **When we set the upper limit of PC-DOS at 640K, we thought nobody would ever need that much memory.**
>
> *William Gates, Founder and CEO, Microsoft Software*
>
> Quoted in "Give Me Power," *Infoworld*, April 29, 1985, p. 5.

FIGURE 2-2
Types of PC Memory

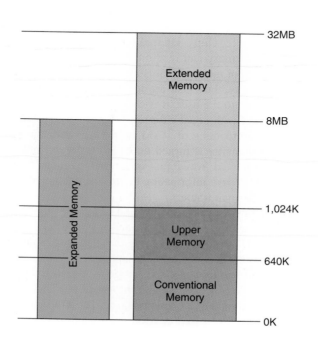

KEEPING THE TRAINS ROLLING WITH COMPUTERS

After running for many years on equipment designed in the first half of this century, the railroad industry is now beginning to use computers to dispatch and control trains. The industry's main objectives in using computers are to improve safety, cut maintenance costs, save fuel, and more efficiently use its 221,000 miles of track and 1.3 million freight cars. Currently, most railroads use a system of in-track sensors and radio transmitters to track the trains. This system has an accuracy of about 3 miles, which means that, for safety's sake, dispatchers have to give each train a 6-mile cushion. This causes trains to run more slowly than needed, wait at sidetracks for long periods, and, in general, run very inefficiently.

Consider the system being tested by Burlington Northern on 250 miles of its track. Custom-designed computer chips are installed on the test locomotives, which communicate with the air force's Global Position System (GPS) satellites to determine the exact location of a given train. The location of the locomotive is sent to a minicomputer used by the dispatchers.

The new system can determine the locomotive's location to within 150 feet, allowing Burlington Northern to operate its trains more frequently and get them to their destinations more quickly. During the test period, the company determined that installing the computer system in all its locomotives would have prevented *all* accidents that occurred on the railroad. Most such accidents were caused when trains exceeded normal speeds and ran through signals. Burlington Northern has decided to install the computer system in all its trains and expects a $1 billion payoff over a 15-year period.

Sources: Hal Straus, "Railroads Rolling into the Space Age," *The Atlanta Journal*, May 2, 1989, pp. D1–D2; and interview with Edward Butt of Burlington Northern, November 7, 1991.

The computer monitors shown here give the train dispatcher almost instantaneous control over the trains at this trackyard.

Secondary Storage

Because of the limited amount of internal storage and the volatility of RAM, some form of storage external to RAM is necessary to permanently store data and programs. This **secondary storage** usually comes in one of two forms of magnetic storage media—disk or tape. With either of these, stored information is accessed by internal memory when the control unit decides that this information is needed. Because the secondary storage unit must locate the information, read it from the disk or tape, and then transfer it to internal memory, secondary storage is a much slower form of memory than internal memory. However, this slow transfer of information is balanced by the virtually unlimited storage capacity.

Disk secondary storage uses a **computer disk** to store information as a form of **direct-access storage** in which information may be accessed in any order, regardless of the order in which the information was stored. A disk is a thin, recordlike piece of metal or plastic that is covered with an iron oxide whose magnetic direction can be arranged to represent symbols. This magnetic arrangement is accomplished by a device known as a **disk drive,** which spins the disk while reading and writing information onto it. This process of transferring information to and from the disk is accomplished by the **read/write head,** which, depending on the type of disk, rides either directly on or immediately above the disk. In a sense, a disk is like a CD that is "played" by the disk drive. However, there are two crucial differences between a computer disk and a CD. First, signals on the computer disk are recorded magnetically rather than by a laser beam burning pits into the surface of the compact disk. Second, the computer can record data on a disk in addition to playing it.

Mainframe computers have large **disk packs** made up of ten disks, each about the size of a record album. These disk packs usually remain in the disk drive except when a special need requires a transfer. Because these disk packs can hold so much information, many users can store data on a single disk pack. When a user connects to the mainframe, his or her user number tells the computer where to look on the disk pack for the user's data.

To store information, personal computers use both plastic disks, called **floppy disks,** and metal disks, called **hard disks.** Floppy disks, which are made of Mylar® and covered with an iron oxide, are easily moved, but they hold only a fraction of the data stored on a hard disk or a mainframe disk pack. For this reason, a user may need several floppies to store all needed data or information. Floppies come in two sizes, $5\frac{1}{4}$ inches and $3\frac{1}{2}$ inches in diameter; the size required depends on the type of disk drive being used. A hard disk is a scaled-down version of a mainframe disk pack. The hard disk rotates at a much faster speed than the floppy and stores a great deal more information.

The **optical** or **video disk,** the newest form of secondary storage, can hold *billions* of characters. Optical disks are similar to compact disks used for music except that they are larger and can hold more information. Currently, most optical disks, like audio CDs, are *read-only* storage devices, but more and more read and write optical disk systems are coming into use.

Magnetic tape that is used for secondary storage can be either reel-to-reel or cassette. Like a disk, tape is covered with iron oxide that is arranged magnetically to store symbols. A tape can easily store millions of characters. However, it is much slower than a disk for transferring information since the tape

Mainframe computers use tape for much of their secondary storage.

Because of the amount of data they can store and their smaller size, microfloppy disks (3½ inches in diameter) are becoming very popular for use on all types of personal computers.

OPTICAL DISK SYSTEM FINGERS CRIME SUSPECTS

In television detective stories, a fingerprint is always a crucial clue, since it enables the detective to determine the identity of the suspect. Unfortunately, finding a fingerprint does not always result in an identification in actual police work. For example, at the State of Georgia Crime Information Center, there are almost 10 million fingerprint cards to be checked when a suspect or "latent" print comes in. Obviously, it is almost impossible to check all these fingerprint cards manually, and as a result, many latent prints go unmatched. In one year, 40,000 latent prints from crime scenes were handled, but only 952 suspects were identified. As a result of this horrendous matching problem, latent prints can usually be used only to check against suspects in custody.

To match fingerprints more expediently, the state of Georgia implemented, in 1989, the Automated Fingerprint Identification System (AFIS). Fingerprint information is stored on an optical disk and when a latent print comes in for checking, its characteristics are entered into the computer and compared to fingerprints on the optical disks. In the first three years of use, AFIS identified 170 suspects from previously unsolved crimes—mostly burglaries. In one murder case, a latent print was entered into the system and, 22 minutes later, a match was found. This led to the arrest of a previously unconsidered suspect. "It was a cold hit," said a Georgia Bureau of Investigation spokesman. "We didn't even know he existed. We had no idea he was involved."

The AFIS program is now integrated with the Computer Crime History (CCH) to enable easy updating of information in the CCH based on fingerprint "hits." This allows authorities to compile a suspect's criminal history in a day rather than the previously required three weeks. AFIS is also configured to accept fingerprint cards created using a "live scan" process, which digitizes the print images rather than using the traditional ink printing method, once local law enforcement agencies install the necessary equipment to carry out this process.

Source: Elizabeth Coady, "New Computerized System Fingered Slaying Suspect," *The Atlanta Journal-Constitution,* February 17, 1989, p. 17-A, as updated by the author in 1991.

After the computer selects possible matches to the latent fingerprint, the matches are displayed on a computer monitor for further comparison by a human user.

must first be *mounted* on a **tape drive,** where a read/write head similar to that used on a disk drive transfers information to and from the tape. Another drawback of a tape system is that the information must be accessed in the *same* sequence in which it was stored on the tape. This type of access is termed **sequential access.**

Mainframe computers depend upon reel-to-reel tapes to store information not needed immediately, such as financial statistics, payroll records, student academic records, and so on, and to make backups of information from disk packs. A **backup** is a copy of the information on the disk; it can be used to restore information if an equipment problem causes the disk to fail. Personal computers use a form of **tape cartridge** to back up hard disks.

Output

The two most popular output devices are the printer and the video screen, or monitor. A **monitor** is required for almost any computer system for two reasons. First, the data or instructions being input from the keyboard or other input device are shown on the monitor. A blinking rectangle or underline called a **cursor** moves on the screen as the data or instructions are input. Second, the monitor is an almost instantaneous outlet for the result of the processing.

Several varieties of monitors are available, but the primary distinction is between **monochrome monitors** and **color monitors.** Monochrome or single-color monitors display light symbols on a darker background—as compared to color monitors, which can display many colors on the screen. The question of which monitor—monochrome or color—is better depends on the task to be completed and the budget of the user. This question will be addressed in more detail in Chapter 5.

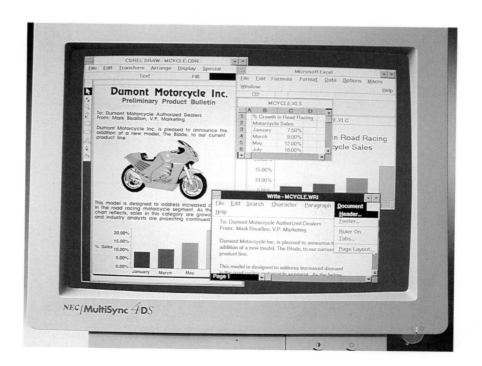

Color monitors are often a necessity—as, for example, when colorful graphics are needed to show the exact color of a product.

Often a user will view the results of processing on the monitor screen and then decide that **hard copy** is needed, in the form of a printed page. Such hard copy is useful because the output to the monitor is not permanent. For mainframe users, it is usually very easy to divert the output on the monitor to a page printer at a computer center. A **page printer** is a high-speed printer that can print an entire page in one motion. For personal computer users, a large number of printers are available today in varying speeds, qualities of print, and price ranges. The most commonly used printer for personal computers is the **dot matrix printer,** which creates symbols on the page by printing a matrix of dots. Other types of printers commonly used with PCs are ink jet printers and laser printers. The **ink-jet printer** sprays ink on the page to create letters and pictures. The **laser printer** is much like a copier except that instead of photocopying an existing document, it converts output from a computer into a printed form.

We can also use secondary storage for input and output by outputting results to a disk or tape for storage or by reading data or instructions from disk or tape. Read-only secondary storage, such as cartridges or video disks, is also designed to be used as an input to the computer.

Terminals

A type of input/output device that is used for work with mainframes or with a computer network is the terminal. A **terminal** is made up of a keyboard and a monitor and is used primarily for input and output. It may or may not have its

DALLAS POLICE TAKE BYTE OUT OF CRIME

In police work, not knowing the adversary can lead to an officer's being wounded or even killed. However, in Dallas, Texas, officers on patrol now use computers in their cruisers to speed the identification process. Each patrol car is equipped with a mobile data terminal that is linked via radio to the city hall data center. Instead of calling the dispatcher to make inquiries about a car license tag or the identification of a suspect, officers simply type in the tag number and the information is relayed to the data center computer, which then returns the status of the automobile. Since the data terminals were installed, the number of license checks has doubled, and many officers agree that, by itself, this capability makes the system worthwhile.

Beyond making license checks easier, however, the mobile terminals can relay information on the status of the driver of a vehicle that has been stopped. Instead of having to read the information over the radio and wait for a response, the new system quickly provides information that can save lives. The terminal screen also acts as a link between an officer and the dispatcher as well as with other officers. In effect, it acts as electronic mail on the roads. For example, when an officer returns to the vehicle, he or she can check the screen for a list of calls to be answered, with high-priority calls being highlighted in a different color. In addition, the officer can trade information with other Dallas police personnel. In one case, it was possible to relay the tag number of a shooting suspect to the data center and have a patrol car waiting for the suspect when he returned home!

Source: Clinton Wilder, "City Cops Take Byte Out of Crime," *Computerworld,* October 29, 1990, p. 76.

> ## We work the crud out of it, that's for sure.
>
> *Dallas Police Officer*
> *David Vestal*
>
> Quoted in "City Cops Take Byte Out of Crime," *Computerworld,* October 29, 1990, p. 76.

The mobile computers installed in Dallas police squad cars give officers access to the police data center.

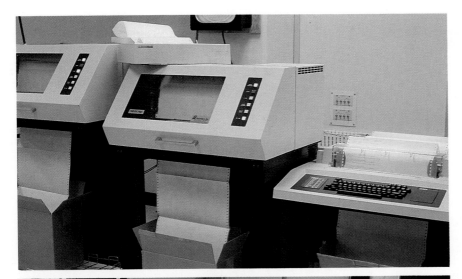

The personal computer printer sitting on top of the mainframe printer monitors the operation of the larger printer.

Employees use this mainframe printer to obtain a hard copy of the results shown on the terminal screen.

own CPU or secondary storage. When it does not have either of these, it is usually referred to as a **dumb terminal.** A PC can also be used as a terminal when it acts as an input/output device for a mainframe or network. Another name for a terminal is **VDT,** for **video display terminal.**

Input/Output Telecommunication

A device that facilitates both input and output is the **modem,** which sends and receives information between computers over telephone lines. The modem converts the electrical signals from RAM in the computer into the type of electrical signals that can travel over telephone lines. In other words, the digital output from the computer must be modulated into an analog form before it can be sent over a telephone line, and the analog input received over the telephone line must be demodulated into digital form before it can be used for input into the computer.

Terminals are often used to link multiple users to the mainframe computer.

The term *modem* is used because the device MOdulates/DEModulates signals. With a modem, a computer terminal or a personal computer can be used to communicate with a mainframe or another personal computer. In either case, the modem acts as both an input device and an output device so the computer can send and receive information over the telephone lines. This is very useful

A modem can link a PC to other PCs or to a mainframe computer.

for persons who wish to work at home, access a computerized information service to research some topic, or simply communicate with other computer users.

Now that we have considered the four major components of computer hardware in detail, we can put together a basic computer system. By a **system** we mean all the items that will go together to produce a working whole. The mainframe computer system shown in Figure 2-3 includes multiple terminals (keyboard and monitor) for input and output, a CPU for processing/internal memory, a disk drive with disk pack and reel-to-reel tape for secondary storage, and a page printer for output.

A corresponding personal computer system is shown in Figure 2-4. As with the mainframe computer, a keyboard and a monitor are used for input and output. In addition, a mouse is shown as a source of input. The processor/internal memory unit includes both RAM and ROM, while secondary storage is made up of a floppy disk drive and a hard disk. For output, a portable printer is used in addition to the monitor. A modem is also included for communication with a mainframe or other personal computers.

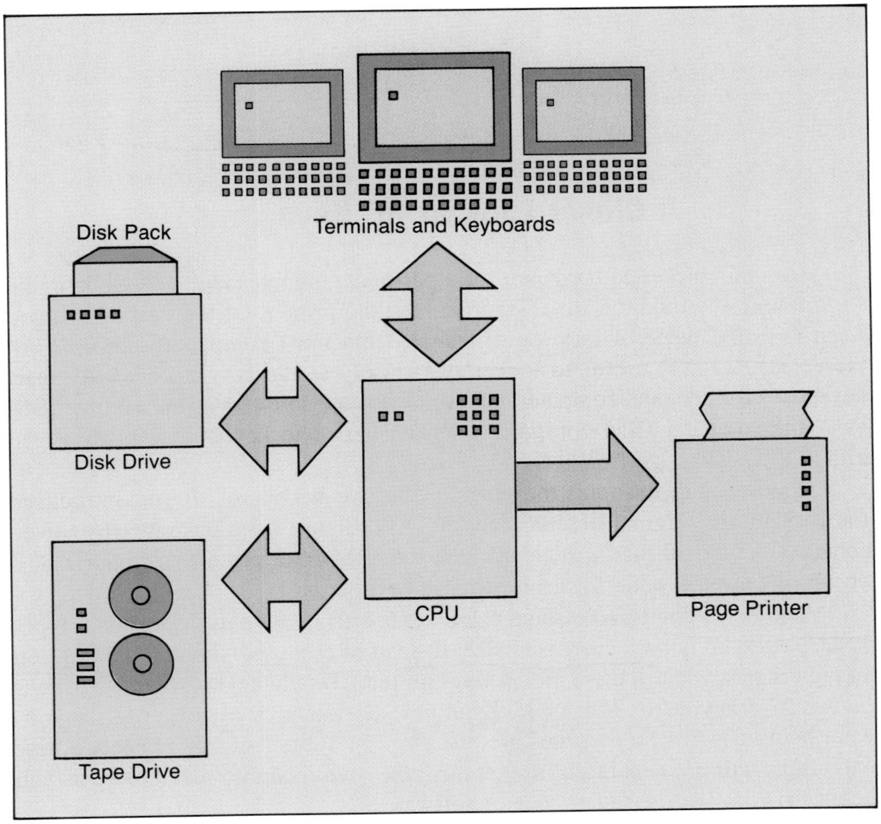

FIGURE 2-3
Mainframe Computer System

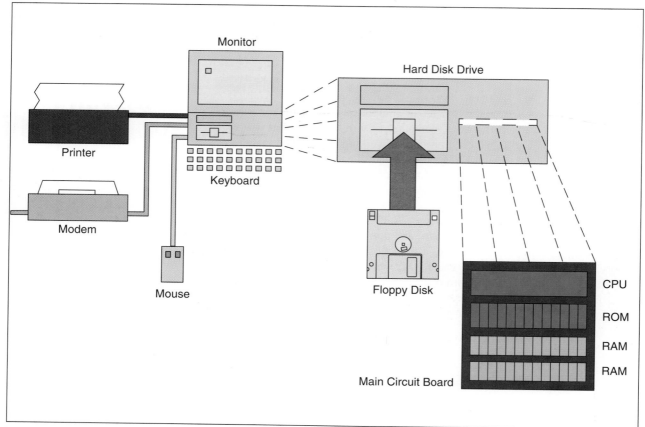

FIGURE 2-4
Personal Computer System

A Closer Look at PC Keyboards

The five main pieces of hardware for a personal computer are the keyboard, the system unit, the monitor, the disk drive, and the printer. Of these, the keyboard is an essential piece of hardware; it is also the most complicated to use. For these reasons, it is useful to look more closely at the two most widely used keyboards for personal computers that run the same software as the original IBM PC—the so-called **IBM compatible PCs.** These two keyboards are shown in Figure 2-5.

Figure 2-5a illustrates the older of the two keyboards. It was introduced for use with the original IBM PCs and PC ATs. Figure 2-5b illustrates the newer, enhanced keyboard that is standard with the IBM PS/2 personal computer. The operations are the same for each of these keyboards.

The first thing to note about these keyboards relative to the standard typewriter keyboard is their increased size. Instead of the approximately 50 keys on a typewriter keyboard, there are 84 keys on the AT-style keyboard and 101 keys on the PS/2 keyboard. These additional keys are for uses particular to the software being used; their purposes are discussed in Table 2-1. While not all these operations will be meaningful to you now, they will come to mean more as you begin to work with various types of software.

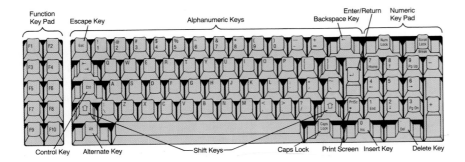

FIGURE 2-5a
Original IBM Compatible
Keyboard

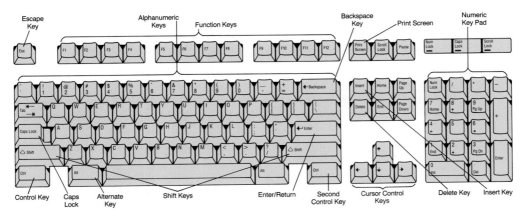

FIGURE 2-5b
Newer Enhanced IBM
Compatible Keyboard

TABLE 2-1
Keys on IBM Keyboards

Key	Name	Purpose
F1–F12	Function keys	Operation depends on package
0–9	Numeric keypad	Cursor control; if Num Lock key is pressed, same action as keys on calculator
$\uparrow, \rightarrow, \leftarrow, \downarrow$	Arrow keys	Cursor control
Esc	Escape key	Aborts the current operation
Tab	Tab key	Tabs the cursor to the next tab stop
Ctrl	Control key	Gives special operating commands when used with other keys
Shift	Shift key	Shifts to opposite case
Alt	Alt key	Gives another meaning to a key when pressed simultaneously with that key
Backspace	Backspace key	Deletes character to left of current position
Ins	Insert key	Switches between insert and replace modes in word processing
Del	Delete key	Deletes character under cursor
Enter	Enter key	Designates the end of a command or line of input
PrtSc	Print screen	Causes the screen contents to be printed when pressed simultaneously with the shift key
Caps Lock	Uppercase lock	Shifts the alphabetic keyboard to upper case until pressed again
Scroll Lock/Break		When combined with Ctrl key, aborts current operation

A Closer Look at Floppy Disks

Floppies were the first low-cost breakthrough satisfying users' needs for on-line memory.

James Adkisson, president,
Insite Peripherals

Quoted in "View from the Top,"
Personal Computing, October 1989,
p. 260.

For personal computers, the floppy disk is the most common form of secondary storage. **Floppy disks,** also called **diskettes,** come in sizes of $5\frac{1}{4}$ inches and $3\frac{1}{2}$ inches (8-inch diskettes were, at one time, used for minicomputers and dedicated word processing computers, but their use has been almost discontinued). The smaller, $3\frac{1}{2}$-inch floppy disk is commonly referred to as a **microfloppy disk.** Both sizes are made of plastic, but while the larger size is flexible neither size is really "floppy." In fact, the microfloppy is encased in a rigid cover that protects the entire disk from dust and other contaminants. Figure 2-6 shows the makeup of both sizes of floppy disks, with the various parts pointed out.

Both sizes of diskette have a **head window,** which is the area of the diskette that is in contact with the read/write head of the disk drive. Over the head window, the microfloppy has a spring-loaded metal shutter that is pushed back when the diskette is inserted in the disk drive. The head window on the $5\frac{1}{4}$-inch floppy is uncovered, and users must be careful not to get oil from their fingers or other contaminants on the diskette. In both cases, the disk drive's read/write head actually rubs against the floppy disk rather than flying above it, so the rotation speed of 300 rpm is less than a tenth that of a disk pack.

For the $5\frac{1}{4}$-inch floppy, the **hub ring** is where the disk drive clamps onto the diskette and rotates the disk. This occurs automatically when the diskette is inserted in the disk drive on the personal computer and the drive door is closed. The hole in the vinyl cover of the diskette is the **index hole;** it is used to indicate to the computer where the disk is in its rotation. There is another hole in the plastic disk itself so that, when the inner and outer holes match up, a light can shine through the combined hole and activate a photoelectric cell underneath the diskette. This signals the computer that the index hole has passed, and the position of the desired information can then be determined from this information. There is also a **write-protect notch,** which, when covered by a piece of opaque tape, will not allow information to be written onto the disk. This is a security device that keeps data on the disk from being destroyed by new information being written over it.

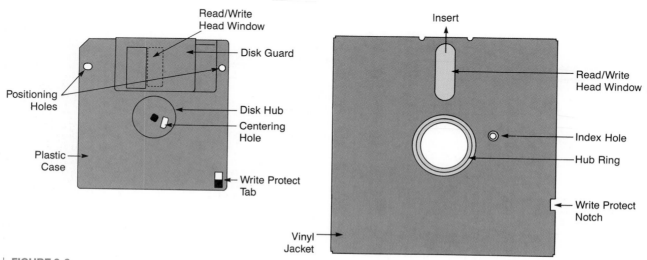

FIGURE 2-6
Floppy Disks

Often, both 3½-inch and 5¼-inch floppy disk drives are used on the same computer.

(Bottom left) The original IBM XT and compatible computers use a 360K, 5¼-inch floppy disk. (Right) The IBM AT and compatible computers use a 1.2M, 5¼-inch floppy disk.

FIGURE 2-7
Diskette Sectoring

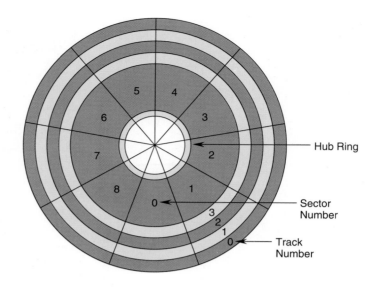

For the microfloppy, different mechanisms replace the hub ring, index hole, and write-protect notch used on the $5\frac{1}{4}$-inch floppy. Instead of a hub ring and an index hole, the microfloppy has a metal hub with a hole in it that is engaged by the disk drive. The position of this engagement of the disk drive with the hub determines the position of the disk in its rotation. Instead of a write-protect notch, the microfloppy uses a sliding tab that can be opened to write-protect the disk. When the tab is moved to uncover the hole, no information can be written onto the diskette.

Since personal computers use only one floppy disk at a time, rather than a group of platters as in a disk pack, the cylinder storage system discussed earlier is not appropriate here. Instead of the cylinder system, a sectoring system is used. The tracks on the disk are divided into **sectors,** and the number of sectors on the diskette depends on the type of diskette and the operating system. A typical sectoring of a diskette is shown in Figure 2-7.

The sectoring plan shown in Figure 2-7 is called **soft sectoring** since it is dependent on the machine being used and the software system that manages the disk, called the **disk operating system (DOS)** (to be discussed in more detail in Chapter 4). Soft sectoring is currently used on all personal computers.

The process by which the disk operating system soft-sectors the disk and records codes on the diskette to identify each track and sector is called **formatting.** The disk must be formatted before it can be used. For example, the $3\frac{1}{2}$-inch microfloppy disk used on many IBM compatible PCs has 80 tracks and 18 sectors. Each track-sector has 512 bytes, so the total storage capacity of the diskette on one side is $18 \times 80 \times 512$ bytes = 720 Kbytes. Since this is a double-sided diskette, it can hold a total of 1.44 Mbytes.

In the process of formatting, a list of the diskette's contents called the **file allocation table (FAT)** is recorded on a specific sector and track. The disk controller (part of the personal computer's hardware) and the DOS use the FAT to locate the programs and files so that the read/write head can move to the proper position on the disk.

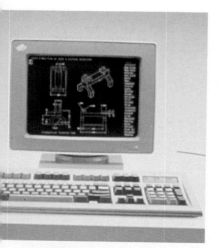

The IBM PS/2 Model 80 is one of many personal computers that use the 1.44M, $3\frac{1}{2}$-inch microfloppy disk.

Storage Capacities

As we said earlier, floppy disks primarily are made in two sizes: $3\frac{1}{2}$ inches in diameter—the microfloppy—and $5\frac{1}{4}$ inches in diameter. In both cases, data are stored on both sides of the diskette. Within these two sizes, there are different storage capacities, depending on the density used to store data on the disk. The density of the diskette is determined by the disk's number of bits per square inch. Currently, there are two categories of density: double and high. High-density diskettes store more data than do double density. Diskettes are commonly described by density abbreviations, with "DD" or "2D" indicating double density and "HD" indicating high density.

The storage capacities of the two sizes and two densities of diskettes used on IBM compatible computers are shown in Table 2-2 along with an example of the machine on which such diskettes are commonly used.

In each case in Table 2-2, the storage capacity is for a formatted disk; that is, the amount of storage available after the required formatting process, which uses some of the disk storage for the directory information. The same diskette can be formatted to have more or less storage space depending on the computer and the disk operating system. This is why a Macintosh can format a double-density microfloppy to have 800 Kbytes of information instead of the 720 Kbytes on the IBM PS/2.

The Apple Macintosh uses an 800M, 3½-inch microfloppy.

TABLE 2-2
Floppy Disk Storage Capacity

Density	Size	Storage Capacity	Typical Machine
Double	$5\frac{1}{4}''$	360 Kbytes	IBM PC XT
High	$5\frac{1}{4}''$	1.2 Mbytes	IBM PC AT
Double	$3\frac{1}{2}''$	720 Kbytes	Toshiba Laptop PC
High	$3\frac{1}{2}''$	1.44 Mbytes	IBM PS/2 Model 80

One impact of high-capacity floppies will be the low-cost distribution of software and data.

James Adkisson, president, Insite Peripherals

Quoted in "View from the Top," *Personal Computing,* October 1989, p. 260.

It appears that the current trend is toward increased use of microfloppies relative to the older $5\frac{1}{4}$-inch floppies. All laptop computers now use this size of disk, and the trend toward it was undoubtedly accelerated by IBM's decision to use this size of disk on its PS/2 series. The convenience and security of the microfloppy has also made it the first choice of many users of other types of machines. Being able to stick the microfloppy in your shirt, blouse, or jeans pocket or in your purse without fear of damage gives it clear advantages over the larger floppy disk.

Another desirable feature of the microfloppy is its increased storage capacity. Special preformatted microfloppies with storage capacities of 20 Mbytes—comparable to a hard disk of only a few years ago—are now available. These microfloppies require their own drive system, which works only with them. These super-high-density microfloppies may soon become very important for transporting large amounts of data and software.

TLC FOR FLOPPIES

Even though floppy disks are pretty tough storage devices that do not require a great deal of special care, they still must be protected from some environmental hazards. While many of these cautions pertain only to older, $5\frac{1}{4}$-inch floppies, care must also be taken in working with the microfloppies. Remember that the diskettes are made of plastic and use a magnetic field to store data. Here are a few rules for using diskettes:

- Don't bend or try to fold the diskette.
- Don't store the diskette in extremely high temperatures or let it be exposed to direct sunlight.
- Store the diskettes in a vertical position.
- Don't lay the diskette on the television or other appliances that create a magnetic field, as this will destroy the data.
- Don't use magnets to secure diskettes to a bulletin board. (Don't laugh—this has been done with disastrous consequences.)
- Avoid touching the disk surface with your fingers and keep other contaminants (such as pizza sauce) off the surface.
- Do not attempt to clean the surface of the diskette with any type of cleaning fluid. This can prevent the disk drive from properly reading information stored on the disk.
- Don't expose the disk to static electricity—such as that caused by a combination of dry air and carpeting—as this can destroy the data on the disk.

BITS, BYTES, AND BINARY NUMBERS

In the earlier discussion of the conceptual computer, we noted that the CPU handles the actual processing of data into information, following instructions input by the user. We also discussed the importance of the two types of internal memory and the use of secondary storage in the processing operation. To handle this processing and storage, computer chips contain microscopic transistorized switches that are either "on" or "off." Because of this system of processing and storing data, the base 2, or **binary**, **number system** is used for both processing and storage. Each transistorized switch corresponds to one **bit** (BInary digiT) of storage. This means that instead of the 10 digits, 26 letters (upper- and lowercase), and various punctuation marks used by humans for processing data into information, the computer represents these symbols with a group of switches, each with just these two conditions—"on" or "off," 1 or 0.

For storing the nonnumeric data, processed information, and instructions in the form of letters, punctuation marks, and special symbols, a standard representation involving groups of eight bits, called a **byte,** has been devised. Each pattern of eight bits represents a given symbol. Several patterns of bits have been suggested, but the two most commonly used codes are **EBCDIC** (pronounced "eb-suh-dick"), which is an acronym for Extended Binary Coded Decimal Interchange Code, and **ASCII** (pronounced "as-key"), which is an acronym for American Standard Code for Information Interchange. EBCDIC was developed by IBM for use on its mainframe computers, while ASCII has become the standard code for personal computers. For example, the letter *A* is coded as 01000001 in ASCII and as 11000001 in EBCDIC. Note that each of these groups of eight bits is either 1 or 0. Because each character can be represented by one byte in either ASCII or EBCDIC, the terms *byte* and *character* are commonly used interchangeably.

These codes are used for transmitting information between the keyboard and internal memory and between internal memory and the display screen as well as for storing information in internal memory and secondary storage. Figure 2-8 shows the letter *A* being transmitted from the keyboard into internal memory with the ASCII code, and the ASCII codes for letters and symbols are shown on pages 328 and 329.

Storing Information

As discussed earlier, data, information, and instructions must be stored in both the internal memory and the secondary storage of a computer. In internal memory, both random-access memory and read-only memory use memory chips to store data, information, and instructions in binary form. The amounts of RAM and ROM available in a particular computer are measured in **Kbytes** (kilobytes) where 1 Kbyte = 1,024 bytes or characters. The letter *K* stands for *kilo,* which is Greek for 1,000. Even though 1,024 (which is 2^{10}) does not exactly equal 1,000, the term *Kbyte* or simply the letter *K* has become a standard measure of storage capacity meaning roughly 1,000. For example, 64K of memory means $64 \times 1,024 = 65,535$ bytes of memory. The next measure of memory after a

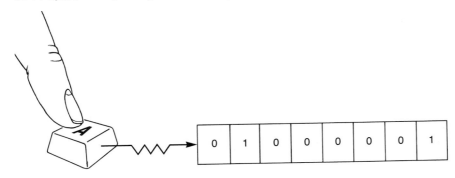

FIGURE 2-8
Transmittal of Letter *A*
from Keyboard

BITS OF HISTORY

50 Years of Development

The First Computer

For a machine as important as the computer, it is strange to think that the question of who built the first computer was settled in court. A 1973 lawsuit invalidated early patents on the computer, because the judge decided the wrong persons had received credit for developing the first computer.

The early history of the computer involves three individuals, or groups of individuals, and the machines they built. One pair of individuals were John V. Atanasoff of Iowa State University and his graduate assistant, Clifford Berry, who began work on an electronic computer before World War II and finished a working prototype in 1942. Although there was a great deal of interest in computers that could compute artillery tables during the war,

the Atanasoff–Berry Computer, or ABC, did not receive much attention. Iowa State did not even attempt to patent the device, and neither man followed up on this early work. The ABC was eventually forgotten and only a few parts of the original machine remain.

Another important individual in the development of the computer is Howard Aiken. In 1944, Aiken completed the MARK I computer for IBM in cooperation with Harvard University. Even though the MARK I had 760,000 electrical parts connected by 500 miles of wiring, it was not completely electronic, because it used 3,000 electromechanical relays as switches. It was so big that an entire building on Harvard's campus was set aside for it.

The pair of individuals who usually receive the credit for developing a purely electronic computer are J. Presper Eckert, Jr., and John Mauchly. Eckert was working on a government project to build a fast computing device when he visited Atanasoff at Iowa State to learn about the ABC. After his meeting, Eckert and Mauchly built the ENIAC (Electrical Numerical Integrator And Calculator) for the war effort. Unfortunately, it was not

finished until 1946, after the war. The ENIAC contained 18,000 vacuum tubes and 80,000 resistors and capacitors, weighed 30 tons, and occupied over 15,000 square feet. It was much faster than the MARK I, because it could multiply two numbers in 0.0003 second, compared with over 0.05 second for the MARK I. However, ENIAC used so much electricity that the lights in the section of Philadelphia in which it was located supposedly dimmed each time the computer ran. The ENIAC, which ran for nine years, is now on exhibit at the Smithsonian Institution.

An important advance over the ENIAC was the EDVAC (Electronic Discrete Variable Automatic Computer) developed by John von Neumann. The EDVAC utilized the concept of the stored program, which meant the computer did not have to be rewired for each job as the ENIAC did.

The 1973 court decision named the Atanasoff–Berry team as the builders of the first computer, rather than Eckert and Mauchly. Aiken is best known for getting IBM interested in computers, but the MARK I contributed little to

The Atanasoff–Berry computer was the first electronic computer built, but only a few parts of this computer exist today.

The MARK I computer was the first computer built by International Business Machines Corporation.

J. Presper Eckert, Jr., is shown with the ENIAC computer that he and John Mauchly jointly designed and built.

later developments of the computer. Von Neumann is remembered for adding the stored program concept to the computer.

Generations of Computers

The subsequent development of computers is usually described as occurring in generations. The first generation, which began with Eckert and Mauchly's ENIAC, is considered to span the period 1946–1959. This generation of computers is characterized by the use of vacuum tubes in the CPU and internal memory units, the first commercial computers, and many fundamental advances in computing. The first commercial computer was the UNIVAC 1 (UNIVersal Automatic Computer), which was sold to the Census Bureau in 1951.

In the second generation of computers, 1959–1964, the vacuum tube was replaced by the transistor. The transistor, a solid-state device, was the major breakthrough that allowed computers to have reasonable size and

UNIVAC 1, a first-generation computer and the first computer available commercially, was used to predict the outcome of the 1952 presidential election.

The IBM 360 series of mainframe computers was an extremely popular third-generation computer that played a large role in making IBM a dominant force in the computer industry.

The four generations of computers as exemplified by vacuum tubes, transistorized circuit boards, integrated circuits, and microprocessors.

power. A solid-state device is made of minerals so that it can be instructed to allow or not allow a flow of current. Because solid-state devices did not use the hot filament that was in vacuum tubes, the use of transistors reduced the computer's heat output and power requirement. Transistors also increased the reliability of the computer, because they did not burn out the way vacuum tubes did. This breakthrough in turn reduced the cost of owning and operating a computer. This period saw tremendous growth in the use of computers by government, business, and industry.

The introduction of the integrated circuit in 1965 was the beginning of the third generation of computers. With this technological advance, an entire circuit board containing transistors and connecting wires could be placed on a single chip. This development meant greater reliability and compactness combined with low cost and power requirements. During this period, IBM controlled the mainframe market with its 360 (later to be 370) series of computers. This series was so well

designed and built that its successors are still in heavy use today.

The fourth and current generation of computers began in 1971 with the introduction of the microprocessor—a central processing unit on a chip. This generation includes the introduction of supercomputers. These "monster computers" are in heavy demand for military and meteorological applications that require a high speed of operation. Another important advance of this generation has been the introduction of the personal computer, because the power of the computer has been made available to anybody who wishes to use one.

A possible "fifth generation" of computers has recently been discussed in the media. The Japanese government has a broad-ranging plan to leapfrog American superiority in hardware with a fifth-generation computer that will include parallel processors—several CPUs working in parallel to speed up execution time. No one knows how successful this particular plan will be, but we probably won't have to wait long to find out.

TABLE 2-3
Memory Relationships

1 bit	=	1 on/off switch
1 byte	=	8 bits
1 Kbyte	=	1,024 bytes
1 Mbyte	=	1,024 Kbytes (1,048,576 bytes)
1 Gbyte	=	1,024 Mbytes (1,073,741,824 bytes)

Kbyte is a **Mbyte** (megabyte), which is 1,024 Kbytes, or approximately 1 million (2^{20}) bytes, of storage. Finally, the largest commonly used measure of storage is the **Gbyte** (gigabyte), which is 1,024 Mbytes or approximately 1 *billion* (2^{30}) bytes of storage. Table 2-3 shows these memory relationships.

Early personal computers had less than 16K of RAM, but current machines can have over 16 Mbytes of RAM with 1 Mbyte being a common amount of memory. Mainframe computers usually have at least 64 Mbytes of internal memory available. Less ROM is needed because it is used for a special purpose that the computer designer knows in advance and because the amount varies from computer to computer.

Secondary storage is also measured in Kbytes, Mbytes, and Gbytes. Tape and disk storage on mainframe computers is measured in megabytes, and personal computer hard disks storing 40, 80, and over 100 Mbytes are common today. Personal computer floppy disks and microdisks hold from 360 Kbytes to 2.88 Mbytes. Optical disks can store gigabytes of data and information!

1. A conceptual computer is composed of input, output, processing/internal memory, and secondary storage units.
2. The input unit sends data and instructions to the computer; the keyboard is a common input device, with the mouse coming into more common use for personal computers.
3. The processing/internal memory unit performs the manipulation and storage of symbols within the computer.
4. The processing unit is usually referred to as the central processing unit (CPU). It is made up of the control unit and the arithmetic–logic unit (ALU).
5. Internal memory is made up of random-access memory (RAM) and read-only memory (ROM). RAM is accessible to the user for storage of data, programs, and processed information. ROM is built into the computer by the manufacturer and is needed to start up the computer and handle certain operations within the computer.
6. Both the CPU and internal memory are built onto silicon chips that can contain 1 million transistors to handle memory and processing operations.
7. Secondary storage is needed because RAM is both limited and volatile; tape and disk are common secondary storage devices. Mainframe computers use disk packs while personal computers use floppy and hard disks.
8. The output unit transmits the results from the computer to the user; the monitor and printer are common output devices.
9. Communication with another computer is accomplished with a modem that translates computer data into a form that can be transmitted over telephone lines.
10. The binary number system is used in computers because the computer uses on/off switches to handle processing and storage.
11. The EBCDIC or ASCII codes are systems for representing letters, digits, and symbols in eight bits each (a byte); one character corresponds to one byte. EBCDIC is used on IBM mainframes; ASCII is used on all personal computers.
12. Memory is measured in Kbytes (1,024 bytes), Mbytes (1,024 Kbytes), or Gbytes (1,024 Mbytes). Mainframes usually have at least 64 Mbytes of internal storage while personal computers commonly have at least 1 Mbyte of RAM.
13. Secondary storage for mainframes and hard disks for personal computers can store Mbytes of information. Floppy disks and microdisks hold from 360 Kbytes to 2.88 Mbytes.

KEY TERMS

arithmetic–logic unit (ALU)
ASCII (American Standard Code for
    Information Interchange)
backup
binary number system
bit
booting process
byte
cartridge
central processing unit (CPU)
chip
color monitor
computer disk
conceptual computer
control unit
conventional memory
cursor
direct-access storage
disk drive
disk operating system (DOS)
disk pack
dot matrix printer
dumb terminal
EBCDIC (Extended Binary Coded
    Decimal Interchange Code)
expanded memory
extended memory
file allocation table (FAT)
floppy disks
formatting
Gbyte
hard copy
hard disk
hardware
head window
hub ring
IBM compatible PCs
index hole
ink-jet printer
input
integrated circuit

internal memory
Kbytes
keyboard
laser printer
light pen
magnetic tape
Mbyte
memory manager
microfloppy disk
microprocessor
modem
monitor
monochrome monitor
mouse
optical disk
output
page printer
pen-based computing
printer
processing/internal memory unit
random-access memory (RAM)
read-only memory (ROM)
read/write head
secondary storage
sectors
sequential access
soft sectoring
system
tape
tape cartridge
tape drive
terminal
touchscreen
transistor
upper memory
video disk
video display terminal (VDT)
voice recognition
volatile
write-protect notch

1. List the four main parts of the conceptual computer.
2. Which part of the computer is comparable to the human brain? to the use of file cabinets?
3. List four items commonly used to input data to a computer.
4. List the two main parts of the processing unit of the computer. What is this combination called?
5. Why are both units needed in the CPU?
6. Differentiate between RAM and ROM. Which is accessible to the user for storage of data, programs, and information?
7. Why is RAM considered to be a volatile form of internal memory? Why is ROM not volatile?
8. Which type of secondary storage device is a direct-access device? Which is a sequential-access secondary storage device?
9. What sizes of disks are available for personal computers? What are the sizes called?
10. List two commonly used output devices for a computer.
11. How are monitors differentiated?
12. Explain the meaning of the term *modem* in computer communications. What is the purpose of a modem?
13. Explain why computers use the binary number system.
14. What are the EBCDIC and ASCII representations of the letter *A*?
15. How much random-access memory is available on most personal computers? What amounts of storage are available for mainframe and personal computer secondary storage?

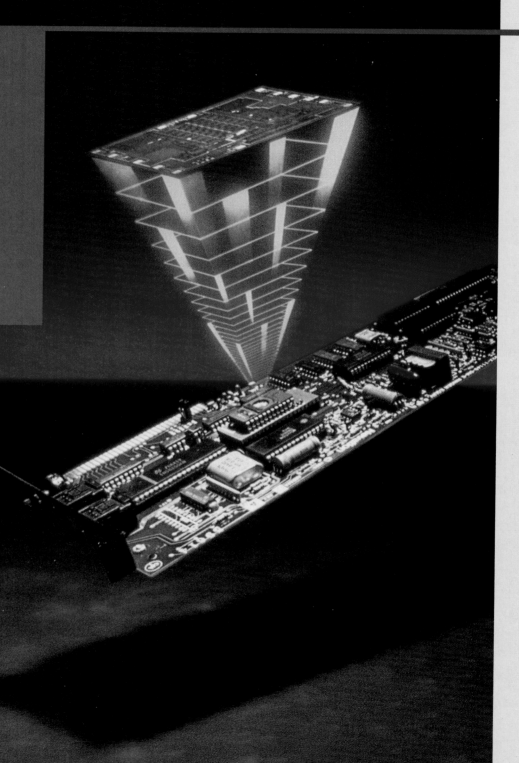

An Introduction to Computer Software

In this chapter, we will introduce the other half of the computer, that is, the software that directs the actions of the hardware. The discussion will cover the importance of software for the successful use of the computer; the three major types of software—systems software, utility software, and applications software; and some important terminology of software packages. (Chapter 4 provides a more complete discussion of systems and utility software.) Six important types of applications packages are introduced in this chapter: word processing, graphics, financial analysis, accounting, data base management, and telecommunications. In each case we will show examples of their use. (Chapters 5 through 8 provide more detailed discussions of these packages.) An introduction to integrated software and desktop publishing is also included in this section.

STUDY OBJECTIVES

After reading this chapter, you should be able to

- understand the importance of software in the successful use of a computer;
- discuss the three major types of software: systems, utility, and applications software;
- recognize the most important terminology of software packages;
- discuss types of user interfaces;
- discuss the difference between a menu-driven package and a command-driven package;
- explain the use of graphical user interfaces;
- list the six important types of applications software widely available for personal computers: word processing, graphics, financial analysis, accounting, data base management, and telecommunications;
- discuss the use of integrated packages and desktop publishing.

SOFTWARE DOWN ON THE FARM

A computer investment doesn't compare [in cost]. It's about the same price as a used pickup truck, and not a very good used pickup.

Norlin Hein, Professor of Agricultural Economics, The University of Missouri

Quoted in "Computer Has Grown into a Useful Piece of Farm Equipment," *Atlanta Journal and Constitution,* Aug. 21, 1989, p. B9.

In the world of agribusiness, the key to success is cutting costs. Because farmers have little or no control over the prices they will receive for their crops, their profit often depends on how little they spend on the production side. In the past, much of this cost-cutting depended on experience, guesswork, and just plain luck. However, today, many farmers are using computers to help them run their businesses. In fact, it has been estimated that almost half of all full-time farmers use a computer to help run the farm.

In managing a farm, computer software is used for a wide variety of tasks, ranging from basic accounting to making decisions about crops. One estimate put the number of software packages available to farmers at close to 2,000. Examples of the applications of computer software on the farm are

- ranking milk cows according to volume of milk produced so that less productive cows can be culled, which may result in a significant reduction in feed costs;

- assisting potato farmers in determining when to apply pesticides to their crops and when to irrigate their fields, depending on the temperature and humidity;
- allowing farmers to draw their fields to scale, indicating crops, drainage problems, pest control problems, fertilizer applications, and other pertinent information, some of which can be obtained from satellite photos, about each field.

While the computer produces important information in the planning process, the farmer still must make the final decisions about when to plant, when to harvest, and when to buy and sell. For farmers who are used to paying over $100,000 for their equipment, the cost of a personal computer and the associated software is small potatoes compared to the savings it can produce.

Sources: "Computer Has Grown into a Useful Piece of Farm Equipment," *The Atlanta Journal,* August 21, 1989, p. B9; and interview with John Brunz, executive director of the Association of Agricultural Computing Companies, November 4, 1991.

Computers are becoming a crucial element in managing the modern farm.

Software has been described as the "driving force" of computers and the "wizard in the machine"; its importance to the use of computers cannot be minimized. Even though the hardware advances of the recent decade have been mind-boggling, the computer without software—without the instructions given it by the user or the manufacturer—would be nothing except a well-constructed combination of silicon chips and electronic circuitry. While there are only so many ways that chips and circuitry can be combined to build a computer, the number of different activities a computer can be instructed to perform by software is virtually limitless. The idea of a computer without software has been described as everything from a car without a driver to a camera without film. Any such analogy makes the point: Computer hardware *must* have software to direct it.

In 1990, worldwide sales of computer software were estimated to be over $80 billion, but it is expected that over $1 *trillion* of software will be sold annually by the year 2000. Because each software program must be created by one or more human programmers, not all software has decreased in price as hardware has. Programs that sold for around $500 when introduced in the mid-1980s still sell for that price or for even more.

Uses of software include just about every application imaginable—from playing games to running the family farm as discussed in the opening box. In this chapter, we will introduce the various types of software and the terminology involved in using software. Detailed discussions of the applications software material introduced here are given in Chapters 4–9.

Programs and Programming

In Chapter 2, we discussed the idea that a computer manipulates and stores symbols by turning switches on and off. For the computer to know which switches should be on and which off, it must be given very specific instructions or rules. This set of instructions is called a **computer program.** The process of developing the set of instructions that will control the computer and direct it to per-

> ## I believe the average businessperson thinks of software as the real power behind computer technology.
>
> *Gari Grimm, president,*
> *WordStar International*
>
> Quoted in "View from the Top,"
> *Personal Computing,* October 1989,
> p. 268.

> ## The software people are the driving force in the computer market and are at the leading edge of computer development.
>
> *John Imlay, chairman,*
> *Management Science America;*
> *past president, Association of*
> *Data Processing Service*
> *Organizations*
>
> From an interview with the author.

Without software, the computer—whether mainframe or personal—can do nothing.

form a desired action is called **programming.** All software, whether built into the machine by the manufacturer, purchased by the user, or developed by the user, is the result of a person or a group of people creating the set of instructions for the computer.

Since the computer knows only what the program tells it, the program must tell it *everything* it needs to know about the process being executed or the problem being solved. This requires a step-by-step approach, developed by the programmer in such a way that no steps are assumed to be known by the computer. These steps are then converted into a program that is written in a **computer language.** There are many (well over 100) computer languages that can be used to communicate with a computer. Each computer language, like a human language, has its own vocabulary and grammatical rules, but most share a similar logical approach to communication with the computer. Commonly used languages are BASIC, COBOL, FORTRAN, Pascal, LOGO, and C.

Many would-be computer users think programming is the only role of a computer and do not purchase a computer because they do not want to have to learn to program. However, as we have discussed previously, the abundance of software available makes it unnecessary to learn programming to be a successful computer user.

TYPES OF SOFTWARE

An ever-growing number of software packages are available to the computer user. In fact, nobody can make even a reasonable estimate of the number of programs that are available. With this wide variety of software, beginning users can become confused about what they need to purchase. To unravel all of the talk about software packages, we must first categorize the types of software that are used in a computer. The three major categories are systems software, utility software, and applications software. Usually, all three of these software types are at work in the computer at the same time, each serving a different purpose.

The first of these, **systems software,** is extremely important because it controls the operations of the other two types of software as well as controlling the computer itself. The most important part of systems software is the **operating system,** which directs the operations of the computer.

Utility software controls day-to-day "housekeeping" operations. These include such operations as making copies of information, displaying a list of user information, and using different computer languages on a computer.

Applications software constitutes the greatest proportion of the software used on computers. This software performs the specialized tasks that we hear so much about, including calculating payrolls, guiding space shuttles, doing word processing or home budgeting, and playing games. The box at the beginning of the chapter describes the use of applications software in farming.

We can view these three types of software and the way they work concurrently in the computer as an "onion," shown in Figure 3-1. The outer layer of the onion is applications software, which is evident to the user since it is the software that actually performs the desired task. Underneath the applications software is the utility software, which is invisible to the user until a housekeeping chore—such as copying information—is required. Finally, at the core of our "onion" is the systems software, which is almost completely invisible to the user.

Information processing is driven by innovative applications software of a wide variety.

David S. Samuels, president, State of the Art Accounting Software

Quoted in "View from the Top," *Personal Computing,* October 1989, p. 268.

FIGURE 3-1
The Onion View of Software

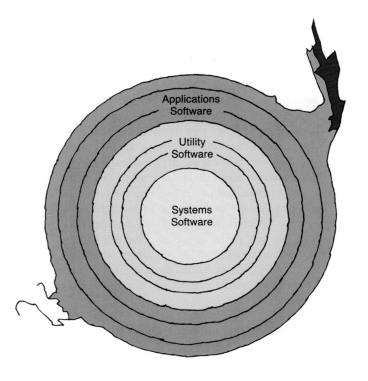

Systems Software

Systems software controls the operation of the computer and makes it possible for the other types of software to execute their tasks. The primary component of systems software is known as the operating system. The operating system manages the many tasks that are going on concurrently within a computer, such

Mainframe operating systems manage the allocation of computer time and resources to multiple users.

as handling the input and output operations and managing the transfer of information between internal memory and the secondary storage. On mainframes, the operating system manages the allocation of processing capability to each of the numerous persons who may be using the computer simultaneously. In this environment, the operating system must also handle all of the requests for different types of operations that come from each of the users.

On a personal computer, the operating system deals with only one user, so an important operation is managing the transfer of information between the internal memory and secondary storage. Since all PCs in use today have the capability of using magnetic disks as secondary storage, the term **disk operating system (DOS)** is commonly used to describe a PC's operating system. Several different brands and types of computers can use the same operating system, so it has been possible to achieve some degree of standardization among personal computers through the operating systems. Three commonly used **generic operating systems** that are not machine specific are MS-DOS (Microsoft DOS), OS/2 (Operating System/Two), and UNIX, all of which run on a variety of makes and models of PCs. In addition, there are several machine-specific or **proprietary operating systems** for machines such as the Apple II series and the Macintosh series of PCs.

These three generic PC operating systems are differentiated by the number of tasks and users they can control. **MS-DOS** is directed toward the use of a single machine to run a single piece of applications software. It is currently the most popular of the three operating systems, with millions of PCs using it. The capability of a personal computer to run MS-DOS software is usually considered

Personal computer operating systems are directed primarily at single-user computer systems.

the criterion for determining whether or not it is an **IBM compatible PC,** that is, a PC that runs software written for the original IBM PC or one of its successors, the IBM PC XT, PC AT, or PS/2 series of computers. Computers that are *not* IBM compatible include the Apple II and Apple Macintosh series.

OS/2 is a single-user, multitasking operating system that was jointly developed in 1987 by IBM and the country's largest PC software developer, Microsoft. With OS/2, a user can run multiple tasks concurrently. For example, the user can work with a word processing package and, at the same time, run a mathematical model that requires several hours to complete its calculations. Finally, **UNIX,** which was originally developed by AT&T for use on minicomputers, has been converted to run on PCs and can direct multiple machines running multiple tasks in a network.

Utility Software

Working on a computer—either a mainframe or a personal computer—requires that the user keep track of a library of information that is organized into files. **Files** are units of information (programs, documents, data, and so on) to which the user or software can assign a name. The systems, utility, and applications software all work with files. A common utility software command is to provide a list of the names of the files. Files are often modified, copied between disks or between disk and tape, or combined with language software to write and run programs. These and numerous other operations fall into the utility software category.

In many cases, the utility software is integrated with the system software in such a way that the user gives a single command and the combination of operating system and utility software carries it out. For example, Figure 3-2 shows the result of using the MS-DOS directory command (DIR), which lists

```
A:\-> dir

 Volume in drive A is MSWARE1-400
 Directory of  A:\

RESUME           24751    1-20-90    1:04p
PRESNTED 390      5558    1-01-80    1:40a
RAGSDALE VPI      2827    1-22-90   10:05a
FLAATL   CHR      4119    1-01-80   11:49a
MISC             2842    2-27-90    6:03a
WORDPROC DOC      2268    4-17-90    4:20p
CHRISLTR 221      3050    2-21-90   12:50a
RESUME   290     26852    2-27-90    6:07a
SUMMARY  90       2955    1-01-80    8:10a
PUBS     390     10758    1-01-80    1:36a
DRAFT    DAT       528    3-02-90   12:29a
DATA1    DAT       528    3-02-90   10:35a
EXAM2    F88      3484   11-14-88    6:51a
PROJECTE INP       936    3-02-90    5:58a
PLAYER   DAT       230    3-07-90   12:08a
MS815            3286    2-18-88   12:08p
FIG3-13  PIX      2317    4-19-90   12:06p
      17 File(s)    256000 bytes free

A:\->
```

> **We're going to create the software that puts a computer on every desk and in every home.**
>
> *William Gates, founder and CEO, Microsoft Software*
>
> Quoted in Susan Lammers, *Programmers at Work* (Redmond, Wash.: Microsoft Press, 1986), p. 82.

FIGURE 3-2
MS-DOS Directory Command

GETTING HELP WITH ALGEBRA

For many students entering the ninth grade, the prospect of studying algebra gives them chills. They have heard "horror" stories from older students about the difficulties they will face with such arcane topics as graphing, factoring equations, solving systems of equations, and formulating word problems. When students go into an algebra class, they see teachers writing strange symbols on the blackboard, and they find it is much more fun to send a note to a friend than it is to pay attention. As a result, many students fall behind and lose interest. Now, however, a new educational software system may take much of the fear out of learning algebra.

Learning Logic is a system developed by the National Science Center Foundation, a nonprofit group dedicated to improving mathematics education in the United States. It allows students to work on a progression of lessons at their own pace. When a student fails to solve a problem, Learning Logic explains why the answer was wrong and provides another similar problem to be solved. In a year-long study in one high school, the system dramatically improved test results in the Algebra I class. Prior to the introduction of Learning Logic, 35 percent of the ninth graders dropped the course. Subsequently, only 12 percent dropped the course. Similarly, only 23 percent of the students failed Algebra I, as compared to 44 percent the previous year.

> **This system is designed to teach a process that's understandable, to keep students in the pipeline, and let teachers be mentors, be tutors.**
>
> *Dr. Fred Davison, President, National Science Center Foundation*
>
> Quoted in McKay Jenkins, "Count on Computers to Solve the Problem," *The Atlanta Journal-Constitution,* August 21, 1991, p. G2.

the names of files on the user's disk. This is an operating system command that actually carries out a utility software operation. There also exists utility software, separate from the operating system, for working with files. Examples include PC Tools and the Norton Utilities.

Applications Software

By far the largest amount of software available to the computer user is in the area of applications software. The applications for which software has been writ-

The Learning Logic system runs on a UNIX-based system using a special type of workstation called an **x-terminal,** which uses high-resolution graphics to display subscripts and special symbols on the screen. When fully implemented, the Learning Logic system will be composed of three online systems—Calculator, Graphulator, and Formulator—that, respectively, allow the student to make complex calculations, graph as many as four equations on the screen, and enter equations for which various operations can be carried out. The Formulator allows the student to carry out factoring, expanding, line multiplication, line addition, and root finding. Initial experience suggests that this system will foster student exploration and problem-solving skills and allow the teacher to become a mentor to the students.

Source: McKay Jenkins, "Count on Computers to Solve the Problem," *The Atlanta Journal-Constitution,* August 21, 1991, p. G2.

Students at the National Science Center are using Learning Logic software to learn scientific concepts at their own pace.
From National Science Center Foundation.

ten cover the entire range of human activities. Applications software is available for a wide range of topics, such as religion, politics, astronomy, marriage counseling, contract bridge, horse racing, generation of lottery numbers, genealogy, finance, word processing, and ham radio. All the computer applications discussed in Chapter 1 are examples of the use of applications software. In fact, it would be safe to say that software exists (or will soon exist) for any topic you can think of.

Most applications software is available in the form of **software packages,** which include programs and a written description, called the **documentation,** of the program. The documentation will often include a **user's manual** that provides detailed instructions on using the package.

A problem with applications software is how to find the proper software for a given application. Mainframe computer centers usually have libraries that contain information on new software as well as offer classes on using software. Personal computer software is widely advertised in specialty magazines such as *Byte* and *PC/Computing* and is sold through retail outlets and by mail. Software packages are often reviewed in newspapers and magazines, and seminars and classes on using existing software are also available.

Software Package Terminology

The use of computer packages has spawned a new software terminology, which a new user needs to learn. One overused term in reference to computer packages and to computers in general is "user friendly." A **user-friendly** package is supposed to be easy to use. Unfortunately, many packages that are advertised as user friendly are really quite difficult to use because of their complexity. In some cases it is not possible for sophisticated business packages to be totally user friendly because they are designed to solve complicated problems. Successful use of these packages may actually require many hours of instruction.

Different software packages have different types of **user interface,** that is, different ways to enter data and commands. The three most common of these user interfaces are menu driven, command driven, and graphical. In a **menu-driven package,** a **menu** either gives the user a list of commands from which to choose or requests that data be entered, in a particular form. Two very common methods of menu selection are (1) to enter a letter or a number and (2) to move the highlighting to the desired selection. In many cases, the user will not only select from a menu, but will also be asked to enter a file name or specific data. For example, in an accounting package, a menu may request users to enter the amounts they wish to budget for various categories. Figure 3-3 shows the

(Left) Many computer magazines carry information on software as well as reviews of various packages. (Right) Software for personal computers is often sold in boxes that contain both a software disk and written instructions.

menu system from the WordPerfect word processing package, in which the user makes a selection simply by entering a number. Figure 3-4 shows the menu system for Lotus 1-2-3, in which the user can move the highlighting to make a selection or can enter the first letter of the desired option.

One widely used type of menu system is the **pull-down menu,** so called because making a selection from a menu results in the appearance of a submenu, from which a choice can be made. Figure 3-5 shows the use of a pull-down menu system on the Apple Macintosh.

At the opposite extreme from menu-driven packages are command-driven packages. A **command-driven package** does not provide a list of commands to choose from or request a specific type of data; instead, it simply waits for the user to enter the appropriate command or data. It may show a **prompt** to alert

```
Format

    1 - Line
              Hyphenation                    Line Spacing
              Justification                  Margins Left/Right
              Line Height                    Tab Set
              Line Numbering                 Widow/Orphan Protection

    2 - Page
              Center Page (top to bottom)    New Page Number
              Force Odd/Even Page            Page Numbering
              Headers and Footers            Paper Size/Type
              Margins Top/Bottom             Suppress

    3 - Document
              Display Pitch                  Redline Method
              Initial Codes/Font             Summary

    4 - Other
              Advance                        Overstrike
              Conditional End of Page        Printer Functions
              Decimal Characters             Underline Spaces/Tabs
              Language

Selection: 0
```

FIGURE 3-3
Menu System in WordPerfect 5.1

FIGURE 3-4
Menu System in Lotus 1-2-3

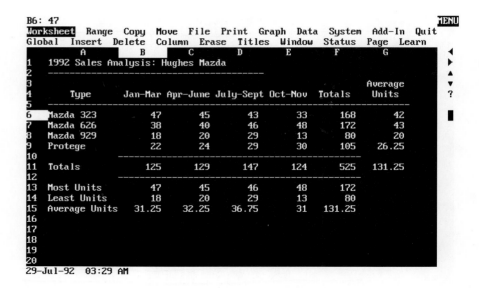

FIGURE 3-5
Pull-Down Menu Interface

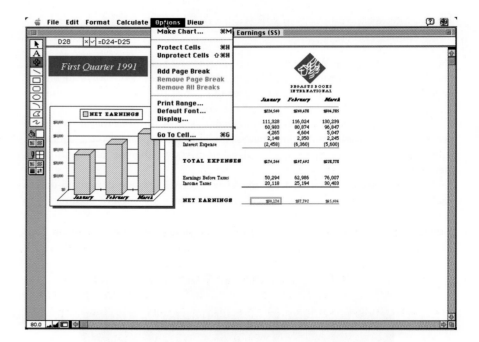

the user that it is time to enter a command or data and to indicate where to enter it. Using a command-driven package requires that the user read the package documentation to learn the necessary commands, or take classes in using the package. Examples of command-driven packages are the MS-DOS operating system and the dBASE data base management software. In Figure 3-2, shown earlier, the DIR (directory) command was entered at the MS-DOS prompt (the > symbol).

The type of user interface that is currently gaining popularity is the **graphical user interface,** or **GUI.** In a GUI, **icons** (pictures) are used to represent the functions to be performed, and a mouse is used to position the cursor or pointer

over the desired function. Once you have positioned the cursor over an icon, you press a button on the mouse and the function is carried out. With a little practice, it is possible to make choices from the menu—enter commands—very quickly. The use of GUI was pioneered on the Apple Macintosh, but many packages for IBM compatible computers now use a GUI. In fact, one of the reasons the popular Windows operating environment was developed was to provide MS-DOS users with this type of interface. Figure 3-6 shows the use of a GUI on the Apple Macintosh, and Figure 3-7 shows its use in Windows 3.1.

There are advantages and disadvantages to all three types of interfaces, and what appears to be an advantage in one may be a disadvantage in another. For packages with a menu-driven interface or a GUI, the advantage is that the user does not have to learn a series of commands before using the package. The user has only to make a selection from a menu or choose the appropriate icon. However, once the user has learned the commands for the package, it can be bothersome to wait for the the next menu or set of icons before making a selection. For a novice user, a command-driven interface can be difficult to use because it is necessary to know both the proper commands and the appropriate spot on the screen to enter them. Of course, once the data format and list of

It's just a different world [Windows] and just a dramatically better way of using a PC.

Bill Gates, founder and CEO of Microsoft

Quoted in Russell Glitman, "Windows 3.0: The Realization of Bill Gates' Grand Plan," *PC Week,* May 22, 1990, p. S–15.

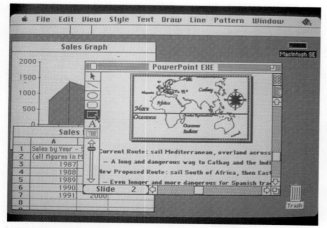

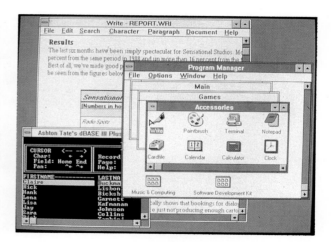

FIGURE 3-6 (left)
Graphical User Interface on
Apple Macintosh

FIGURE 3-7 (right)
Graphical User Interface in
Windows 3.1

commands are learned, data or commands can be quickly entered to a command-driven package.

Some packages allow users to begin with a menu-driven format and then move to a command-driven format as they become familiar with the package. For example, the package may have you enter the first letter of a command rather than moving the highlighting to the command, or may permit you to actually turn off the menu system. Lotus 1-2-3 is an example of the first type of package and dBASE is an example of the second.

APPLICATIONS SOFTWARE FOR THE PERSONAL COMPUTER

Currently, a great deal of business applications software is used on mainframe computers to handle the many large-scale processing tasks that businesses face. At the same time, personal computer applications software is becoming more and more important both in business and at home. While mainframe computers are used for large-scale data processing applications, applications software on a PC is often used to perform various types of analyses, handle record keeping, carry out text preparation, and so on. Because PC applications software allows individuals to increase their productivity, it is often referred to as **personal productivity software.** The six most widely used types of applications software for the PC are word processing, graphics, spreadsheets, accounting software, data base management, and telecommunications. Figure 3-8 shows the distribution of sales of PC software packages in 1991.

The discussion here briefly describes what each type of package can do for a user. (The packages are discussed in much more detail in Chapters 5–8.) Integrated software and desktop publishing are also introduced in this section.

Word Processing

One of the most useful functions of a personal computer is the ability to easily compose, edit, and print various types of documents with **word processing software.** While text entry, editing, and printing are important capabilities of word processing software, they are not the only ones. In fact, the software can do a

The user was empowered by the [PC] technology rather than being alienated from it.

Mitch Kapor, founder of Lotus Development Corporation

Quoted in Richard March, "Explosive PC Decade Ends on Cautious Note," *PC Week*, January 1, 1990, p. 10.

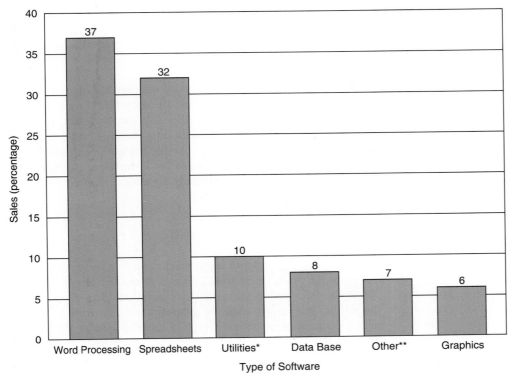

FIGURE 3-8
1991 PC Software Market Share

Source: Computer Intelligence, La Jolla, CA.

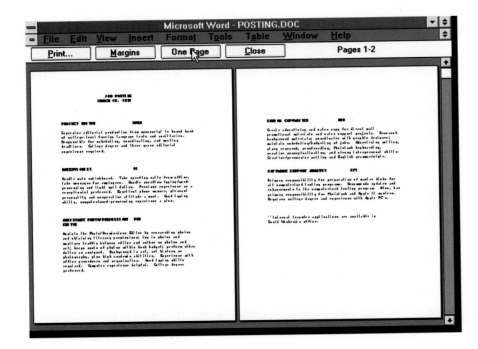

Microsoft Word, an extremely popular word processing package, allows the user to preview the document before printing it.

great many more tasks. For example, it allows easy setting of margins, line spacing, and tabs to arrive at a desired page format. When the text is entered from the keyboard, lines will "wrap around" the margins by automatically continuing to the next line. All these free the user from having to monitor the margins and "return" the cursor at the appropriate time.

Other useful functions of word processing software are inserting, deleting, or striking over material on the screen; searching the document for a particular sequence of characters; centering material; paginating automatically; and, on most packages, underlining, boldfacing, or italicizing material. An important operation with word processing software is the ability to "cut" electronically a block of material from the document and "paste" it somewhere else either in the current document or in a completely different document. Figure 3-9 shows a document being created in WordPerfect 5.1.

Graphics Software

The old saying that "a picture is worth a thousand words" is never more true than when applied to the portrayal of results from a computer. Using a bar or pie chart to show the information generated by analysis of data gives added meaning to the results. Businesses often use **graphics** software for analysis of data or to make a dramatic presentation. Graphics are also used in the design process to speed up the laborious job of designing anything from a computer chip to an airliner. Artists are also using "paint packages" to create fantastic artwork on the computer.

For business analysis and presentation purposes, the most commonly used types of graphics are the line chart, which simply connects a series of points; the pie chart, which assigns a section of a round pie proportional to the quantity of data; the bar chart, which draws a series of either horizontal or vertical bars

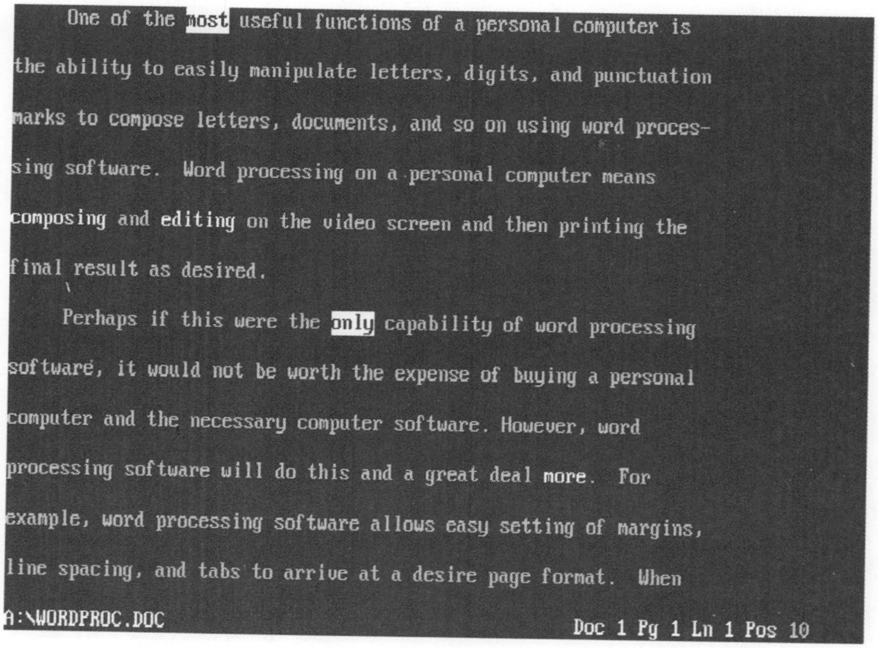

```
      One of the most useful functions of a personal computer is
the ability to easily manipulate letters, digits, and punctuation
marks to compose letters, documents, and so on using word proces-
sing software.  Word processing on a personal computer means
composing and editing on the video screen and then printing the
final result as desired.
      Perhaps if this were the only capability of word processing
software, it would not be worth the expense of buying a personal
computer and the necessary computer software. However, word
processing software will do this and a great deal more.  For
example, word processing software allows easy setting of margins,
line spacing, and tabs to arrive at a desire page format.  When
A:\WORDPROC.DOC                                    Doc 1 Pg 1 Ln 1 Pos 10
```

FIGURE 3-9
Document in WordPerfect 5.1

FIGURE 3-10
Presentation Graphics

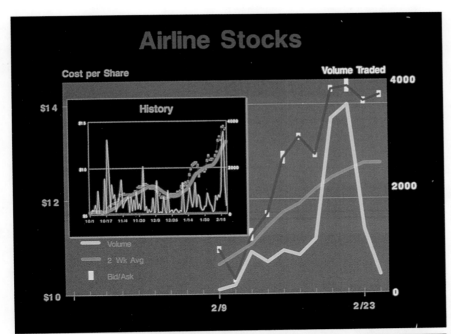

Paint packages can be used to develop beautiful, complex pictures on the computer screen.

GETTING HELP FROM YOUR PC IN GETTING THERE

Have you ever wanted to go across the state or across the nation but were unsure of the best route to follow? If you ask your friends which route to follow, you will probably get different answers, each of which is the "best," according to each friend. If you have faced this problem, then AUTOMAP, the PC-based software package, may answer your question.

AUTOMAP, which runs on both IBM compatible PCs and the Apple Macintosh, will provide an onscreen map showing the fastest, prettiest, or most convenient route between any two points in the United States. You can look at the entire United States or zoom in on a particular region to obtain more detail. The software will print the map and detailed driving instructions that list the roads you will be traveling, the exact distance you will travel on a particular road, where to turn, and which signs to look for. AUTOMAP contains information about 359,220 miles of roads and 51,921 places. It is programmed to find the best route for your requirements and to provide you with alternative routes, in case you decide to wander. Surveys show that AUTOMAP can reduce driving time and related costs for its users.

Source: Allison Sprout, "PC Road Atlas," *Fortune,* October 7, 1991, p. 116.

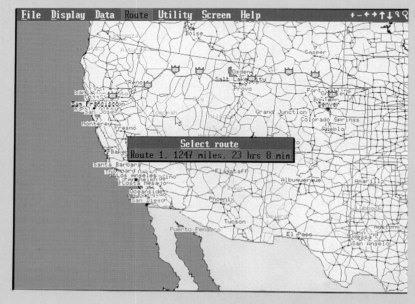

Automap software can help travelers find the fastest, prettiest, or most convenient route between two locations.

depicting the data; and the scatter diagram, which plots points on the X–Y scale. Figure 3-10 shows a presentation graph created with Harvard Graphics—a popular presentation graphics program.

Spreadsheets

Also known as **financial analysis software,** this use of the personal computer is built around a table of rows and columns called a **spreadsheet.** The user enters values and labels into **cells** at the intersection of the rows and columns. Various relationships between the values in the table are then defined using formulas that are also entered in cells. Whenever the user changes a value, the package uses the formulas to recompute all other values that depend on the changed value.

This sort of analysis allows the user to determine the effect of changing the values or assumptions in the spreadsheet. The capability of spreadsheet software to recalculate all values whenever a single value or assumption is changed is extremely important. A manager working with the budgetary or planning process can test many assumptions or scenarios by changing a few values or formulas and then letting the spreadsheet do the work. Most spreadsheets now also incorporate both graphics and data base management capabilities. Figure 3-11 shows a spreadsheet and corresponding graph created in Lotus 1-2-3.

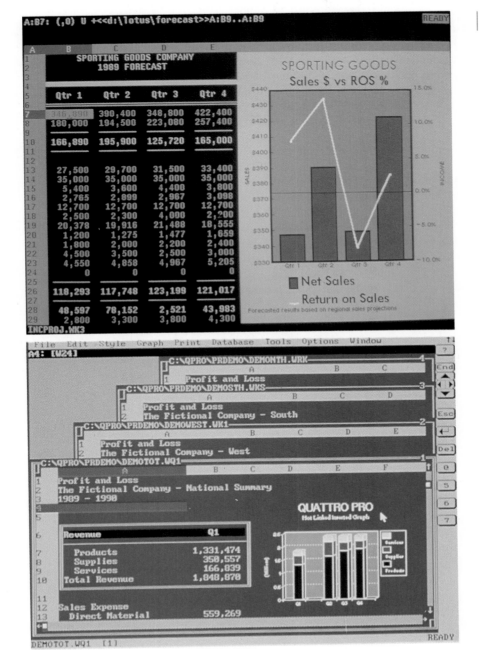

FIGURE 3-11
Lotus 1-2-3 Spreadsheet

Quattro Pro from Borland is a competitor of Lotus 1-2-3.

Accounting Software

For businesses, **accounting software** is extremely important since the accounting function enables a business to keep up-to-date and accurate records of its financial position. Using the output from accounting software, a firm is better able to make both short-term and long-term plans. Accounting packages come in various levels of specialization, ranging from general packages to industry-specific packages and even firm-specific packages.

While it is unrealistic to think that a family needs full-scale accounting software, there are home budgeting software packages available that meet the needs of the average family. These packages allow a family to computerize its budget and to record cash inflows and outflows in a manner similar to business accounting packages. Figure 3-12 shows the use of a popular **personal budgeting package**—Managing Your Money.

Data Base Management Software

A common operation both at work and at home is that of storing information. This storage may be as simple as a 3- by 5-inch index card box of recipes or as complex as rows of filing cabinets containing personnel records. We may wish to rearrange the information or search for a particular element or group of elements that has specific attributes. With **data base management software,** a user can perform the same operations on a computer. In a sense, this type of package acts as an "electronic filing clerk." The term **data base** refers to *a collection of information that is arranged for easy manipulation and retrieval.*

The simplest data base management packages enable their users to create a single data base file that can be rearranged or searched as needed. More sophis-

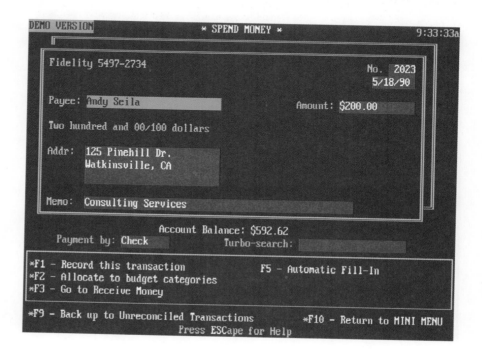

FIGURE 3-12
Personal Budgeting Package

ticated packages enable the user to work with multiple data base files to find and manage information. An important operation using data base management software is **sorting.** When a data base file is sorted, it is arranged according to characteristic, for example, in alphabetical order or in numerical order, depending on the user's need.

Another important operation in working with a data base is that of retrieving elements that match a given criterion. The user can also specify a second and even a third criterion, and the elements that match all of the criteria can then be output. Data base management packages are very important when an individual or a firm must manage large volumes of data in such a way that information needed to make a decision is easily found. Figure 3-13 shows a list of data base records from dBASE IV.

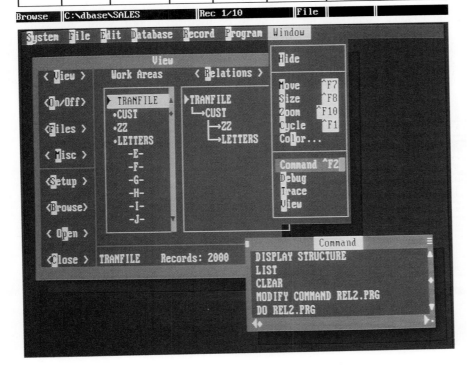

FIGURE 3-13
Data Base Records from dBASE IV

FoxPro is another popular data base management package for use on personal computers.

Telecommunications Software

In our discussion of computer hardware, we mentioned that the computer could be used for communication. Software and hardware are now available that allow us to use a personal computer for communication with other computers. The **telecommunications software** is combined with a modem to make the computer output and input compatible with telephone transmission signals. The combination of the communication package and the modem then allows the personal computer user to communicate with mainframe computers or with other personal computers. There are national networks that can be used via the communication package/modem combination to send electronic mail, post messages on an electronic bulletin board, or access national general-purpose or special-interest data bases. Figure 3-14 shows a list of telephone numbers that have been stored in a popular telecommunications package—Procomm Plus—for future calls.

Telecommunications links also allow both mainframes and personal computers to be linked in what are called **computer networks.** A computer network can be a **wide area network (WAN)** that connects computers over great distances or a **local area network (LAN)** that connects computers within the same geographic area. LANs have generated a great deal of interest because of the need for personal computer users to share information and peripherals. Another important consideration is the micro-to-mainframe link, which allows users of personal computers to communicate with mainframes to obtain information or to carry out processing projects that are too big for a personal computer. It has been said that the stand-alone computer (one that is not connected to other computers) will soon be a thing of the past.

Integrated Software

As personal computers have come to be used to perform word processing, graphic design, spreadsheet analysis, data base management, accounting, and telecommunications, users have needed the capability of moving back and forth between these and other types of packages. For example, a person using a word processing package to write a report may need to include in the document a table

FIGURE 3-14
(Left) Telephone Numbers Stored on Procomm Plus. (Right) Prodigy offers its subscribers many options, such as this market update service.

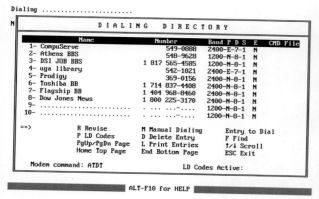

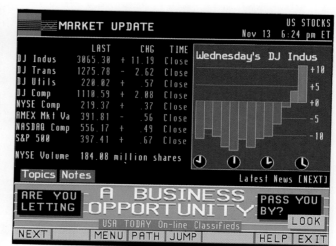

from a spreadsheet package or a bar chart from a graphics package. One way to handle this task is to cut the table or chart physically from the hard copy of the spreadsheet or graphics document and paste it into the hard copy of the word processing document. However, this can be very inconvenient and can result in a document with an unprofessional appearance.

What the user would like to do is electronically shift the table or chart from the spreadsheet or graphics package into the word processing document. This too can be a problem if the form in which a table or chart is saved is incompatible with the form the word processing package can accept. To provide an easy-to-use method for working simultaneously with multiple operations—that is, graphics, spreadsheets, word processing, and so on—integrated packages have been developed. An **integrated package** contains some or all of the most commonly used operations, with a specific procedure for shifting between operations. Popular integrated packages for personal computers include Lotus Works from Lotus, Framework from Ashton-Tate, and Microsoft Works. Because of their importance to users today and their close relationship to spreadsheets, integrated packages are discussed in Chapter 6 on financial analysis packages.

The use of multiple operations and the capability to transfer information between operations are often tied together through windows. A **window** is a section of the monitor screen that displays the current status of an operation. For example, an integrated package may use a window to display the status of a spreadsheet while a word processing document is being edited. Windows may also be used to display the current status of multiple operations that are using the same data. For example, an integrated package may use one window to display a spreadsheet and another window to display the graph associated with that spreadsheet. Windows are also used with some operating systems to show the output from different packages that are running concurrently on the computer and to show full-motion video on the screen. Figure 3-15 shows an example of the use of windows in an integrated package.

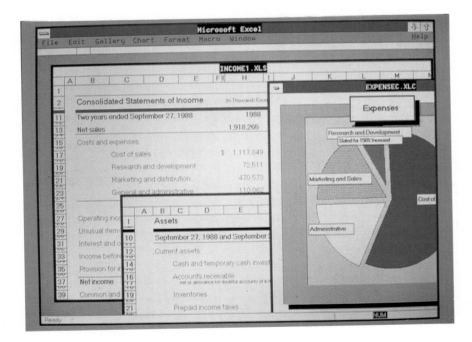

FIGURE 3-15
Uses of Windows

An **operating environment** is a type of software that is growing in use. It works with MS-DOS to provide one or more of the following features: a graphical interface, the capability to concurrently run multiple tasks, and the capability to use windows to see the output for programs that are running concurrently. The growing popularity of operating environments tends to reduce the need for integrated packages, since operating environments allow a user to switch between applications without leaving the package. Popular types of operating environment packages are Windows 3.1, Desqview, and GEOS. Operating environments will be discussed in detail in Chapter 4.

Desktop Publishing

One of the best examples of the power of personal computing lies in the area of desktop publishing. **Desktop publishing** combines word processing, graphics, and special page definition software to create documents that rival those available from professional typesetting houses. That is, a document created on a word processor is combined with graphics and then transformed into a form like that seen on the pages of this textbook. This involves such operations as the use of various sizes and types of fonts and typefaces, the use of proportional spacing to lead to a flush-right margin and an attractive text layout, and the combination of text and graphics on the page in a meaningful manner. Desktop publishing is covered in more detail as a part of Chapter 5 on word processing and graphics. Figure 3-16 shows a document being worked on with a popular desktop publishing package—Pagemaker from Aldus.

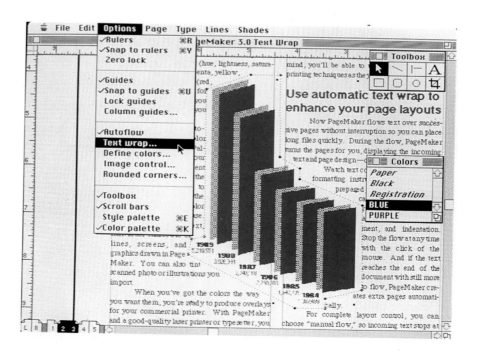

FIGURE 3-16
Document in Desktop Publishing Package

Buying Computer Software

While it is impossible to give a complete guide to buying all types of software in a paragraph or two, some general guidelines for would-be software users may be helpful. A more complete discussion and purchase guidelines for each type of software will be given in later chapters where the various types of software are discussed.

The most general guideline that can be given is the same one that you would apply to buying a car: Try it before you buy. First, determine the software that you think will fit your needs. Second, find a source of this type of software, such as a computer store. Then go to that store and try out the software on your type of computer. Be sure to allow enough time to try all of the functions of the software needed for your particular use. If the software fails to perform as advertised or the store does not want you to take the time to try out the software, go elsewhere. Remember, a piece of software that works fine on an Apple II will not work on an IBM PS/2, Compaq Deskpro, or even an Apple Macintosh. For this reason, it is crucial to match up your hardware and operating system with the prospective software before buying.

If you have not yet purchased a personal computer, select the software first, determine which computer runs the software, and then buy the two—hardware and software—as a package. This approach comes closest to ensuring that you will be happy with both.

When you are buying the software, you should be aware of two types of inexpensive utility and application software: freeware and shareware. **Freeware** is software that is distributed at a very low (often zero) cost by computer users' groups or by individuals. It is not copyrighted; therefore, it is in the **public domain** and may be copied legally. In fact, it is usually placed on electronic bulletin boards, so anyone with a modem and telecommunications software can transfer it to his or her computer. One shortcoming of freeware is that, usually, there is little or no support beyond that included with the software.

Whereas freeware is distributed without support, **shareware** is software for which support is available for a small fee (often from $25 to $89). Users who pay the fee are then registered and become eligible to receive new versions of the software as they become available, as well as continuous support for the product.

> ## With the right match of user and software, positive results are almost assured.
>
> *Fred Gibbons, chairman,*
> *Software Publishing Company*
>
> Quoted in "One Size of Software Doesn't Fit All," *Personal Computing,* October 1987, p. 232.

BITS OF HISTORY

A Software Time Line

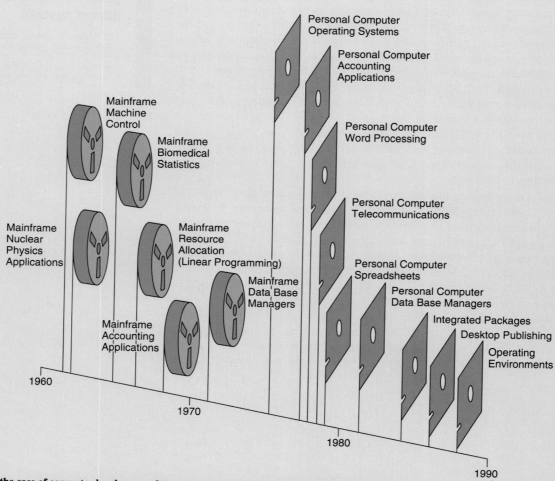

Personal Computer
Operating Systems

Personal Computer
Accounting
Applications

Personal Computer
Word Processing

Personal Computer
Telecommunications

Personal Computer
Spreadsheets

Personal Computer
Data Base Managers

Integrated Packages

Desktop Publishing

Operating
Environments

Mainframe
Machine
Control

Mainframe
Biomedical
Statistics

Mainframe
Nuclear
Physics
Applications

Mainframe
Resource
Allocation
(Linear Programming)

Mainframe
Data Base
Managers

Mainframe
Accounting
Applications

1960

1970

1980

1990

As in the case of computer hardware, software has moved—almost explosively since the late 1970s—from being the tool mainly of large research institutions to contributing immensely to the productivity of small businesses and interest groups and individual users.

1. The computer hardware must have software, in the form of computer programs, to control its actions. Software is the crucial element in the computer.

2. A software package is made up of one or more computer programs and some type of documentation. Software packages allow nonprogrammers to use the computer to achieve a desired objective.

3. Computer programs are written in one of many computer languages and provide the instructions that the computer must follow.

4. There are three types of software: systems, utility, and applications. Systems software manages the computer's operations; utility software handles housekeeping chores, including keeping track of a user's files; applications software performs the actual tasks as directed by the user.

5. The key part of the systems software is the operating system that manages the operations of all other parts of the computer. On a personal computer, this is usually referred to as a disk operating system, or DOS.

6. Applications software packages have become very popular.

7. Packages can also be menu driven or command driven depending on whether the user chooses from a menu or must already know the information to be entered.

8. Graphical user interfaces combined with a mouse have been found to be very easy to use.

9. The six most important types of business software packages for the personal computer are word processing, graphics, spreadsheets, accounting, data base management, and telecommunications.

10. Word processing software allows a user to compose, edit, and print documents from the computer keyboard. Graphics packages are useful in analyses of data, in presentations, and for creating art forms using the computer.

11. Financial analysis software creates budgets or forecasts from a table (also called a spreadsheet) of values, labels, and formulas. Accounting packages enable a business to monitor its financial well-being; personal budgeting packages do much of the same for the individual.

12. With a data base management package, a user can manipulate large files of data to find desired information.

13. Telecommunications software enables the computer to use a modem and telephone lines to link up with other computers.

14. Integrated software combines all of the applications software capabilities into one package. An operating environment allows MS-DOS – based machines to carry out multitasking.

15. Desktop publishing combines word processing, graphics, and page layout to publish documents of a professional standard.

KEY TERMS

accounting software
applications software
cells
command-driven package
computer language
computer network
computer package
computer program
data base
data base management software
desktop publishing
disk operating system (DOS)
documentation
files
financial analysis software
freeware
generic operating system
graphical user interface (GUI)
graphics software
IBM compatible PC
icons
integrated package
local area network (LAN)
menu
menu driven package

MS-DOS
operating environment
operating system
OS/2
personal budgeting software
personal productivity software
programming
prompt
proprietary operating system
pull-down menu
shareware
software
software package
sorting
spreadsheet
systems software
telecommunications software
UNIX
user friendly
user's manual
utility software
wide area network (WAN)
window
word processing software
x-terminal

1. Discuss the importance of software to the use of a computer.
2. Explain the role of programming in the preparation of computer software.
3. Name the three major categories of software that work concurrently in a computer. Discuss the purpose of each type of software.
4. What is a DOS? What role does it play in the use of the personal computer?
5. What type of software allows a user to keep track of a library of files? What is a common operation performed with a library of files?
6. Explain why the availability of software packages opens up the use of computers to many people.
7. What is the difference between a menu-driven package and a command-driven package? Discuss the advantages and disadvantages of each.
8. How is a mouse used in selecting commands? What is an icon? What is a pull-down menu?
9. List the six different business applications software packages discussed in the text. Which of these would you like to have available for your use? What would you use it for?
10. Discuss a situation in your home, school, club, fraternity, or sorority in which a financial analysis package (spreadsheet) would be useful to you.
11. Discuss a use for a data base management package. (Hint: Such packages can generate mailing lists by matching the names and a desired criterion.)
12. Discuss the use of a graphics package to analyze the data from a midterm examination.
13. Discuss how you might use a telecommunications software package.
14. Discuss how you might use an integrated package. How does an integrated package differ from an operating environment?
15. Discuss how you might use desktop publishing.

4

An Overview of Operating Systems

As we discussed in Chapter 3 on software, it is impossible to run applications software without an operating system. For this reason, it is useful to understand how operating systems work before we go into the various types of applications software. Operating systems for mainframes will be discussed first, followed by a section on MS-DOS, OS/2, and UNIX—the most commonly used personal computer operating systems that will work for different types of computers. Each system will be discussed in some detail, with attention given to the hardware that is compatible with that operating system. We will also cover the concept of operating systems that run on only one type of computer as well as RAM-resident software and operating environments such as Windows 3.

STUDY OBJECTIVES

After reading this chapter, you should be able to

- understand the functions of operating systems on all sizes of computers;
- discuss the terminology of mainframe operating systems;
- explain how a mainframe operating system handles multiple users and multiple tasks;
- describe the purpose of channels, buffers, and preprocessors on a mainframe computer;
- recognize differences in mainframe and personal computer operating systems;
- list the functions of a personal computer operating system;
- discuss the terminology of personal computer operating systems;
- name the three most common operating systems for personal computers and explain the differences between them;
- discuss the most popular proprietary operating systems for PCs;
- explain the use of operating environments and RAM-resident programs.

MAKING THE DESERT BLOOM WITH OS/2

OS/2 was the best choice for this system because of its graphical user interface that fully integrates point-and-click technology, dialogue boxes, and robust graphics capability.

Dennis Runo, Customer Automation, Inc.

Quoted in "OS/2 Makes the Water Flow, Changing Desert to Farmland."

Controlling the flow of water diverted from the Colorado River is crucial for the Palo Verde Irrigation District of southeastern California and western Arizona. With too much water, fields can become flooded; with too little water, crops wither and die. Until 1990, the system of ditches, gates, and pumps created in the 1970s was controlled by a teletype-like system that required an operator to enter cryptic commands that sent radio signals to a network of remote control units. Each remote control unit, in turn, controlled three or four separate gates or pumps. The remote control units also collected data on water level, gate position, and pump status. Based on the information gathered by the remote units, water was distributed to farmers who pay a water toll, which is based on the number of acres that are irrigated.

Beginning in 1988, a new system was developed to control the flow of water. It uses an IBM PS/2 Model 80 personal computer and the OS/2 operating system. This operating system was chosen by the software developer because of its graphical user interface, which is called the Presentation Manager, and its capability to run multiple tasks concurrently. Operators now use a mouse to initiate all configurations and controls. They also view the system status via color-coded graphics. For example, if there is a ditch failure, the screen flashes red to alert the operator to close a gate to avoid loss of water. Because the OS/2 system has been so effective, the water district is now planning to automate the system of gates and pumps, which would allow the PC to automatically, without operator intervention, take whatever action is required to prevent water loss.

Source: Jennifer Curry, "OS/2 Makes the Water Flow, Changing Desert to Farmland," *PC Week,* April 16, 1990, pp. 69, 80; and interview with Dennis Runo of Customer Automation, Inc., Phoenix, Arizona, December 6, 1991.

The OS/2 system controlling the Palo Verde Irrigation District's water flow has an easy-to-use, graphical-user interface.
Source: *PC Week,* April 16, 1990, pp. 69, 80.

It has been called the computer's "traffic cop," "office manager," "nervous system," and "chauffeur." *It* is the computer's operating system. In the boxed insert, the OS/2 operating system for IBM compatible personal computers is discussed. This operating system allowed the software developer to write software with a graphical user interface that made the operation of the irrigation system easier and more efficient. For any computer, the **operating system** is a collection of software programs that manages the tasks that are performed concurrently in the computer, regardless of whether the computer is a mainframe, minicomputer, or personal computer. For example, the operating system must monitor the keyboard to determine when a key has been pressed to provide input to the computer. It must also manage the video screen and printer to provide output from the computer. The operating system controls the operation of secondary storage to transfer data back and forth between secondary storage and main memory. On mainframes and minicomputers, the operating system is responsible for additional tasks that cannot be performed on a personal computer. A mainframe or minicomputer operating system manages many different hardware sites and terminals and ensures that users have the proper user identification to access the computer. A mainframe operating system also handles the very important task of allocating resources to multiple users. Finally, the operating system for any size of computer controls the execution of applications programs.

The primary differences between the operating systems for mainframes and those for personal computers are the number of users and the complexity of the peripheral devices to be managed. Mainframes usually are multiuser

> ## An operating system is just a vehicle to run an application.
>
> *Tim Paterson, creator of the first version of MS-DOS*
>
> Quoted in "An End to the DOS Dynasty," *PC Week*, July 29, 1986, p. 52.

Personal computer operating systems usually support only one user at a time.

machines, while most personal computers are single-user machines. There are exceptions, especially in the case of personal computers, for which multiple-user systems are becoming available. Mainframes must manage a large number of disk and tape drives, input devices, and printers, while a personal computer system usually has only one or two disk drives and a printer. As a result of these differences, mainframe operating systems are extremely large programs that require a maintenance staff of **systems programmers** to maintain them. On the other hand, personal computer operating systems are less complex and must be able to operate without any day-to-day maintenance.

Another difference between mainframe and personal computer operating systems is that operating systems for mainframes are all *proprietary* and will work on only one variety of machine. For personal computers, there now exist *generic* operating systems, which will run on many different types of personal computers. Some personal computers are set up to run multiple operating systems to take advantage of a larger variety of software. While there are still proprietary operating systems for personal computers, the trend is toward the use of generic systems.

Functions of the Operating System

In Chapter 3, the operating system was depicted as the core of an "onion," with outer layers made up of utility software and applications software. The operating system is the core of the "onion" because it is the least visible form of software in a computer. It can require many commands but does not require data. There is no visible output from an operating system to either the screen or the printer except when an error occurs, in which case an error message is shown on the screen. Even though it is usually invisible, the operating system is crucial to the operation of the computer.

> As measured by the number of moving parts, [the IBM] System/370 [mainframe] operating system is undoubtedly mankind's most complex single creation.
>
> *Gary D. Brown, author of*
> System/370 Job Control
> Language
>
> Quoted in "Workhorse Operating Systems Square Off," *Computerworld,* January 4, 1988, p. 18.

Systems programmers are responsible for maintaining a mainframe operating system.

The functions of the operating system can be summarized as follows:

- provides an interface between the user and the computer;
- controls access to the machine;
- works with ROM to start up, or "boot," the computer;
- schedules an efficient use of the CPU while eliminating the need for human intervention;
- manages data and information in internal memory;
- manages files on secondary storage, making them available as needed while providing security to multiple users;
- executes other computer programs;
- manages peripheral devices such as printers, disk drives, and tape drives.

We will look next at operating systems for personal computers.

PC OPERATING SYSTEMS

Operating systems for personal computers share the same characteristics as mainframe operating systems, but, as we noted earlier, personal computer operating systems are primarily single-user systems. At one time, all PC operating systems were also single-tasking systems (that is, they could work on only one job or "task" at a time), but today the move is toward multitasking PC operating systems. Table 4-1 compares the mainframe and personal computer operating systems.

Before going into specific PC operating systems, we will consider personal computer operating systems in general. Like mainframe operating systems, personal computer operating systems perform four important functions for the user:

1. *Handle the startup or* **booting** *process.* For a PC, the booting process is usually very simple, often requiring the user merely to insert a disk and turn on the computer.
2. *Control the hardware.* The keyboard, mouse, video screen, secondary storage, modem for communications, printer, and any other hardware devices are all under the control of the operating system. Because the operating system controls this portion of the process, the user can easily add new peripheral devices such as a hard disk without having to learn a lot of new commands.

TABLE 4-1
Comparison of Operating System Features

Feature	Type of Computer	
	Mainframe	*Personal Computer*
Machine use	One brand of computer	Many brands
Number of users	Multiple	Single
Number of tasks	Multiple (concurrent)	Single/multiple
Support	Systems programmers	User/consultants

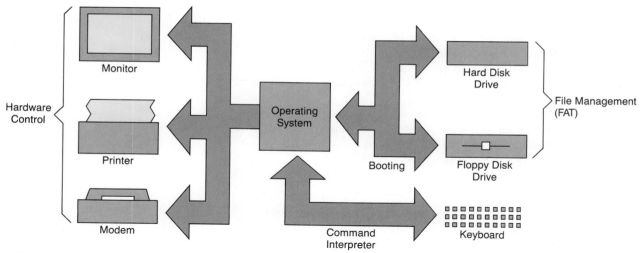

FIGURE 4-1
Functions of a Personal
Computer Operating System

3. *Interpret the user's commands.* When the user types in a command like COPY, the **command interpreter** determines what these keystrokes mean and sends a message to the appropriate utility or applications program to carry out the command. If there is an error in spelling or if an unknown command is entered, an error message is displayed to the user. When the requested procedure is complete, the operating system looks for new instructions from the keyboard (or other input devices).

4. *Maintain a* **file allocation table (FAT)** *on secondary storage.* Computers are heavily dependent on disk secondary storage, and must be able to save files to disk and retrieve them later. The FAT makes this possible.

These four operations of a personal computer operating system are demonstrated in Figure 4-1.

Because most personal computers use disks for secondary storage, the name **disk operating system (DOS)** is almost always used to describe the operating system of a personal computer. For each file, the DOS file system uses a unique name that the user supplies and then uses for future retrievals. The list of the files on the disk is known as the **disk directory.** Figure 4-2 shows a disk directory for a commonly used DOS.

Generic Operating Systems

The operating system is important to the computer because *everything* that runs on the computer depends on it for instructions. For this reason, the capabilities of a computer depend, to a large extent, upon the capabilities of the operating system. It is also true that different brands and types of personal computers that

```
A:\-> dir

Volume in drive A is MSWARE1-400
Directory of  A:\

RESUME           24751   1-20-90    1:04p
PRESNTED 390      5558   1-01-80    1:40a
RAGSDALE VPI      2827   1-22-90   10:05a
FLAATL   CHR      4119   1-01-80   11:49a
MISC              2842   2-27-90    6:03a
WORDPROC DOC      2268   4-17-90    4:20p
CHRISLTR 221      3050   2-21-90   12:50a
RESUME   290     26852   2-27-90    6:07a
SUMMARY  90       2955   1-01-80    8:10a
PUBS     390     10758   1-01-80    1:36a
DRAFT    DAT       528   3-02-90   12:29a
DATA1    DAT       528   3-02-90   10:35a
EXAM2    F88      3484  11-14-88    6:51a
PROJECTE INP       936   3-02-90    5:58a
PLAYER   DAT       230   3-07-90   12:08a
MS815             3286   2-18-88   12:08p
FIG3-13  PIX      2317   4-19-90   12:06p
       17 File(s)     256000 bytes free

A:\->
```

FIGURE 4-2
Disk Directory

use the same DOS can run the same applications software. This is very different from a mainframe environment, in which each operating system tends to be very different from all others and applications software must be written to run on specific brands and types of machine. The need for a single DOS to run the same applications software on different personal computers has led to the development of **generic operating systems.** There currently exist three common generic disk operating systems and several others that are not so well known. The three are MS-DOS (Microsoft DOS), from Microsoft; OS/2 (Operating System/2), from Microsoft and IBM; and UNIX, originally developed by AT&T. These systems can be broadly identified by three characteristics:

1. the number of tasks that may be run concurrently under the operating system;
2. the number of machines the operating system will support;
3. the types of computers on which the operating system can be used.

As we said at the beginning of this section, at one time almost all PC operating machines were single-user, single-task systems. Even today, the predominant PC operating system—MS-DOS—is of that type. However, the other two systems—UNIX and OS/2—go beyond this to offer either multitasking or multiuser control or both, similar to the control offered by mainframe operating systems. Even MS-DOS has been expanded to handle some multitasking in versions starting with 5.0 and through operating environments such as Windows. MS-DOS and OS/2 can be used only on IBM PS/2s and IBM compatible PCs, whereas UNIX is not restricted by type of machine. OS/2 is further restricted to computers that use the Intel 80286, 80386, or 80486 (now commonly referred

TABLE 4-2

Comparison of Generic PC Operating Systems

Operating System	Number of Tasks	Number of Users	Machine
MS-DOS	One	Single	IBM PS/2 or IBM compatible PCs
OS/2	Multiple	Single	Computers using the Intel 80286, 80386, or i486 chips
UNIX	Multiple	Multiple	Not restricted

to as the i486) CPU chips; it will not run on the original IBM PC, PC XT, or compatibles that use the Intel 8088 or 8086 CPU chips. Table 4-2 summarizes this information.

MS-DOS

Today, the most widely used operating system for PCs is **MS-DOS.** It was first used on the IBM PC, under the name "PC-DOS." MS-DOS and PC-DOS are often jointly referred to simply as "DOS." MS-DOS was chosen in 1981 as the operating system for IBM's entry into the personal computer market, which immediately stamped MS-DOS as an industry standard operating system for 16- and 32-bit IBM compatible computers. IBM's choice of MS-DOS also had a great deal to do with the emergence of Microsoft Corporation as one of the world's leading developers of PC software. Currently, at least 10 million people use MS-DOS as their computer operating system, and a vast majority of all applications packages in existence today will run on MS-DOS.

Like most software, MS-DOS has undergone several revisions since it was first released. These versions were numbered sequentially, that is, 1.0, 2.0, 2.1, 3.0, 4.0, 5.0, and so on. Each subsequent version added new features and power to the operating system. For MS-DOS, the most commonly used versions are those numbered between 3.0 and 6.0. Versions 4.0 and 5.0 departed from the earlier, strictly command-driven form to offer either a menu-driven or a command-driven structure. DOS 5.0 also added a full-screen program editor and the capability to swap between programs.

There have been many predictions that MS-DOS would be superseded by other, more "modern" operating systems such as OS/2. However, there is little evidence that this will occur any time soon, especially with the continued release of updated versions. In addition, the release of Windows has solved many of the problems with MS-DOS.

Regardless of the version being used, the user must know or at least understand some of over 50 MS-DOS commands. Most of these commands can be input from the keyboard *interactively* or selected from a menu, but some are **batch commands** that can be combined into a program that will execute the commands sequentially. All interactive commands are entered at the **prompt,** which signals that the computer is awaiting a command.

MS-DOS is divided into two sets of commands: the **internal commands,** which are stored in RAM as a part of the booting process, and the **external commands,** which are located on disk storage. Since they are stored in RAM, the internal commands can be accessed immediately by the CPU. The external commands must be read from floppy or hard disk storage as needed.

(Top) This IBM compatible PC runs under the MS-DOS operating system. (Center) This IBM PS/2 Model 80 computer runs under the OS/2 operating system. (Bottom) This RISC System/6000 Powerserver 320 computer runs under the UNIX operating system.

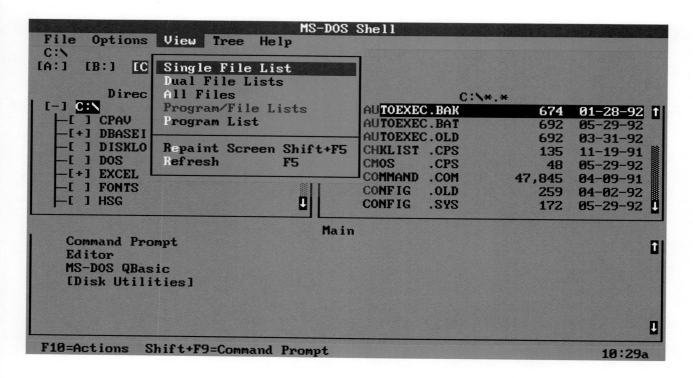

MS-DOS Shell

File   Options   View   Tree   Help

C:\

[A:]   [B:]   [C

Single File List
Dual File Lists
All Files
Program/File Lists
Program List

Repaint Screen   Shift+F5
Refresh   F5

Direc

[-] C:\
├─[ ] CPAV
├─[+] DBASEI
├─[ ] DISKLO
├─[ ] DOS
├─[+] EXCEL
├─[ ] FONTS
└─[ ] HSG

C:*.*

AUTOEXEC.BAK		674	01-28-92
AUTOEXEC.BAT		692	05-29-92
AUTOEXEC.OLD		692	03-31-92
CHKLIST	.CPS	135	11-19-91
CMOS	.CPS	48	05-29-92
COMMAND	.COM	47,845	04-09-91
CONFIG	.OLD	259	04-02-92
CONFIG	.SYS	172	05-29-92

Main

Command Prompt
Editor
MS-DOS QBasic
[Disk Utilities]

F10=Actions   Shift+F9=Command Prompt   10:29a

Beginning with Version 5.0, MS-DOS has a menu-driven option.

Commonly used internal MS-DOS commands include COPY, for copying files from one disk to another; TYPE, for displaying the contents of a text file; and DIR, for listing the contents of a disk or section of a disk. Commonly used external MS-DOS commands include FORMAT, which prepares a disk to receive files, and DISKCOPY, which copies the entire contents of one floppy disk to another.

Subdirectories

As long as personal computers had only floppy disk drives, keeping up with files was relatively easy: Each original $5\frac{1}{4}$-inch floppy held a maximum of 360 Kbytes of storage. However, when hard disk drives holding megabytes of information came into widespread use, working with all the files on a hard disk became a problem. To rectify this, MS-DOS was modified to allow the user to break up the files into **subdirectories.** Each subdirectory can be given a name and can be thought of as being analogous to a separate floppy disk. This **hierarchical** or **tree structure** divides a long list of files into several shorter lists that are easier to keep track of.

As an example of the use of subdirectories, assume that a college professor stores on disk both the chapters for a book she is working on and exams for the courses she teaches. If the book has 20 chapters and she has created 25 exams at one time or another, with one file for each book chapter and one for each exam, then there would be at least 45 files on the disk. With a single directory on the hard disk, it would be difficult to look through all the files to find a

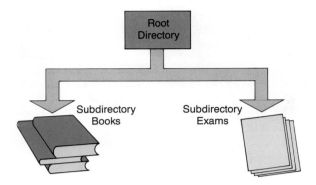

FIGURE 4-3
Tree Structure

particular chapter or exam. However, a tree structure with one subdirectory for book chapters and one for exams would allow the professor to look much more easily for a desired chapter or exam. MS-DOS has commands that allow the user to create subdirectories or to switch between subdirectories. Other PC operating systems have similar commands to work with subdirectories. Figure 4-3 shows how such a tree structure would appear.

OS/2

On April 2, 1987, IBM and Microsoft jointly announced the development of OS/2—the operating system that would "succeed" the almost "ancient" MS-DOS. Created in 1981 to run the then new IBM PC, MS-DOS has gone through several upgrades. Yet even with all its upgrades, MS-DOS has remained primarily a command-driven operating system aimed at running a single task or job. Also, without the use of memory management software, MS-DOS can use only 640K of RAM, regardless of the memory capacity of the machine.

The new system, named **OS/2,** provides users with a **graphical user interface (GUI)** called the Presentation Manager, allows for the use of up to 16 Mbytes of RAM, and runs multiple tasks on personal computers using the Intel 80386 or i486 chips.

OS/2 has gone through several stages of development, culminating in the recently released OS/2 2.0. This latest version of OS/2 was written to run only on 80386- and i486-based machines, and it features a Macintosh-like graphical interface and the capability of running multiple MS-DOS applications concurrently.

While MS-DOS continues to be the operating system of choice for many people who use PCs based on the Intel 80386 or i486 chips, many analysts believe that OS/2 will come to be used on many of these types of machines. This move to OS/2 is likely to be driven by three considerations: limited access to RAM with MS-DOS, trends toward graphical interfaces for all types of software, and the desire of many PC users to be able to carry out multiple tasks concurrently. As noted earlier in this section, without the use of programs like Windows or the so-called "DOS extenders," MS-DOS users can only access 640K of RAM, regardless of the amount of RAM on the PC and the size of the

> **[OS/2 2.0] is a better DOS than DOS, a better Windows than Windows, and a better OS/2.**
>
> *Lee Reiswig, general manager of IBM's system software development effort*
>
> Quoted in "The New OS/2: Impressive Rival for Windows," *The New York Times,* October 27, 1991, p. 8.

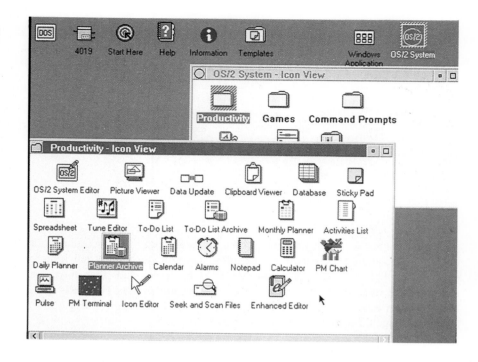

When multiple tasks are being processed, the OS/2 Presentation Manager allows them to be displayed simultaneously on the screen.

program being executed. This limitation is an inherent feature of MS-DOS and is a very real limitation to "power users" who work with very large programs. OS/2 is designed to take full advantage of the memory capacities of the Intel 80386 and i486 chips, so it can address up to 16 Mbytes of memory—almost 30 times that available with MS-DOS.

A widespread movement in computing is toward a graphical interface in which a mouse is used to point to **icons** that represent the desired action and to press one or more mouse buttons. If the user knows the meaning of the icon, then it is not necessary to learn any operating system commands. For example, if a file folder represents a file and a trash can represents the erasure of a file, the user can erase a file by pointing to the file folder and then "dragging" it to the trash can. This type of operating system interface was pioneered by the Apple Macintosh, and its ease of use has caused many IBM compatible PC users to ask for the same type of interface on their PCs. In response, a graphical interface called the **Presentation Manager,** similar to the interface on the Macintosh, is incorporated into OS/2 and, as discussed in the opening box, is important to many users.

As noted earlier, MS-DOS is primarily a single-task operating system. This was acceptable to PC users as long as they worked with slow PCs and floppy disk systems. Now, with the heavy use of high-volume hard disks and faster processors, PC users are finding that they need to be able to work on multiple tasks concurrently. For example, a user may wish to use telecommunications to transfer files concurrently with working on a word processing package. Users also want to be able to switch around among applications without actually exiting any of the applications. The introduction of the Intel 80386 and i486 chips will make multitasking more widely available because these chips can be used to run multiple applications concurrently.

STEVE JOBS AND THE NeXT COMPUTER

On April Fool's Day of 1976, Steve Jobs and Steve Wozniak founded the Apple Computer Company to sell the personal computers they were building in a garage. For nine years, Jobs served in various positions with the company, including president and chairman of the board, as it grew into a giant in the personal computer field. During this time, he was instrumental in developing both the extremely popular Apple II and Macintosh lines of computers, the latter being notable for its graphical

user interface and easy-to-use operating system.

In 1985, Jobs left Apple to found a new company—NeXT, Inc. Three years later, on October 12, 1988, Jobs introduced a high-performance personal computer called the NeXT computer. It was originally aimed at the academic market but has since been modified for use in nonacademic situations. The NeXT is based on the Motorola 68040 chip—the same series of chip used in the Macintosh.

While the NeXT contains several technological innovations, including a 256-Mbyte erasable and removable optical disk, a 2.88-Mbyte microfloppy disk drive, and a new chip technology that gives "mainframe performance," possibly the greatest long-term contribution of the NeXT will be its operating system. The NeXT uses a variation of the UNIX operating system with a graphical user interface called NeXTStep. Although UNIX has long been known for its power, especially for multiple users and multitasking, it

has also been criticized for being difficult to use. The graphically oriented NeXTStep offers an easier way to use the power of UNIX. In fact, IBM thought so much of NeXTStep that it has licensed its use on its UNIX-based machines.

Major software applications have been modified to run on the NeXT computer using the NeXTStep operating system. These include packages from Lotus, WordPerfect, and Oracle. Possibly, the crucial new application that will lure new users to NeXT is the Improv spreadsheet from Lotus Development Corporation. Designed specifically for the NeXT, Improv is said to clear up some complications associated with using spreadsheets by using English commands rather than a numerical syntax.

Source: James Daly, "Job's NeXT Unveils Do-or-Die Systems, Software," *Computerworld*, September 24, 1990, p. 7.

Steve Jobs

Lotus' IMPROV software has a graphical-user interface and pull-down menus.

Source: Lotus Corp.

A key advantage of OS/2 over MS-DOS is that multitasking is a part of OS/2. This allows multiple applications written for the operating system to run concurrently as long as there is sufficient internal memory. The latest version of OS/2, 2.0, can run applications written for OS/2, Windows, and MS-DOS concurrently.

UNIX

MS-DOS and OS/2 are both single-user operating systems that can control only one machine at a time. The third generic PC operating system, **UNIX,** is a multiuser, multitasking operating system. UNIX was originally developed by AT&T for use on its own minicomputers, but has since been modified to be used on all sizes of computers, from supercomputers down to some of the more powerful personal computers that have sufficient memory and disk space. Because UNIX is a multiuser system, it is the most widely used operating system for controlling systems of workstations. IBM has also developed a version of UNIX called AIX, for use on its midsize and mainframe computers.

Microsoft has developed a version of UNIX called XENIX, which will run PCs using the Intel series of chips. Apple also has developed a version of UNIX that will run on its more powerful Macintosh computers. Finally, as discussed in the box on Steve Jobs, a version of UNIX with a graphical interface was developed for use on the NeXT computer. This interface has been licensed by IBM for use with its version of UNIX.

The reason UNIX can be used on many different sizes and types of computers is that it is written in two parts. One part is written in a high-level (English-like) language that can run on various types of computers. The second part is written in a low-level language that is specific to the type of computer.

> **A lot of people criticize UNIX, but my question is, what out there is better for multitasking/ multiuser?**
>
> *David Carlson, senior vice president of information systems, K mart*
>
> Quoted in "UNIX Jumps Into the Breach," *Computerworld*, May 20, 1991, p. 100.

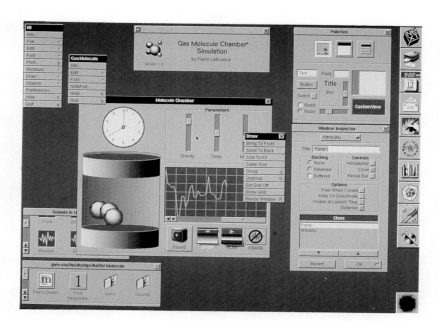

The NeXTStep graphical interface for the UNIX operating system, with icons and windows, is an important feature of the NeXT computer.

This means that only the low-level language portion must be rewritten to convert the UNIX program to run on a new computer. Another attractive feature is that UNIX can run other operating systems as a job. For example, it is possible to run MS-DOS as a task under UNIX and then to run applications written for MS-DOS as subtasks.

UNIX is a very complete system, offering hierarchical file structures and the ability to send data from one program to another through a system called *piping*. In **piping,** the output from one program is "piped" to another program, for which it becomes the input. This very powerful feature allows programs to be combined to solve complicated problems. UNIX also has over 200 utilities that can perform almost any task a user could desire. These utilities can be joined together through piping to handle many operations. To the knowledgeable user, this wealth of commands and utilities can be very useful.

A problem that has limited the widespread use of UNIX is that the command structure can be somewhat difficult to learn. Systems like NeXTStep from NeXT, Inc., are aimed at providing a special interface that will make UNIX easy for beginners to use. Another reason often given for the lack of widespread acceptance of UNIX is the many variations of this operating system that exist today. Currently, there is a great deal of discussion as to what version of UNIX should be the "standard," and at least two groups of companies are competing to have their version accepted as the standard.

Proprietary Operating Systems

While MS-DOS, OS/2, and UNIX may be purchased separately from the computers they control, several computer manufacturers use **proprietary operating systems** for their computers. These are operating systems that are closely tied to the computer on which they run. Currently, the most popular proprietary operating systems are those for the Macintosh and the Apple II. Other systems include the Commodore and Amiga lines of computers.

The Apple II series of computers uses a chip—the Motorola 6502—on which MS-DOS and OS/2 will not work. This is not surprising; since the original Apple II was built *before* either of those operating systems were developed, its operating system was developed specifically for the Apple II series. While it is possible to purchase special hardware to rectify this problem, most Apple users have continued to use Apple DOS (or its more recent version, ProDOS). This operating system is aimed at the student and the home user and is fairly easy to use compared to MS-DOS, OS/2, or UNIX. At the same time, the Apple II operating systems do not offer the power and capabilities of these generic operating systems.

Of the operating systems currently available, possibly the easiest to use is the Macintosh operating system. This system provides icons, a mouse, and pull-down menus for selecting commands, enabling the user to concentrate on the job to be accomplished rather than on how to get the computer to do the job. Files are stored in folders, which are analogous to MS-DOS subdirectories. To retrieve a file, the user makes the mouse move the pointer to a folder, clicks the mouse to "open" the folder, and then clicks the mouse a second time to retrieve the file. This Macintosh operating system has a unique approach to applications

The Apple Macintosh user interface has provided a standard environment that is easy to understand.

*J. Garrett Fitzgibbons,
president, Mouse Systems*

Quoted in "View from the Top,"
Personal Computing, October 1989,
p. 263.

FIGURE 4-4
Macintosh Operating System

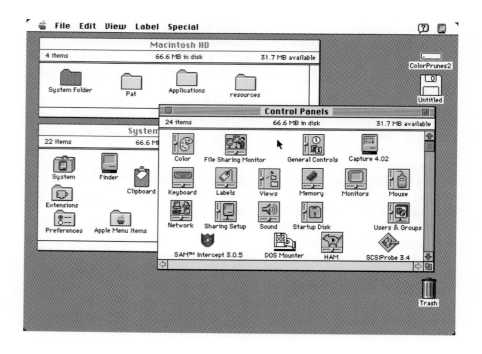

software in that when a data file is retrieved, the appropriate applications software is also retrieved and executed. For example, if the user retrieves a spreadsheet file that was created with Excel, then the Excel package is also retrieved and executed. This is the reverse of many MS-DOS applications in which the user executes the applications software package first and then retrieves a file.

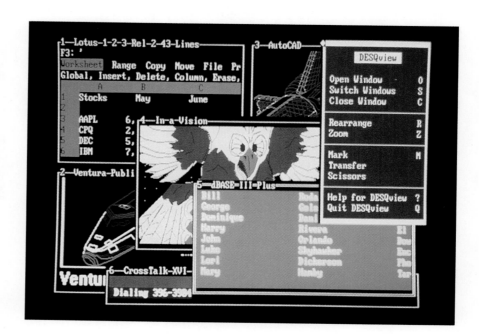

DESQview is a popular operating environment for computers running under MS-DOS.

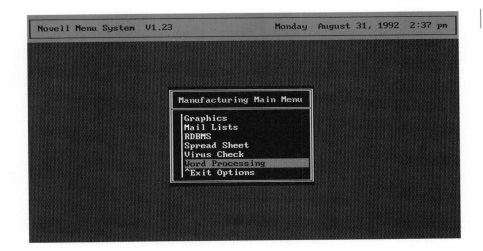

FIGURE 4-5
LAN Menu System

Executing other tasks on the Macintosh is also very easy using the icon and mouse system. Recall our discussion in the section on OS/2 of the deletion of a file on Macintosh. In the case of tasks requiring multiple operations, the user may need to pull down a submenu to expose an expanded list of commands. Again the mouse is used to position the cursor over the appropriate command in the submenu, and the button is pressed to carry out the task. Figure 4-4 shows the Macintosh operating system in use.

Many popular applications packages have been rewritten to run using the Macintosh operating system. The ease of use of the Macintosh operating system was the primary reason that Microsoft and IBM put so much effort into developing similar interfaces in the OS/2 Presentation Manager and Microsoft has placed such emphasis on Windows. In response to these moves by Microsoft and IBM, in 1991, Apple released a new version of the Mac operating system, called System 7, which offers numerous improvements over previous versions.

Local Area Network Operating Systems

As more and more organizations are moving to local area networks (LANs) composed of PCs, there has been an increasing interest in LAN operating systems. **LAN operating systems** operate at a level above the basic operating system (usually MS-DOS) to allow users to access software and files on the file server. At the same time, the LAN operating system must also ensure that software licenses of commercial software are not being violated by having too many users accessing a package or by users illegally copying software. In addition to the LAN operating system's primary function of managing the file server, it must allow users access to printer facilities; provide security against unwanted users accessing the network through a system of account IDs and passwords; and add communication capability between the PCs. Currently, the three most popular LAN operating systems are Netware from Novell, which is the most popular system; LAN Manager from Microsoft; and Banyan Vines. Figure 4-5 shows a menu system on a LAN running under Novell Netware.

OPERATING ENVIRONMENTS AND RAM-RESIDENT PROGRAMS

In our discussion of PC operating systems, we have placed a great deal of emphasis on multitasking and easy-to-use graphical interfaces. However, the most widely used PC operating system—MS-DOS—is primarily a command-driven operating system that was designed to be used on a single machine for a single task. Fortunately, ways have been found to get around these shortcomings of MS-DOS to implement such features as graphical interfaces and multitasking. Graphical interfaces and multitasking are being incorporated into a type of software known as an *operating environment* that acts as a "shell" around MS-DOS. Another type of software called a *RAM-resident program* offers a form of multitasking. While these are not operating systems, they are related closely to operating systems, so we will discuss each briefly in this section.

Operating Environments

An **operating environment** (also called a **shell**) is a software application that works with MS-DOS to provide one or more of the following additional features: a graphical user interface (GUI), the capability to run multiple tasks concurrently, and the capability to use onscreen windows to view the output for programs that are running concurrently. Figure 4-6 shows how an operating environment is situated between the applications software and the operating system.

These operating environments are sold like applications programs and include such packages as Microsoft Windows 3.0/3.1, DESQview from Quarterdeck Office Systems, NewWave from Hewlett-Packard, and Ensemble from GeoWorks. In addition to making the use of MS-DOS easier, these systems can give users fast access to their programs, and they allow them to switch applications or shift data from one application to another. Windows and DESQview are currently the most popular of these operating environments. Windows offers all three of the features described, whereas DESQview is aimed primarily at multitasking and displaying output in onscreen windows.

Windows

Windows 3.0 was introduced in May 1990, and since its introduction, it has become the single largest-selling application package in the short history of personal computers. In its first 18 months, *4 million* copies of Windows 3.0 were sold. Windows offers a GUI that many users find easy to use. The basic interface for all programs is the desktop, on which users work with icons that represent applications and files. There are also "groups" of applications and files that are contained in resizable windows.

In addition to allowing users to "point-and-click" to access application programs and utilities, all programs written for Windows display the same menu bar with menu choices at the top of the screen, a scroll bar at the right, and arrows to reduce or expand the application's window. Non–Windows-based programs usually do not have these consistent features. For example, help is accessed in 1-2-3 by pressing the F1 function key but is accessed in WordPerfect 5.1 by pressing the F3 function key. Users can run several Windows applications

FIGURE 4-6
Relationship of Operating
Environment to Operating
System

```
        Applications
         Software
     Operating Environment
      Operating System
         Hardware
```

FEASTING ON WINDOWS AT TACO BELL

Taco Bell has a legal department, as do all large corporations, that makes wide use of both personal computers and mainframes. At this national fast-food chain, the legal department has moved to improve the personal productivity of its staff by installing Windows on its IBM compatible personal computers.

Although Macintosh computers are widely used throughout Taco Bell, the corporation's legal department uses IBM compatible personal computers and, thus, had to retain its MS-DOS compatibility while moving to a graphical user interface. To do this, a Windows application called deskMinder, a desktop manager, was installed. deskMinder presents the user with a graphical desktop onscreen, complete with drawers, shelves, telephone, clock, and other items. Icons were also added for a word processor, spreadsheet, data base management package, and corporate mainframe.

With this system, in addition to accessing the software packages, the user can select the computer icon to access the mainframe or the telephone icon to dial external sources such as a legal data base.

deskMinder also made many Windows utilities, such as the calculator and calendar, more accessible by creating onscreen buttons for them. Today, with Windows and deskMinder on their PCs, the 40 staff members of Taco Bell's legal department can have a graphic user interface while retaining MS-DOS compatibility.

Source: Ben Myers, "Taco Bell Feasts on deskMinder's Accessibility to Windows," *PC Week,* September 16, 1991, p. 121.

Taco Bell installed the deskMinder desktop management software in their legal department to improve productivity.

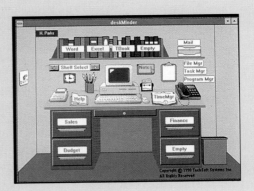

FIGURE 4-7
Multitasking in Windows 3.0

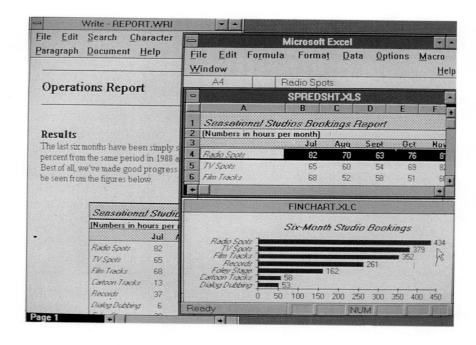

simultaneously, cutting and pasting data among them. In late 1991, Windows 3.1 was introduced as an improved version that cleaned up some of the problems found in the earlier version.

A disadvantage of Windows is that existing MS-DOS programs must be rewritten to take advantage of its many features, and this is not always an easy task. For example, it took the WordPerfect Corp. well over 18 months to create WordPerfect for Windows. However, almost all popular MS-DOS packages will soon be rewritten to work with Windows, if they have not already been rewritten. A second disadvantage is that Windows cannot run on all hardware because it requires at least an 80286 machine with a hard disk and a minimum of 2 Megabytes of memory. However, even an 80286 machine is still often too slow to adequately run Windows, and most experts recommend at least an 80386 machine to take full advantage of all of Windows's features. Figure 4-7 shows two applications running concurrently on *Windows*.

RAM-Resident Programs

Another way of getting around some of the restraints that MS-DOS puts on the personal computer is RAM-resident programs. A **RAM-resident program** is an applications program that once run is, as the name implies, resident in RAM until the computer is turned off. The RAM-resident program "hides" in a part of RAM that is not used by the operating system or any application program. By remaining in the background, it does not interfere with other programs that are run in the foreground. However, it can be called up as needed to overlay the existing application with one or more windows in which a function is executed.

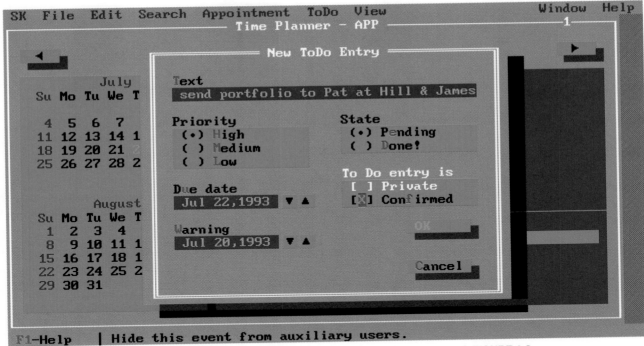

FIGURE 4-8
RAM-Resident Program

The first example of a RAM-resident program, and still one of the most popular, is Sidekick from Borland. This is a utility software application that the user activates into the foreground by simultaneously pressing the Ctrl and Alt keys on an IBM compatible PC keyboard. When these two keys are pressed, a menu "pops up" over any existing software on the screen. From this menu, the user can choose to view a calendar, use a text editor, use a calculator, use a dialer to dial a phone number, view an ASCII table, set up the Sidekick system, or exit Sidekick. It is possible to use more than one of these applications simultaneously with multiple windows on the screen. The text editor can also be used to "cut and paste" information from the screen for later use in other programs. Figure 4-8 shows the Sidekick Time Planner.

There are numerous RAM-resident programs besides Sidekick, and it is possible to load more than one such program into RAM at one time as long as there is no conflict between the programs. For example, many of the photographs of computer screens, including Figure 4-7, used in this book were "captured" from the screen by a RAM-resident program that can convert a screen image into a digital form on disk. Other RAM-resident programs can capture a series of keystrokes and play them back when needed. As you go further into using the computer, you will certainly find a use for a RAM-resident program.

A shortcoming of RAM-resident programs is that they can occasionally interfere with the operation of a foreground program or with each other. When multiple RAM-resident programs are being used, they sometimes must be loaded into memory in a specific order. Also, it is not always possible to remove a RAM-resident program from memory without rebooting the computer.

BITS OF HISTORY

Operating Systems

Mainframe Operating Systems

Before 1960, computers were set up to execute or "run" one application program at a time. Only after one job had been input, executed, and output could the next job begin. This process wasted a lot of time by causing the CPU to be idle while each job was entered and the output printed. To avoid this wasted CPU time, the first operating systems were written to allow for concurrent execution of jobs. In this way, the CPU would never be idle and the number of jobs completed would be greater. The overall effect of this approach was a dramatic increase in the amount of work that could be performed by the computer.

The first operating systems were written not by computer companies, but by groups of computer users called SHARE in 1958 to 1959. The computer companies initially considered themselves to be hardware vendors only and did not become involved in writing software. However, once it was established that an operating system would enhance computer sales, the user-designed systems were purchased and developed by the hardware companies. The first operating system that allowed multiple users and concurrent jobs was the Master Control Program for the Burroughs 5500 series of machines in 1964 to 1965. This was followed by the operating system for the IBM 360 series of machines (OS-360), which, with the addition of many enhancements, has remained in use for IBM mainframes since 1966.

Personal Computer Operating Systems

Pre–MS-DOS In the early 1970s, a computer scientist named Gary Kildall was consulting for the semiconductor manufacturer Intel, developing compilers to convert high-level languages into machine languages. In the process of working on languages for desktop computers, he discovered a need for an operating system to run all these languages on the same machine. To continue his work, he developed the first operating system for personal computers, which he named CP/M (for Control Program/Microcomputers). As other computer scientists and hobbyists heard about CP/M, Kildall began to get requests for it. To meet this need, in 1974 he and his wife formed a company, Digital Research, to market the product. CP/M was the first operating system for small computers and allowed users to develop a program to suit a particular operating system rather than a particular machine. As a result it became a best-seller, with over 15,000 programs written for it at one point.

Other pre–MS-DOS operating systems included those developed to control the operation of the Apple II, Commodore, and Amiga computers.

The Burroughs 5500 series of computers was the first to accommodate multiple users and concurrent job execution.

> **They needed to get something really quick. I figured later I'd go back and work out the finished operating system with multitasking and all that.**
>
> *Tim Paterson, original designer of MS-DOS*
>
> Quoted in "PC-DOS, also 10, Has Its Own Storied Past," *Infoworld,* August 12, 1991, p. 48.

MS-DOS   Shortly after Intel first offered the 16-bit 8086 chip in 1979, a small hardware firm called Seattle Computer Products needed an operating system for an 8086 product under development. To satisfy this need, it developed an operating system called QDOS (for Quick and Dirty Operating System) with an eye to making it as compatible as possible with CP/M. This operating system was renamed 86-DOS and licensed to Microsoft for development of 16-bit software to run on Intel chips. Microsoft eventually bought the system, renamed it MS-DOS, and later licensed it to IBM for use on the original IBM PC as PC-DOS.

UNIX   The oldest operating system for small computers, UNIX was developed in 1970 by Bell Labs (now AT&T) for use on its in-house minicomputers. When personal computers became popular in the early 1980s, UNIX was modified to run on these smaller computers. It has since been licensed to other companies, such as Microsoft, to be sold for 16-bit computers under the name XENIX. IBM has a version called AIX, and a version of UNIX is the operating system used on Steve Jobs's NeXT computer.

OS/2   The newest PC operating system, OS/2, was developed jointly by Microsoft and IBM and announced in April 1987. Designed as a successor to MS-DOS that offers multitasking and expanded memory management, OS/2 has gone through various stages of development leading up to the current version. Currently, OS/2 offers an easy-to-use graphical interface and robust multitasking capabilities.

Macintosh   The graphical interface approach of the Macintosh operating system is based on work done in the 1970s at the Palo Alto Research Center (PARC) of Xerox (the same people who were involved in the development of the computer mouse). Of central importance at this laboratory was finding ways to make the computer easier to use rather than requiring the user to become an expert on a given machine. It is said that Steve Jobs—a co-founder of Apple Computers—visited this center in the late 1970s, saw what they were doing, and decided that this same approach should be used for future Apple computers. The people at Apple adapted the earlier work to develop the operating system on the Lisa computer and then on the Macintosh computer.

(Left) Gary Kildall, founder of Digital Research, developed the CP/M operating system—the forerunner of MS-DOS. (Right) Andrew Hertzfeld was one of the architects of the original Macintosh operating system.

1. All types of computers need operating systems.
2. An operating system performs various important functions that allow the user to execute utility and applications programs.
3. Currently, most personal computer operating systems are aimed at single users performing single tasks.
4. Personal computer operating systems control the hardware, interpret the user's commands, and maintain a file system on secondary storage.
5. Generic operating systems can run on many different computers; proprietary systems run on only one.
6. The most widely used generic operating systems for personal computers are MS-DOS, OS/2, and UNIX.
7. Of these three, OS/2 and UNIX are multitasking operating systems, and UNIX can also control multiple machines. OS/2 has a graphical user interface (GUI).
8. Apple is one of several computer manufacturers that use proprietary operating systems, with the Apple Macintosh offering an extremely easy-to-use, icon-based operating system.
9. Local area network operating systems are becoming more important as more organizations use LANs.
10. Operating environments and RAM-resident programs allow an MS-DOS user to circumvent some of the difficulties of that operating system. Microsoft Windows is an extremely popular operating environment.

KEY TERMS

batch command
batch mode
booting
command interpreter
disk directory
disk operating system (DOS)
external command
file allocation table (FAT)
generic operating system
graphical user interface (GUI)
hierarchical structure
icon
internal command
LAN operating system
MS-DOS
operating environment

operating system
OS/2
piping
Presentation Manager
prompt
proprietary operating system
queue
RAM-resident program
remote job entry (RJE) site
shell
subdirectory
systems
systems programmer
time-slice
tree structure
UNIX

1. Name the functions of an operating system.
2. How does a mainframe operating system differ from a personal computer operating system?
3. In a computer system, how is concurrent execution different from simultaneous execution?
4. How does the computer run concurrent jobs with no perceptible loss of speed for each job? What is a time-slice?
5. What is an RJE site? Why is it needed?
6. What is the purpose of the supervisor program?
7. What is JCL? How is it used?
8. What is the difference between a channel, a buffer, and a preprocessor?
9. How does a mainframe operating system use a system interrupt? How does it use virtual memory?
10. What are the functions of a personal computer operating system?
11. What is the difference between a generic operating system and a proprietary operating system? Which does a mainframe use? Why?
12. Name the three most commonly used generic operating systems for personal computers.
13. Which operating system is primarily a single-user, single-task operating system?
14. Which operating system is primarily a single-user, multitask operating system? Which can be used to control multiple machines and multiple tasks?
15. What functions does an operating environment perform? What is a RAM-resident program?

5

Word Processing, Graphics, and Desktop Publishing Packages

We noted in earlier chapters that the computer can work with symbols as well as numeric data. In this chapter, we discuss computer software packages for processing words and pictures. These packages are commonly known as word processing, graphics, and desktop publishing packages. Word processing packages enable the user to format a document in a desired form, enter text to create a document, edit the document to reach a final version, and save and print the final version of the document. If additional changes are needed, the word processing package allows them to be made with ease. Graphics packages are used to create pictures to present ideas. Four types of graphics packages will be discussed, including analysis graphics, presentations graphics, computer-aided design, and paint packages for developing computer art. The importance of hardware in selecting and using graphics packages will also be covered. Finally, we discuss a type of software package—desktop publishing—that combines features of word processing and graphics packages to produce near-typeset-quality documents on laser printers.

STUDY OBJECTIVES

After reading this chapter, you should be able to

- understand how the key operations of a word processor make this type of computer package superior to a typewriter;
- describe the process by which a document is formatted;
- discuss the word processing text entry and editing operations in the creation of a document;
- distinguish between the replace mode and the insert mode for word processing packages;
- describe the process by which a document is saved and printed;
- list and discuss other important word processing operations, including block-action commands, search and replace, and spellchecking;
- recognize the key concerns in selecting a word processing package for a personal computer;
- understand how a computer creates graphic images;
- discuss the difference between character and bit-mapped graphics;
- list and discuss the four types of graphics packages that are commonly available on computers;
- explain the importance of hardware in the selection and use of a graphics package;
- discuss the use of desktop publishing to create near-typeset-quality documents on laser printers.

TRYING SOMETHING NEW

Publishing Books at Clarke Central High

Desktop publishing has revolutionized the capabilities of small print shops and offices which previously had to rely on high-cost professionals to do specialized work in typesetting and design. The revolution continues with multimedia and the widespread use of color.

Albon "Buddy" Woods, printing and photography instructor, Clarke Central High School, Athens, Georgia

Quoted in interview with author, March 30, 1991.

Albon "Buddy" Woods is the printing and photography instructor at Clarke Central High School in Athens, Georgia. He had just begun experimenting with desktop publishing when the author of this textbook called him in November 1988 to ask him to publish, on a tight schedule, a computer lab manual. Although Buddy had never published anything as complex as a lab manual, he agreed to give it a try. Using an IBM compatible PC, laser printer, and Ventura desktop publishing package, he and the author were able to convert word processing text and screen-captured graphics into a complete product by the following February.

Since that first success with desktop publishing, Buddy has expanded his operation to produce several books for the same publisher, including two additional versions of the lab manual, two versions of a programming book, and the software tutorial section of another book.

With the money the school earned from these projects, Buddy expanded Clarke Central High's computer facilities: It now has four i486-based PCs, all with large, high-resolution monitors. In addition, the school now has three laser printers, one that produces output equal to that of a commercial typesetting machine; two scanners; optical character reading (OCR) software; and an ink jet printer for color output.

With the new equipment, Buddy and his students have completed numerous other jobs, including two family history books, each with over 300 pages and 600 photos; brochures for a local firm; sports brochures; graduation programs; and programs for Black History Week for the school district. Some of his students now use desktop publishing to layout the school newspaper and yearbook. Since the first project, over 200 Clarke Central students have experienced desktop publishing.

When Buddy was asked to comment on desktop publishing, he said, "It's easy to overdesign a project by including too many fonts or design elements. The rule should be 'keep it simple.'"

Source: Interview with author, March 30, 1991. Reprinted with permission of Mr. Albon "Buddy" Woods, Printing & Photography Instructor at Clarke Central High School in Athens, Georgia.

Buddy Woods uses the Ventura desktop publishing package for his work in and out of the classroom.

In our initial discussions of computer usage, we described computers as **symbol processors** capable of storing and manipulating symbols. While computational work is an extremely important aspect of computer use, manipulating characters and creating pictures are growing uses of the computer. In fact, studies have shown that word processing is the number one use of personal computers. On the other hand, generating graphics to represent ideas is fast becoming one of the most exciting uses of computers today. Computer graphics are used extensively for games; animation and special effects in movies; analysis of business, scientific, and engineering data; presentation of ideas to groups; design of industrial and electronic equipment; and artistic purposes. In both word processing and graphics, the computer is helping to facilitate the communication of ideas from the user to other people. And, as discussed in the box, desktop publishing is being used more and more often to combine words and pictures into a professional-quality document that can be printed on a laser printer.

For word processing, graphics, and desktop publishing, we will not discuss the operation of any one package in detail. Instead, we will present the key ideas and functions that are common to all such packages. Tutorials on the use of commercial word processing and graphics packages are presented in separate lab manuals available with this textbook.

WORKING WITH CHARACTERS AND SYMBOLS

WORD PROCESSING PACKAGES

Software packages with names like WordPerfect, WordStar, and Microsoft Word are all examples of word processing packages for personal computers. These and many other **word processing packages** allow the user to define the form of a document, input and modify text using a keyboard, and then print the document.

The four key operations of a word processing package are

- defining the form of the document;
- entering a document from a keyboard;
- editing (modifying) the document;
- printing the document.

Two of the most popular word processing packages are WordPerfect and Microsoft Word.

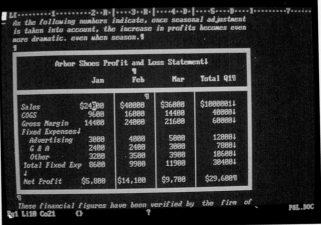

All word processing packages offer these same operations; the deciding factors between packages are most often the ease of using a particular package and the manner in which the operations are carried out. Other differences involve price, specialized features, documentation, and the amount and type of technical support offered after the package is purchased.

Defining the Form of the Document

Usually, before a document can be entered from the keyboard, its form must be defined. This process is known as **formatting,** and it involves entering values for left and right margins, tab stops, vertical spacing (single, double, or other spacing), number of lines per page, and number of characters per inch. For example, a user may format a document to double space each 56-line page, with left and right margins of 1 inch each. If ten characters per inch are selected, then these margins would be ten characters per inch per side.

Once these parameters have been defined, the user usually sees a blank screen, except for a **status line** at the top or bottom of the screen that provides information about the current status of the screen. An example of a status line for WordPerfect 5.1 is shown in Figure 5-1. Note that the status shows that this is Document number 1 (of 2) and that the cursor is on Page 1, Line 1, Position 1 (the left margin) of the document.

Another common formatting decision concerns the right margin. With word processing packages, the left margin is always justified; that is, the text always lines up on the left. The user may also decide to have the right margin justified. **Right justification** means that the word processing package adds extra spaces within the lines to make the ends of the lines line up on the right margin. This may not be shown on the screen, but will occur when the document is

Doc 1 Pg 1 Ln 1" Pos 1"

FIGURE 5-1
WordPerfect Status Line

printed. As examples of documents with and without right justification, Figure 5-2 shows the same section of the Gettysburg Address printed under each condition.

A feature that more word processing packages are including is the capability to display the document on the screen in exactly the same form it will have when it is printed. This is known as *What You See Is What You Get* and is referred to as **WYSIWYG.** This is an important feature for onscreen creation of documents because the user can see clearly what the document will look like when it is printed.

Entering Text

For a word processor, as for a typewriter, the text must first be entered from a keyboard. But even as early as the text entry stage, the word processor has a very useful function called *word wrap*. In **word wrap,** the user simply enters text and lets the computer worry about whether there is enough room for a particular word on the current line. If the computer decides that a word will not fit on a line, it moves the word to the next line. The typist needs to use the Enter key only at the end of each paragraph.

Editing Text

The ability to edit (modify) text easily is an important and useful characteristic of a word processing package. **Text editing** in its simplest form means replacing, inserting, or deleting characters from existing text. With most word processors, editing means much more than this. For example, blocks of text can be deleted, copied, or moved to other points in a document, or copied or moved to an entirely different document. The editing function on a word processor also allows the user to search for a string of characters or even to replace that string with another string.

To accomplish the editing operations requires a way of controlling the blinking square of light or underline called the **cursor,** which designates where the computer is expecting text to be entered or deleted. It is also necessary to be able to give the word processor commands to carry out insertion, replacement, or deletion of text; to work with blocks of text; and to search for strings of text.

Cursor Control   Recall from our discussion of keyboards in Chapter 2 that several keys are specifically for cursor control. The **cursor control keys** with Up and Down arrows move the cursor one vertical line at a time; the keys with

FIGURE 5-2
Unjustified and Justified Printed Documents

Four score and seven years ago, our forefathers brought forth on this continent a new nation, conceived in liberty, and dedicated to the proposition that all men are created equal. We are now engaged in a great civil war testing whether that nation, or any nation so conceived, can long endure.

Four score and seven years ago, our forefathers brought forth on this continent a new nation, conceived in liberty, and dedicated to the proposition that all men are created equal. We are now engaged in a great civil war testing whether that nation, or any nation so conceived, can long endure.

Left and Right arrows move it one character at a time in the direction of the arrow. Holding down any of these keys will cause the movement to repeat. Moving the cursor either up or down off the screen results in an action known as **scrolling,** in which new material appears from that direction. The **PgUp** (page up) and **PgDn** (page down) keys provide larger vertical movements and often are used to scroll to a new page of the document or to a new **video page,** which is the amount of text that can be seen on the screen at one time. The effect of the **Home** and **End** keys depends on the word processing package being used. For some word processing packages, the gray plus and minus on the right side of the keyboard can also be used for larger up and down movements.

Entering Commands   The method of entering commands depends greatly on what word processing package is being used. Some packages, such as WordPerfect, use the function keys—either by themselves or in conjunction with the Ctrl, Shift, and Alt keys—to send commands, while other packages, such as WordStar, use the Ctrl key in conjunction with letter keys. One of the most difficult parts of learning a new word processor is learning the command structure; this is probably one of the reasons that many longtime users appear to be reluctant to change word processors.

Composition houses use specially designed word processing terminals for typesetting documents of all kinds.

Replacement or Insertion of Characters   This is performed in either the **replace mode** or the **insert mode.** In the replace mode, characters that are entered at the cursor location replace or type over the existing characters. In the insert mode, characters entered at the cursor location push existing text to the right. Because of this typeover or pushover action, the replace and insert modes are also referred to as the **typeover** and **pushover modes.** On most word processors, the Ins key is used to *toggle* or switch between these two modes. For example, if the insert mode is on, then the user inserts text by locating the cursor where the insertion is to be made and then entering text, pushing existing text to the right. In this same situation, the user would replace characters at the cursor by first pressing the Ins key and then typing over the existing text. Either mode continues until the Ins key is pressed again.

Deleting Material   To delete material, we place the cursor over the character to be deleted and press the Del (delete) key. If the delete key is held down, characters to the *right* will be pulled under the cursor and deleted. This will continue until the Del key is released. After an insertion or deletion, the text is **reformatted** automatically to account for the removal of text—that is, the text is moved to fill out lines to the margin.

With most word processors, we can also delete text to the *left* of the cursor by using the **Backspace key,** which works like the Del key but in the opposite direction.

Even though we have discussed insertion and deletion as parts of the *editing* process, both of these procedures are also used during the *text entry* process to modify text as it is being entered. The edit operation can be used to correct errors or to add or delete text at any time while material is being entered.

Block-Action Commands   The user can delete a large amount of material simply by holding down the delete command keys. With a large section of text, however, it is easier to perform a block-action command to accomplish this task. In a **block-action command,** the user first defines a block of text. The cursor is then positioned at the beginning of the block and the block-define command is given. The same procedure is performed at the end of the block of text. After a block is defined in this way, a series of actions can be performed on the block, including the deletion of the entire block. We could remove a sentence from a paragraph by defining it as a block and giving the appropriate block-delete command.

Another block-action command is in the text block movement. This process is also called **cut-and-paste,** because using a block-action move is the same as cutting out a block of material from a manuscript and pasting it down somewhere else in the manuscript. For example, a user might decide that a particular paragraph should be located somewhere else in a document. With block-move commands, the paragraph could be lifted from its current location and shifted to the new spot. A block of text can also be copied to other locations in the document or to entirely different documents. A block of text used in many locations is referred to as **boiler plate material,** because it can be used over and over again. The boiler plate is copied to those other locations with a block-action command. Figure 5-3 shows a block being marked and then deleted.

Search   Most word processors can search for the occurrences of a word or some sequence of characters. In this operation, the user defines the desired word

TWP: WHAT A RELIEF

From the time that she began working in the Department of Management Science and Information Technology at the University of Georgia in 1977, one of Linda Keith's primary jobs has been typing highly technical or mathematical papers. Initially, Linda used a typewriter with interchangeable printheads to convert the professors' handwritten manuscripts into a typewritten form. This would often result in the paper going back and forth several times between the writer and Linda for retyping until all of the symbols and equations were represented exactly. Even after several typings, Linda would still have to make liberal use of "whiteout" to correct

T-Cubed reduces the amount of work necessary to produce a final mathematical manuscript.

errors. The introduction of word processors helped to some extent since the text did not have to be retyped each time. However, most word processors did not handle mathematical symbols and equations very well; Linda still had to type those on a typewriter.

Today, Linda uses a technical word processor (TWP) called T-Cubed (produced by TCI Software) to create mathematical and scientific papers. This TWP makes it much easier to type

equations and to include mathematical or scientific symbols, providing the needed symbols or even enabling Linda to create her own. "What You See Is What You Get" onscreen creation of equations allows her to be sure the equation is being entered correctly. And, of course, they can be easily changed when a professor modifies the paper or adds new material.

Source: Interview with the author, 1991.

Revising	T3 Demo		Full	Keyboards	Same as keys		Same as keys
Pg	16:1	Pos	1	29 +0.0	.50 in	Line format	Single Space	H 0 D 0

Benchmark 6:
Allen F. Henry, *Nuclear Reactor Analysis*, MIT Press, Cambridge, Mass, 1982, 495, equation 11.4.19, subequations 4 and 5.

$$iB_r\left[\tilde{\alpha}_{k\ell}^n\right] \equiv \frac{1}{2}(k_{n-1} + k_n)\int_0^R 2\pi r \, dr \left[\rho_{k*}^n(r)\right]\frac{d}{dr}\left[\Psi_\ell^n(r)\right],$$

$$\left[p_{r,k\ell}^n\right]^{-1} \equiv \int_0^R 2\pi r \, dr \int_{z_n^- - \frac{1}{2}h_n - 1}^{z_n^+ + \frac{1}{2}h_n}\left[\rho_k^{n*}(r)\right]\left[D^{-1}(r,z)\right]\left[\rho_\ell^n(r)\right],$$

Benchmark 7:
E. I. Guendelman and Z. M. Radulovic, "Infrared Divergence in Three-Dimensi Gauge Theories", *Physical Review. D (Particles and Fields)*, American Physic 30, No 6, 15 Sept 1984, page 1347, Figure 13.

This benchmark requires three symbols used in the Feynman diagrams which are not supplied with the standard release system. However, you can use the T³ font edi these symbols very quickly.

11:41 am ▭▭▭▭▭ ACN3

and then enters the appropriate command to initiate the search. When the defined word is found, the computer positions the cursor over the word and waits for user action. An extension of this process is the **search and replace** operations, in which the user defines both the object of the search and a replacement word. A search and replace operation is commonly used to find misspelled words in a document and to replace them with the correct words. For example, if a user suspects that the word *compiler* has been spelled *compilor* throughout a document, the simple procedure of the search and replace operation could be used to correct this error. The object of the search is the word *compilor,* and the replacement word is *compiler.*

Most word processors can perform a **wildcard search,** which locates a word when only part of the word is known. For example, assume that both *insure* and *ensure* are used in a document and that the user wishes to search for both

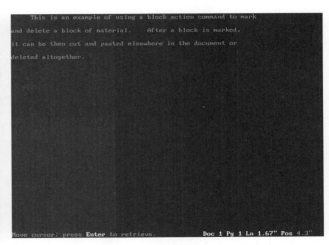

FIGURE 5-3
Block-Action Command to
Delete Material

of these words. The user substitutes a special character, such as *?*, for the first letter. The computer would then search for *?nsure* to find all occurrences of both *insure* and *ensure*.

The insertion, deletion, block movement or copy, and search and replace operations make the editing function a useful part of word processing. Editing really sets a word processor apart from a typewriter.

Other Text Entry and Editing Operations

In addition to the text entry and editing operations discussed so far, most word processors can perform many operations, including centering, boldfacing or underlining text, and indenting entire paragraphs. It is also possible to include subscripts, superscripts, headers or footers, and footnotes in the document and to paginate it automatically.

Centering allows the user to center a line of text between the margins as it is being entered or after it has been entered. A good example of WYSIWYG is the display of **boldfaced** or underlined words on the screen. Many word processors are being written to work under Windows to take advantage of its WYSIWYG capabilities. Windows word processors can show different types and sizes of fonts as well as graphics on the screen. Figure 5-4 shows WYSIWYG in one such Windows word processor.

In **paragraph indentation,** one or both margins of a paragraph can be indented. This feature is useful for documents in which long quotations must be indented but changing the margins for each quotation would be awkward. With technical or mathematical papers, it is important to be able to include subscripts (S_1) or superscripts (2^{10}) in the document to create equations and mathematical or chemical formulas. Inclusion of **headers** or **footers** (text that is displayed at the top or bottom of each page) is an important feature when copyright notices or other information must be included on each page of the text.

For writers of research papers, the capability of a word processor to handle the numbering of **footnotes** for references is very useful. When the paper is printed, the package also allocates the proper spacing at the bottom of the page for the footnotes cited on that particular page. An especially useful footnoting

FIGURE 5-4
WYSIWYG Word Processing
under Windows 3.0

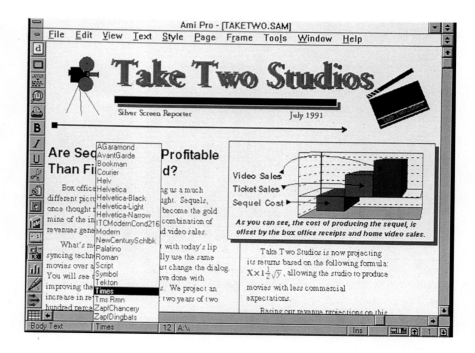

feature is the capability of the word processor to renumber footnotes when new references are added.

Automatic pagination of documents allows the user to include a page number automatically on each page of the text. Most packages will allow the user to select the position of the number on the page and the type of number (arabic or roman) to be used.

Saving and Printing a Document

Once a document has been formatted, entered, and edited, the next steps are to save the document to secondary storage and then print it. It is always a good idea to save the document first—before printing it—so that if a problem occurs during the printing process the document is still saved on secondary storage. In fact, it is a good idea to save the document at several points during the document creation process.

Printing requires a special type of software known as a printer driver. A **printer driver** converts the special characters that the word processing software has inserted in the document—for underlining, boldface, subscripts, and so on—into instructions that the printer can use. For some word processors, these **printer codes** show up on the screen next to the plain text; in others, the material itself will actually appear boldfaced, underlined, or subscripted on the screen. While many printers need specific drivers, others are able to use drivers written for one or the other of the two most popular types of printers—Epson or IBM. Word processing software usually comes with a driver for these two types of printers as well as drivers for various other types of printers. Before printing a document, the user selects a printer driver. Usually this selection needs to be done only once, and the same driver will work for all future documents. Figure 5-5 shows the printer codes for a document in WordPerfect 5.1.

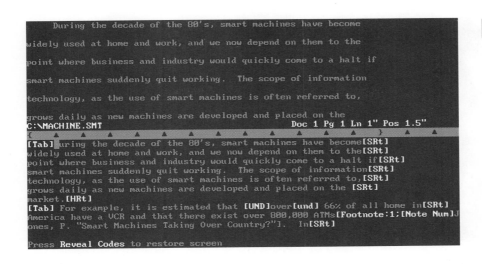

FIGURE 5-5
Printer Codes in WordPerfect 5.1

Another feature of word processing packages relating to printing is the use of print spoolers. A **print spooler** enables the user to print one document while working on another. This software uses the slices of time between keystrokes to have the CPU print the document. This is a very useful feature when several documents (letters, reports, and so on) are being prepared at the same time.

Other Operations

In addition to text entry, editing, formatting, and printing, there are many special features available on most popular word processors. Among the more popular of these are a speller and thesaurus, mail-merge, outlining, document translation, and macros. A **speller** checks the spelling in a document by consulting an electronic dictionary of commonly used words and alerting the user when a word is entered that is not in the dictionary. Words may not need to be changed—for example, if they are personal names or technical terms—and it is usually possible to add special words to the dictionary. Figure 5-6 shows the speller for WordPerfect in operation. In this case, it has highlighted the word *thse* as possibly being misspelled and has provided a suggested correction.

One problem with depending too much on a speller to find misspelled words in a document is that the speller will *not* find words that are spelled incorrectly in the context in which they are used. For example, if *their* is used when the correct word is *there,* the speller will not recognize the error. For this reason, a speller should never be used as the sole proofreader of any document.

An electronic **thesaurus** provides synonyms and, possibly, antonyms for specified words. Unlike the speller, the thesaurus usually requires that the user select a word for which synonyms and antonyms are desired before invoking the thesaurus. Figure 5-7 shows the thesaurus for WordPerfect providing synonyms for the word *fool.*

The word processor with language, spelling, and grammar checkers became a way to make communications more personal and more effective.

Camilo Wilson, chairman and CEO, Lifetree Software

Quoted in "View from the Top," *Personal Computing,* October 1989, p. 260.

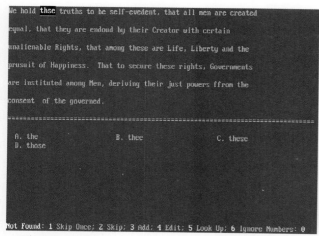

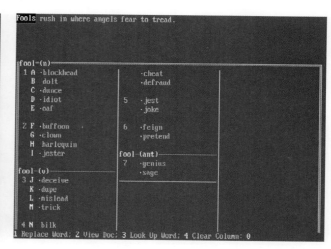

We hold thse truths to be self-evedent, that all men are created
equal, that they are endoud by their Creator with certain
unalienable Rights, that among these are Life, Liberty and the
prusuit of Happiness. That to secure these rights, Governments
are instituted among Men, deriving their just powers ffrom the
consent of the governed.

A. the   B. thee   C. these
D. those

Not Found: 1 Skip Once; 2 Skip; 3 Add; 4 Edit; 5 Look Up; 6 Ignore Numbers: 0

Fools rush in where angels fear to tread.

fool-(n)
1 A ·blockhead   ·cheat
  B dolt   ·defraud
  C ·dunce
  D ·idiot   5 ·jest
  E ·oaf   ·joke

2 F ·buffoon ·   6 ·feign
  G ·clown   ·pretend
  H harlequin   fool-(ant)
  I ·jester   7 ·genius
                       ·sage
fool-(v)
3 J ·deceive
  K ·dupe
  L ·mislead
  M ·trick

4 N bilk
1 Replace Word; 2 View Doc; 3 Look Up Word; 4 Clear Column: 0

FIGURE 5-6 (left)
Word Processing Speller

FIGURE 5-7 (right)
Word Processing Thesaurus

Mail-merge is a function that allows a word processor to be used to prepare form letters. The letter is prepared in the same manner as any other document, except that the inside address and salutation are left blank. The names and addresses are then entered into another file, one after the other. Upon a command from the user, the two files are merged with a name and address being added to each letter as it is printed.

Since most writers do an outline before beginning the actual writing of a document, some word processing packages now include an **outline processor.** The outline processor helps the user plan the project by automatically numbering the various levels of the outline.

Another useful feature of a word processor is the **document translation** function that converts documents from other word processing packages. For example, WordPerfect can convert WordStar files into a WordPerfect format.

In word processing packages, a **macro** is a sequence of commonly used keystrokes to which the user assigns a name. The computer then executes the keystroke sequence whenever the user invokes the macro. For example, the sequence of keystrokes to save a document and exit the package might be named Alt-S and would be executed anytime the user presses the Alt and S keys simultaneously.

SELECTING A WORD PROCESSOR

Word processing software comes in many different forms, ranging from very complex to fairly simple and likewise varying in price from $500 down to less than $100. To select the package that fits your needs you must decide what the package will be used for, what type of computer it will be used on, and how much money you can spend. Keep in mind that word processing is probably the most personal of all types of PC software, with no one package defining the market. For this reason, you can choose from a wide variety of packages. Also, if you ask two friends who use different packages to tell you which is better, you will probably receive two different answers. Word processor users are often very loyal to "their" package and will advise you to use the same one they do. For this reason, it is extremely important to define your needs and try out the packages that appear to fit your criteria. By doing this rather than buying a bestseller or one that is recommended by a friend, you have a better chance of being satisfied with your purchase.

If you are going to be doing math or scientific word processing, then you need to purchase a specialized word processor like the TWP discussed in the earlier box. If you wish to combine word processing with desktop publishing, then you should look for a package that will allow you to incorporate graphics as well as multiple fonts and type sizes. Finally, if you have no special needs, then almost any package may be adequate.

Be sure that your computer has the amount of memory needed for a particular package. If you are going to be using a WYSIWYG-oriented package, be sure you have the correct type of video system. Also, while in some cases there are different versions of the same package for the Apple Macintosh and IBM compatible computers, they are not the same package and cannot be switched between machines. Finally, note that although price is not always a good indicator of the features that are available with the package, less costly packages usually cannot afford the same level of online telephone help as may be available with more expensive packages such as WordPerfect. Table 5-1 shows some popular word processors for both the Apple Macintosh and IBM compatible computers.

In selecting a word processor or any other personal computer software, it is extremely important that you try out the package before purchasing it. Insist upon being able to sit down with the software at a computer of the type that you will be using and try sample applications of your choosing. To help in the selection of software packages (and hardware, too), there are numerous computer magazines that review software and hardware. Some of the magazines are directed toward a particular type of computer; others are more general. Table 5-2 lists some of the more popular computer magazines and the particular computer, if any, toward which each magazine is directed. Virtually every piece of software available on the market has been or will be reviewed in at least one of these magazines. These reviews can help a potential buyer determine whether a particular package fits his or her needs.

There also exist various surveys of software that keep track of the top-selling packages. These surveys appear weekly and monthly in newspapers and computer magazines and are useful in determining the most popular software.

On the Apple Macintosh, word processing has always been able to include graphics and various fonts and to show the result on the screen.

TABLE 5-1
Popular Word Processing Packages

Package	Machine	List Price	Use
WordPerfect	IBM	$495	General/DTP
Microsoft Word	IBM	495	General/DTP
WordStar	IBM	495	General
Ami Pro	IBM/Windows	N/A	General/DTP
PC-Write	IBM	$ 89	General
EXP	IBM	299	Technical
Lotus Manuscript	IBM	495	Technical
Mac WordPerfect	Mac	395	General
Microsoft Word	Mac	395	General/DTP

TABLE 5-2
Computer Magazines

Magazine	Computer Orientation
Byte	General
Creative Computing	General
InfoWorld	General
MacWeek	Apple Macintosh
MacWorld	Apple Macintosh
PC/Computing	General
PC Magazine	IBM and compatibles
PC Week	IBM and compatibles
PC World	IBM and compatibles

Remember, though, that a popular software package may not suit your needs, so don't select software on the basis of its popularity.

GRAPHICS PACKAGES

If word processing packages are used to communicate ideas via words, then **graphics packages** communicate ideas via pictures. These pictures are designed by the computer software to present material in a form that is easy to understand and easy to work with. For example, graphics on supercomputers have been used to represent such diverse physical relationships as the amount of light coming from parts of a distant galaxy, to the effect of a steam pipe breaking within a nuclear power plant, to the reconstruction of a tornado to reveal unexpected downdrafts. The combination of color, three-dimensional representations, and motion can reveal the effect of changes in data over time in a way that would otherwise not be possible. In these cases, a supercomputer is needed to handle the mass of data and the calculations that must be made to represent the relationships as a picture. However, mainframes and personal computers can be used for similar graphic analyses that require less computational effort.

Graphics packages can also be used for artistic purposes, to produce dramatic and beautiful pictures. Graphics is a very exciting area in computers, with new and different uses emerging almost every day. For example, many of the special effects in *Terminator 2: Judgment Day* were created using computer graphics. Similarly, graphics are being used to analyze baseball pitches on TV.

With high-resolution monitors, it is possible to use graphics in such areas of scientific research as genetics, microbiology, and medicine. It is also possible to design automobiles, tools, and space shuttles using computer graphics.

Types of Graphics

There are four types of graphics packages currently in use on both mainframes and personal computers: analysis graphics, presentation graphics, computer-aided design (CAD), and paint packages. **Analysis graphics** are used to help analyze data to determine if patterns exist or to gain a better understanding of

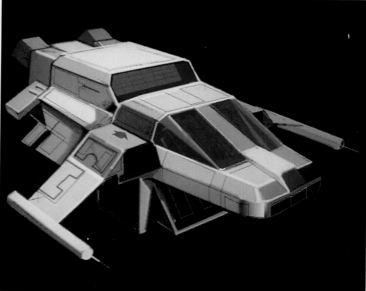

A.D.A.M.: A COMPUTERIZED ANATOMY BOOK

One of the most important courses in any medical program is human anatomy—the structure of the human body. Historically, students have learned anatomy through textbooks, slides, and cadavers. However, now a new software package called A.D.A.M.—Animated Dissection of Anatomy for Medicine—may replace all these learning tools. With A.D.A.M., the student can actually dissect, without a cadaver, any part of the human body without worrying about making mistakes.

The A.D.A.M. program uses an optical disk that stores information about the human body. The disk generates high-resolution graphics of various parts of the human body, and the graphics are displayed on either an Apple Macintosh or IBM compatible PC. Users can choose to watch a simulation of a complete pathology example or an unlimited number of dissectible views and animations of common surgeries. It is possible for students to peel the skin and muscles, layer by layer, to see deep within the body or to use the mouse as a scalpel to simulate an incision into the body. With a color printer, users can prepare a printed version of the screen.

In addition to the obvious uses of A.D.A.M. for medical students, other groups are also interested in it. For example, insurance companies have shown an interest in this system, because it allows a physician to "walk" a patient through an entire operation. That way, the patient has a better understanding of the procedure and, therefore, is less likely to initiate a lawsuit against the doctor or hospital after the surgery. Similarly, companies that make medical items, such as artificial hip joints, may wish to equip their salespeople with this system to demonstrate to the physician–consumer how the product works.

Source: Bill Husted, "New Computer Program Handles Medical Needs," *Atlanta Journal-Constitution,* May 30, 1991, p. G2.

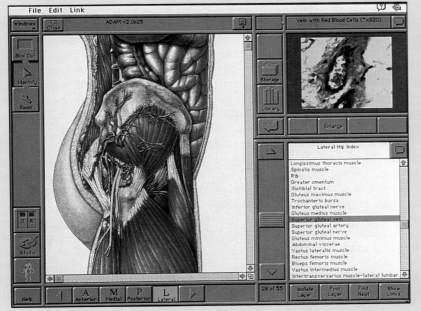

Animated Dissection of Anatomy for Medicine (A.D.A.M.) software eliminates some of the need for animal dissections.

the data. The results of an analysis graphics package are primarily charts and diagrams and usually are not meant to be used for presentations. When the impact on the audience is important, **presentation graphics** are used. These are usually full-color graphics, sometimes in three dimensions, that are meant to vividly portray an idea to an audience. The use of presentation graphics is growing rapidly—up to 36 percent in 1990 alone—as more organizations find ways to use them. If the object is to use graphics to design a building or an electronic or mechanical device, then **computer-aided design (CAD)** is needed. Using CAD, an engineer, architect, or draftsman can greatly reduce the time necessary to develop a blueprint for an electronic or structural design. Finally, if the objective is to use a computer for artistic purposes, then a **paint package** is needed. With such a package, the user may pick a type of "brush," choose colors from a "palette," and then use the cursor to draw on the screen.

We will discuss each of these types of packages in some detail. However, first we will explain how graphics are created and discuss the importance of hardware in graphics.

Understanding Graphics

To understand how graphics work, look at a picture in a newspaper. These *half-tone* pictures are made up of black dots on a white background. The black areas are completely covered with dots, and the gray areas are a mixture of dots and white background. Graphics on a computer screen work exactly like the half-tone picture in the newspaper except that the background is usually dark and the dots are light colored. Each dot corresponds to a **pixel** or picture element on the screen that is turned either on or off. The letters of the alphabet, digits, punctuation marks, and graphics symbols all are formed this way. Figure 5-8 demonstrates how the letter A and a rectangle can be portrayed on the screen using pixels.

If the dots are controlled individually, the graphics are said to be **bit-mapped,** and the on–off condition of each pixel corresponds to the on–off condition of a bit in internal memory. The number of dots on a screen determines the **resolution** of the screen, with the lowest resolution screens in use today having 320 pixels horizontally and 200 pixels vertically. High-resolution monitors have 1,024 horizontal pixels and 768 vertical pixels. High resolution becomes important when the user attempts to draw complex figures. Without high resolution, figures may be ragged and have a "stair-step appearance" on the screen.

If the dots on the screen are controlled as a group, the graphics are called **character graphics.** Special symbols are combined to create bar charts, borders around the screen, boxes, and the like. However, character graphics cannot be used to create any type of picture. The symbols used in character graphics correspond to various ASCII characters, as shown in Figure 5-9. Some early com-

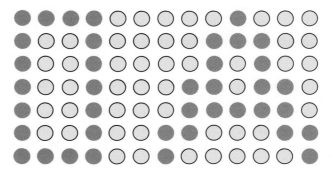

FIGURE 5-8
Dot Representation

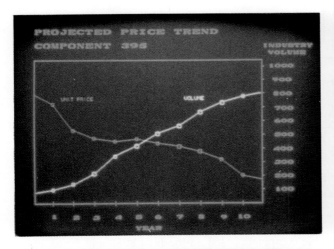

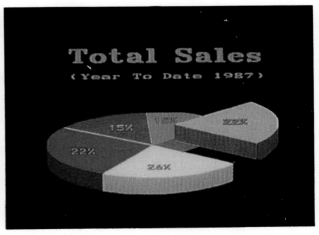

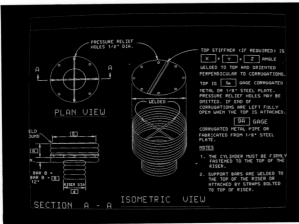

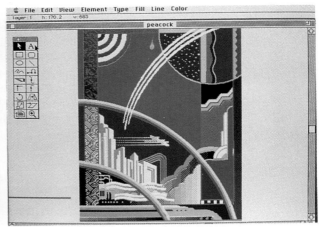

(Top left) When researchers are studying trends, they find that line graphs are a highly practical, informative type of analysis graphics. (Top right) "Exploded" pie graphs in multiple colors are often used in presentation graphics. (Bottom left) Computer-aided design (CAD) is commonly used to create engineering designs. (Bottom right) Paint packages can be used to create elaborate works of art.

puters could work only with character graphics, but today virtually all computers can work with both types of graphics. Character graphics are often used to create boxes and borders in software packages.

The Hardware Connection

Of all the packages commonly used on personal computers, graphics packages are most dependent upon hardware. This is true at both the mainframe and personal computer levels. With mainframes, very powerful graphics chips are used to generate the desired picture. Quite often, special graphics workstations using graphics chips and extremely high-resolution monitors are connected to mainframes.

For personal computers, different chips are more or less suited to displaying graphics. For example, the Motorola 68000 series of chips used by the Apple Macintosh, Commodore Amiga, and NeXT series of computers supports very-high-resolution graphics, while the Intel 8088 and 80xxx chips used in IBM compatible computers, including the PS/2 line, can support only character graphics, unless additional graphics hardware is added.

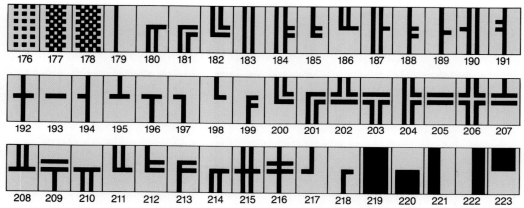

| 176 | 177 | 178 | 179 | 180 | 181 | 182 | 183 | 184 | 185 | 186 | 187 | 188 | 189 | 190 | 191 |

| 192 | 193 | 194 | 195 | 196 | 197 | 198 | 199 | 200 | 201 | 202 | 203 | 204 | 205 | 206 | 207 |

| 208 | 209 | 210 | 211 | 212 | 213 | 214 | 215 | 216 | 217 | 218 | 219 | 220 | 221 | 222 | 223 |

FIGURE 5-9
Character Graphics Symbols

For IBM compatible computers based on the Intel 8088 and 80xxx chips (80286, 80386, and i486) to work with bit-mapped graphics, an additional piece of hardware is needed. This is a **graphics adapter board,** which supports color and graphics and is installed in one of the slots in the back of an IBM compatible PC. To understand the hardware–graphics relationship on the PCs that use the Intel chips, we need to look at five commonly used options: the Hercules Graphics Card and monochrome display, the Color/Graphics Adapter (CGA) and CGA display, the Enhanced Graphics Adapter (EGA) and EGA display, and the Video Graphics Array (VGA) and VGA or multiscanning display, and the Super VGA system.

The Apple Macintosh has long been used to create outstanding graphics.

File   Edit   Search   Windows   Volumes

A photograph has been digitized on the Macintosh and displayed on the screen.

When the original IBM PC was introduced in 1981, it was sold with a text-only monochrome (single-color) monitor. Many users still prefer this type of monitor because of the high-quality text it supports, but, without an add-in board, it cannot show even monochrome bit-mapped graphics. The needed add-in board, called a **Hercules Graphics Card,** was introduced in 1982 and enables the display of high-resolution (720 × 348 pixels) monochrome graphics on the monochrome monitor.

The first board that was developed to display color graphics was the **Color/Graphics Adapter (CGA),** which, when combined with an RGB color monitor, would show low-resolution graphics (320 × 200 pixels) in four onscreen colors. In response to a need for higher-resolution graphics and more colors, the **Enhanced Graphics Adapter (EGA)** was created in 1984. When this board is combined with an Enhanced Color Display monitor, medium-resolution graphics (640 × 350 pixels) can be shown in 16 onscreen colors.

Introduced at the same time as the PS/2 line of IBM computer in 1987, the **Video Graphics Array (VGA)** differs from previous graphics adapters in several ways. First, instead of being digital like all previous video systems, VGA is analog like a television screen. This allows the VGA system to show up to 32 shades of 8 colors, whereas EGA could show only bright and soft shading

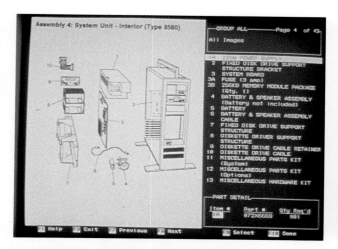

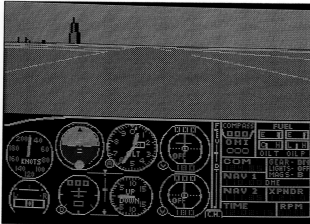

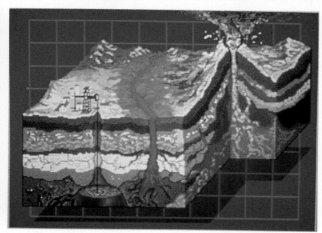

(Top left) Hercules systems can display high-resolution graphics in one color. (Top right) CGA video systems can display medium-resolution graphics in four colors. (Bottom left) EGA video systems can display high-resolution graphics in up to 16 colors. (Bottom right) VGA video systems can display high-resolution graphics in up to 256 colors.

XGA, the very latest video system from IBM, surpasses even the VGA in high-quality resolution and number of colors.

Graphics boards combine with IBM compatible PCs to display graphics on the monitor screen.

of its 16 colors. Second, the resolution is increased up to 640 × 480, offering high-quality text and graphics. A VGA board can use a VGA analog monitor, or a **multiscanning monitor** that can show display analog VGA, or any of the digital graphics adapters.

The newest and most expensive video system for personal computers is the **Super VGA system,** or XGA on IBM systems. This system provides a resolution of 1,024 × 768 pixels and 262,000 colors from which to choose to display 256 colors on the screen. Figure 5-10 shows the letter R as it is represented by the various video systems.

Selection of the appropriate graphics adapter and monitor for your purposes will be discussed in more detail in the Guide to Buying a PC following Chapter 10.

As mentioned earlier, there are four types of graphics packages: analysis graphics, presentation graphics, CAD, and paint packages. All four types are available for both mainframe and personal computers, but we will consider in detail only those that are available on the personal computer. Graphics workstations connected to mainframes and minicomputers provide higher-quality graphics than do PCs, but they are also much more expensive.

> **[Super VGA] will be the next standard for the high-end computer market, and eventually the standard for all graphics applications.**
>
> *Michael Castro,*
> *senior industry analyst for*
> *Dataquest, Inc.*
>
> Quoted in "IBM Touts XGA as New High-End Graphics Standard," *PC Week,* November 5, 1990, p. 8.

A CLOSER LOOK AT GRAPHICS PACKAGES

FIGURE 5-10
Examples of Video Systems

Souce: From *PC/Computing,* October 1989, p. 225. Diagrams by Mary Ellen Zawatski.

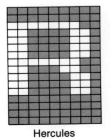

Hercules

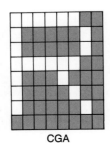

CGA

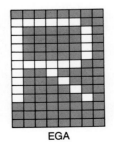

EGA

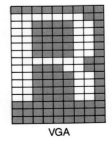

VGA

SVGA

Analysis Graphics

Analysis graphics are those that help a decision maker understand or analyze the data. Since the computer is capable of handling large amounts of numerical data and the human mind is able to conceptualize pictures better than numbers, analysis graphics help us understand the numerical data. Thousands of pages of numerical data can be reduced to a single picture to reveal relationships that might otherwise go unnoticed.

On personal computers, the emphasis for analysis graphics has been in business, so they are also often referred to as **business graphics.** Common uses include pictorial representations of sales, budgets, or expenses, or comparisons either over time or between different groups at the same time. A personal computer is well suited for this type of graphics because of its immediate access.

Most analysis graphics are created with spreadsheet packages like Lotus 1-2-3. These graphics include bar graphs, stacked-bar graphs, pie graphs, scatter diagrams, and line graphs.

A **bar graph** uses vertical or horizontal bars to compare quantities; the length or height of the bar represents each quantity. For example, monthly regional sales could be compared using a bar graph. **Stacked-bar graphs** place multiple quantities on the same bar.

A **pie graph** can be used to compare parts of some overall quantity (budget, income, etc.), for example, regional sales for a year, with the regions divided into slices proportional to their sales. A **scatter diagram** can be used to compare two groups of data, for example, the number of salespeople in each region compared to the sales in that region. Finally, a **line graph** can be used to show trends over time, for example, to show the trend of total sales over the last five years. The incline or decline of each line segment demonstrates the change in values on the vertical axis for each unit change on the horizontal axis. Figure 5-11 shows a Lotus 1-2-3 spreadsheet along with a bar chart created

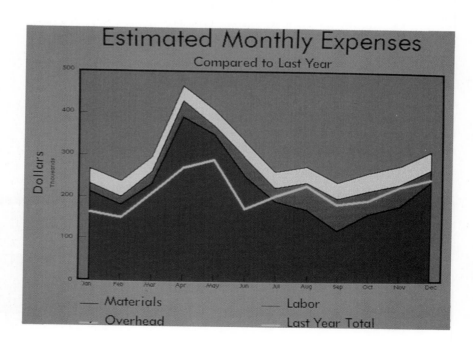

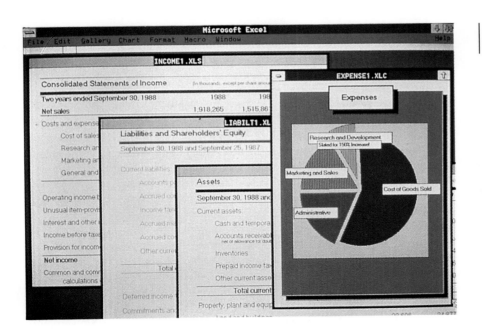

Microsoft Excel can display graphics simultaneously with the spreadsheet data.

from this spreadsheet. Note the use of color to differentiate parts of the graph. Each release of a new spreadsheet seems to bring better, more colorful graphs, including three-dimensional capabilities.

Presentation Graphics

While analysis graphics are used to help the user understand data, presentation graphics are used to present results to others. Consequently, they must have a much more "professional" look to deliver the message with a "punch." The actual graphs used in presentation graphics may include those used in analysis graphics, but they are much more elaborate: They use more colors to add emphasis to key points in the graph, and three-dimensional graphs are frequently used

FIGURE 5-11
Spreadsheet (left) and Analysis Graphics (right)

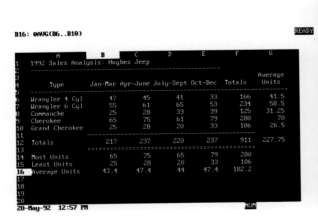

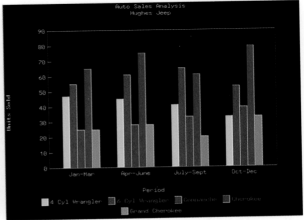

to compare more than two variables or to add depth to a picture. Another strategy is to combine different types of graphs on the same screen.

Using a presentation software package to create a slide or overhead presentation can dramatically reduce the time it takes to prepare a well-thought-out presentation. Some presentation software now allows each graphic to be handled as if it were part of a series of slides or makes it easy to create reference notes about each slide as it is prepared. This software can be divided into three types: charting, diagramming, and drawing. A **charting package** shows the relationship between sets of numerical information. Many times these packages generate enhanced graphics from the information on a spreadsheet. Figure 5-12 shows a pie chart created by Charisma, a presentation charting package.

A **diagramming package** works with shapes to graphically display a set of facts, such as organizational charts, schedules, or office layouts. Usually a series of shapes is assembled on the screen and then the size, location, and orientation of these shapes are manipulated. The third type of presentation package is the **drawing package,** which allows the user to add lines to the shapes, usually with a mouse as an input device. It is also possible to add motion to the output from a presentation package to achieve some degree of animation if the output is being shown on monitor. Popular presentation software packages include Harvard Graphics, Micrografx's Charisma, Freelance, and Powerpoint.

While a black-and-white dot matrix or laser printer is usually sufficient for hard copy of analysis graphics, a jet printer, a laser printer, or 35mm slides are needed to obtain a hard copy for presentation graphics. A color ink-jet printer uses different colored inks that are "shot" on the page to form the multicolored graph. Color laser printers are replacing black toner with multicolors.

The most common method of producing 35mm slides of a screen image is to "capture" the image on disk using special software and then have the image converted to film or slides by a company specializing in that technology. These service bureaus can also produce hard copy of the screen. Many of the screen shots in this textbook were produced using this technology.

Computer-Aided Design

CAD (for computer-aided design) has been in use on mainframes and minicomputers since the 1960s for design of airplanes, automobiles, semiconductor chips,

FIGURE 5-12
Presentation Graphics

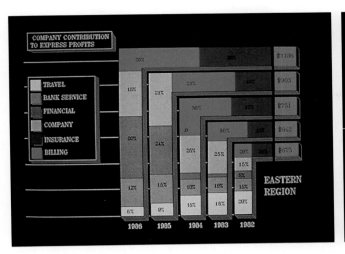

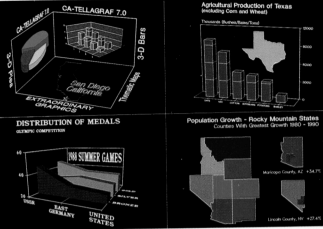

Both PCs (left) and mainframes (right) can be used to generate interesting presentation graphics.

buildings, and the like. With CAD, an engineer or designer can look at a particular design in detail or from a different angle. Frequently, a light pen is used to point to the specific part of the design that is to be enlarged or rotated. Special large screens are often used with CAD to allow the designer to see every detail of the object he or she is working with. Up until 1984, most CAD packages were used in a mainframe environment and cost in the $100,000 range. Now, as the computing power and storage capacity of PCs have increased, so too have the number and variety of PC CAD programs, with some now costing as little as $500. These lower-priced systems are moving CAD into many new areas. For example, some dentists are now using CAD to help fabricate porcelain fillings. In 1991, $333 million was spent on CAD hardware and software.

With a CAD package, a series of commands enables a designer or an architect to create and manipulate designs based on a series of graphics objects called **primitives** (points, lines, circles, and so on). Once a primitive is selected to be used, the user places it on the screen by using a mouse or other pointing device or by specifying the X and Y coordinates of the location. While the design may not be drawn a great deal faster with CAD than with paper and pencil, it can be revised much faster with the CAD package. Removing a line, room, or gear from a paper drawing can require redoing the entire picture, but CAD can do it with only a few keystrokes. Objects also can be easily moved, copied, or magnified with CAD, and the dimensions of a drawing can be computed by the computer rather than with a ruler.

The user may also create new designs by drawing with a stylus or **puck** onto a digitizer tablet or may use previously entered designs from a library in secondary storage. A joystick or mouse can also be used to create designs on the screen or to move the cursor to make menu selections. Figure 5-13 shows the use of CAD in an engineering design.

Both black-and-white and color plotters are used to provide a printed version of CAD graphics.

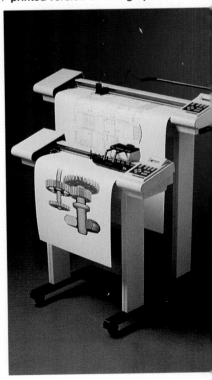

Paint Packages

If you are interested in the beauty that can be created with graphics, then you need a paint package. This type of software allows the user to manipulate pixels to produce freehand or combination freehand and library drawings of various

FIGURE 5-13
Use of CAD

shapes, colors, and textures. "Library" shapes are various geometric shapes (circles, squares, etc.) that are available in internal memory. With a paint package, the user has control over the screen through the cursor, and, depending upon the type of graphics available with the hardware, pictures may be "drawn" or "painted" using a mouse or other input device. There are also palettes of colors to choose from or groups of textures to use in "filling" areas on the graph. Shapes can be enlarged, reduced, or distorted as needed to meet the user's needs. The resulting picture can be saved as one of the standard graphic file types such as Paintbrush (.PCX) or Tagged Image Format File (.TIFF). These files can then be imported into documents as needed. With modern personal computers using bit-mapped graphics and a color monitor, the results can be amazing.

The paint package that really started the expansion in this field was MacPaint, for the Apple Macintosh, which was introduced in 1984. Even though it was originally available only in black and white, the results that were obtained with MacPaint were amazing. Other manufacturers soon jumped into this market for both the Macintosh and IBM compatible computers. It is now possible to obtain a paint package in color for almost any computer that can support bit-mapped graphics. Figure 5-14 shows the results of using various paint packages.

DESKTOP PUBLISHING

Possibly the most exciting trend in computers today is what is known as desktop publishing. **Desktop publishing** is the use of personal computer hardware and software to create and publish newsletters, advertisements, magazines, books, and so on, at a fraction of the cost required for commercial typesetting. For example, the computer lab manual that accompanies this textbook was desktop published using a popular package—Ventura Publishing from Xerox.

ENGINEERING WITH CAD

CAD is an important tool of many large industries, but it can also make a small company more profitable. For example, Grecon Manufacturing Co., a small engineering and consulting company, depends heavily on a PC-based CAD system to design automated production operations. In fact, Grecon's use of CAD led to a dramatic change in the way the company does business. Originally, Grecon was a metalworking shop, and the owner, Gregory Roberts, used a CAD system for many purposes: to design parts for production, analyze customer orders and blueprints before turning them over to machinists, and measure the least-cost size of sheet metal blanks required to produce a finished part. Mr. Roberts discovered, however, that his design skills with the CAD system were in sufficient demand for him to specialize in the engineering and design side of the business.

Today, Mr. Roberts designs production devices that automate secondary manufacturing operations. For example, if two metal plates are to be joined by a spring as part of a production process, Mr. Roberts uses CAD to design a production device that will automatically insert the spring. He does this by using CAD to draw the device to scale and then using the computer to check any problems with the design. If necessary, he subcontracts the actual production of the device to a third party. Designing a part correctly the first time, before it goes into production, is crucial to profitably creating a part. As Mr. Roberts puts it, "A mistake in designing the part costs you three times the amount of money—not just double—because you have to spend the time to undo the mistake and then to make the part over again." For Grecon, VersaCAD is a great help in avoiding these costly mistakes.

Source: John Pallatto, "CAD System Makes a Profit," *PC Week*, February 24, 1987, pp. 51 and 57, and author's interview with Mr. Roberts, December 10, 1991.

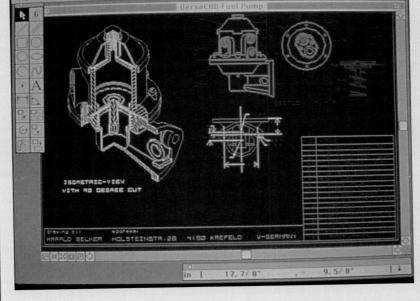

VersaCAD is one of several popular CAD packages that can be used for sophisticated design work on a personal computer.

Just in its infancy, desktop publishing can trace its beginnings to the Apple Macintosh personal computer, which allows text and graphics to be combined on the screen. The Macintosh also can handle proportional spacing like that used in printing this textbook, different type fonts, and various type sizes. In **proportional spacing,** different letters are given different amounts of space. By combining graphics with proportionally spaced text, and then printing the result on the Apple LaserWriter printer, people found they could create professional-looking documents ranging from in-house newsletters to magazines and text-books. The desktop publishing market has grown significantly over the last five

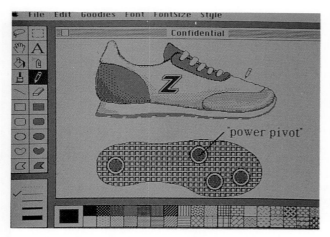

FIGURE 5-14
Some Paint Package Creations.
(Clockwise from top left)
MacPaint; PC Paintbrush IV Plus;
DeluxePaint, enhanced version
on a 20-inch color monitor; GEM
Artline.

years. In 1991 alone, almost $200 million of hardware and software was sold for use in desktop publishing.

The key elements of a desktop publishing system are a personal computer, a word processing package, a graphics package, a desktop publishing package, and a laser printer. It is important to remember that the desktop publishing package must be capable of importing the results of the word processing and graphics packages. An important part of a desktop publishing package is the **page description language (PDL),** with the most widely used page description language being Postscript from Adobe. The PDL is crucial to the success of desktop publishing since it handles the important operation of combining text and graphics into a final page format that fits the needs of the user. Another useful element is **clip art**—previously created art images—that can be imported into a document.

Current Methods

To understand desktop publishing fully, we first need to look at the steps involved in commercially publishing a newsletter or book:

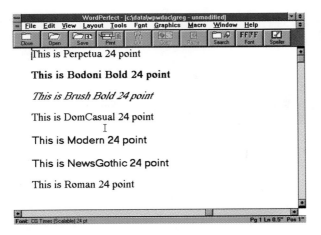

1. The document is created on a typewriter or with a word processing package.
2. A commercial typesetter sets the document in long columns of text called *galleys*.
3. The galleys are proofread and corrected.
4. A production artist "pastes up" the corrected galleys into pages, leaving spaces for photographs and drawings.
5. The completed pages are sent to an offset print shop for final reproduction.

Currently, most publishing companies use paste-up artists, who combine text and graphics manually.

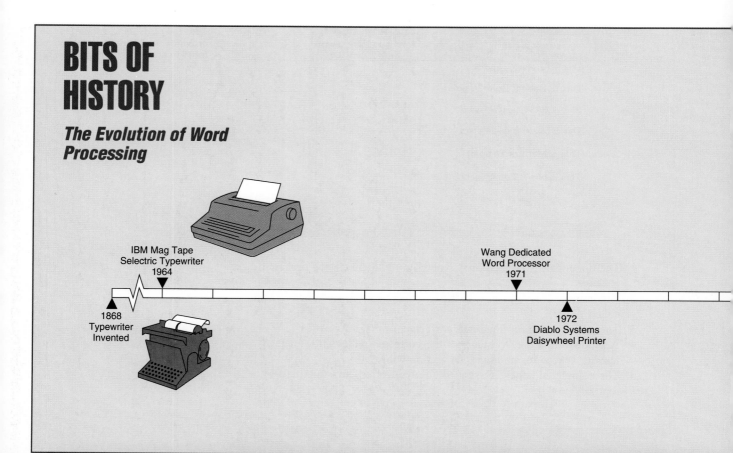

BITS OF HISTORY

The Evolution of Word Processing

IBM Mag Tape
Selectric Typewriter
1964

Wang Dedicated
Word Processor
1971

1868
Typewriter
Invented

1972
Diablo Systems
Daisywheel Printer

In the final production process, the print shop combines the pages of text and the various graphics elements into a single film overlay. This film is then used to produce a plate for the printing press that will produce the final pages. The cost of the typesetting and paste-up operations alone run anywhere from $50 to $250 per page.

Publishing with a PC

The steps that replace the commercial methods just discussed with a personal computer are these: The user

1. creates a document with a word processor;
2. creates a **stylesheet** with the desktop publishing package. The stylesheet assigns fonts and type sizes to the various elements of the document, defines the margins, and in general specifies the format of the document;
3. flows the text from the word processor into columns on the page;
4. inserts graphic elements;
5. prints the completed pages using a laser printer.

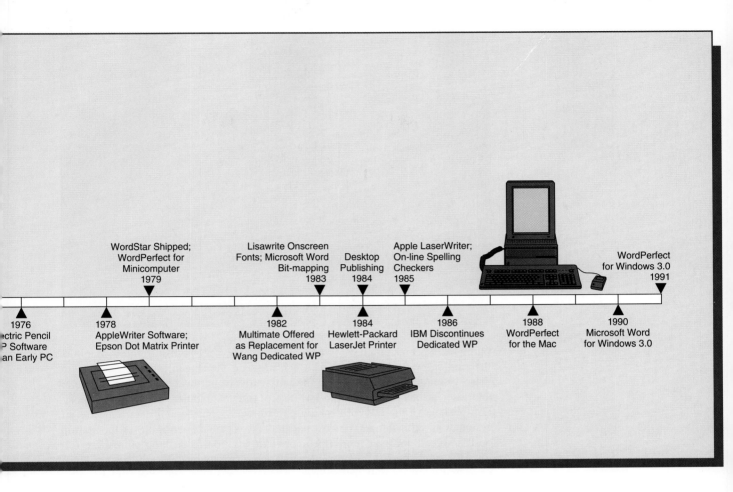

Timeline labels (above line):

WordStar Shipped;
WordPerfect for
Minicomputer
1979

Lisawrite Onscreen
Fonts; Microsoft Word
Bit-mapping
1983

Desktop
Publishing
1984

Apple LaserWriter;
On-line Spelling
Checkers
1985

WordPerfect
for Windows 3.0
1991

Timeline labels (below line):

1976
ectric Pencil
P Software
an Early PC

1978
AppleWriter Software;
Epson Dot Matrix Printer

1982
Multimate Offered
as Replacement for
Wang Dedicated WP

1984
Hewlett-Packard
LaserJet Printer

1986
IBM Discontinues
Dedicated WP

1988
WordPerfect
for the Mac

1990
Microsoft Word
for Windows 3.0

During step 3, holes or **frames** for graphics can be left in the text, and drawings, photographs, or graphic images created with graphics packages can be transferred to the page in the desired shape and orientation. It is for this step that a system that supports WYSIWYG is crucial; otherwise the user cannot see the appearance of the completed page in order to adjust the positioning of various elements and to decide on the size and style of fonts, the italics, boldfacing, headlines, and so on. Figure 5-15 shows a page being electronically "pasted up" on a computer screen.

In step 5, a laser printer is used because it can output text and graphics at 300 dots per inch. While this is less than the 1,200-dots-per-inch quality possible with commercial typesetting equipment, it is acceptable for many purposes. The printed pages can be used as camera-ready copy for creating a plate that will be used in the printing process, or, if only a small number of copies is needed, they can be printed on the laser printer.

In addition to needing a laser printer for output, users need a high-resolution graphics display to distinguish between various fonts and an **image scanner** for converting graphics, drawings, or photographs to a graphic form that can be included with the text. In addition to the popular combination of Apple Macintosh PC and LaserWriter printer, 80386 or i486 IBM compatible computers can be combined with any number of laser printers for desktop publishing

FIGURE 5-15
Example of Desktop Publishing

purposes. Special graphics systems that include very-high-resolution monitors that can show an entire $8\frac{1}{2} \times 11$–inch page on the screen are often used with these systems. Even considering the initial cost of hardware (personal computer and laser printer) and software (word processing, graphics, and page-composition packages), the cost of desktop publishing is considerably less than that of commercial publishing. The cost per page goes down even more as the startup cost is spread out over more documents. In addition, if desktop publishing follows the same road as previous personal computer applications, the cost of hardware and software will come down as more companies enter the market.

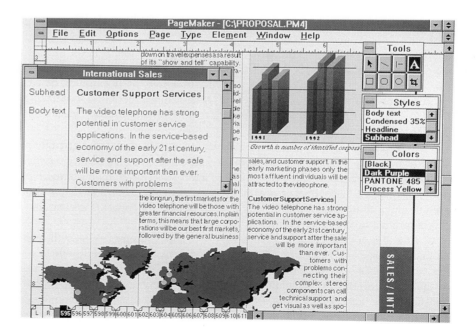

PageMaker software is one of the most popular desktop-publishing packages.

With an appropriate combination of computer hardware and software, image scanner, and laser printer, it is possible to create near-professional-quality documents.

1. Word processing, graphics, and desktop publishing packages help the user communicate ideas to other people.
2. Word processing is divided into formatting the document, entering and editing text, and saving and printing the document.
3. Formatting consists of setting up the margins, the tab stops, the vertical spacing, the right justification, and the number of characters per inch. WYSIWYG means that the text appears on the screen as it will when printed.
4. During text entry, word wrap is a useful feature that speeds the process.
5. During editing, the insert (push-over) mode and replace (type-over) mode can be used to insert or replace text. Deletion and backspacing can be used to delete existing text.
6. Other text entry and editing capabilities include using block-action commands to delete, copy, or move blocks of text; search or search and replace for finding and editing strings of text; center-

ing text; paragraph indention; pagination; and use of macros.

7. Printing consists of converting the electronic form of the document to hard copy, and it requires printer driver software.

8. Other labor-saving devices on a word processor include a speller, a thesaurus, mail-merge, outlining, and macros.

9. Graphics packages use the picture elements, or pixels, to display pictures on the screen. Graphics can be character or bit-mapped, depending on whether or not each pixel is individually controlled.

10. Graphics are hardware dependent: The quality of the graphics displayed depends on the CPU chip used and the add-on hardware included in the system.

11. There are four types of graphics packages: analysis graphics, pre-sentation graphics, computer-aided design (CAD), and paint.

12. Analysis graphics display the results of data analysis using bar graphs, pie graphs, line graphs, or scatter diagrams.

13. Presentation graphics present material graphically and dramatically to someone besides the user. For personal computers, such graphics include chart, diagramming, and drawing packages.

14. CAD is used to facilitate and improve the design process, while paint packages enable the user to design art on a computer.

15. In desktop publishing, the user creates publishable documents by combining word processing and graphics packages on a personal computer with page composition software and a laser printer.

KEY TERMS

analysis graphics
automatic pagination
Backspace key
bar graph
bit-mapped graphics
block-action command
boiler plate material
boldface
business graphics
centering
character graphics
charting package
clip art
Color/Graphics Adapter (CGA)
computer-aided design (CAD)
cursor
cursor control keys
cut-and-paste
desktop publishing
diagramming package
document translation
drawing package

End key
Enhanced Graphics Adapter (EGA)
footers
footnotes
formatting
frames
graphics adapter board
graphics packages
headers
Hercules Graphics Card
Home key
image scanner
insert mode
line graph
macro
mail-merge
multiscanning monitor
outline processor
page description language (PDL)
paint packages
paragraph indentation
Pg Dn key

Pg Up key
pie graph
pixel
presentation graphics
primitives
printer codes
printer driver
print spooler
proportional spacing
puck
pushover mode
reformatted
replace mode
resolution
right justification
scatter diagrams
scrolling

search and replace
speller
stacked-bar graphs
status line
stylesheet
Super VGA system
symbol processors
text editing
thesaurus
typeover mode
Video Graphics Array (VGA)
video page
wildcard search
word processing packages
word wrap
WYSIWYG

REVIEW QUESTIONS

1. How are word processing and graphics packages similar? Dissimilar?

2. What four operations are performed on a word processor? How does word wrap speed text entry?

3. What does WYSIWYG have to do with formatting?

4. What is the difference between the insert mode and the replace mode in editing? Why are they termed *pushover* and *typeover?*

5. What does "cut-and-paste" mean in a word processing package? What does "block-delete" mean?

6. Why are imbedded print commands and printer drivers needed to print a word processing document?

7. Discuss the purposes of spellers, mail-merge, outlining, and macros in a word processor.

8. What is the difference between bit-mapped and character graphics? Which is used the most now?

9. How are graphics depicted on the screen? What is a pixel?

10. What is the hardware connection for graphics packages? What type of graphics will an IBM compatible PC display without additional hardware?

11. List the various types of graphics adapters used on IBM compatible PCs. Which have the lowest resolutions? The highest resolutions?

12. Name the four types of graphics packages. Discuss a commonly used application for one of these.

13. What graphs are used most often for analysis and presentations?

14. Why do we say that desktop publishing combines word processing and graphics into a single application?

15. What hardware and software items are needed for desktop publishing?

6

Financial Analysis and Accounting Packages

Since financial matters are very important to both individuals and companies, there exist numerous software packages to manage and analyze financial information. These packages can be broadly divided into two types: financial analysis and accounting. Financial analysis packages—or, as they are also called, spreadsheets—allow a user to analyze data in a tabular format and determine what will happen if either the data or the assumptions change. Integrated packages, which combine operations such as data base management and graphics with spreadsheets, are powerful extensions of the spreadsheet. Accounting packages are divided into those for businesses and those for individuals. Business accounting packages are designed to track the financial status of a firm, while personal accounting packages are meant to help manage an individual's finances. Business accounting packages have separate package elements for such operations as general ledger, accounts receivable, accounts payable, payroll, order processing, and inventory control. Personal accounting packages include functions for managing investments, preparing income taxes, and managing personal finances.

STUDY OBJECTIVES

After reading this chapter, you should be able to

- recognize financial software packages for computers;
- explain how a spreadsheet works and describe the types of entries used in a spreadsheet;
- discuss the various functions available on many spreadsheets;
- understand how a spreadsheet can be used for planning budgets and making forecasts;
- discuss the concept of an integrated package as it relates to spreadsheets;
- list and discuss the various types of packages that are available to the individual for managing personal finances;
- explain personal budgeting packages and how they may be used to track an individual's finances;
- understand the purpose of business accounting software and the modules that go into a business accounting package.

SURVIVING IN KUWAIT ON 1-2-3

It was impossible. We had no clue how much food we had or how long it would last.

Dr. Robert Morris, dental consultant to the Kuwaiti government

Quoted in Lynda Radosevich "A Template for Survival," *Lotus,* July 1991, pp. 28–29.

When Dr. Robert Morris first heard in August 1990 that Iraq had invaded Kuwait, where he was working as a health care consultant, he assumed that he and other Westerners would be allowed to leave routinely. However, his assumption proved wrong, and he and 20 other non-Kuwaitis found themselves in hiding. His PC and a copy of Lotus 1-2-3 became crucial to the group's survival.

When it became clear to Dr. Morris and the rest of the group that the invading Iraqis were not going to let them leave, they decided to hide in an abandoned apartment house in downtown Kuwait City, from where

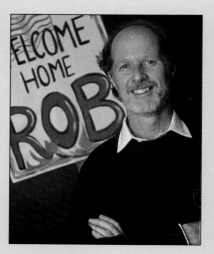

they formulated security policies to avoid Iraqi army patrols and sought to secure a food source. They contacted Kuwaiti restaurants to obtain bulk food shipments. However, when they had trouble keeping track of the amounts of food and its location, Dr. Morris created a spreadsheet to handle the task.

The spreadsheet tracked the amount and types of food received, the storage location of each type of food, and the average daily consumption required to sustain the group. It also computed the number of days they could exist if no more food was acquired. Much of this information was coded, in case it fell into Iraqi hands. It took Dr. Morris three days to create the spreadsheet but only five minutes to update it each night after the midnight delivery had been distributed.

The food was distributed in amounts and types that provided each person with a nutritionally balanced diet of 1,800 calories per day. The spreadsheet became the focal point of the group as each member came to offer comments or suggestions on a daily basis.

As it turned out, all the food was not needed. Most members of the group were allowed to leave the country in December when Iraq released Western hostages.

Source: Lynda Radosevich, "A Template for Survival," *Lotus,* July 1991, pp. 28–29.

INTRODUCTION TO FINANCIAL PACKAGES

Shortly after computers were first available on a commercial basis, large corporations and institutions discovered that a computer could be very useful for handling finances, since storing numerical data and then quickly adding and subtracting them are natural applications of computers. Initially, only large companies could afford computers—mainframes. As personal computers have become widely available, however, financial management by computer has become possible for small companies and individuals as well.

Financial management software for mainframes and minicomputers has been developed for use by institutions and companies that deal with large amounts of data. On the other hand, there exist financial management software packages for all varieties of computers that both small companies and individuals can use to manage their finances. Software for the various sizes of computers is necessary because of the differences in the needs of users. For example, a mainframe could handle the payroll for a large university, a government agency, or an automotive assembly plant. Toward the other end of the computer use spectrum would be the small, family-run interior decorating store with two part-time employees. In this case, a personal computer with a hard disk could handle the inventory control and accounting needs very easily. Finally, the individual who wishes to use a computer to keep track of finances and tax records would be able to use almost any personal computer on the market today with a disk drive.

Since a financial management software package intended for use on a mainframe is primarily developed for a specific type of mainframe, we will concentrate on the software that is available for the wide range of types and brands of personal computers. There are three broad categories of financial management software, and among the three of them, all the functions listed earlier can be accomplished. The three broad categories of software we will discuss are financial analysis packages (often referred to as spreadsheets), personal financial management packages, and business accounting packages.

A **spreadsheet** can be used for almost any financial management operation, but its greatest applications are in the areas of analysis, budgeting, and forecasting. With a spreadsheet package, it is possible to set up an entire budget or sales forecast and then determine the results of making changes to one or more of the anticipated values. In the box at the beginning of this chapter, a spreadsheet was used to analyze a food "budget" to ensure that the western hostages would have sufficient supplies. A forecast of the future needs of the hostages was a part of the analysis.

Personal financial management packages are aimed at helping the individual keep track of finances. The three major operations carried out by this type

> ## 1-2-3 has made the investment business more complex. We analyze a lot more structures.
>
> *Henry Ford, vice president,*
> *Merchant Banking Group,*
> *Bankers Trust Co.*
>
> Quoted in "Where 1-2-3 Makes Deals in a Hurry," *Lotus,* June 1989, pp. 52–55.

```
D30: {H13 Bold} U [W11] 32000                                    MENU
Worksheet  Range  Copy  Move  File  Print  Graph  Data  System  Enhance  Quit
Retrieve  Save  Combine  Xtract  Erase  List  Import  Directory  Admin
```

A	B	C	D	E	F	G

Personal Budget
1992

INCOME	ANNUAL	MONTHLY	%
Salary #1	$35,000	$2,917	39%
Bonus #1	0	0	0%
Salary #2	32,000	2,667	36%
Bonus #2	4,000	333	5%
Estimated Stock Options	12,000	1,000	14%
Dividends	1,400	117	2%
Interest	625	52	1%
Tax Refund	1,200	100	1%
Other: Summer Rental	2,400	200	3%
Other:			
TOTAL INCOME	$88,625	$7,386	100%
EXPENSES	ANNUAL	MONTHLY	%
Charitable Donations	$700	$58	1%

26-Mar-92 04:13 PM

Families can use financial software on a personal computer to monitor their investment portfolio.

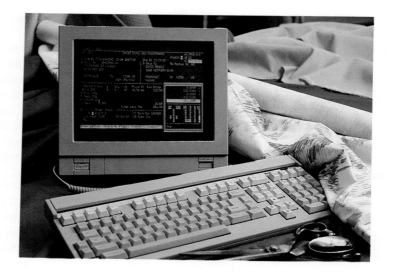

Small businesses have come to depend on personal computers to handle much of their accounting and financial work.

of software are personal accounting (classifying and summarizing all financial transactions during a month), investment analysis, and tax planning. Each of these will be discussed later in this chapter.

A **business accounting package** usually has several modules or software elements, each of which handles a single task involved with tracking the financial health of the firm. Modules for such operations as payroll, accounts receivable, accounts payable, and inventory control are often included. Business accounting packages will be discussed in more detail in a later section of this chapter.

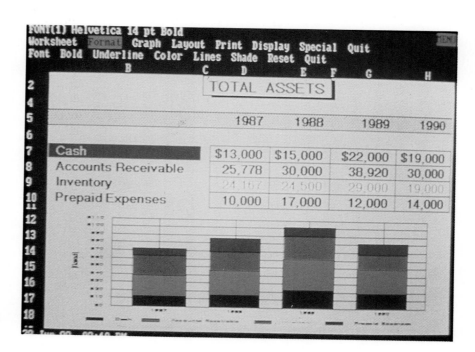

Spreadsheets like Lotus 1-2-3 are used for financial analysis by individuals and by companies of all sizes.

The explosion in the use of personal computer software packages can be traced directly to the introduction in 1979 of VisiCalc, the first spreadsheet for the Apple II computer, developed by a group of Harvard and MIT students. Since that time, numerous packages containing many variations and improvements on VisiCalc have been released. These packages include Lotus 1-2-3, Microsoft Excel, Quattro Pro, PlanPerfect, and SuperCalc[5] for IBM compatible PCs and Microsoft Excel and 1-2-3 for the Apple Macintosh. Spreadsheets are one of the most popular types of computer package in use, with an estimated 3 million packages sold in 1991 alone. Lotus 1-2-3, alone, is the all-time best-selling computer applications package. PC spreadsheet packages have been rewritten to run on minicomputers and mainframes to give the users of these larger machines the machines the capabilities of these packages. Similarly, MS-DOS–based spreadsheet packages are being rewritten to run under the Windows operating environment, as well as on the Macintosh. In addition, a spreadsheet called Improv has been written specifically for the NeXT computer. It takes full advantage of NeXT's graphical nature.

Spreadsheets have also been used for many purposes other than financial analysis. Professors use them to keep electronic gradebooks, and scientists use them to model physical systems, analyze data, and plan processes. Some of the most popular spreadsheet packages combine the spreadsheet with data base and graphical operations that allow users to work with all three at one time. Finally, integrated packages that add word processing and telecommunications to the spreadsheet–data base–graphics combination are becoming increasingly popular.

However, regardless of the name of the package and the operations that have been added to it, the general concept of using a table of numbers to represent budgets, sales forecasts, and so on remains the same. The name *spreadsheet* originated with the accountant's ledger pad, with printed row and column lines. The budget or sales forecast figures were entered in pencil on this "spreadsheet"; whenever a value was changed, all values had to be recalculated by hand. Before discussing the computerized spreadsheet packages, let us consider a manual spreadsheet in more detail, in the following budgeting example.

Jill Bradley is a recent college graduate who has taken a position with a local computer store as a salesperson/consultant. In this position, Jill will receive a salary of $700 per month plus a commission of 6 percent of her gross sales. Out of this combination of salary and commission, payroll taxes and health insurance of $250 per month are deducted to arrive at her "take-home income." The manager has told Jill that most employees have sales of about $10,000 their first month and that the sales volume usually increases by 5 percent per month for the next two months. After the first three months, the rate of increase in sales differs from employee to employee.

Jill's estimates for the first month's income and expense values are shown in Table 6-1. Jill has to pay $300 a month to rent an apartment that she shares with a co-worker. Also, she has bought a new car that carries a monthly payment of $150. While these expenses are **fixed,** in that they do not change from month to month, Jill also has **variable expenses** for food, utilities (electricity and telephone), fuel for her car, and miscellaneous expenses.

Jill also wants to save as much as possible over the next three months to purchase a high-quality compact disk player and speakers. The cost of the CD

TABLE 6-1
Estimated Income and Expense Values

Item	Estimated Value
Commission	$ 600 (0.06 × $10,000)
Salary	$ 700
Net Income	$1,050 ($600 + $700 − $250)
Rent	$ 300
Car Payment	$ 150
Food	$ 250
Utilities	$ 150
Gas	$ 50
Other	$ 100

system is $500, so this is the minimum Jill wants to save over the three months. Summing rent, utilities, food, car payment, gas, and "other" expenses and subtracting this amount from the take-home income gives the amount Jill will be able to save each month. While this sounds complicated in text form, it is very easy to see in tabular form, as shown in Table 6-2. The remainder of our discussion of the functions of a spreadsheet will depend on this case, so be sure you understand it.

In Table 6-2, we have assigned letters to the various quantities to show the relationships among the various values, and we have marked estimated values (like utilities) with an asterisk (*) since these values are subject to change. We have also shown the formulas used to compute dependent values. For example, we used the equation $C = 0.06 \times MS$ to show the commission (C) to be equal to 0.06 times monthly sales (MS). Finally, we have shown the monthly sales for July to be $10,000, with increases of 5 percent each month in monthly sales for August and September. Note also that the total of Jill's savings for the three months starting with July is only $242. Based on this budget, it will take Jill more than three months to save enough money to buy the CD system. How-

TABLE 6-2
Jill Bradley's Budget in Tabular Form

Item	Month			Totals
	July	August	September	
Monthly Sales (MS)*	$10,000	$10,500	$11,025	$31,525
Commission (C = 0.06 × MS)	600	630	662	1,892
Base Salary (BS)	700	700	700	2,100
Net Income (NI = C + BS − 250)	1,050	1,080	1,112	3,242
Rent (R)	300	300	300	900
Car Payment (CP)	150	150	150	450
Food (F)*	250	250	250	750
Utilities (U)*	150	150	150	450
Gas (G)*	50	50	50	150
Other (O)*	100	100	100	300
Expenses (E = R + CP + F + U + G + O)	1,000	1,000	1,000	1,000
Savings (S = NI − E)	50	80	112	242

ever, if her sales are higher than average, then her take-home pay and amount saved will increase.

Let us now analyze the effect of changes in assumptions in the spreadsheet. In other words, we can ask some "What if?" questions to determine the effect of changes in Jill's anticipated values. Note that changing Jill's monthly sales has the greatest effect on the spreadsheet since this value controls the amount of commission, the net income, and the level of savings each month. For example, to see how changing Jill's monthly sales will affect the spreadsheet, assume that instead of selling the "average" sales volume of $10,000 the first month, Jill sells $11,000 worth of goods. The effect of this change is shown in Table 6-3.

Note in Table 6-3 that the increase in monthly sales from $10,000 to $11,000 for the first month also increased the forecast sales for August and September. This occurred because each of them is based on the first month's sales. These increases, in turn, increased each month's Net Income and Savings values in such a way that a 10 percent increase in monthly sales actually resulted in a 78 percent increase in the total savings after three months!

According to the revisions in Table 6-3, Jill is much closer to saving enough to buy the CD system after three months. But what if food expenses are greater than expected and a heat wave during this period drives up the cost of utilities? On the other hand, what if Jill has a greater than 5 percent increase in sales volume in August and September? These and many other such "What if?" questions might be checked with this spreadsheet. However, doing it with pencil and paper would very quickly become tedious, especially if the number of months was extended to include an entire year or if the number of expense categories was increased.

Before the VisiCalc spreadsheet package was introduced, a manager in a large company would assign a staff member the task of manipulating a spreadsheet with paper and pencil. The time required to work with the spreadsheet manually was too great for a busy manager. For small firms, it was not possible to perform even this manual manipulation because of the time and effort it involves. With the advent of the electronic version of the spreadsheet, the

> **PC technology permits me to efficiently carry out tasks that I once would have delegated and then repeatedly reviewed in pre-PC days.**
>
> *Don M. Lyle, president,*
> *Emerald Systems*
>
> Quoted in "View from the Top,"
> *Personal Computing,* October 1989,
> p. 252.

TABLE 6-3
Revised Jill Bradley Budget

Item	July	August	September	Totals
		Month		
Monthly Sales (MS)*	$11,000	$11,550	$12,128	$34,678
Commission (C = 0.06 × MS)	660	693	728	2,081
Base Salary (BS)	700	700	700	2,100
Net Income (NI = C + BS − 250)	1,110	1,143	1,178	3,431
Rent (R)	300	300	300	900
Car Payment (CP)	150	150	150	450
Food (F)	250	250	250	750
Utilities (U)*	150	150	150	450
Gas (G)*	50	50	50	150
Other (O)*	100	100	100	300
Expenses (E = R + CP + F + U + G + O)	1,000	1,000	1,000	1,000
Savings (S = NI − E)	110	143	178	431

manager of any size of firm can now personally do this manipulation quickly and easily. And since having the manager involved in this process usually leads to better planning and forecasting, better management should result.

Setting Up an Electronic Spreadsheet

Conceptually, an **electronic spreadsheet** on a computer works exactly like the manual spreadsheet we showed earlier. However, once the values and the formulas that carry out the relationships among the values are entered, the computer takes care of recalculating all affected values when one value changes.

A spreadsheet is made up of horizontal **rows** identified by numbers, and vertical **columns** identified by letters. The intersection of a row and a column is called a **cell** and is identified by the row number and column letter. Movement from cell to cell in a spreadsheet is handled via the **cell pointer,** a rectangle highlighted in **reverse video.** Figure 6-1 shows a blank Lotus 1-2-3 spreadsheet (also referred to as a **worksheet**), with the cell pointer located in cell A1 (row 1 and column A). Rows and columns are also pointed out in this figure. The cell pointer can be moved with the cursor control keys (or, for some packages, a mouse).

One of three entities can go into a cell: a label made of letters and digits, a number called a value, or a formula that shows the relationship between cells containing values. A **label** is any combination of letters and numbers that describes the contents of a row or column. It is not meant to be used in any sort of calculation. The months at the top of each column and the items on the left of each row in the Jill Bradley spreadsheet are examples of labels. **Values** are numbers, either positive or negative, with or without a decimal. They may be placed in any cell and then used to make other calculations. The original values

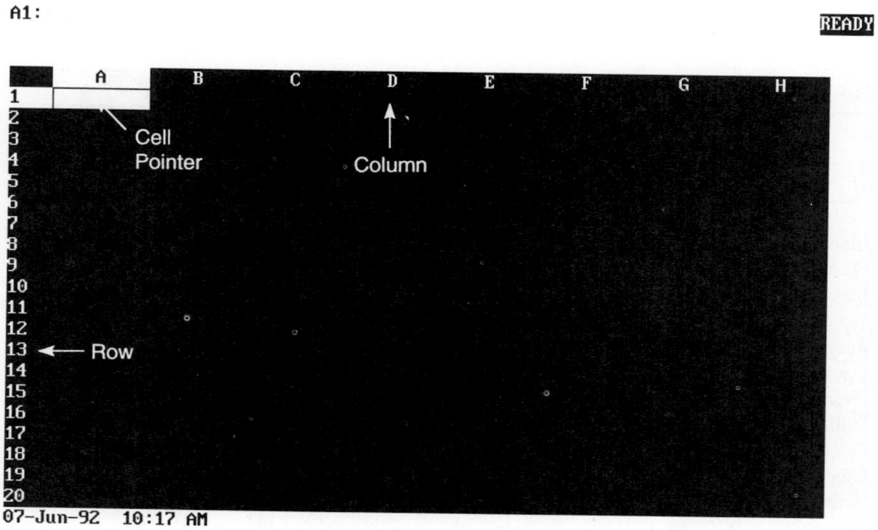

FIGURE 6-1
Blank Lotus 1-2-3 Spreadsheet

for sales, base salary, rent, car payment, and so on in the Jill Bradley spreadsheet are examples of values. **Formulas** are combinations of cell identifiers, constants, and arithmetic symbols. Calculation of the commission amount is handled through a formula.

Using this notation, we can set up Jill Bradley's budget in electronic spreadsheet form by entering labels and values into the blank spreadsheet in Figure 6-1. Entering the labels and values is simply a matter of moving the cell pointer into the cell where the entry is to be made and typing the label or value. The entry does not actually appear in the cell while it is being entered. Instead, it appears on an **edit line** above or below the spreadsheet during the entry process and then in the cell after the Enter key is pressed. Figure 6-2 shows the Jill Bradley spreadsheet after labels and values were entered. A label and a value are pointed out in this figure.

Note in Figure 6-2 that row 1 is used for the column headings and column A is used for the item names. Note also that column A is wider than the other columns in Figure 6-2 to allow for the length of the labels in this column. The column width can be changed for either the entire spreadsheet or individual columns. Changing the column widths for the entire spreadsheet is an example of a **global change;** changing the column width for an individual column is an example of a **local change.**

While labels and values are important elements in a spreadsheet, the formulas are the key elements that make it a powerful analytic tool: They represent the assumptions underlying the spreadsheet and they carry out the calculations. When a formula is entered in a cell, the value calculated by the formula is displayed. Table 6-4 shows the meaning of various symbols in spreadsheet formulas. These operations are arranged in the order in which the computer will carry them out, that is, grouping, raising to a power, multiplication and division, and addition and subtraction.

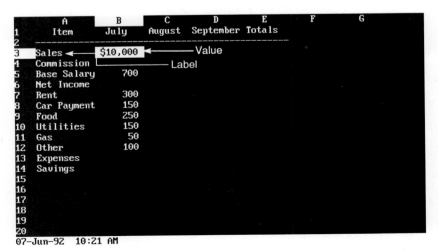

FIGURE 6-2
Electronic Spreadsheet with
Labels and Values

TABLE 6-4
Symbols Used in Spreadsheet Formulas

Symbol Name	Symbol	Operation
Parentheses	( )	Grouping
Caret (Shift-6)	^	Raising a number to a power
Asterisk	*	Multiplication
Slash	/	Division
Plus sign	+	Addition
Minus sign	−	Subtraction

It is important to understand that **cell identifiers** such as A10, B2, and so on are used in formulas wherever possible so that any change in the values in those cells will automatically be reflected in the formula. For example, in the Jill Bradley spreadsheet, cell B4 contains the July commission value, which is equal to 6 percent of the July sales in cell B3, so the formula 0.06*B3 would be entered in the B4 cell. If the sales value entered in B3 is $10,000, the result of this formula would be $600. If the sales value changes, the commission value will also automatically change. Figure 6-3 shows the entry of this formula in the Jill Bradley spreadsheet. Note that the formula is shown in the Edit line but the result appears in cell B4.

The next step is to enter the remaining formulas into the spreadsheet. As in the entry of labels and values, the cell pointer is moved to the proper cell and the formula is entered. For example, to enter the formula for July Net Income in cell B6, we move the cell pointer to B6 and enter the formula +B4+B5−250 there (the first + is used to show that this is a formula, not a label). Whatever values are in the cells in the formula will be used to calculate the value in the

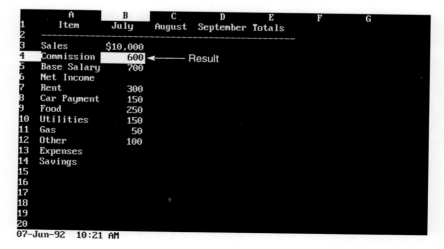

FIGURE 6-3
Entry of July Sales Commission Formula

B6 cell. The other formulas that must be entered in the July column are for Expenses, in cell B13, and for Savings, in cell B14. The formula in B13 is +B7+B8+B9+B10+B11+B12 and the formula in B14 is +B6−B13.

The formulas for the corresponding August and September cells will substitute C and D, respectively, for B in each of the formulas for the July cells. In addition, the August and September Sales values will be calculated with formulas that represent the 5 percent expected increase in sales volume each month. For August, the formula in cell C3 will be 1.05*B3; for September, the formula in cell D3 will be 1.05*C3. The formulas in the Total column will be the sum of each row. For example, the total of the sales volumes will be in cell E3 and will be equal to +B3+C3+D3. The formulas for other rows in this column will be the same except for a change in the row number. For example, in cell E4, the formula will be +B4+C4+D4.

After we enter each formula in the appropriate cell, we obtain the spreadsheet shown in Figure 6-4. Note that this electronic spreadsheet is similar to Table 6-2.

Working with an Electronic Spreadsheet

Now let's try changing some anticipated values on this electronic spreadsheet. Assume that July sales, instead of being $10,000 as was expected, are $11,000. Changing all the entries by hand would be tedious since the August and September sales values are also affected, as well as the net income and savings values for all three months. With an electronic spreadsheet, however, it's very easy. All we need to do is move the cursor to the B3 cell and change the value in that cell. The resulting spreadsheet is shown in Figure 6-5 and is the same as that shown earlier as Table 6-3.

E3: (C0) +B3+C3+D3   READY

	A	B	C	D	E	F	G
1	Item	July	August	September	Totals		
2	------	------	------	------	------		
3	Sales	$10,000	$10,500	$11,025	$31,525		
4	Commission	600	630	662	1,892		
5	Base Salary	700	700	700	2,100		
6	Net Income	1,050	1,080	1,112	3,242		
7	Rent	300	300	300	900		
8	Car Payment	150	150	150	450		
9	Food	250	250	250	750		
10	Utilities	150	150	150	450		
11	Gas	50	50	50	150		
12	Other	100	100	100	300		
13	Expenses	1,000	1,000	1,000	3,000		
14	Savings	50	80	112	242		
15							
16							
17							
18							
19							
20							

07-Jun-92 10:24 AM

FIGURE 6-4
Jill Bradley Spreadsheet with Formulas Added

FIGURE 6-5
Jill Bradley Spreadsheet with
New Sales Value

```
B3:  (C0) 11000                                                        READY

       A       B        C          D        E        F        G
1     Item     July    August   September  Totals
2    ---------------------------------------------------
3    Sales     $11,000  $11,550  $12,128   $34,678
4    Commission   660      693      728      2,081
5    Base Salary  700      700      700      2,100
6    Net Income 1,110    1,143    1,178      3,431
7    Rent         300      300      300        900
8    Car Payment  150      150      150        450
9    Food         250      250      250        750
10   Utilities    150      150      150        450
11   Gas           50       50       50        150
12   Other        100      100      100        300
13   Expenses   1,000    1,000    1,000      3,000
14   Savings      110      143      178        431
15
16
17
18
19
20
07-Jun-92  10:26 AM
```

With an electronic spreadsheet, it is easy to test various assumptions, as we have done with Jill Bradley's budget. In the final case, the amount available in savings after three months is still not quite enough to purchase the CD system, but it is much closer than before. Using a spreadsheet in this way, Jill can test the effect of a change in any of her original anticipated expense figures. The same is true in many business situations in which managers want to test assumptions in the process of developing an annual budget or forecasting the coming year's income.

Common Spreadsheet Features

Although commercial spreadsheet packages all differ in their ease of use and scope, most spreadsheets share a group of features. To understand the power of spreadsheets, we should discuss each feature briefly. Spreadsheets usually have the following capabilities:

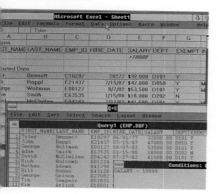

Microsoft Excel is a very popular spreadsheet for use on the Apple Macintosh.

- Copy the contents of one cell or a group of cells—called a **range**—into another location.
- Move the contents of a range of cells to another location.
- Insert or delete a row or a column.
- Format the rows and columns to take a desired form.
- Work with ranges of cells.
- Save a spreadsheet to a disk or load one from a disk.
- Print an entire spreadsheet or just a part of a spreadsheet.
- Use windows that allow the user to look at two parts of a big spreadsheet.
- Include functions that perform specialized operations.
- Perform a series of operations using macros.

TRACKING HEALTH COST WITH A SPREADSHEET

For all levels of government, tracking the skyrocketing cost of providing health and social services is an important part of controlling costs. In San Mateo County in Northern California, this task falls to the county controller's Health and Welfare Claiming Department, which is responsible for monitoring and filing claims for many county departments, including Social Services, Mental Health, Public Health, and Drug and Alcohol Abuse.

The department must process the hundreds of claim forms required by the state and federal governments. Until 1990, staff members often worked overtime to manually complete the government-supplied health and welfare claim forms. They used typewriters to transfer the data received from the hundreds of program facilities to the government forms and then spent weeks checking the forms for accuracy.

To reduce the cost of completing and checking the claims forms, the department's manager, George Lumm, moved much of the claims operation to Lotus 1-2-3 Release 3.1 in 1990. He chose this package because its graphical capabilities allowed him to duplicate on the computer the government forms and then copy the data from his spreadsheet, where calculations are performed automatically and error free. Lumm, single-handedly, was able to do the same operations his entire staff of seven had done manually, and Lumm did it in one-tenth the time.

Lumm chose Lotus 1-2-3 Release 3.1 also for its data linking capabilities, which allow him to compare data electronically from different spreadsheets. For example, by using linked spreadsheets, he can compare the amounts of money that the mental health facilities received in a given period from the state, insurance companies, Medi-Cal, and Medicare. He can also determine how much time was spent on each patient to compute the cost per unit of service.

Source: "Spreadsheets Add Up for County," *Government Technology*, February 1991, p. 47.

> ## The benefits my group derives by being able to duplicate state forms in 1-2-3 are enormous.
>
> *George Lumm, San Mateo County*
>
> Quoted in "Spreadsheets Add Up for County," *Government Technology*, February 1991, p. 47.

■ Create and display graphics based on spreadsheet data.
■ Perform data base operations on the rows of the spreadsheet.

When an entry in one cell of a spreadsheet is to be the same as that in another cell, the *copy* command may be used to make the value or formula the same in both cells. When a formula is involved, a relative copy of it can be made. A **relative copy** uses the same formula structure in the new cell, but changes the formula to match the location of the new cell. For Jill Bradley's budget spreadsheet, the values in each row were summed to generate a Total column. Each formula is the same except for the row number. The relative copy of the first row formula—that is, B3 + C3 + D3—would be inserted into each cell of the last column but the row numbers would change. *Moving* the contents of one cell to another is similar to copying, except that the original cell is empty after the move.

If Jill Bradley wanted to know how much she could save in two months rather than three, she could *delete* the September column and the spreadsheet would recalculate all values based on only the first two months. The September component of any formula would be given a value of zero in the spreadsheet calculations. Similarly, if Jill decided to save for an additional month to buy the CD player, she could *insert* a column for October after September and then use the copy command to enter the correct values and formulas.

To make the spreadsheet appear a certain way, a user can *format* the spreadsheet. Formatting can move all values as far to the left or right as possible in a cell for a pleasing appearance. It can also be used to add commas in large numbers, to place negative values in parentheses, or to treat all numeric entries as dollar amounts with two places to the right of the decimal point. Formatting also includes changing individual column widths. The Jill Bradley spreadsheet in Figure 6-5 was formatted as currency with no places to the right of the decimal point.

The copying, moving, formatting, and printing operations can also be applied to a group of cells called a range. A range of cells can be made up of a part of a row, a part of a column, or a rectangle of cells. For example, a range copy would define a group of cells as a range and then copy this range to a designated location in the spreadsheet. It is also possible to move, format, and print a range of cells.

It may be necessary or useful to *save* a spreadsheet to a disk for future reference. For example, if an incomplete spreadsheet is saved, the user can *load* the spreadsheet at some later point and begin work again. A spreadsheet template may also be saved on disk. A **template** is a skeleton spreadsheet that matches a particular application. For example, the labels and formulas from Jill Bradley's budget could be used as a template. When new values are input for salary, rent, and so on, the template provides the formulas needed to calculate the values for the blank cells.

> In automating the process of cranking out numbers, business plans, and forecasts [with spreadsheets], people are producing analyses 50 to 100 times more frequently than when they used only paper.
>
> *Said Mohammadioun,*
> *president, Samna*
>
> Quoted in "View from the Top," *Personal Computing*, October 1989, p. 266.

H1: [W4] 'Wee-B-Dry Corporation: Lease Versus Purchase Decision (Page Two) `READY`

	H	I	J	K	L	M	N	O	P	Q
1	Wee-B-Dry Corporation: Lease Versus Purchase Decision (Page Two)									
2	===									
3										
4		------- OWNERSHIP COSTS AND DEDUCTIONS -------							LEASE VALUE	
5		INTEREST		DEPREC-			TAX	AT LOAN	PV LOAN	LEASE	PV LEASE
6	YEAR	EXPENSE	MAINT	IATION	TOTAL	SAVINGS	OUTFLOW	OUTFLOW	PMT (AT)	PMT
7	1	2,000	2,000	4,000	8,000	2,720	4,556	4,556	4,620	4,620
8	2	1,672	2,000	6,400	10,072	3,425	3,851	3,501	4,620	4,125
9	3	1,312	2,000	3,840	7,152	2,432	4,844	4,004	4,620	3,683
10	4	916	2,000	2,300	5,216	1,773	5,503	4,134	4,620	3,288
11	5	480	2,000	2,304	4,784	1,626	5,650	3,859	4,620	2,936
12	6	0	2,000	1,156	3,156	1,073	6,203	3,852	4,620	2,622
13										
14	==									
15								$30,607	$23,905	$27,720	$21,274

20-Jul-92 08:36 PM

An important use of spreadsheets is to help managers make decisions involving financial questions.

Once a spreadsheet has tested various assumptions and is formatted to a desired form, some or all of the spreadsheet can be printed. The part of the spreadsheet that is printed depends on the commands given. A user can have just one cell printed, or the entire spreadsheet.

When a spreadsheet's rows and columns cannot all appear on the screen at one time (the number of rows and columns differs from package to package and machine to machine), the **windowing** feature of the spreadsheet is useful. In this situation, the user can see two different parts of a spreadsheet at the same time. *Windowing* can be vertical, which shows two sets of columns, or horizontal, which shows two sets of rows. As an example of the use of windowing, assume that Jill Bradley's budget spreadsheet covers 12 months rather than just 3 months. With a spreadsheet this large, **horizontal scrolling** moves the columns off the screen on the left as more columns are viewed on the right. When this occurs, the row labels are no longer visible, and the values in the right-hand columns are not easily identified. With windowing, the user can see the labels in the left-hand window and the monthly columns in the right-hand window on the screen at the same time. Figure 6-6 shows the result of using windows to view the labels in column A simultaneously with the June and Totals columns for Jill Bradley's budget. In this figure, the left window contains the row labels in column A and the right window contains columns M and N. It was assumed in this yearly budget that Jill's July sales were $11,000 and that sales initially increased 5 percent per month for the first two months but increased by only 2 percent per month for the months October through June. Note that with even these small increases in sales, Jill had a sizable total sales, net income, and savings by the end of the year.

To help the spreadsheet user make many common calculations, such as finding sums and averages and making financial calculations, spreadsheets have a set of **functions.** These are essentially a group of built-in formulas for carrying

N3: (CO) @SUM(B3..M3)   READY

	A		M	N	O	P	Q	R
	Item	1	June	Totals				
1								
2	----------	-2	-------	-------				
3	Sales	3	$14,493	$155,343				
4	Commission	4	870	2,081				
5	Base Salary	5	700	2,100				
6	Net Income	6	1,320	3,431				
7	Rent	7	300	900				
8	Car Payment	8	150	450				
9	Food	9	250	750				
10	Utilities	10	150	450				
11	Gas	11	50	150				
12	Other	12	100	300				
13	Expenses	13	1,000	3,000				
14	Savings	14	320	431				
15		15						
16		16						
17		17						
18		18						
19		19						
20		20						

07-Jun-92   10:34 AM

FIGURE 6-6
Budget Spreadsheet with Windowing

out specific operations. For example, to find the sum of a series of cells in Lotus 1-2-3, we would use the @SUM function; to find the average, we would use the @AVG function. In addition to these simple functions, there are statistical, financial, mathematical, date and time, data base, and character string functions. In 1-2-3, we use them by entering the @ symbol (the "at" symbol), the function name, and the range of cells to be included. For example, let's say we want to find the total savings after three months. Instead of placing the formula +B3+C3+D3 in the E3 cell, we can use the function @SUM(B3..D3). The ellipses (..) show that the function should sum everything in row 14 between columns B and D.

Frequently, a user will want to perform the same series of actions or commands a number of times. To facilitate this repetition, most spreadsheet packages allow the user to save the series of actions or commands under a name. The unit of actions or commands is referred to as a **macro**, and the user can perform the same operation again simply by giving the name of the macro. For example, an instructor may wish to find the sum of a series of quiz grades, subtract the lowest grade, and then find the average of the remaining values. The instructor can do this for one student, save the keystrokes as a macro with a name of QUIZAVE, and then use this macro for all the other students.

A powerful function of almost all current spreadsheets is the capability of converting the data from one or more columns or rows of the spreadsheet into graphs. The most common graph options are bar, line, pie, and stack-bar graphs and scatter (x−y) diagrams. Titles, legends, and labels may also be added to the graph to facilitate an analysis of the spreadsheet data.

Another useful spreadsheet operation is data base management. The rows of the spreadsheet are treated as records of a data base, so it is possible to sort entries or search for records with specific characteristics. Spreadsheets also contain a special set of data base functions that allow you to perform a variety of

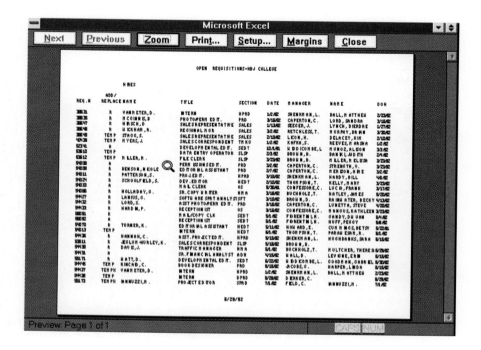

Some spreadsheet software features WYSIWYG screen layout.

operations, such as summing or averaging only those rows that meet a specified criterion.

Most new versions of spreadsheet packages include three new features: presentation graphs, WYSIWYG (What You See Is What You Get), and linking capabilities. Presentation graphs with three-dimensional graphics and elaborate titles and labels are becoming common in many packages. Similarly, multiple type sizes and fonts, which are displayed on the screen, are being added to spreadsheet packages. Finally, **spreadsheet linking** capabilities allow the user to link data and formulas to multiple spreadsheets, so that a change in one

NOT JUST FOR FINANCES

Spreadsheets as "Electronic" Gradebooks

With the availability of spreadsheets, many college instructors are replacing their traditional gradebooks with a spreadsheet equivalent. There are several good reasons to make this replacement: A blank spreadsheet with appropriate labels and formulas can be used over and over again for different grading periods; corrections can be made easily when errors in exam scores are detected; the spreadsheet's mathematical functions can be used to compute averages and other values; and the data base facilities can be used to sort the students by name alphabetically or by some numerical value.

As an example of using a spreadsheet as an electronic gradebook, consider the situation faced by the author in teaching 300 students in an Introduction to Computer class for which students attend both a lecture

For a large class especially, an electronic gradebook saves valuable time and helps to ensure accuracy.

section and a computer laboratory section each week. There are three lab instructors, all of whom use the same spreadsheet form to record scores for the students in their sections. This spreadsheet form has columns for each student's name, ID number, quiz scores, exam scores, and project scores, along with formulas to compute total and average scores for each student's overall grade and for each quiz, exam, and project. Because five quizzes are given during the term and only the four highest scores are retained, the @MIN function is used to determine the lowest quiz score, which is then subtracted

from the total of the five quiz scores. The @SUM function is then used to sum the quiz scores, exam scores, and project scores to find the total for the term. The spreadsheets for all 11 sections are combined into one massive spreadsheet, and the students are sorted alphabetically by name to match the university grade rolls. With the @IF function, the total scores are converted into letter grades, which are then transferred (by hand!) to the university grade rolls. While this is still a big job, it is much easier than doing the same job with traditional paper and pencil gradebooks.

`H7: [W5] @IF(F7>895,"A",@IF(F7>795,"B",@IF(F7>695,"C",@IF(F7>595,"D","F")))` **READY**

	A	B	C	D	E	F	G	H
1		CS 101						
2		Fall Semester 1992						
3								
4								
5	Student Name	Student #	EXAM ONE	EXAM TWO	FINAL	TOTAL		Grade
6								
7	ADHERN, D.	9503	275	250	385	910		A
8	ARMENTO, S.	8199	225	235	361	821		B
9	BAXLEY, S.	7868	200	173	325	698		D
10	BRIGHT, T.	3898	195	280	309	784		C
11	BROUN, G.	2407	285	217	387	889		B
12	BRUN, R.	0812	235	216	326	777		C
13	CHAX, G.	0713	220	236	263	719		C
14	DRAZLE, M.	7768	295	289	285	869		B
15	HOWLETT, J.	6010	185	132	356	673		D
16	KEVLAR, S.	8423	145	184	216	545		F
17	LOWRANCE, K.	5841	200	151	329	680		D
18	MCCORMICK, J.	4905	195	290	376	861		B
19	MILLMAN, M.	3428	215	253	352	820		B
20	CHANANA, P.	1850	225	239	278	742		C

`07-Jun-92  10:46 AM`   `CALC`   `CAPS`

spreadsheet is transferred to other spreadsheets requiring the same value or formula. More powerful spreadsheets, such as Microsoft Excel and Lotus 1-2-3 Release 3.1, can simultaneously display multiple-linked spreadsheets.

Integrated Packages

The popularity of spreadsheets has led software companies to create packages that add other packages to the spreadsheet. The first such package was the extremely successful Lotus 1-2-3, which included graphics and data base management functions along with the spreadsheet. After 1-2-3 came the **integrated package,** which allowed a user to do even more work with only one package. Examples of integrated packages for IBM compatible PCs are Symphony from Lotus, Framework III from Ashton-Tate, Enable OA from Enable, First Choice from Spinnaker Software Publishing Corporation, and Microsoft Works, which is also made for the Apple Macintosh.

These packages all have spreadsheet, data base, word processing, graphics, and telecommunications functions. Each package works differently, but all have the same objective—*to allow users to do all their processing in one package with a common interface and command structure.* For example, it is possible with an integrated package to begin writing a report, decide a graph is needed, switch to the graphics part of the integrated package, design the graph, then move the graphic into the report. With integrated packages, any change in one part of the package is immediately known to all other elements of the package. For example, if the results of a spreadsheet are being included in a graph and the values of the spreadsheet are changed, the graph will also reflect the changes.

Purchasing a Spreadsheet and Integrated Packages

When shopping for a spreadsheet package, you should know that all choices for IBM compatible PCs have been standardized on the Lotus 1-2-3 file format, that is, .wk1 files. This means that no matter which spreadsheet you choose, it will work with spreadsheets developed on another package. Price probably will not be a determining factor in your decision because most packages cost about the same: They list for about $500 to $600 but usually can be purchased for considerably less from a discount dealer. SuperCalc[5], however, is quite a bit less costly. With this in mind, your choice of spreadsheet will depend on your hardware and on whether you are using the Windows operating environment. Several packages run on virtually any PC. They include Quattro Pro from Borland, SuperCalc[5] from Computer Associates, PlanPerfect from WordPerfect Corporation, and Lotus 1-2-3 Release 2.4. However, Lotus 1-2-3 Release 3.1 and Microsoft Excel require an Intel 80386 or i486 computer.

For PCs running under the Windows operating environment, there is Lotus 1-2-3 for Windows and Microsoft Excel. Both packages use the Windows graphical interface, high-quality graphics, and multiple text fonts, but as we mentioned, they require a CPU with either the Intel 80386 or i486 chip. Other spreadsheets are being rewritten to run under Windows and may be available at the time this textbook is published. Macintosh users can choose between 1-2-3 for the Mac and Microsoft Excel.

Integrated software packages can be divided, roughly, by price into two categories: high end and low end. At the high end are the packages that sell for

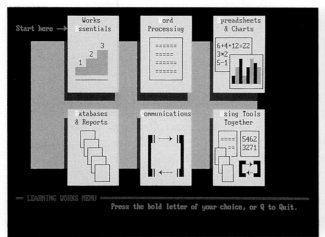

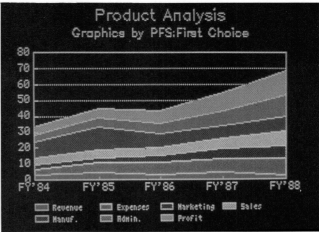

more than $600. For IBM compatible PCs, these include Framework, Symphony, and Enable. At the low end are the packages that sell for less than $200. They include for IBM compatible PCs, First Choice and LotusWorks from Lotus. Microsoft Works is available for both the Macintosh and IBM compatible PCs and can interface Microsoft's spreadsheet package, Excel. The low-end packages are very popular today among two groups: first-time users and laptop computer users. First-time users can have all their software in one package with a single interface. Laptop users find that a low-end integrated package fits very nicely their fairly inexpensive portable computer. At the high end, sophisticated users are discovering that there are more features in the later versions of these packages than there were in earlier versions.

> **Lotusworks enables us to serve those users in small businesses, home offices, and education with an extremely capable, cost efficient, all-in-one solution.**
>
> *Tim McManus, director of marketing for integrated software at Lotus Development*
>
> Quoted in "Integrated Software for Entry-Level Users," *Lotus Quarterly,* Fall 1990, p. 3.

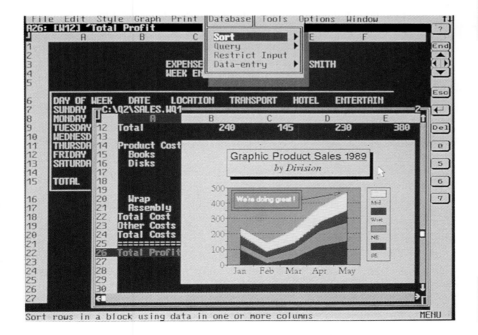

Quattro is capable of annotating graphs that can be displayed simultaneously with the spreadsheet data.

Unit sales of low-end packages increased 46 percent between 1989 and 1990, whereas sales of the high-end packages increased only 5 percent during the same period.

PERSONAL FINANCIAL MANAGEMENT PACKAGES

Personal financial management is a popular use for a personal computer. Studies have shown that close to 50 percent of all personal computer owners use their computers for some sort of financial management. Personal financial management packages fall into three major categories: personal budgeting (accounting), tax planning and preparation, and investment analysis. **Personal budgeting packages** allow a user to perform a number of tasks on a computer, including the following:

- Assign checks to various expense classifications and keep a running total of each budgeted amount.
- Record checks as they are written and then use the computer to do a bank reconciliation (comparing the checkbook balance to the bank balance).
- Track tax-deductible expenses as they occur and sum them at the end of the tax year.
- Provide a calculation of net worth.
- Keep an inventory of home furnishings and valuables.

Tax planning and preparation packages may be used to keep tax records throughout the year and determine the effects of financial decisions as they are made throughout the year. At year-end, a tax package can help in the preparation of state and federal income tax returns. Such packages can be useful if the user knows the tax laws well and is in a financial situation that could benefit from careful tax planning. However, annual software updates are needed because the government constantly modifies the tax code.

Investment analysis packages may be stand-alone packages or they may be tied into a national data bank that updates the information in the package. Portfolio management and security analysis are two basic types of investment analysis software. Portfolio management software is primarily a stand-alone package that helps the investor manage a list of stocks, bonds, mutual funds, treasury bills, and so on. Such packages can also determine the effect of selling a stock by calculating the gain or loss and the resulting tax effect. Security analysis software is usually tied into a national data base that updates the prices of a selected list of securities to aid the investor in making investment decisions.

Although the tax preparation and investment analysis software are designed for a specific group of users, the personal budgeting software can be used by almost anyone.

Personal Budgeting Software

While double-entry bookkeeping is the standard form of accounting for most companies, most individuals use a single entry for each expenditure. This is called single-entry bookkeeping, checkbook accounting, or cash-basis accounting. For each expenditure or deposit, the individual enters a check number, the person or institution to whom the check is paid or the source of the deposit, and

THE ELECTRONIC TAXMAN

Recent years have seen increasing numbers of professional tax preparers sending electronic tax returns instead of bulky paper returns. In a program begun for the 1985 tax year, the Internal Revenue Service is accepting digital submission of certain tax filings; in 1990, the IRS started accepting electronically submitted tax returns from every state in the nation. While this program includes only those income tax returns that involve a refund and those submitted by a person or company approved by the IRS, the process promises to speed refunds to taxpayers and to result in fewer errors and reduced paperwork for the IRS. Currently, a paper tax return must be opened, numbered, and sorted before data entry operators read and key in the figures on each return. While most errors can be blamed on the taxpayer or the tax preparer, some errors do occur in the data entry process. It usually takes two weeks for the IRS to process a paper return.

In contrast to the paper return process, with electronic returns the IRS does not have to key in all the forms, make corrections, store the paper returns, or try to decipher a taxpayer's handwriting. The IRS can also electronically transfer a refund directly to the recipient's bank account. The IRS hopes that the software used to digitally prepare tax returns will catch many of the errors that go unnoticed during the submission of the paper return. The result for the taxpayer? The IRS has said that digital returns can result in a refund in as few as 17 days—as compared to 10 weeks for a paper return. However, there is a cost. The IRS estimates the cost of filing electronically is between $5 and $50.

With all of these advantages to both the IRS and the taxpayer, many commercial tax preparation firms are getting set up to handle digital returns. An H & R Block spokesperson said that many of its employees will be among the over 40,000 professional preparers using the electronic filing program.

Sources: Steve Rosenthal, "The Taxman Goes High-Tech as IRS Accepts Electronically Filed Returns," *PC Week*, January 27, 1987, pp. 111–113; and Kathy Kristof, "Does Filing Taxes Electronically Make Sense?" *LA Times*, March 10, 1991, p. D4.

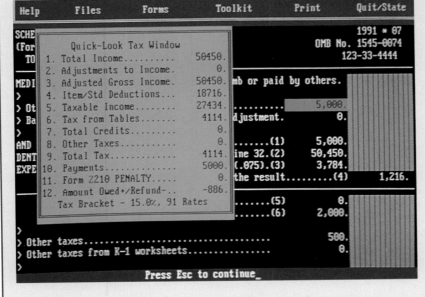

Tax preparation software is becoming very popular with individuals who prepare their own federal income tax returns.

the amount in a checkbook ledger. The person keeps a running balance in the checkbook, which shows the current level of funds in the bank account. At the end of each month, the individual compares the balance shown in the checkbook with the balance provided by the bank. The individual must first modify the bank balance by subtracting checks that have not cleared and adding deposits that have not cleared and then compare this modified balance to that in his or her checkbook.

One welcome feature of personal budgeting packages is their ability to help users balance the family checkbook quickly and easily.

To reduce the time and effort involved in personal accounting, numerous software packages have become available. While each is different in some way, they all have similarities:

- A user can set up a budget with some number of accounts.
- Each check that is written is entered with a number or name that matches an account in the budget.
- A running total is kept of all expenditures in each account.
- At the end of the month, the actual expenditures in each account are compared with the budgeted amounts.
- Also at the end of the month, the software can be used to reconcile the check returns.

The central problem of personal finance software is that people won't use it if it doesn't save time.

Scott Cook, founder and president, Omtiot (maker of Quicken personal budgeting package)

Quoted in "What's New in Personal Finance Software," *Personal Computing,* January 1989, p. 131.

Most such personal budgeting packages use completion screens to prompt the user for the needed information. A **completion screen** has questions to be answered and places for category names and amounts to be entered. Usually, these packages ask the user to define income and expense categories and to enter budgeted amounts.

A second common type of completion screen is the transaction screen. A **transaction screen** prompts the user to enter the actual income and expenses. This screen may request such information as the check number (or other code), the date, a description of the transaction, whether it is an income transaction or an expense transaction, the amount, and the category from the budget screen into which this transaction falls. Another characteristic of personal budgeting packages is that they can show a monthly income and expense summary that compares actual amounts to budgeted amounts.

Personal accounting packages can help keep track of an individual's or even a small business's finances. In addition to the screens discussed earlier, some software can generate reports involving check reconciliation, assets, liabilities, credit cards, and summary reports. Also, an entire group of packages is now available that has the primary purpose of writing checks. The user enters all the information necessary and the computer generates checks that are printed on the user's printer.

Selecting Personal Budgeting Software

When selecting personal budgeting software, you should answer several questions to determine which package is most suitable for your needs. First, how easy is the package to use and how flexible is it? It should be easy to enter and edit transactions. Second, what is the capacity of this package? If the package handles only 50 checks a month and the user normally writes more than 50, the package will not be useful. Third, will the package print checks? For those who write a large number of checks, this may be an important feature. Fourth, can the package suitably search for and report transactions? This function can be important if the user must recall previously entered transactions. Finally, can the package track and report tax-deductible transactions, and will it interface with a tax program? This feature can make tax preparation much easier.

If you are trying to decide whether to purchase personal budgeting software, and you do not own or have access to a computer and printer, you should also know that it will be difficult to justify buying the hardware, because it will probably cost far more than the amount of money you can save by using personal budgeting software.

BUSINESS ACCOUNTING PACKAGES

Tracking the inflow and outflow of money is crucial to the management of a business of any size. This tracking operation is referred to as **accounting.** High interest rates and the increasing complexity of the tax laws emphasize the importance of the accounting function to businesses. Because of the importance of accounting and the large amounts of data involved, for almost 30 years large corporations and institutions have used mainframe computers to handle this function. When minicomputers and personal computers were developed, accounting packages were among the first packages made for these smaller computers. Today, many commercial accounting packages are available for standard accounting systems. Many small software companies get their start by developing packages for special situations in which a company could not use a standard package.

Six major operations exist within business accounting—general ledger, accounts receivable, accounts payable, payroll, order processing, and inventory control. Usually, each operation is developed as a module. A **module** is a separate program that performs a specific task and shares data with the other modules to lead to an integrated system. Let us take a closer look at each accounting operation.

The **general ledger** is the record that contains all the firm's financial transactions. The term **double-entry bookkeeping** originated here, because each transaction must be recorded twice, once as a **credit** to some account and once as a **debit** to some account. For example, the purchase of a delivery truck for

$10,000 is recorded in two accounts: The asset account is debited for $10,000, and the cash account is credited for the same amount. All business accounting software packages have some form of general ledger module.

The **accounts receivable** module of a business accounting software package keeps track of money owed to a firm and when payments are due. Some packages generate sales reports on sales volume and print reminders that can be sent to past-due accounts. The software also ages the various accounts from current status to past due to uncollectible. Most firms must track credit accounts, so all business accounting software packages have some form of accounts receivable module. This module accounts for all money that is owed to the firm. Figure 6-7 shows the opening screen for an accounts receivable summary from a typical business accounting software package.

The **accounts payable** module of a business accounting software package monitors the money the firm owes its suppliers. Because creditors may give some form of discount if bills are paid before the due date, an accounts payable module can save money as well as ensure that all bills are paid. An accounts payable module can also print checks to suppliers and generate reports on amounts paid to each supplier. Like the general ledger and accounts receivable modules, the accounts payable module is found in all business accounting software packages. Figure 6-8 shows an accounts payable screen from an accounting package.

To speed payment of employee wages, a **payroll** module is commonly included in business accounting software packages. This module computes employees' gross wages due from regular-time work, overtime, and tips. It then determines the deductions from the wages for taxes, Social Security, health insurance, union dues, and so on. After subtracting the deductions from the gross wages, the payroll package can then print a check for each employee. At the end of each tax year, a payroll package can also generate the W-2 forms for employees based on the total wages for the year.

The **order processing** module helps the retail or wholesale operation by making sure that customers' orders are filled in a timely manner. With this mod-

Accounting data used to be just a historical record of what happened to a company. But more and more companies are now using it as a means of running their companies on a day-to-day basis.

Sal Catania, New York partner of the accounting firm Coopers and Lybrand

Quoted in "Accounting Systems," *Computerworld,* February 24, 1992, p. 73.

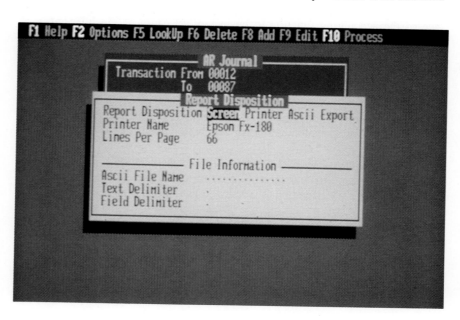

FIGURE 6-7
Opening Screen of Accounts Receivable Summary

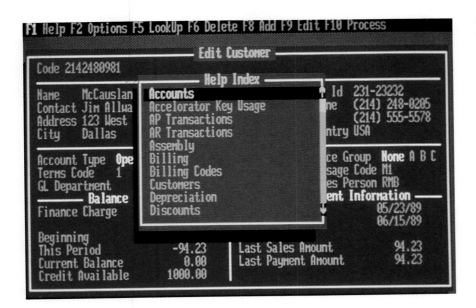

FIGURE 6-8
Accounts Payable Screen

ule, orders can be received, entered, and managed. Once the order is entered, the module can print an order confirmation for the customer and the packing slip used to select the ordered goods. If out-of-stock goods are input, the module generates an order to replace these items. If standing orders exist, the order processing module prints a reminder that these orders should be filled.

Along with order processing, the **inventory control** module manages the flow of goods into, within, and out of the firm. Inventory is the storage of raw materials, work in process, and finished goods. An inventory module keeps track of the numbers of items that are kept in inventory at any one time. It is not unusual for even a small company to have over $100,000 tied up in inventory.

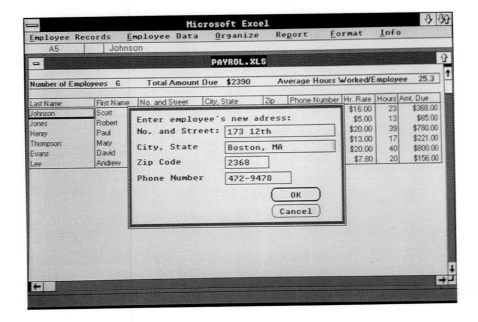

Even spreadsheet packages, such as Excel from Microsoft, can be set up to act as payroll modules in an accounting system.

BITS OF HISTORY

It All Began with VisiCalc

> [VisiCalc] was the catalyst that launched the personal computer out of the hobbyist garages and into small businesses.

Paul Saffo, research fellow, Institute for the Future

Quoted in "Looking at VisiCalc 10 Years Later," *Personal Computing*, November 1989, p. 233.

If there was one event that made the public aware that the personal computer was indeed a "mind tool" that could make work easier, it was the introduction of VisiCalc. By allowing the recalculations to be done on a personal computer, this software package relieved the user of the drudgery of constantly recalculating by hand the many values in budget and forecasting tables. VisiCalc allowed a user to enter the values once, tell the software what formulas to use to make the calculations, and then let the computer do the work. This was such a revolutionary idea that 200,000 copies were sold in the first two years on the market. Since VisiCalc was initially available only on the Apple II computer, it is also credited with selling 20,000 of these machines.

The history of VisiCalc is a classic story of one person trying to find a way to make a task easier. In this case the person was Dan Bricklin, who in 1978 was an MBA student at Harvard. Harvard uses the case method of teaching in its MBA program, and this involves using spreadsheets. Bricklin got the idea of computerizing this process. Even though a Harvard professor told him the idea would never work, Bricklin enlisted the aid of an MIT student, Bob Frankston, to program the project and named the finished product VisiCalc, for VISIble CALCulator. Another Harvard MBA, Dan Fylstra, also became involved—in the marketing of the finished product.

The success of VisiCalc spawned many other "Calcs," the most successful of which are Lotus 1-2-3 and Excel. Although VisiCalc is no longer on the market, having been purchased by Lotus Development Corporation, it is clearly the "grandfather" of all current spreadsheets.

Bob Frankston.

Therefore, the inventory module can be a key element in the management of a firm's resources.

Selecting and Using a Business Accounting Package

Why does a company use a specialized accounting package rather than a spreadsheet? Although a spreadsheet is a flexible financial tool that can be used for a wide range of applications, accounting packages also have a wide range of uses. The answer to the question depends on the size of the firm and the consistency of the applications. If the firm is small or the applications vary a great deal, then a spreadsheet probably could be chosen. On the other hand, accounting packages are a necessity for most firms, because the same operation is carried out many times. Such repetition on a spreadsheet would be very tedious.

Another advantage of accounting packages is that they are usually *menu driven*. A menu-driven package is easier to use because a user need only answer the questions shown on the screen. Many packages have an **error trapping** mechanism that keeps a user from entering an incorrect type of data. For example, if the package requests an employee's name and the user tries to enter the number of hours worked, the package would flash an error message and refuse to accept the input.

Business accounting software packages can be very complex because they perform so many tasks. Users should read the documentation carefully before proceeding, since one step may affect the next. Because of the complexity of the accounting packages and of the accounting function in a firm, a great deal of thought must be given to the selection of a package. The package should match the firm's accounting system. If a firm's accounting system does not match a standard software package, the firm has two choices: Have an accounting package written to match the company's accounting system or change the accounting system to match an available software package. Having a software package specifically developed for an existing system can be a time-consuming and expensive process with no guarantee that an acceptable package will result. On the other hand, changing the accounting system to match an existing package may seem like a radical solution. However, the user is guaranteed a computerized accounting system that works as expected. Recent decreases in the prices of accounting systems have made it possible for a small company to buy a package and try it out for an outlay of less than $200.

REVIEW OF KEY POINTS

1. Software packages for handling finances are very popular programs for personal computers.
2. The following three types of packages can be used to manage or analyze finances: spreadsheets, personal financial management packages, and business accounting packages.
3. A spreadsheet allows a user to use a table of numbers, labels, and formulas to analyze relationships between the values.
4. Spreadsheets are commonly used to analyze data and to work with budgets and forecasts.
5. Once a spreadsheet has been created with labels, values, and

formulas, the user can ask "What if?" questions by changing values to determine the resulting changes in other values.

6. Common operations on spreadsheets include copying or moving ranges of cells, printing some or all of the spreadsheet, saving or loading the spreadsheet, and using functions and macros.

7. Integrated packages combine spreadsheets with other software packages.

8. The three types of personal financial management packages are personal budgeting, investment analysis, and tax planning and preparation.

9. Personal budgeting packages are used to help individuals track their expenditures and compare these payments against a budget.

10. Investment analysis packages are used to help individuals analyze and manage investments in various types of securities.

11. Tax planning and preparation packages can help individuals plan their tax strategy and prepare income tax returns.

12. Business accounting software packages are designed to keep track of a company's finances.

13. Modules in most business accounting packages include general ledger, accounts receivable, accounts payable, payroll, order processing, and inventory control.

KEY TERMS

accounting
accounts payable
accounts receivable
business accounting package
cell
cell identifier
cell pointer
column
completion screen
credit
debit
double-entry bookkeeping
edit line
electronic spreadsheet
error trapping
fixed expense
formula
function
general ledger
global change
horizontal scrolling
integrated package
inventory control
investment analysis package

label
local change
macro
module
order processing
payroll
personal accounting package
personal budgeting package
personal financial management
    package
range
relative copy
reverse video
row
spreadsheet
spreadsheet linking
tax planning and preparation package
template
transaction screen
value
variable expense
windowing
worksheet

1. Why is a financial analysis package also referred to as a "spreadsheet"?

2. What three types of elements can be entered in a spreadsheet? How do they relate to each other?

3. How can a spreadsheet be used to ask "What if?" questions of a budget or forecast?

4. What is a *cell* in a spreadsheet? How is a cell location denoted?

5. Why are cell locations, rather than values, used in formulas?

6. What is "windowing" in a spreadsheet? Why is it useful?

7. What is a relative copy? What is a range?

8. How is a template used with a spreadsheet? How do functions make working with a spreadsheet easier?

9. Under what circumstances could a spreadsheet be used instead of a business accounting package? Instead of a personal accounting package?

10. What problem can occur in the use of a tax planning and preparation software package?

11. What is the difference between double- and single-entry bookkeeping?

12. How does a personal budgeting package differ from a business accounting package?

13. Why are there different modules in a business accounting package?

14. In a business accounting software package, what is the accounts receivable module? The order processing module?

15. Why is *error trapping* important in a business accounting package?

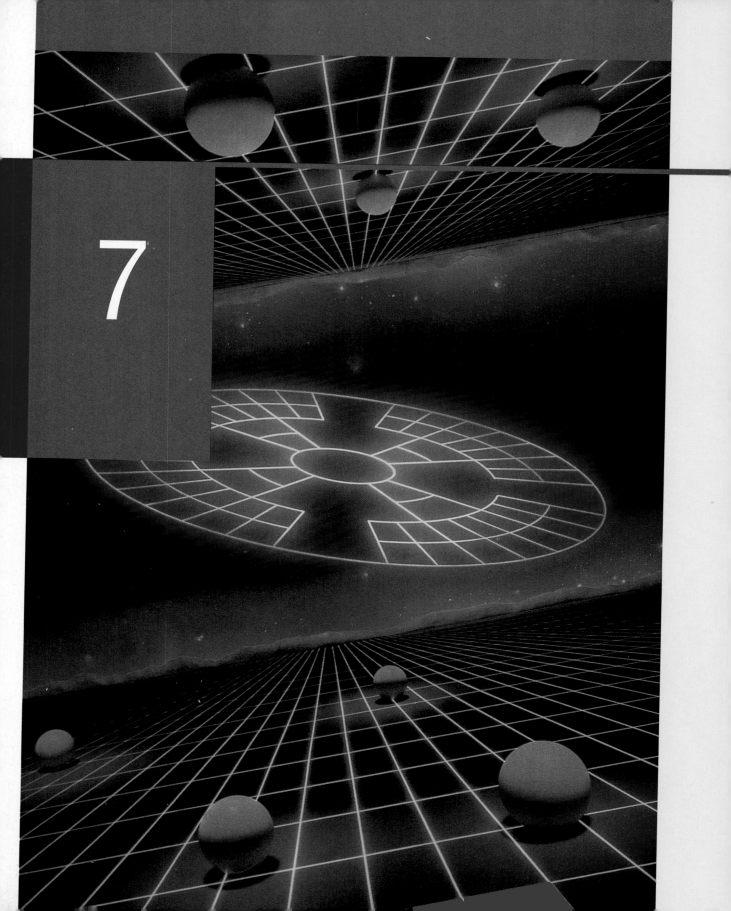

7

Data Base Management Packages

Because the management of large amounts of information is crucial in many situations, the use of a data base is extremely important. This chapter presents the general concepts and terminology of data base management software, beginning with a discussion of the use of fields, records, and files for storage and manipulation of information. Types of data base management software are discussed and the differences between file processing systems and data base management systems are emphasized. The various operations that are common to all file processing systems are explained. The three types of data models—relational, hierarchical, and network—for data base management systems are then discussed and demonstrated. Finally, data base management packages for personal computers are discussed and suggestions are made for selecting and purchasing data base management software for personal computers.

STUDY OBJECTIVES

After reading this chapter, you should be able to

- discuss the importance of data bases and data base management software;
- understand the concepts and terminology of data bases, including fields, records, and files;
- discuss the differences between file processing and data base management systems;
- understand the various operations available on file processing systems;
- describe the use of indexing and pointer systems for sorting data base records;
- explain the differences between relational, hierarchical, and network data models;
- describe three common operations for working with a relational data base management system;
- discuss the use of SQL with relational data base systems;
- list some popular data base management packages for personal computers and differentiate file management systems from data base management systems;
- understand the facts that affect the selection of a data base management package for a personal computer.

DATA BASE HELPS FIGHT ON AIDS

In the fight against Acquired Immune Deficiency Syndrome (AIDS), the computer has become an important weapon for researchers in their search for drugs that might be effective in deactivating the Human Immunodeficiency Virus (HIV) that causes AIDS. Studies have shown that inhibiting the HIV enzyme, called a protease, deactivates the AIDS virus; therefore, researchers have been looking for a chemical compound that will match and thus cripple the enzyme.

The traditional approach to this type of research would involve randomly testing thousands of chemicals, a time-consuming process that would not guarantee that a suitable chemical would be found. Instead, scientists at the University of California at San Francisco used three computer programs to search the Cambridge Crystallographic Data Base for molecules that mirror the HIV enzyme. The data base contains structural images of more than 60,000 existing drugs.

The first program narrowed the search to 10,000 possibilities. The second program, called Dock, then searched for chemicals whose shape would fit an indentation in the HIV enzyme. Dock reduced the list of possible chemicals to 200. A stereo image of each chemical was produced by the third program, Midas Plus. This enabled the scientists to reduce the list to 20 chemicals, including Haldol, a psychotropic drug that doctors often prescribe to their patients who suffer from schizophrenia.

The researchers were encouraged by their discovery that Haldol closely matches the HIV enzyme. However, they also determined that the drug would have to be administered in doses 1,000 times that of normal—enough to kill a patient—to block the HIV virus. Although Haldol is not an immediate "cure" for individuals suffering from the HIV virus, it provides researchers with a starting point in developing a chemical compound that is less toxic than Haldol but effective in blocking the HIV enzyme.

Source: Michael Alexander, "Fight Against AIDS Takes to the Screens," *Computerworld*, July 1, 1991, p. 17.

INTRODUCTION TO DATA BASE CONCEPTS

For as long as humans have been keeping records, they have been storing information. Usually, the information has been stored in a manner that makes specific elements easy to find. The information may be stored as phone books, dictionaries, encyclopedias, stock quotes in the newspapers, mailing lists, and lists of batting averages for major league baseball players. Cooks often use 3- by 5-inch index cards to store recipes; students use them to store term paper notes. You undoubtably can think of other ways to store information; but in every case, it is organized in a form that is easy for the user to retrieve.

A collection of information stored on a computer is referred to as a data base; specifically, a **data base** is *any collection of information stored on a computer and arranged in such a way that the information can be easily manipulated and retrieved.* Data bases are often used to access particular pieces of information or to rearrange the information in some order. For example, when a mailing list is stored as a data base, it is possible to output only those names in certain ZIP codes or to output the entire list in numerical order by ZIP code. In the box on p. 192, a data base facilitates the search for a drug that will help in the fight against AIDS. The information in a data base can be output as a summary, or a report can be generated based on the collected information.

As mentioned, before the era of computers, information was stored as lists, on index cards, in file folders, in filing cabinets, and so on—and in many cases it is still stored in these forms. However, these nonelectronic forms can involve a great deal of paper or card shuffling for any summary information or report to be obtained. Because the computer is a machine that stores and manipulates information electronically, **data base management software** can do the same work more easily and in less time than humans. Data base management software can be used to create the data base, enter information into the data base, and then rearrange the data base or retrieve desired information from the data base. The information that is retrieved can then be output in a report format if desired.

In this chapter, we will discuss data base terminology and types of data bases, and then give an example of the creation and use of a PC data base. Finally, we will discuss the need for larger data bases and the various approaches used to work with them.

Data Base Terminology

Like any field of study, data base management has its own specific terminology that defines the various elements and operations used in working with data bases.

Many college libraries now have computers to search for books and articles by author, title, or subject.

The first concept to be considered is the data hierarchy. The **data hierarchy**—the way data or information is organized in the computer—is made up of fields, records, files, and data bases. In this section, we provide an overview of this terminology, starting with the concept of a field.

A single fact or data item under consideration is called a **field.** Examples of fields include a name on a mailing list, a part number, or a sales amount. Fields are usually identified within a file by a **field name** that is unique to that field. For example, we might have a field called SALES_AMT to refer to a sales amount field. A collection of fields that pertains to a single person, thing, or event is termed a **record.** For example, we might have a transaction record that contains numerous fields, including sales invoice number, customer name, date of purchase, product number, sales amount, and salesperson number. A related collection of records, all having the same fields, is referred to as a **file.** For example, a mailing list file would have a record for each person on the mailing list, with each record having the same fields but having different names and addresses on each record. Figure 7-1 shows a mailing list file with the fields and records pointed out.

Finally, if we have multiple files that are accessed together to generate needed information, then we have a data base. For a company that maintains a mailing list file, the data base might also have a sales file that contains the customer name and information on previous sales—including the date and amount of each transaction and the person responsible for the sale—and an inventory file that contains the product numbers and the current price and number of units in stock of each product. By accessing the data base made up of these files, we can generate various reports, including one that shows which products are being sold by which salesperson to which customers. This information could be helpful in deciding whether to hire an additional salesperson and, if so, where he or she should be located.

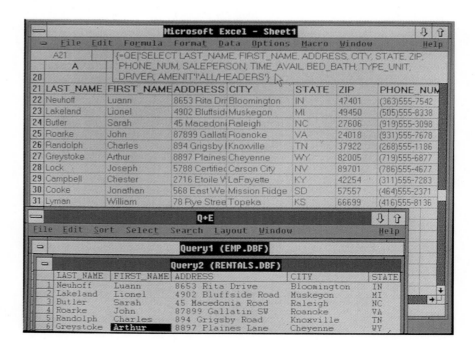

A popular use for computerized data bases is to set up mailing lists.

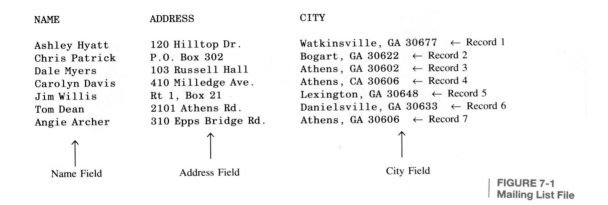

NAME	ADDRESS	CITY	
Ashley Hyatt	120 Hilltop Dr.	Watkinsville, GA 30677	← Record 1
Chris Patrick	P.O. Box 302	Bogart, GA 30622	← Record 2
Dale Myers	103 Russell Hall	Athens, GA 30602	← Record 3
Carolyn Davis	410 Milledge Ave.	Athens, CA 30606	← Record 4
Jim Willis	Rt 1, Box 21	Lexington, GA 30648	← Record 5
Tom Dean	2101 Athens Rd.	Danielsville, GA 30633	← Record 6
Angie Archer	310 Epps Bridge Rd.	Athens, GA 30606	← Record 7

Name Field   Address Field   City Field

FIGURE 7-1
Mailing List File

Figure 7-2 shows the concept of a data base made up of a mailing list file, a transaction file, and an inventory file.

Types of Data Base Management Packages

Computer software for working with data bases can be broadly divided into two groups—file processing systems and data base management systems—with the primary difference between the two types of packages being the number of files the package can manage. A **file processing system (FPS)** can work with *only* one file at a time, while a **data base management system (DBMS)** can work with multiple files. An FPS can work with many types of lists including mailing lists, membership rolls, customer lists, and parts lists. Many data base management packages for personal computers are designed to work with single files. However, whenever the needed information appears on different lists in separate files, a DBMS must be used. Mainframe data base management software is almost always of the multifile variety (DBMS) since mainframes are used to work with very large and sophisticated data bases. As PCs are becoming more powerful and have larger amounts of secondary storage, multifile data base management systems are being used on them as well. In the next section we consider file processing systems. Data base management systems will be taken up in a later section.

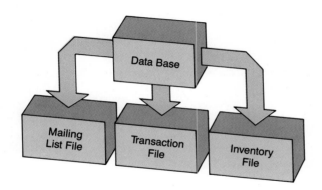

FIGURE 7-2
Data Base

File processing systems are often used to maintain up-to-date records on retail inventories (left) and to control patient records in hospitals (right).

Another institution that has benefited greatly from the use of data bases is the city or county blood bank.

As we said earlier, one of the two types of data base management package is the file processing system—or, as it is also known, a **file processor.** File processing systems are important because almost all organizations, regardless of size, require some form of recordkeeping that involves lists. In some cases, these records are simply lists of the members or employees of the organization; in larger organizations, the records go into great detail about the people, products, or services involved in the organization. Before computers, the only way to keep these records was on cards, on paper lists, or in folders in filing cabinets. When information was needed from these records, someone had to go through the cards, lists, or folders manually to collect the information.

Today, file processors are essentially electronic forms of these record-keeping systems that allow the user to go through the file quickly and easily. These software packages work with one file made up of many records to organize the information and to generate reports. File processors are often used on personal computers when the list management operations can be restricted to one file. Some of the more popular file processor packages for personal computers are RapidFile; Professional File; the data base manager in Lotus 1-2-3; and a shareware package, PC-File. dBase III PLUS, one of the most popular data base management packages, is often used as a file processor even though it is capable of working with multiple files.

Operations Using a File Processor Package

All data base management packages that include file processors have some operations in common: the file management operations and report generator operations. The **file manager** controls the actual creation of the file, including giving it a name, setting up the structure of the file with its fields, and entering data into the file. The file manager also handles file manipulation tasks such as sorting (rearranging) the file according to some field and searching for records that meet some criterion. It is also possible for the file manager to output only those

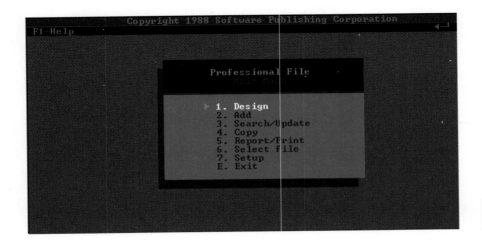

Professional File from Software Publishing Co. is an easy-to-use file processing system.

COMPUTERIZED HITMAN HELPS LA POLICE

> A couple of years ago, we could have spent days going through unsolved cases and we may never have found the one. The killer probably would have walked.

Lt. Edward Hocking, Los Angeles Police Department

Quoted in "Police Have Their Own 'HITMAN': Computer File on Killings," *Los Angeles Times,* February 20, 1988, p. cc/Part II.

When Los Angeles police detectives need information on a homicide or suspected killer, they go to HITMAN— Homicide Information Tracking Management Automation Network. HITMAN is a data base management package that catalogs information about homicides in metropolitan Los Angeles, which number approximately 1,000 per year. HITMAN originally ran on a personal computer, but as its size continued to grow, it was moved to a mainframe. Currently, HITMAN contains over 7,000 records. Each record can contain over 100 fields, and detectives can search many fields simultaneously.

With HITMAN, detectives can electronically track individuals who are suspected of being involved in not only murder but other criminal activities such as prostitution, drug dealing, and gang-related or domestic violence. The data base provides the police with a list of suspects that has been narrowed by such factors as weapon, neighborhood, race, and motive. It is especially useful in finding a serial killer's MO (*modus operandi,* or mode of operation), because it can merge information from multiple crimes.

Another important use of HITMAN is linking new information to unsolved crimes. Frequently, individuals arrested in jurisdictions outside Los Angeles provide information about crimes that occurred in LA. The new information, regardless of how brief or seemingly insignificant, is entered in HITMAN, which performs the link function. Many homicide cases have been solved in this way. For example, a prisoner in Texas confessed that he had robbed and killed someone in Los Angeles several years before his arrest in Texas. He did not know the name of his victim or even the neighborhood in which he committed the crime, but he did remember that he shot the victim in the face several times and that he threw the body in a dumpster next to a bar. Texas authorities gave the information to LA police, who fed it into HITMAN, which linked the details to those of unsolved homicide cases and found only one case in which a victim with face wounds was found in a dumpster behind a bar. Case closed.

Without HITMAN, detectives would have had to spend several days manually searching case files to link the data. The suspect probably would have been released for lack of evidence before the detectives could manually link the new information to the unsolved crime.

Source: Jill Stewart and Boris Yaro, "Police Have Their Own 'HITMAN': Computer File on Killings," *Los Angeles Times,* February 20, 1988, p. CC/Part II; and interview with Los Angeles Police Department, December 11, 1991.

records that match a desired characteristic. For example, the first three fields of a file can be output for all records that meet some criterion.

The **report generator** handles the output of some or all of the fields either in the original order or in a sorted order with appropriate headings and a specific format. It can also be used to sum or average the contents of one or more fields.

Operations within the file manager and report generator functions include but are not limited to the following:

- creating the data base file;
- defining the structure of the file in terms of the fields;
- using a data entry screen in entering the information in each record;
- listing records on the file in some desired order;

- searching for a particular record or listing all records on the file with some special characteristic;
- creating the report format to be used;
- outputting the information in the desired report format.

The best way to understand these operations is to actually set up and use a data base. To do this, we will look at a data base example that involves a familiar situation—a professor's grade roll. There will be four fields: student name, student Social Security number, number of absences, and quiz average.

Creating the Data Base File   With the data base management software, creating the data base file is usually very easy—often requiring only that a unique but meaningful name be assigned to the file. In the case of the student data base, the professor might assign a name of STUDNTDB.

Defining the Structure   To work with this student data base, the professor must determine the type of information that will go into each field. This is known as creating the **data base structure**—defining the data base fields in terms of the field names, widths, and types.

The field name is a unique name given to each field in the data base. For example, the professor might use field names of NAME for the student names and SS_NUMBER for the student Social Security numbers. For many data base packages, field names must be made up of only letters, digits, and underscores.

The **field width** is the number of positions needed to store the information in each field. In our example, a field width of 20 should be satisfactory for the student name field; a field width of 11 (nine digits and two dashes) is needed for the student Social Security field.

The **field type** is the type of information that will be stored in that field. The allowable field types depend on the package being used, but four common field types are character, numeric, date, and logical. A **character field** can store any type of information but *cannot* be used for any type of calculation, while a **numeric field** can store numeric information and also can be used for making calculations. Numeric fields often designate the number of decimal positions that can be included in the value, or whether the field can include decimals at all. A **date field** can store only a date in dd/mm/yy format while a **logical field** can only be true or false (or yes or no). Table 7-1 shows the field names, field widths, and field types for the student grade data base. Table 7-2 shows the information that will be entered for this class. If the field type is numeric, the number of decimal positions is also shown. Note that while both the ABSENCES field and the QUIZ_AVE field are numeric, the ABSENCES field

TABLE 7-1
Structure for STUDNTDB Data Base File

Field Name	Field Width	Field Type	Decimal Positions
NAME	20	Character	
SS_NUMBER	11	Character	
ABSENCES	3	Numeric	0
QUIZ_AVE	6	Numeric	2

TABLE 7-2
Student Data Base Information

NAME	SS_NUMBER	ABSENCES	QUIZ_AVE
McCormick, Charles	999-89-1234	4	63.40
Deplant, Susan	999-40-2773	4	82.00
Factor, Ben E.	999-04-3043	3	74.90
Quay, May	999-99-1532	2	91.50
Fields, Samuel	999-09-0744	0	94.25
Boat, Rhoda	999-21-9876	2	48.50
Hyatt, Ashley	999-80-2269	1	85.50
Monk, Chip	999-13-4321	0	57.90

has zero decimal positions (sometimes referred to as an **integer field**) and the QUIZ_AVE field has two decimal positions (sometimes referred to as a **real field**). Be aware that the decimal point may be included in the field width of a real field and that the absolute maximum number of digits or letters to be entered should be considered when the field width is selected.

Entering Information   To enter the information in the data base, we commonly use a data entry screen. A **data entry screen** prompts the user to enter information for each record through a series of "fill-in-the-blank" questions that are shown on the monitor screen. Usually, the field name will be shown with the cursor next to it in a blank area in which the information for that field is entered. After the professor enters the information for a particular field and presses the Enter key, the cursor moves to the next field and awaits entry of information in that field. When all information for a record is entered, a blank data entry screen is shown for the next record.

Listing the File in Some Order   Once the information is entered in the data base, the records may be listed in the order in which they were input or the file may be rearranged or sorted according to some field. Figure 7-3 shows the student grade data base listed in the order in which it was input.

It is very common, in a data base file containing names, to sort alphabetically by name. Figure 7-4 shows the student data base listed alphabetically. The same data base can be sorted on another field if the professor wants it in another order. For example, the grade data base can be sorted from the highest QUIZ_AVE to the lowest. We will discuss the process of sorting in more detail in a later section.

Listing Particular Records   A very important operation with any data base is the process of finding records that meet some criterion. This may involve matching a single record or listing a group of records that meet the criterion. In our example, the professor may wish to see the record for the student "Hyatt, Ashley" or the records of all students with fewer than three absences. In either case, the data base management software will search the data base for records meeting the criterion and then list them on the screen or on the printer. Figure 7-5 shows a listing of students with fewer than three absences.

It is also possible to perform more complex searches by combining two or more fields. For example, the professor may want to list all students with

```
NAME              SS_NUMBER    ABSENCES QUIZ_AVE       NAME              SS_NUMBER    ABSENCES QUIZ_AVE
McCormick, Charles 999-89-1234     4     63.40         Boat, Rhoda       999-21-9876      2     48.50
Deplant, Susan    999-40-2773      4     82.00         Deplant, Susan    999-40-2773      4     82.00
Factor, Ben E.    999-04-3043      3     74.90         Factor, Ben E.    999-04-3043      3     74.90
Quay, May         999-99-1532      2     91.50         Fields, Samuel    999-09-0744      0     94.25
Fields, Samuel    999-09-0744      0     94.25         Hyatt, Ashley     999-80-2269      1     85.50
Boat, Rhoda       999-21-9876      2     48.50         McCormick, Charles 999-89-1234     4     63.40
Hyatt, Ashley     999-80-2269      1     85.50         Monk, Chip        999-13-4321      0     57.90
Monk, Chip        999-13-4321      0     57.90         Quay, May         999-99-1532      2     91.50
```

FIGURE 7-3 (left)
Listing of Student Data Base

FIGURE 7-4 (right)
Alphabetical Listing of Student
Data Base

fewer than three absences *and* a quiz average greater than 80. The result of this search is shown in Figure 7-6.

Finally, it is possible to list records depending on a computation involving numeric fields. For example, our professor has a policy of subtracting the number of absences from the quiz average, and wants to see a listing of all students with a resulting modified quiz average greater than 90 to determine which students will receive a grade of "A." That is, the professor wants a listing of students who meet the requirement QUIZ_AVE − ABSENCES > 90. This listing is shown in Figure 7-7. Note that May Quay, who had an average of 91.50 before the absences were subtracted, was not listed in Figure 7-7 because her two absences dropped her modified quiz average below 90.

Generating Reports While a simple listing of records may be acceptable in many cases, other situations require a more formal report from the data base. Most data base management packages have a report generation function built into the software. This function may allow for special formats or headings, the summing of fields, and the creation of new columns by combining existing

FIGURE 7-5 (left)
Listing of Students with Fewer
than Three Absences

FIGURE 7-6 (right)
Listing of Students with Fewer
than Three Absences and Quiz
Average Greater than 80

```
NAME              SS_NUMBER    ABSENCES QUIZ_AVE       NAME              SS_NUMBER    ABSENCES QUIZ_AVE
Quay, May         999-99-1532      2     91.50         Quay, May         999-99-1532      2     91.50
Fields, Samuel    999-09-0744      0     94.25         Fields, Samuel    999-09-0744      0     94.25
Boat, Rhoda       999-21-9876      2     48.50         Hyatt, Ashley     999-80-2269      1     85.50
Hyatt, Ashley     999-80-2269      1     85.50
Monk, Chip        999-13-4321      0     57.90
```

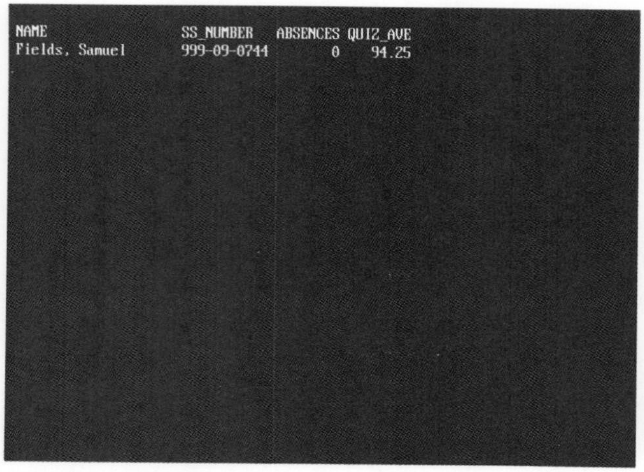

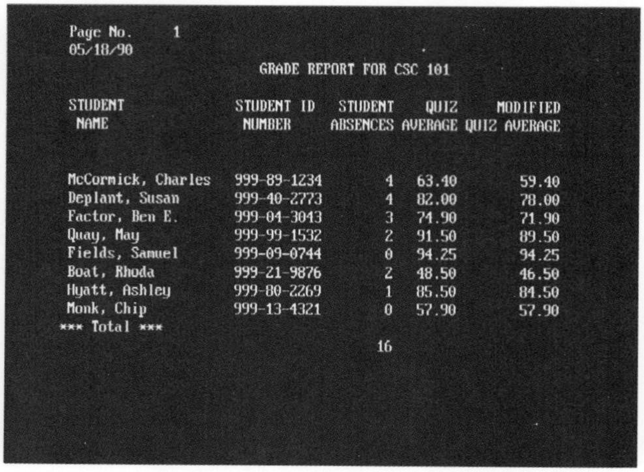

```
NAME              SS_NUMBER  ABSENCES QUIZ_AVE
Fields, Samuel    999-09-0744        0    94.25
```

```
Page No.    1
05/18/90
                        GRADE REPORT FOR CSC 101

STUDENT              STUDENT ID  STUDENT    QUIZ     MODIFIED
NAME                 NUMBER      ABSENCES AVERAGE QUIZ AVERAGE


McCormick, Charles   999-89-1234       4   63.40        59.40
Deplant, Susan       999-40-2773       4   82.00        78.00
Factor, Ben E.       999-04-3043       3   74.90        71.90
Quay, May            999-99-1532       2   91.50        89.50
Fields, Samuel       999-09-0744       0   94.25        94.25
Boat, Rhoda          999-21-9876       2   48.50        46.50
Hyatt, Ashley        999-80-2269       1   85.50        84.50
Monk, Chip           999-13-4321       0   57.90        57.90
*** Total ***
                                          16
```

FIGURE 7-7 (left)
Listing of Students with
QUIZ_AVE − ABSENCES >90

FIGURE 7-8 (right)
Final Report for Student Data
Base

columns. A report thus created is essentially a template for the output of some or all of the data base. The professor may wish to use more descriptive headings in the final report, find the total number of absences for the class, and create a new column that subtracts the number of absences from the quiz average. Figure 7-8 is a report showing this result. Note the difference between the QUIZ AVERAGE column and the MODIFIED QUIZ AVERAGE column, which resulted in three students dropping a letter grade on a 60–70–80–90 scale.

More on Sorting a Data Base

As we mentioned earlier, an important operation in working with a data base is **sorting,** or rearranging the information in some specific order. The resulting list is in either ascending or descending order (ascending order is the default on many data base managers) based either on the alphabetical or numerical sequence, depending on what is in the key field. When the student data base is listed alphabetically, it is sorted in ascending order based on the alphabet. It could also have been sorted in descending order according to the QUIZ_AVE field to list the students from highest to lowest quiz average.

Usually, the computer does not sort information by actually rearranging the records on the disk. Physically rearranging data base records to create a new, sorted file is a very slow process, and the new file must be used anytime a sorted version of the data base is needed. Instead of physically sorting the data, the computer can handle the rearrangement process via **indexing,** which is a system of using record numbers to keep track of the record locations. A **record number** refers to the physical position of the record in the list. Indexing schemes are usually implemented by a **pointer system,** wherein the value of a given pointer denotes the location of the *next* record in the indexed ordering. Such a system avoids the need for a search through the record numbers to find the *next* record in the indexed ordering. It also allows additions and deletions to be incorporated easily into the ordering: The computer simply changes the pointers. As an example of a pointer system in use, consider again the STUDNTDB data base file shown in Table 7-2, which we have listed again as Table 7-3 with the records numbered. In this case, the alphabetical ordering can be expressed through a

TABLE 7-3
Student Data Base Information Using Pointer System

Record Number	Pointer	NAME	SS_NUMBER	ABSENCES	QUIZ_AVE
1	8	McCormick, Charles	999-89-1234	4	63.40
2	3	Deplant, Susan	999-40-2773	4	82.00
3	5	Factor, Ben E.	999-04-3043	3	74.90
4	–	Quay, May	999-99-1532	2	91.50
5	7	Fields, Samuel	999-09-0744	0	94.25
6	2	Boat, Rhoda	999-21-9876	2	48.50
7	1	Hyatt, Ashley	999-80-2269	1	85.50
8	4	Monk, Chip	999-13-4321	0	57.90

pointer system. This alphabetical ordering is shown in Table 12-3, with the pointer system in a separate column.

To use the pointer system shown in Table 12-3, we must first know that record 6 is first in the ordering. Note that there is no pointer to record 6 since nothing points to it. Note also that no pointer follows record 4 since it is the last record in the ordering and points to no other record. To use the pointer system to determine the alphabetical ordering, go first to record 6. The pointer value from 6 is 2, so 2 is the next record. Go to record 2 and note that the pointer value is 3; go to record 3 and its corresponding pointer, and so on, down to record 4, the last record in the ordering. This procedure yields an alphabetical ordering of 6–2–3–5–7–1–8–4 in terms of record numbers.

If a record is added to or deleted from a data base that is using a pointer system, only the pointers need to be changed to reflect this. For example, if Sue Dodd adds the class late, her information would become record 9. Then the pointer system for an alphabetical order would become 6–2–9–3–5–7–1–8–4, since Dodd comes before Factor (record 3) and after Deplant (record 2). Only the pointers for records 2 and 9 would be affected by this change. The new pointer system for this ordering is shown in Table 12-4, with the added record and changed pointers highlighted.

TABLE 7-4
Modified Student Data Base Information Using Pointer System

Record Number	Pointer	NAME	SS_NUMBER	ABSENCES	QUIZ_AVE
1	8	McCormick, Charles	999-89-1234	4	63.40
2	9	Deplant, Susan	999-40-2773	4	82.00
3	5	Factor, Ben E.	999-04-3043	3	74.90
4	–	Quay, May	999-99-1532	2	91.50
5	7	Fields, Samuel	999-09-0744	0	94.25
6	2	Boat, Rhoda	999-21-9876	2	48.50
7	1	Hyatt, Ashley	999-80-2269	1	85.50
8	4	Monk, Chip	999-13-4321	0	57.90
9	3	Dodd, Sue	999-83-6900	2	74.50

Advanced Features

In addition to the features just discussed, which are common to all file processing systems, some packages offer the capability of combining fields from separate files and combining commands into programs. In the first case, for example, we might want to combine the student grade information in STUDNTDB with other grade information, say, student grades on projects, which is kept in another file. As long as the two files have at least one field in common, we can create a third file by combining fields from records that have the same entry in the common field. In our situation, if the student Social Security number is common to both grade files, we could match Social Security numbers to create a new file that contained some or all the information in the two existing files.

In the second case—creating files made up of commands—file processing systems offer the capability to have the package run through an entire series of commands for the data base file. These file processing programs are often referred to as **command files,** and they greatly extend the power of these packages. Figure 7-9 shows one such command file that uses dBASE III PLUS to create a list of student names and quiz averages.

The newest version of dBASE, dBASE IV, goes a step beyond command files. It also has an applications generator that allows the user to create menus to tie together forms, queries, and reports without having to actually write a program.

DATA BASE MANAGEMENT SYSTEMS

As we discussed in the previous section, file processing systems are very useful for working with lists of information that can be contained on a single file. They are often very easy to use and can be quite inexpensive. Frequently, however, information is needed that is stored on multiple files. For example, a college or university could have one file for the registrar's office with application and admissions data similar to the file discussed earlier, another file with housing information, and still another file for the financial aid office with information

```
********** Program STUDENT *************
SET TALK OFF
SET ECHO OFF
* Select data base file
USE STUDNTDB
?
? "Student Name          Quiz Average"
?
* The program loop ends when end of file is reached
DO WHILE .NOT.EOF()
    ?NAME,QUIZ_AVE
* Skip to next record
    SKIP
ENDDO
RETURN
```

FIGURE 7-9
dBASE Command File

Colleges may use several different data bases to store various types of information about students.

on scholarships and loans. When information is stored on separate files, accessing the various elements is not an easy task and fundamental questions about data redundancy, data integrity, and data dependence are raised.

Data redundancy is the repetition of the same data on different files. The college or university offices mentioned earlier may have separate files containing much of the same information, for example, name, Social Security number, address, and so on. Such redundancy is costly in terms of money required to collect and process the data for computer storage and in terms of computer storage itself.

The second problem mentioned, **data integrity,** is closely related to data redundancy. When the same information is stored in multiple files throughout an organization, any change in the data must be made in *all* files. For example, a student's change of address has to be entered in all the university files mentioned earlier. A change missed in only one file can lead to severe problems for the users of the data and for the person referred to by the incorrect data.

Whenever different departments in an organization collect, process, and store information, it is altogether possible that they will use different software to perform this operation. One department might use a computer language like COBOL to create its files on a mainframe computer, another department might use a file processing package to do the same operation on a personal computer, and still another department might use a minicomputer to process and store information. When this occurs, there is a problem with **data dependence** between the software and the files. The files of one department are incompatible with the files of another department and, as a result, it is often very difficult to combine the information from the two files.

Taken together, the problems of data redundancy, data integrity, and data dependence mean that any effort to combine files from different departments can be a very painstaking task. Consider again our example of the three departments at a university or college. If a college administrator wished to write a report on the number of students who were accepted who also requested financial aid and on-campus housing, the process of collecting the necessary data from three different files created by three different departments could be quite slow and awkward.

The solution to the problems that result from each department in an organization creating its own files is for the institution to install a data base managed by a DBMS. A data base management system will create all files with the same software, and this software will be used by all units to access the data base. Further, a file processing system that can handle only one file at a time will not be acceptable for the demands of working with a data base made up of numerous files, so we will need a data base management system that can manage multiple files.

Data Models

In working with data base management systems, the user has a choice of how the data will be organized on the data base. Three **data models** have been developed for organizing the data base: the hierarchical data model, the network data model, and the relational data model. In a hierarchical data model, there is a hierarchy from top to bottom, with each lower-level element linked to only one upper-level element. In a network model, there is also a hierarchy, but a lower-level element may be linked to multiple upper-level elements. In a relational model, a series of tables is used to show the relationships between the data elements. Figure 7-10 shows each of the data models schematically.

Each of the three models has been implemented in various commercial DBMSs, and each has its strong and weak points. We will give a brief overview of each data model and show examples of each.

The Hierarchical Data Model

The **hierarchical data model** can be used to handle situations in which data elements have an inherent superior–subordinate relationship in that every data element has one and only one **parent** or owner but a parent may be linked to

FIGURE 7-10
Schematic of Various Data
Models

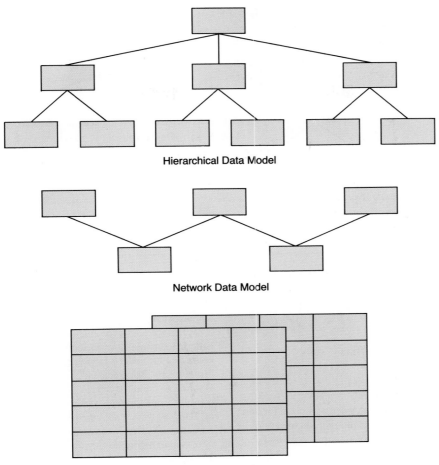

Hierarchical Data Model

Network Data Model

Relational Data Model

multiple lower-level elements called **children.** Such linkages are referred to as **one-to-many** and **one-to-one relationships;** a parent (the "one") is linked to many children or to one. A hierarchical model is similar to the charts that organizations use to describe their superior–subordinate relationships. As an example of the use of a hierarchical data model, consider a data base made up of family names, the cars owned by family members, and any outstanding parking tickets on each car. Figure 7-11 shows how this automobile data base would be represented as a hierarchical data model.

Note in Figure 7-11 that the family name is the highest-level data type, the automobiles are the next level, and the parking tickets for each automobile are at the bottom. There is always only *one* upper-level data element for any number of lower-level elements. This is a one-to-one or one-to-many relationship.

The Network Data Model

If there are **many-to-many relationships,** the **network data model** can be used, which allows each data element to have more than one parent. The hierarchical

FIGURE 7-11
Hierarchical Data Model for
Automobile Data Base

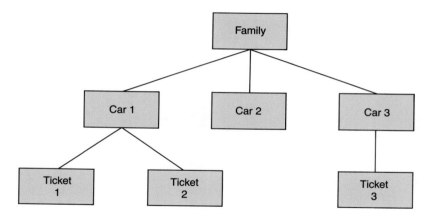

"I'LL HAVE THE USUAL"

It seems that ordering a pizza for home delivery is as familiar to college students as buying textbooks and studying for exams. Now, Domino's Pizza has a data base system called OASIS that makes it even easier for students and other pizzaphiles to indulge.

The next time you call Domino's to place an order, an employee may request your telephone number and then simply ask if you want "the usual." This is possible because OASIS, which is installed on each store's UNIX-based personal computer, gathers information about the store's customers. Types of information the data base stores include the customer's address, favorite toppings, number of pizzas usually ordered, method of payment, and special requests, such as delivering the pizza to a dorm room. The data base also knows if the caller is telephoning from a number that has been used by someone who refused to

pay for a pizza or by a prankster who, for example, requested pizza delivery to a nonexistent address.

When the employee enters the caller's telephone number in the store's computer, the caller's buying habits are displayed on the screen and the Domino's employee can ask, "Do you want the same toppings as last time?" or "Do you want it delivered to your dorm room?" Drivers have all this information before leaving the store. If a customer does not want to provide his or her telephone number, the system allows the employee to key in the order rather than pull up the information from the customer data base.

In addition to speeding the order process for both the customer and the Domino's employee, the OASIS system automates order preparation and delivery by creating a "door slip" when an order is taken. The slip tells the pie maker exactly what the customer ordered and tells the driver exactly where to deliver the pizza. Further, OASIS provides Domino's management with the demographic characteristics of each store.

Source: "New Domino's Computer System Could Help the Company Avoid Those Noids," *The Atlanta Journal-Constitution*, September 11, 1989, p. C14; and interview with Domino's on December 12, 1991.

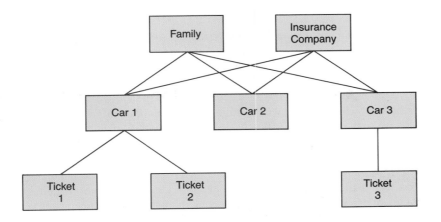

FIGURE 7-12
Network Data Model for
Automobile Data Base

model described previously is actually a special case of the network model in which the number of parents per child is restricted to one. Figure 7-12 shows how the network model could be used to represent the automobile data base when another upper-level data element has been added—the insurance company that insures each automobile.

In the network data model for the automobile data base, each automobile now has *two* parents: the family that owns the cars and the insurance company that insures the cars.

The Relational Data Model

While the hierarchical and network models use a tree or a network structure to show the linkages between fields, the **relational data model** uses a table structure. These tables—or, as they are also called, **flat files**—have columns that

Data base software on mainframe computers helps brokers on the New York Stock Exchange manage the tremendous number of transactions that take place each trading day.

correspond to the various fields and rows that correspond to the records. Each row must have the same number of columns, and the same specific format must be followed throughout. The word *relational* comes from the capability of a relational data model to relate all of the tables to each other to find needed information.

As an example of the use of a relational data model, we will use another situation with which you may be familiar—an admissions office at a college or university. Assume that this office has a data base with four fields: an applicant name field (NAME), a Social Security number field (SSNUMBER), a high school grade point field (GPA), and a Scholastic Aptitude Test (SAT) score field. With just these four fields, the admissions office has been able to handle applications with a file processing system of the type discussed earlier. Assume that now the college admissions committee wants the admissions office also to consider recommendations that have been written for each applicant and any extracurricular activities in which the applicant was involved in high school. In both cases, the number of fields needed to store this information is unknown. All applicants must have two recommendations, but they may have more. Similarly, the majority of applicants will have at least one extracurricular activity, but most will have several. Using a file processing system to handle this data base would lead to many empty fields or to not enough fields. In this case, a data base management system capable of handling multiple files is needed.

Figure 7-13 shows the three tables necessary to represent the admissions data base. The table in Figure 7-13a contains the NAME, SSNUMBER, GPA, and SAT fields; the table in Figure 7-13b contains the SSNUMBER and RECOMMENDATION fields; and the table in Figure 7-13c contains the SSNUMBER and ACTIVITY fields. Horizontal and vertical lines have been drawn in

To research the bloodlines and race records of approximately 1 million thoroughbred horses before making a purchase, many horsebreeders use Bloodstock Research, an online data base service.

NAME	SSNUMBER	GPA	SAT
Stafford, Phyllis	999-23-4321	3.65	1270
Box, Rip	999-31-9776	2.95	1080
Maxwell, Danny	999-99-1234	4.00	1390
Triesch, Martha	999-88-1532	3.50	1250
Campbell, Lange	999-14-3143	2.75	890
DeVane, Samuel	999-19-1744	2.90	980
Roth, Susan	999-74-3343	4.00	1500
Patrick, Ashley	999-89-2269	3.10	1270

FIGURE 7-13a
Applicant Table

SSNUMBER	RECOMMENDATION
999-23-4321	Ben Dyer
999-99-1234	Andrew Seila
999-99-1234	Ron Armstrong
999-99-1234	Robert Brown
999-14-3143	Ann Scott
999-74-3343	Chris Jones
999-74-3343	Roscoe Davis
999-89-2269	Ralph Stam
999-89-2269	Dane Marshall
999-89-2269	James Cope
999-89-2269	Carol Calbos

FIGURE 7-13b
Recommendation Table

SSNUMBER	ACTIVITY
999-99-1234	Football
999-99-1234	Basketball
999-99-1234	Computer Club
999-23-4321	Chorus
999-74-3343	Cheerleader
999-89-2269	Computer Club
999-89-2269	Swimming
999-14-3143	Volleyball

FIGURE 7-13c
Activity Table

the tables in Figure 7-13 to show the row and column nature of the relational data base. The Social Security number, which is common to all three tables, is the factor that determines the relationship between the various tables. When multiple tables are used, the number of recommendations and activities is not limited by the number of fields, as it might be in a file processing system, and there are no blank fields. A relational data base management system provides much more flexibility to add a new table of information related to the existing tables.

For the relational data base management system to use this combination of tables to find the information on a particular individual, it must go through a two-step process. First, a search procedure is used to find the name of the individual in the first table; the corresponding Social Security number is noted. Then, using the Social Security number, the file manager goes to the other tables to find the corresponding information. To do this the file manager needs a data dictionary. The **data dictionary** contains information about the data base,

including the number and names of the fields, the location of the various fields in the tables, and the relationships between the tables. The data dictionary is a necessity for proper documentation of the data base.

Two important operations in the use of a relational data base management system are the SELECT and JOIN operations. The computer uses the SELECT operation to create a new table by choosing only those rows from a table that have a desired attribute. The JOIN operation allows a user to create a new table from two existing tables by combining rows that meet some criterion. For example, if we wanted to create a table made up of those applicants from the first table who had a GPA greater than 3.0, we would use the SELECT operation to find all rows from the main applicant table that meet this criterion. The resulting new table is shown in Figure 7-14. We could then use the JOIN operation to combine the activities with the information in this table. Figure 7-15 shows the result of this second operation.

Another useful operation is the PROJECT operation, which allows a user to choose which fields from a table to use in creating a new table. The PROJECT operation can be combined with the SELECT and JOIN operations as needed to manipulate the tables in a relational data base.

Comparing the Data Models

While you probably feel more comfortable with the relational data model since we constantly work with tables of one sort or another, it is good to know that the hierarchical and network models exist and have an important role in data

NAME	SSNUMBER	GPA	SAT
Stafford, Phyllis	999-23-4321	3.65	1270
Maxwell, Danny	999-99-1234	4.00	1390
Triesch, Martha	999-88-1532	3.50	1250
Roth, Susan	999-74-3343	4.00	1500
Patrick, Ashley	999-89-2269	3.10	1270

FIGURE 7-14
Result of Using SELECT Operation

NAME	SSNUMBER	GPA	SAT	ACTIVITY
Stafford, Phyllis	999-23-4321	3.65	1270	Chorus
Maxwell, Danny	999-99-1234	4.00	1390	Football
Maxwell, Danny	999-99-1234	4.00	1390	Basketball
Maxwell, Danny	999-99-1234	4.00	1390	Computer Club
Roth, Susan	999-74-3343	4.00	1500	Cheerleader
Patrick, Ashley	999-89-2269	3.10	1270	Computer Club
Patrick, Ashley	999-89-2269	3.10	1270	Swimming

FIGURE 7-15
Result of Using JOIN Operation

A data base system in a local pharmacy can help the pharmacist improve customer service and monitor possible harmful drug interactions.

base management. The hierarchical model, used extensively on mainframes and minicomputers, is based on the standards set by a computer industry group called CODASYL (Conference On Data Systems Languages), while the relational model has been used on personal computers for some time and is becoming more popular on mainframe computers.

Hierarchical and network models offer some advantages over the relational model: They have less data redundancy and require less computer time. On the other hand, the relational model tends to be the more flexible of the three, because new tables can be created as needed using the SELECT, JOIN, and PROJECT operations. With the other two models, all of the structure in the data base must be defined as it is being created. Many users also find the relational model the easiest to understand and use. The trend in data base models is definitely toward increased use of the relational model on both personal computers and mainframes.

Examples of hierarchical and network models on mainframe computers are the IDMS and IDS systems; DB2 from IBM is a relational DBMS for mainframe computers. On personal computers, dBASE III PLUS and dBASE IV and R:BASE 5000 are popular relational data base managers, and KnowledgeMan/2 is a network product.

Interfacing with a DBMS

To use any of the commercial data base management systems, the user must learn the command structure that interfaces with the software system. Some popular personal computer data base managers have developed interfaces that are very easy to use, while many of the mainframe systems require either a programming language or a special **query language** to access the software. One such query language is the Structured Query Language (SQL), which is an inherent part of a relational data base and can be used to work with relational data bases on any size computer. An additional advantage of SQL is that it was originally designed to work in multiuser environments, so it can be used with workstations and in the increasing number of PC-based networks. As evidence of the increasing popularity of SQL, it is now included as a part of dBASE IV.

An example of a query using SQL is shown in Figure 7-16. This set of statements requests a list of the names, grade point averages, and SAT scores for all applicants with GPAs greater than 3.0. This list is output in alphabetical order.

Personal computer data base management packages like the very popular dBASE III PLUS and dBASE IV have their own query language in the form of commands that can be entered interactively from the keyboard or combined into a series of instructions that takes the form of a computer program. For example, Figure 7-17 shows the dBASE III PLUS series of commands; the period in front

FIGURE 7-16
Example of SQL

```
SELECT NAME, GPA, SAT
FROM APPLICNT
WHERE GPA > 3.0
ORDER BY NAME
```

```
. USE APPLICNT INDEX ALPHA
. LIST NAME, GPA, SAT FOR GPA > 3.0
```

FIGURE 7-17
Example of dBASE Commands

of the command is the dBASE III PLUS user prompt. The first statement requests that the dBASE file name APPLICNT, which has been indexed alphabetically, be used, and the second statement lists the desired fields for records that meet the GPA criterion.

Because both the mainframe and dBASE III PLUS query languages require the user to develop a *logical procedure* to perform the desired task, they are referred to as **procedural languages.** If the user can perform the desired task by simply answering questions from the software, then the language is **nonprocedural.** Procedural languages are analogous to command-driven software and nonprocedural languages are like menu-driven software. dBASE III PLUS and dBASE IV also have a nonprocedural, menu-driven command system that allows the user to answer questions instead of entering commands.

Some systems go beyond a nonprocedural language structure to use a natural language. As the name implies, a **natural language** allows users to enter

You can spend an awful lot of money on a program, but if it doesn't do what you need it to do, it's a waste of money.

Marlise Parker, small business consultant

Quoted in "The Perfect Small Business Data Base," *PC Today,* June 1992, p. 17.

DBMS software may contain a natural language query feature.

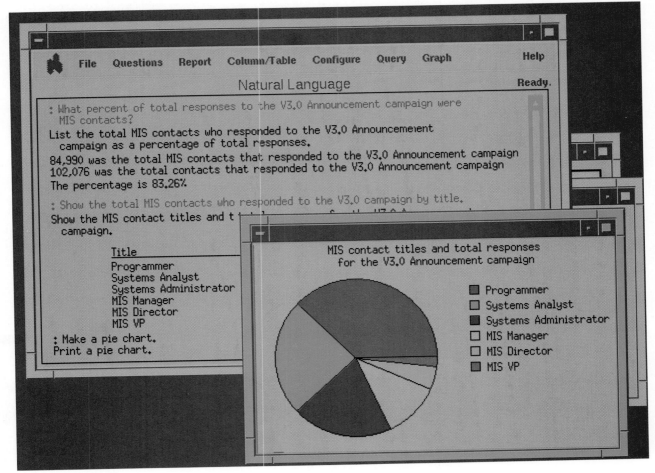

LEARNING A FOREIGN LANGUAGE WITH HYPERTEXT

It [Transparent Language] would make an excellent program to present to our foreign language methods classes to acquaint them with the really fine technology that has become available for second language acquisition.

Prof. Genelle Morain,
Language Education
Department, University of
Georgia

Letter from Genelle Morain to author.
April 5, 1992.

Data bases are primarily used to provide users with needed information. The information is usually stored in fields, records, and files, and specific commands are used to retrieve the information. A form of electronic information retrieval that is becoming more popular, however, is provided by hypertext.

Hypertext allows its users to navigate a data base more freely, because it is largely free of the constrictions imposed by traditional data bases. Unlike traditional data bases, hypertext stores information in discrete nodes or groups that can be reached from any other node. This is possible because hypertext's author created links within the system. The system links, in turn, allow the user to link *anything* in the document, including words, phrases, or specified strings in the file. Therefore, navigation within the data base is motivated by the user's mental connections.

As an example of the application of hypertext to a familiar situation, consider the often painstaking process most high school and college students go through to learn a foreign language. Traditionally, students learn a language's grammar rules and vocabulary before they progress to reading blocks of text. Now, a computer system called Transparent Language uses hypertext to enable a beginning foreign language student to read popular text material almost immediately.

This is possible because the software allows students to translate the

commands in their own "natural language." Examples of this are the Clout system for R:BASE 5000 and the Q&A data base management package. A natural language version of the procedural commands shown in Figures 7-16 and 7-17 might be

```
Show the NAME, GPA, and SAT of all students with
GPA greater than 3.0
```

text as they read. The text is presented at the top of the computer screen, and the student positions the cursor on a line, word, or phrase that he or she wants to translate. The translation, grammatical structure, and verb tense of the selected word or passage appear in a window at the bottom of the screen; therefore, if the reader does not understand a portion of the text, a quick look at the bottom of the screen explains its meaning. The system includes various texts or stories and a linguistic data base for each text. The data base was created by language experts, who entered information at the rate of 5 hours per page, and includes five languages—English, Spanish, French, German, and Latin.

This method of language learning is based on a linguistic theory called "comprehensible input," which proposes that people learn a language better by having repeated encounters with real words in real text, in the same way children learn new words from their parents, than by traditional systems. For example, school administrators traditionally set aside an entire year for high school students and a semester for college students studying Latin to translate the *Aeneid;* but with the Transparent Language hypertext system, the *Aeneid* can be read in a few hours.

Source: Daniel J. Lyons, "Program Eases Learning of Foreign Languages," *PC Week,* October 21, 1991, p. 203.

```
┌──────────────────Original-Language Text──────────────────┐
│ EL SOMBRERO DE TRES PICOS                                 │
│                            ◆                              │
│      XI                                                   │
│                                                           │
│      --Dios te guarde, Frasquita...  --dijo el corregidor a media voz,
│  apareciendo bajo el emparrado y andando de puntillas.
│      --¡Tanto bueno, señor corregidor!  --respondió en voz natural,
│  haciéndole mil reverencias--.  ¡Usía por aquí a estas horas!  ¡Y con el
│  calor que hace!  ¡Vaya, siéntese su señoría!...   Esto está fresquito.  ¿Cómo
│  no ha aguardado su señoría a los demás señores?  Aquí tienen ya preparados
│  sus asientos...  Esta tarde esperamos al señor obispo en persona, que le ha
├──────Word Translation──────┬───────────Phrase Translation───────────┤
│ appearing                  │                                          │
│                            │                                          │
├────────────────Sentence or Clause Translation────────────┤
│ appearing under the grapevine, walking on tip-toe.        │
│                                                           │
│                                                           │
├────────────────────────────┬──────────────────────────────┤
│ Present participle. If used as a noun, it │ Infinitive: aparecer  │
│ is a gerund.                              │                        │
│                                          ├──────────────────────────────┤
│                                          │ Esc=Menu    Location: 4-1  │
└──────────────────────────────────────────┴──────────────────────────────┘
```

Because there are two separate and distinct types of data base packages for PCs—file processors and data base management systems—it is important to decide first which type of package is needed. The user should know how much data is involved, how many fields may be needed, how big the fields will be,

SELECTING DATA BASE SOFTWARE FOR A PERSONAL COMPUTER

BITS OF HISTORY

The Origins of Hypertext

There are so many
ways that computers
can help you get stuff
out of your mind so
you can study it and
look at it; hypertext is
going to be a big part
of that development.

*Douglas Engelbart, inventor
of the mouse*

Quoted in "What's All the Talk about
Hypertext, Anyway?" *PC Week,*
October 6, 1987, pp. 60, 69.

Hypertext, although new to most
computer users, actually predates the
use of computers. The notion of
hypertext was proposed by Vannevar
Bush, President Franklin D.
Roosevelt's science advisor, in a 1945
Atlantic magazine article entitled "As
We May Think." Bush's words were
prophetic, and he actually developed
plans for an electromechanical
hypertext machine that would allow
users to store and retrieve virtually any
amount of information as well as shift
quickly between documents stored on
microfilm. However, he did not give it

the name we use now. That came 20
years later, when computer visionary
Ted Nelson coined the term *hypertext,*
which he described as "nonsequential
writing."

Early hypertext systems were
created in the late 1960s by Doug
Engelbart, the inventor of the mouse, at
the University of Illinois, where at least
one actual hypertext application ran on
an IBM mainframe. Then in the 1970s,
a hypertext system called NoteCards
was developed by researchers at Xerox.
Hypertext remained a largely hidden
concept, however, until the release in
1987 of the HyperCard software system
by Apple for use on the Macintosh.
HyperCard contains hypertext among
its broad array of information
management and programming
capabilities.

Source: Paul Karon, "What's All the Talk about
Hypertext, Anyway?" *PC Week,* October 6, 1987,
pp. 60, 69.

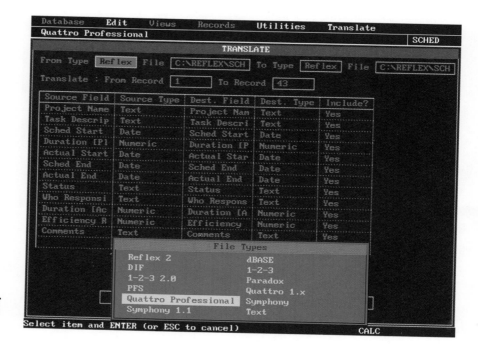

This RapidFile file processor
software can be used in
conjunction with a number of other
packages, as shown in the window
at the bottom of the screen.

and what kind of reports will be required. Prices for file processors range from "almost free" packages that are available from various bulletin boards to over $100 for packages with more power and options, such as Professional File and RapidFile. Relational data base management systems such as Paradox, dBASE IV, and R:BASE are usually much more costly, with prices exceeding $500.

REVIEW OF KEY POINTS

1. A data base is a collection of information arranged for easy manipulation and retrieval. Data bases are found all around us.
2. Data base packages are aimed at manipulating information and outputting it in the form of reports.
3. The data hierarchy is made up of fields, records, files, and data bases. A record is made up of information in the fields, and a file is a collection of records all having the same fields. A data base is made up of one or more files.
4. The field width is the number of positions taken up by a field. Field names are used to identify fields on a record.
5. The two primary types of data base management packages are the file processing system (FPS) and the data base management system (DBMS). An FPS is used for working with a single file; a DBMS can work with multiple files.
6. File processing systems create the data base file, set up its structure, manage data entry, and handle file manipulation tasks. Then the information can be output as lists or as more formal reports.
7. Common file processor operations include sorting the records, searching for a given record, and listing a group of records.
8. Because physical sorting of data base records is very slow, pointer systems are used to perform the sorting process through indexing.
9. More advanced file management operations include merging two files that share a common field and writing command files made up of data base commands.
10. Data base management systems, which work with a data base made up of multiple files, help eliminate problems with data redundancy, data integrity, and data dependence on software.
11. Data models are utilized to organize the information in a data base. The most widely used data models are hierarchical, network, and relational.
12. A hierarchical data model works with one-to-one and one-to-many relationships in a tree structure. A network data model is like a hierarchical data model except that it allows many-to-many relationships.
13. A relational data model uses tables to model the data base. These tables, called flat files, are related by having a field in common.
14. Procedural and nonprocedural languages are used to interface with a DBMS. Now, natural languages are also being used to access a data base.
15. Selecting a data base package requires a great deal of planning: The user's needs and knowledge should be carefully matched to the appropriate package.

character field
children
command file
data base
data base management software
data base management system
    (DBMS)
data base structure
data dependence
data dictionary
data entry screen
data hierarchy
data integrity
data models
data redundancy
date field
field
field name
field type
field width
file
file manager
file processing system (FPS)
file processor

flat file
hierarchical data model
hypertext
indexing
integer field
logical field
many-to-many relationship
natural language
network data model
nonprocedural language
numeric field
one-to-many relationship
one-to-one relationship
parent
pointer system
procedural language
query language
real field
record
record number
relational data model
report generator
sorting

REVIEW QUESTIONS

1. What is a data base? What is the relationship of a data base to files?
2. What is a data base management package?
3. What are the elements of a file? How are they ordered? What are the field width and field name?
4. What is the difference between a file processing system and a data base management system?
5. What are the first two steps involved in using a file manager to work with a data base file?
6. How is information entered in data base management software?
7. How is indexing used to speed up the sorting process? What is a pointer system?
8. Name two advanced features found in many file processing systems and discuss their functions.
9. Name three problems that can occur when separate files exist within the same organization. How can a DBMS help eliminate these problems?
10. List the three data models. Which does not support a many-to-many relationship between fields?
11. Why is the concept of a table important in a relational data base? What is the "JOIN" function for a relational data base package and why is it such a useful operation?
12. Why is a relational data base package more flexible and more powerful than a file processing package? If you were going to set up a membership list of a student

organization, what type of package would you choose? Why?

13. What is SQL? Why is it becoming more popular for working with data bases?

14. What is the difference between a procedural language and a non-procedural language? How are natural languages being used in data base management packages?

15. Name four points that the user should consider when selecting data base management software for a personal computer.

8

Telecommunications and Computer Networks

Combining a computer with a communications link for two-way communications with other computers is called telecommunications, and two or more computers linked together form a computer network. In this chapter, we will cover the related topics of telecommunications and computer networks, including the use of local area networks, which are restricted to a single location, and wide area networks, which may cover the entire globe. The use of PCs for accessing online services and data base vendors, interacting with other users, sending mail via telephone lines, telecommuting, and buying goods and services will be examined. The hardware and software needed to communicate using a PC are also discussed, and some directions for the future are covered.

STUDY OBJECTIVES

After reading this chapter, you should be able to

- understand the many opportunities that telecommunications offers users of personal and mainframe computers;
- discuss computer networks in general;
- distinguish between a local area network (LAN) and a wide area network (WAN);
- list reasons why a LAN can be useful;
- describe the three types of LANs that are commonly used;
- discuss the three types of wide area networks;
- list and discuss the various ways in which a personal computer can be used to communicate with other computers;
- describe how a modem and communications software enable a personal computer user to telecommunicate;
- distinguish between an online service and a data base vendor;
- explain how electronic bulletin boards and electronic mail operate;
- discuss telecommuting and the use of videotex;
- understand the importance of integrated services digital network for the future of telecommunications.

PCs JOIN THE MARINES

We train like we fight. When we go into the field we just unplug [the personal computers] from the wall and go.

Major Robert A. Coates, USMC

Quoted in "PCs in the Trenches," *The Atlanta Journal-Constitution,* May 2, 1989, pp. C1–C2.

When the U.S. Marines were mobilized for Operations Desert Shield and Desert Storm, they packed personal computers for communications along with their rifles and other supplies. The same PCs that you can purchase at the corner computer store were outfitted for war with software able to quickly organize, retrieve, and communicate information on battlefield conditions.

During a battle, large-scale troop movements are directed from division headquarters, which is usually a mile or more behind the front lines. Traditionally, communication with the front has been through couriers, telephone, and radio, all of which have disadvantages. Couriers may be shot or captured, and voice communications over telephones or radios can easily become garbled. Even within division headquarters, there is a great deal of noise and confusion, which may interfere with a commanding general's communication with staff officers.

To solve these problems, the Marines in Saudi Arabia used both radio and cable communications media to set up 20 mobile local area networks (LANs) in various desert locations for communications. They used many innovative methods to keep the PCs cool. In fact, the LANs were repeatedly taken apart, moved, and put back together as various marine units shifted locations. In this way, they created a truly mobile telecommunications system in the middle of the desert.

Documentation about front-line conditions and requests for supplies could be transmitted to division headquarters in seconds, which was far more efficient than it would have been to read a list of conditions or items into a radio. The speed of the communication also prevented the enemy from obtaining a fix on the transmitter.

For transmitting information from a LAN to Marine headquarters in Quantico, Virginia, two mobile data centers on trucks were used. These centers included a minicomputer, a front-end processor, disk drives, and high-speed printers. Data from the mobile data centers were communicated to Quantico via satellite.

Source: Robert Snowdon Jones, "PCs in the Trenches," *The Atlanta Journal-Constitution,* May 2, 1989, pp. C1–C2 and as updated December 1991.

Marines will be using computers and telecommunications extensively in any future military conflicts.

One of the most interesting topics in information systems today is that of telecommunications. **Telecommunications** may be broadly defined as *the electronic transmission of information.* This transmission of information can include voice, data, and pictures. Voice transmissions have been with us since Alexander Graham Bell invented the telephone well over 100 years ago, and radio and television transmissions have become common occurrences over the last 50 years, so these are not new areas. However, the electronic transmission of data between computers is a newer use of telecommunications, dating from the 1960s. Computers and communications have become so intertwined that any communications company that hopes to compete in a national or international market must also be involved with computers—and similarly, computer companies must be into communications.

Almost daily, we read and hear of innovations in this field, for example, teleconferencing, voice and electronic mail, electronic bulletin boards, satellite links, fax machines, fiber optics, and information banks. The military use of computers to ensure that correct information and instructions flow between the front lines and the command post (discussed in the box) is just one of many telecommunications examples that are frequently discussed in newspapers and magazines and on television. It seems that new forms of communications are springing up as quickly as new ways are found to use telecommunications. For example, the **compound document,** which combines written, voice, and computer communications to express an idea clearly, is becoming a popular method of sharing ideas.

Because telecommunications is such a broad topic and could easily take up an entire book by itself, we will restrict this chapter to a discussion of the transmission of data between computers and the use of fax machines.

Computers transmit data over a variety of communications links. (Left) Microwave towers are very important in telecommunications for transmitting voice and data. (Right) Fiber optic cables are replacing the older copper cables because of increased transmission speed and capacity as well as much reduced size.

Types of Telecommunications

Twenty years ago, telecommunications involving computers usually consisted of the use of "dumb" terminals to send instructions and data to the mainframe. A **dumb terminal** and a PC look somewhat alike in that each has a keyboard and a monitor. However, the dumb terminal was so named because it had no CPU or secondary storage. Its sole purpose was as an input/output device for the mainframe. As information systems have grown, so too has the need for much more sophisticated telecommunications systems. While there is still a great need for terminals linked to a mainframe, they quite often are "smart" terminals or PCs that allow the user to carry out some processing at the terminal and to use the mainframe for more complicated or time-consuming operations. PCs are often made to work like mainframe terminals through **terminal emulation** hardware and software.

In addition to terminals linked to mainframes, there is a need for **computer networks** that use telecommunications to link two or more computers together and allow them to share data, to spread out the processing chores, or to serve as huge repositories of information that is available to users. Examples of computer networks include

- banking networks in which one bank card can be used at many automatic teller machines over a widespread area;
- message networks that allow people to use computers to send and receive mail electronically;
- U.S. Department of Defense computer networks that allow users in numerous universities and research centers to exchange results and data;
- airline, car rental, and hotel computer networks that enable travelers to make reservations from anywhere in the country;
- corporate computer networks that transfer the results of data processing operations between corporate locations;

Commonly used networks include (left) banking networks that allow us to withdraw money from an ATM hundreds of miles from home and (right) airline reservation networks that enable us to make reservations for several different airlines with one telephone call.

- commercial information networks—like CompuServe and Prodigy— that serve many roles for individual users, including making different types of information available, acting as a mail drop, and providing an electronic bulletin board;
- PC-based networks that allow individuals to share software, files, and peripherals as well as to communicate with each other.

Computer networks can be wide area networks or local area networks. **Wide area networks** can range in scope from a few city blocks to almost global; **local area networks** are usually thought of as being restricted to a single location. Local area networks also usually involve telecommunications between PCs and are very important in office information systems.

Individuals are also using PCs to search for information, to communicate with other PC users, and to obtain "free" software. Equipped with a PC, a modem, and communications software, a PC user can access commercial information sources, computer bulletin boards, and electronic mail services.

Facsimile Machines

A widespread use of telecommunications technology that does not always involve a computer is the use of **facsimile machines** or, as they are commonly called, **fax machines.** Fax machines are rapidly changing the way we work by making it very easy and quick to send *any* type of document around the corner, across the country, or even around the world. To use a fax machine for telecommunications simply involves dialing the telephone number of the receiving machine and feeding the document into the sending machine; at the same time, the document is reproduced by the receiving machine at another location. The document can be typed or handwritten, can contain pictures, or can be any combination of these. Fax machines are especially useful for sending documents that require signatures, something that is not possible with electronic or voice mail. Over the past five years, facsimile transmission of documents has grown tremendously, with an estimated 1.5 million fax machines in use in the United States today. In fact, the growth in the number of easy-to-use facsimile machines has led to a decline in the use of overnight mail.

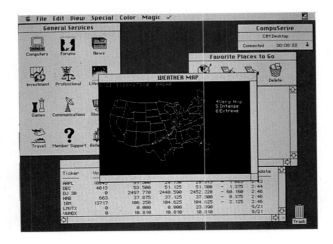

Commercial information networks such as CompuServe offer a tremendous variety of information.

Facsimile uses a scanner to digitize very thin strips of the document (0.005 to 0.01 inch wide) and convert the result into binary. The binary pattern corresponding to the document is then converted into telephone signals and transmitted over telephone lines. At the receiving end, the telephone signals are converted back to binary, which is then used to create on a blank sheet the same black-and-white pattern that was on the sending document. This process is shown in Figure 8-1.

Communications Media

Information transmitted over networks travels over various media, including twisted pairs, coaxial cable, fiber optics, and microwaves. **Twisted pairs** of copper wire are like those used in much of the existing telephone system. **Coaxial cable** is the type of cable used to transmit cable television signals into your home, whereas **fiber optic cable** is the newest medium and consists of thousands of glass fiber strands. **Microwaves** are high-frequency radio transmissions that can be sent between two earth stations or between earth stations and communications satellites, the method commonly used to transmit television signals. Twisted pairs are commonly used only for slow, **voice-grade transmissions,** whereas the other media are used for much higher-speed **broadband transmissions,** which can transmit large amounts of data.

LOCAL AREA NETWORKS

Since the introduction of the mainframe computer in the early 1950s and the personal computer in the late 1970s, computers have rapidly become a fixture in organizations of all sizes, ranging from General Motors and the U.S. government down to the neighborhood hardware store and homeowner's association. Whenever there are two or more computers in an organization, there are also many times when the organization would benefit if the computers could work together to share data and information. As a result, a great deal of interest has been generated in the subject of linking computers together, regardless of whether they are in the same location or on different continents. Computers linked together in the same location form a local area network (LAN); computers located in different geographical locations form a wide area network (WAN). We will discuss local area networks in this section and wide area networks in the next.

FIGURE 8-1
The Facsimile Process

Sending Fax Machine

11000011
10010110

Receiving Fax Machine

11000011
10010110

Uses of LANs

Local area networks can be useful for those frequent situations in which computer users wish to share information, secondary storage, peripheral devices, or a data base. For example, a user may wish to send another user information in the form of a document, a graph, or a spreadsheet analysis. Without a local area network, the usual way to do this is to physically share a floppy disk. This is cumbersome and the disk can become damaged and unreadable. Using a LAN, the user can simply send the information over the network to the other user without having to store it on disk.

A part of the concept of sharing information in a LAN is electronic mail. Using **electronic mail** (also called **E-mail**) on a network involves sending documents, pictures, and messages to one or more persons. The user simply turns on the terminal or PC, enters the proper commands, types in the document, gives the names of those persons who are to receive it, and presses a key. Instantaneously, a message that "mail is waiting" appears at the proper terminals or PCs. If the recipient is working at the terminal at that time, he or she can read the mail immediately; otherwise, the message appears on the screen the next time the terminal or PC is turned on. No more going through the hassle of typing the document; making copies; addressing envelopes; remembering to send the letters; and then waiting for the recipient to receive, read, and reply. With electronic mail, the recipient can receive the message and respond immediately. Figure 8-2 shows electronic mail being sent over a local area network that uses personal computers.

Enabling users to share secondary storage, peripherals, software, or a data base is another way that a local area network can be very useful. By sharing a single hard disk drive, all users have access to certain information, while other information may remain specific to a given computer within the network. This hard disk is usually referred to as a **file server,** because it contains files that all users may access. These files may be data files or software packages, and the user can usually access them just as if they were on a local hard disk. In the

> **File servers are going to blow the doors off traditional mainframes.**
>
> *Larry Boucher, CEO of Auspex Systems, Inc.*
>
> Quoted in "Rethinking the Computer," *Business Week,* November 26, 1990, p. 119.

(Left) Local area networks are often used in colleges and universities to allow students and faculty to use software and printers or to send messages from one to the other. (Right) The terminal displaying this screen from Microsoft Windows 3.0 is linked up to a LAN.

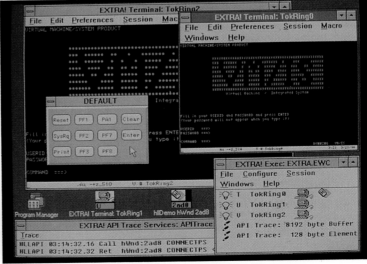

FIGURE 8-2
Electronic Mail over Local Area
Network

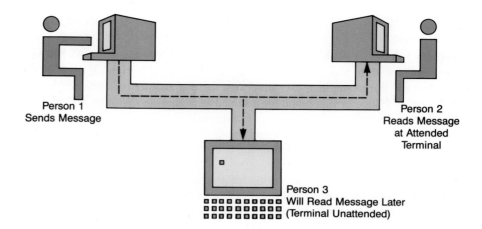

Person 1
Sends Message

Person 2
Reads Message
at Attended
Terminal

Person 3
Will Read Message Later
(Terminal Unattended)

case of a package, the user can retrieve it to his or her machine, load it into RAM, and execute it just as if it were located on the local machine. In some cases, the PC may not even have any disk drives, depending totally on the file server for disk access. These **diskless workstations** make access to software and data easier to control, thereby improving the security of the system.

In terms of sharing peripherals, having one high-speed letter-quality or laser printer or a flatbed plotter in the network that can be accessed by all PCs saves equipment costs. Instead of each PC having its own printer or the user having to carry a floppy disk to the PC that is linked to the printer, print jobs can simply be sent to the print queue to be printed in their turn. Similarly, sharing a single data base gives all users access to the data base information. In most cases, the users can access the data base but cannot change it, thereby ensuring the security of the information. Figure 8-3 shows how information, secondary storage, peripherals, software, and data bases can be shared in a local area network.

A PC on a LAN can not only share files, software, and hardware resources with other PCs on the same LAN but can communicate through gateways and

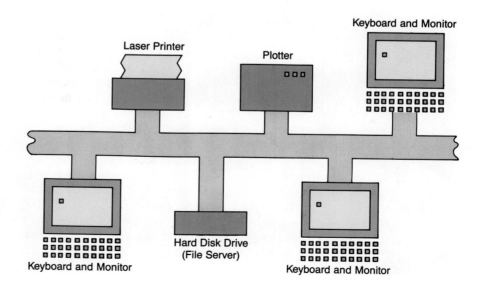

Keyboard and Monitor

Laser Printer

Plotter

Keyboard and Monitor

Hard Disk Drive
(File Server)

Keyboard and Monitor

FIGURE 8-3
Sharing Information, Secondary
Storage, Peripherals, and Data
Bases in a LAN

bridges with other types of computers and with other LANs. A **gateway** is the combination of hardware and software that connects two dissimilar computer networks. A gateway allows a LAN user to access a mainframe network without leaving his or her PC. Similarly, a gateway between a LAN and a WAN enables a LAN user to send E-mail over the WAN. For example, the author of this textbook was able to use a gateway to communicate from his LAN with a colleague in Australia over the WAN.

A **bridge**, on the other hand, connects two similar networks. For example, if two LANs are connected with a bridge, the users of each LAN can access the other network's file server without making any physical changes to their data.

The proliferation of local area networks in organizations has led to a trend called **downsizing,** which occurs when a LAN replaces a mainframe or minicomputer system. Companies downsize for several reasons. First, a mainframe system is much more expensive than a PC network. Second, a mainframe's cost makes it inflexible because a company may be unwilling to change the system once it is up and running, which soon renders the system obsolete. Third, PCs are usually much easier to use than mainframes, and they are becoming even more so with the advent of such graphical-based systems as the Macintosh and, for IBM compatible PCs, Windows.

Classification of LANs

Local area networks can be classified according to the topology of the network. Basically, there are three topologies of LANs: star, bus, and ring. In the **star network,** a **host computer** has multiple "slave" computers connected to it. Since the host controls all **data communications,** any communications between any two computers must be routed through the host computer. If the host fails, then the entire system goes down. Terminals linked to a minicomputer form a star LAN.

A **bus network** has computers that tie into a main cable or **bus,** with no one central computer; the failure of any one computer does not affect the overall performance of the network. To send a message to another computer requires only that the software be able to signal the correct computer to receive the message. An example of a bus network is the popular EtherNet system.

In a **ring network,** all computers are treated the same and any communications between two computers must be processed by any intervening computers. To avoid having the system go down when a single PC fails, ring LANs often have ways to drop the single PC without interfering with the operation of the LAN. IBM's Token Ring Network is a good example of a ring network. Figure 8-4 shows the diagrams of the star, bus, and ring networks.

Since users may not know when another user is sending information over the network, there must be some way to control access. Two procedures are often used to control the sending of information from computer to computer. In a **token sharing network,** a special bit pattern called a **token** is sent to each computer sequentially around the network. Only the computer that has the token at a given instant can transmit. In a **multiple access network,** such as a bus network, all computers are free to transmit at any one time, but collision-detecting software must be in place to control those cases in which two or more computers are trying to transmit at the same time. Figure 8-5 shows the operation of the token ring LAN.

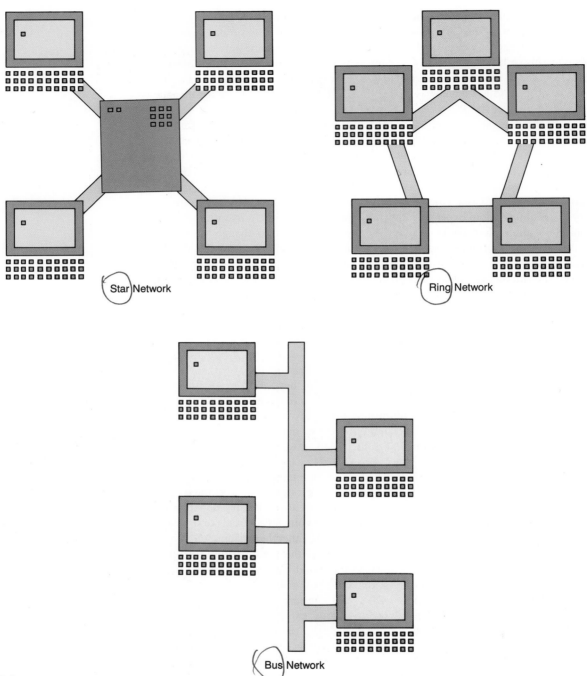

FIGURE 8-4
Star, Bus, and Ring Computer
Networks

LANs can also be classified by their configuration; that is, LANs can be designated as file-server, client-server, or peer-to-peer configurations. Currently, the most popular configuration is the **file-server configuration** in which the files are stored on a central hard disk but local PCs do most of the processing. However, the **client-server configuration,** in which the processing burden is on the central computer, is becoming more popular. In this configuration, the server

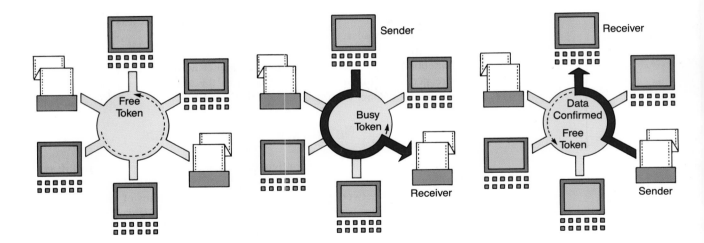

Sender

Free Token

Busy Token

Receiver

Receiver

Data Confirmed

Free Token

Sender

computer is often dedicated to a single purpose, such as a data base engine or communications. This leads to an entirely different approach to networking, where users share the processing device, as well as files or peripherals.

Finally, the **peer-to-peer configuration** is often used for smaller networks in which the emphasis is on users sharing files. With the peer-to-peer configuration, each computer can function as both a server and a workstation, instead of as a single dedicated file server. This configuration is significantly cheaper

LAN BRINGS GOODWILL TO THE GAMES

A 120-node LAN was crucial to the success of the 1990 Goodwill Games in Seattle. The file server LAN was involved in all aspects of the games, from administration and security to reporting and broadcasting. Running on an 80386-based file server with a 660-megabyte hard disk and a laptop data base server, the network handled such tasks as overall games administration, connecting reporters and broadcasters speaking five languages, transmitting

scripts from Turner Broadcasting System (TBS) writers to television host Larry King, and checking the identity of the 2,200 full- and part-time TBS workers. There was also a mainframe gateway that allowed LAN users to retrieve event results from the mainframe used by games officials.

The network used the Novell LAN operating system to manage the 120 PCs connected by twisted-pair wiring. Additional remote users could access the network via modems. With the exception of two custom-written applications, off-the-shelf commercial applications were used on the Goodwill LAN. These applications included an E-mail package, Excel and Word for Windows from Microsoft, Lotus 1-2-3, and WordPerfect.

Source: Stuart J. Johnston, "Goodwill Games Prove LANs Aren't Toys," *Infoworld*, August 6, 1990, p. 31.

The days of the LAN as a toy are over.

Walter Toucher, systems coordinator for the Goodwill Games LAN system

Quoted in Stuart J. Johnston, "Goodwill Games Prove LANs Aren't Toys," *Infoworld*, August 6, 1990, p. 31.

than either the file-server or client-server configuration, but it is not well suited for heavy-duty transaction processing.

The future of local area networks appears very bright, with a great deal of attention being paid to them and to computer networks in general. More and more personal computers are being used in the office, and the advantages of tying them together are rapidly being realized.

Network Operating Systems

LANs that use the file-server configuration must have a **network operating system** that manages the interaction between the various local PCs and the central file server. The network operating system has many features of single PC operating systems, because it, too, must manage disk access, file storage, and memory use. In addition, the network operating system must control access to the server—that is, determine who can log onto the server to use its files. As security becomes more important and more and more of an organization's data reside on the file server, it becomes more crucial for the network operating system to protect data yet allow authorized individuals to log onto the system. Network operating systems are also discussed in Chapter 4.

WIDE AREA NETWORKS

While local area networks are in the process of becoming extensively used in the office, wide area networks have been around for many years—in the form of long-distance telephone networks. Today, as the need for transferring data and information between computers over long distances grows, wide area computer networks are also becoming very important for business, industry, and government. There are basically three types of wide area computer networks in use today: academic and research networks, private networks designed to provide communications between a company's host computer and the employee's and customer's terminals, and value-added networks.

All these wide area computer networks use a special form of telecommunications called packet switching. In **packet switching,** the terminals are linked to the host computer through interface computers. The host computer breaks up long messages into data units called **packets,** which are then given to the interface computers to transmit through the network. The terminal at the destination receives the packets and then reassembles them into a copy of the original message. Figure 8-6 shows a schematic of a typical packet switching network.

Academic and Research Networks

Various wide area networks are used to facilitate interaction between universities and other research institutions. In many cases, the networks allow users on smaller systems to communicate. The biggest such WAN is called Internet, which connects 500,000 computers on 5,000 networks in 33 countries. A subnetwork of Internet is BITNET, which is an electronic mail system subscribed to by over 1,500 colleges, universities, and other academic and research institutions. With BITNET, a user at one of the network's subscribing institutions,

Ninety percent of the people I deal with are on E-mail.

Nicholas Negroponte, director of the MIT Media Laboratory

Quoted in "Electronic Mail: Ready for the 1990's," *Lotus,* February 1990, p. 7.

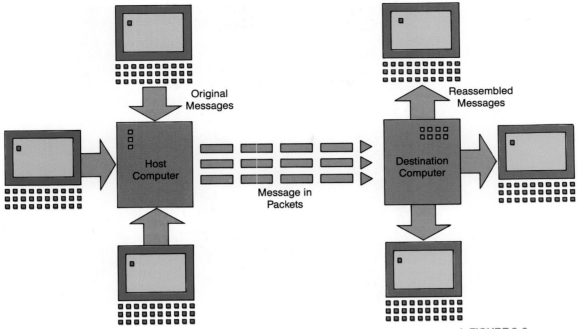

Original Messages

Host Computer

Message in Packets

Reassembled Messages

Destination Computer

FIGURE 8-6
Packet Switching Network

or **nodes,** can send electronic mail to a user at another subscribing institution if he or she knows the other user's network address, PMCK@UGA, for example. This is very useful for professors or researchers, because they can send messages, letters, or even papers to colleagues throughout the United States, Europe, and the Middle East.

A WAN called ARPANet (for Advanced Research Projects Agency Network) was set up by the U.S. Department of Defense to link defense-oriented researchers. ARPANet spans the United States. Its success encouraged the development of several related networks, including NSFNet (National Science Foundation Network), which links many subnetworks of research universities.

Finally, MCI Mail is a commercial electronic mail system that allows subscribers to send messages electronically across the country.

Private Networks

When a private company wants to set up a wide area network to connect its mainframes or to link its own or outside terminals into its mainframes, it must decide the type of telecommunications media that will be used: standard or wide area telecommunications service (WATS) lines, a dedicated private line leased from a telephone company (called a **leased line**), or satellite communications. This decision will depend on the number of transmissions to be made and the quality and speed required of the transmissions. Some computer networks require high-quality, high-speed lines on a frequent basis, making the use of leased lines or satellite transmissions economical. Other networks will find the use of standard, low-speed, voice-quality lines adequate and economical.

In addition to selecting the type of transmission facility, a company using a private network must decide whether it will manage the telecommunications

```
┌─From NFPKP@DUCVAX.TEXAS.EDU,  14 Jul.92  9:19 ──────────────────── 1 of 8 ─┐
│Date:      Tue, 14 Jul 1992 09:19 CST                                        │
│From:      NFPKP@DUCVAX.TEXAS.EDU                                            │
│Subject:   Re: Summer Issue of National Forum                               │
│To:        PMCKEOWN@cbacc.cba.uga.edu                                        │
│                                                                            │
│                                                                            │
│Patrick:                                                                     │
│                                                                            │
│Did you get a reply to your message?  We had your article typeset and it is │
│on the way in the process, but we are not completed here...may be 2-3 more   │
│weeks at least before issue is out...                                        │
│                                                                            │
│Sorry for not getting back to you before now.  Let me know if you have not  │
│seen galleys of your article....I believe Mary Lister has already sent       │
│them to you, has she not?                                                    │
│                                                                            │
│Advise,                                                                      │
│Stephen W. Brown                                                             │
│                                                                            │
│                                                                            │
│                                                                            │
│                                                                            │
└─ +/- <F5>-mark <Del> Copy Forward Headers Move Print Reply eXtract ──── 5% ─┘
```

Professors and researchers at universities and research centers worldwide can send and receive messages electronically using electronic mail.

function itself or hire an outside telecommunications company. This management role includes determining the speed and routing of transmissions and the error-checking mechanisms used to ensure that data are correctly transmitted.

Value-Added Networks

The third alternative for wide area networks is value-added networks. **Value-added networks (VANs)** are public networks that are available by subscription and provide their clients with data communications facilities. The company that runs the VAN assumes complete responsibility for managing the network, including providing conversion between different systems. In addition, VANs often offer other services, such as multiple terminal sessions, electronic mail, and access to network data bases. In a sense, a VAN adds value to the data by ensuring that it reaches its destination with little effort on the part of the subscriber.

A VAN works for its subscribers by providing connections or **ports** to its wide area network through a local telephone call. Once the subscriber accesses the network, data are routed between the local terminal and a long-distance host computer that is connected to the network by a leased line. By using communications channels that are shared among many users, these public data networks take advantage of economies of scale to provide these services at an acceptable cost to their clients. In some cases, it is also possible to forward data from one VAN to another to reach a destination computer that is not linked to the user's VAN. Figure 8-7 depicts a value-added network.

This network control center manages and monitors Tymnet's public (VAN) network worldwide.

FIGURE 8-7
Value-Added Network

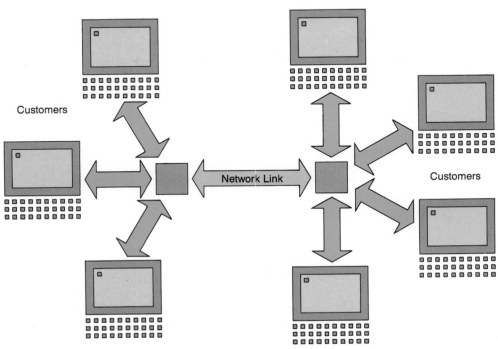

Customers

Network Link

Customers

Examples of VANs include Infonet, Tymnet, GTE Telenet, CompuServe, and AT&T Information Services NET. In some cases, a company will subscribe to multiple VANs—to ensure that its clients will always have a network available to them through a local telephone call and to take advantage of lower rates in different markets.

Computer Networks and DDP

Networks are important in the area of **distributed data processing (DDP)**, which attempts to place computing power as close as possible to the point of actual information processing, as compared to the centralization of computer resources. Using the evolving telecommunications technology, DDP networks are capable of connecting mainframes, minicomputers, and personal computers together. DDP allows a computer-based information system to be designed to match organizational structure, to support unique business strategies, and to provide a more natural use of information systems.

How does DDP work? As an example, assume that a manufacturing plant firm has one central administrative office and several plants located in different parts of the country. A mainframe in the administrative office handles data processing that involves the firm as a whole. Minicomputers and PCs at each manufacturing plant handle the processing for that site. The smaller computers are linked to the mainframe by some form of communications link that allows them to obtain information from the mainframe and send back the result of the processing handled locally. The mainframe stores the company's primary data base, and the smaller computers have local data bases, or **distributed data bases,** that are separate from the primary data base. The smaller computers can also access the primary data base for needed information.

DDP has certain obvious advantages. The users of the smaller computers are not held up by competing for access to the mainframe; at the same time, the mainframe's processing load is reduced. In addition, local users can customize software to fit their individual needs and can develop their own computer-based information systems. At the same time, they can interface with the central computer. These advantages often result in lower costs for the organization as a whole.

On the other hand, problems with DDP include lack of data security of the communications links, inconsistency between the software and hardware at the local sites and the software and hardware at the central computer, and possibly less technical support at the local sites than at the central site. The hardware inconsistency is aggravated when users attempt to interface personal computers with the mainframe or with local minicomputers. Users often find that their personal computers cannot "talk" to the mainframe or transfer data without additional hardware or software.

Electronic Data Interchange

The use of computer networks in business for **electronic data interchange (EDI)** is growing. EDI allows computers to exchange electronic transmissions of data and information and, therefore, automate much routine business between retail stores, distributors, and manufacturers. Instead of sending paper documents, such as purchase orders, invoices, bills of lading, shipping slips, and so forth, back and forth through traditional communication channels, EDI allows companies to transmit the same information electronically between their computers. By combining EDI with point-of-sale inventory systems, a computer at a retail store can automatically order goods, based on sales, from its supplier. The supplier, in turn, can automatically ship the goods to the retail store and electronically transmit the appropriate document. EDI greatly reduces human involvement in the ordering and shipping process, thereby reducing costs and speeding service.

TELECOMMUNICA-TIONS ON THE PERSONAL COMPUTER

One of the most popular uses of the personal computer is for telecommunications, either with a mainframe or with another PC. Using a PC, a modem, and communications software, the user can access a wide range of information sources, goods and services, and other PC users. The uses of the PC for telecommunications fall into five broad categories: accessing information sources, interacting with other users, using electronic mail, telecommuting, and using videotex. Before going into these in detail, we will briefly discuss the concepts and terminology of PC telecommunications.

Personal Computer Telecommunications Concepts and Terminology

To understand how a computer can send and receive data and information, first recall that the information in a computer is stored and manipulated in the form of bits. A **bit** is *an electronic pulse (one) or the absence of a pulse (zero)*. Before the information in this electronic form can be transmitted, it usually must be translated into a form that the communications linkage can accommodate. This translation process has two steps: conversion of data from parallel to serial form and conversion of digital data into an analog form.

To understand the first step, note that, within the computer, data are stored and processed in a **parallel form**—16, 32, or 64 bits at a time, depending on the type of computer. On the other hand, data being transmitted must be sent one bit at a time in what is called **serial form.** To understand the difference, think of parallel form as bits marching through the computer 16, 32, or 64 abreast and serial form as the same bits moving in single file. The computer's **serial port** converts parallel data into a serial form for transmission or converts serial data back into a parallel form.

The second step of the translation process involves converting the data, which are now in a serial form, from the binary "on–off" state that is used in the computer into an **analog equivalent** that can be telecommunicated. The word *analog* refers to a physical relationship that represents data. The physical relationship is an electrical wave form that the communication link can carry. For example, to be sent over an ordinary telephone line, information must be converted to an audio form; that is, a one-bit is translated into one tone and a zero-bit into another tone. The translation from binary to the analog form of data is carried out by a device known as a **modem.** The name *modem* comes from

Prodigy (screen shown right) has proved to be a popular form of telecommunications for all family members.

the conversion of digital data into analog data through a process known as MODulation and the reverse process known as DEModulation.

When a bit is modulated, it is converted into a particular wave form. There exists one frequency that represents the digit 0 and a second frequency to represent the digit 1. When these frequencies are demodulated, they are converted back into a 0 or a 1. Figure 8-8 demonstrates the process of sending information from one computer to another over telephone lines.

Data can be sent between computers in one of two modes: synchronous or asynchronous. In **synchronous communications**, large numbers of characters

are sent as a block, whereas in **asynchronous communications**, the characters are sent one at a time. Synchronous communications are much faster but also require more expensive equipment. Most communications between two PCs or between a PC and a larger computer are asynchronous and involve only the purchase of an inexpensive modem and appropriate software.

Asynchronous communications modulate and demodulate ten bits, usually the first seven bits of the ASCII representation of a character, *plus* three other bits. Only seven ASCII bits are needed because they are enough to represent all characters of the alphabet. The three additional bits are the start bit, parity bit, and stop bit. The **start bit** is before each character and signals the computer that

FIGURE 8-8
Communication between Computers

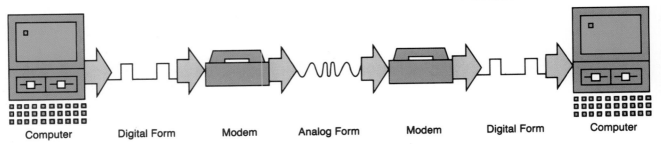

| Computer | Digital Form | Modem | Analog Form | Modem | Digital Form | Computer |

a character is coming. A **parity bit** is immediately after the character and checks the number of 1-bits in the character to see if the computer correctly received the character. If even parity is specified, there should be an even number of 1-bits in the signal; similarly, if odd parity is specified, there should be an odd number of 1-bits. Finally, the **stop bit** is after the parity bit and notifies the computer that the previous character is complete. Characters are always preceded and followed by strings of 1's that fill the gaps between characters. If necessary, all eight bits for a character may be used by dropping the parity bit.

Figure 8-9 demonstrates three different representations of the letter A (1000001 in ASCII) as it is transmitted over a telephone line. In all three representations, the following have been added: a start bit of zero at the beginning of the character, a parity bit of one (even parity) after the character, and a stop bit of one at the end of the bit-string. The first representation is in binary form. Next, the bits are shown as square waves before entering the modem and then as audio waves after the modulation. In all three representations, the part that represents the character is shown in a box to distinguish it from the start and stop bits. Demodulation is simply the reverse of this—sound waves are converted into pulses that are equivalent to the character representation.

The speed at which modems can send and receive information is measured by the number of **bits per second** (bps) that can be transmitted. For modems used with personal computers, rates of 1,200, 2,400, and 9,600 bps are the standard. Since each character in asynchronous communication is equivalent to 10 bits, a rate of 1,200 bps is approximately equal to 120 characters per second. Modems can be either **internal** or **external,** depending on whether they are installed inside the computer or connect to the serial port and sit outside the computer. Most modems now have the capability to dial or answer your phone

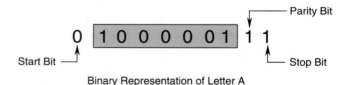

Binary Representation of Letter A

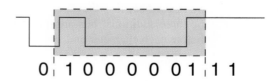

Digital Equivalent of Binary Representation

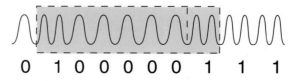

Analog Representation After Modulation

FIGURE 8-9
Demonstration of Modulation
Process

(known as **autodial** and **autoanswer**), to hang up the phone if a busy signal is reached, or even to dial a second number if the first is busy.

If you are buying a modem, a crucial consideration is **Hayes compatibility,** that is, whether it uses the same commands as a Hayes modem. The communications system in Hayes modems has become an industry standard, so it is important to ensure that any modem you purchase is Hayes compatible.

When a modem is used to connect a terminal or personal computer to another computer, the communication can be in one of three modes: simplex, half-duplex, or full-duplex. When the communication is possible in only one direction, the **mode** is **simplex.** Communication between computers is in the **half-duplex mode** if only one computer can send information at any one time. On the other hand, the communication is in the **full-duplex mode** if both computers can send information at the same time. Half-duplex is like a bridge that allows only one car to cross at a time; full-duplex is like a bridge that allows cars to cross in both directions simultaneously. When half-duplex is used, one computer sends and the second receives, then the second sends and the first receives. When half-duplex is used, the screen of the sending computer usually will show the same signal that is being transmitted, but when full-duplex is used, the receiving computer will send the signal back to the screen of the sending computer. Thus, with full-duplex the user can check the accuracy of the signal being received by having it sent back to the originating computer. Most communications involving personal computers use the full-duplex mode. Figure 8-10 shows half-duplex and full-duplex communication between computers.

The final consideration for a modem is what is known as the protocol for the communication. The **protocol** is the set of rules that the two computers will follow in sending and receiving information. With the continuing standardization of modems, this has become much less of a consideration than it once was.

A personal computer is not capable of sending or receiving information without special instructions. The **communications software** used to carry out telecommunications on a PC is another type of "personal productivity" software in that it allows the PC to be used for many tasks, including dialing telephone numbers, answering calls, sending and receiving data and information over the telephone line, and accessing other computers. Software packages like ProComm Plus, PC-Talk, and Crosstalk are all examples of communications software that allows the PC to communicate with other computers.

Now that you know a little bit about the technology of PC communications, we can turn our attention to the five primary uses of a PC for communications: accessing information sources, interacting with other users, using electronic mail, telecommuting, and videotex.

**FIGURE 8-10
Types of Computer
Communications**

Half-Duplex

Full–Duplex

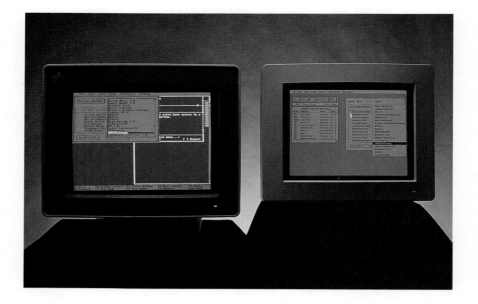

Accessing Information Sources

One of the oldest uses of telecommunications is to obtain information from the various data bases that have been available on a commercial basis since 1972. Information can be obtained from online services, from data base vendors, or directly from the data bases. There are currently over 3,500 data bases that can be reached from a personal computer.

Online services are companies that provide computerized information to their subscribers. Users can reach the online services through a local call or a toll-free (800) number. The services offer a wide range of information, including a general information category of the type found in an encyclopedia. They also offer news services, newspaper articles, business and financial information, stock market quotes, magazine articles, airline schedules, and medical information. Most of them also provide such services as electronic mail, special interest groups (SIGs) on various topics, and gateways into other electronic services such as the American Airlines reservation service and the Official Airline Guide. These online services have an initial subscription charge plus hourly charges that vary according to the time of day and the number of bps. The most popular online services are CompuServe, with close to 600,000 subscribers; GEnie, with over 100,000 subscribers; and Prodigy, with over 1 million subscribers.

Data base vendors offer many full-text data bases from newspapers, magazines, scientific journals, and so on. They also offer data bases with only bibliographic citations, abstracts, or summaries. Data base vendors also tend to specialize in specific topic areas. For example, Lexis offers data bases that cover federal and state court decisions, and the Dow Jones New/Retrieval tends to specialize in business news. Once in a specific data base, a PC user can specify a subject, such as "computer," and then receive a list of all available references on this subject. The information is taken from among the many data bases that are stored in each service. In some cases, the full article may be accessed; in others, only a bibliographic listing and a summary of the article are available. There is often overlap between data base vendors since they do not actually

create the data bases but purchase them from outside companies who collect and compile the information.

Costs for using one of these encyclopedic data base services are charged by the hour and can range from $25 an hour to $300 an hour. This may seem expensive, but remember what the user receives for that cost. When the user initiates a search for a topic, it is possible that *every* reference to that topic will be found in 15 minutes! Compare this with a search in the library that could take days to complete, and you will see why these services are well worth the cost. Examples of data base vendors include BRS, Dialog, Dow Jones New/ Retrieval Service, Lexis, Nexis, and WestLaw.

The actual data bases that may be accessed through an online service or a data base vendor are quite varied. And in some cases, the user may access the data base directly without going through one of the data base services. Table 8-1 will give you an idea of the types of data bases that are available.

Interacting with Other Users

Just as the personal computer enables users to obtain information from mainframe computer data banks and information services, it may also enable them

TABLE 8-1
Examples of Online Data Bases

Data Base	Topics Covered
Dun's Market Identifiers	A directory of 2 million U.S. businesses
Forbes 500 Annual Directory	A ranking of the 500 largest U.S. companies
Business Periodical Index	An index to articles from 476 legal periodicals
CENDATA	Economic and demographic data on 200 countries
Career Placement Directory	Resumés in over 200 occupations
Books in Print	Over 1 million bibliographic references
Insurance Data Bases	Laws relating to insurance
AP Online	News stories from the Associated Press

Source: Scott Spanbauer, "On-line Services and Data Bases," *PC World,* October 1988, pp. 200–202.

THE "WIRED" CAMPUS

Students at Drew University in New Jersey are "wired" to each other, to faculty members, to the library, and to the world through a communication and information network that connects all offices and dorm rooms. So that all students can take advantage of this network, they are provided with a PC that is paid for with part of their tuition. The network includes a data network, voice system, and broadband network. The data network links the academic computing system, the library, all PCs on campus, and external networks that provide electronic mail, data base, and information services. The voice system provides enhanced telecommunications facilities, including voice mail. The broadband network provides every student room and classroom on campus with high-speed video (TV) and data transmission.

Drew students and faculty are using these networks in many ways. Voice and electronic mail are widely used for assigning and submitting coursework and research projects. Voice mail is widely used for class announcements, including updates, reminders, and other timely notifications. E-mail is used by many members of the Drew community to communicate not only among themselves but, at no additional cost, with faculty and students at other institutions. The broadband network enables Drew faculty members to include educational broadcasts in their courses.

The network technology available at Drew is also used in more innovative ways. For example, students discovered that they could create a "chain" voice mail message, which resulted in the creation of a 60-minute version of "The Twelve Days of Christmas" as students added a new verse each time the message was forwarded. In another case, the network was responsible for saving a Drew student's life. The student used her computer to communicate regularly with a friend in Ithaca, New York. When she communicated that she was depressed and had taken drugs and alcohol, the Ithaca student contacted administrators at Drew, who immediately located the Drew student and provided emergency care.

Source: Drew University press release, September 1991.

to interact directly with other users. This interaction can take place in one of two ways: through a bulletin board service or through participation in a teleconference. In a **bulletin board service,** a user, club, or corporation combines a computer with one or more telephone lines, a modem, and a type of communications software that allows users to call in and "post" messages on the electronic bulletin board for other users to see. Both CompuServe and Prodigy have national bulletin board facilities, and there are an estimated 30,000 local bulletin boards around the country. Local bulletin boards get along quite well with a personal computer, while the national bulletin boards require the speed and storage capabilities available only on mainframes.

One of the most popular uses of a bulletin board—whether a national one or a local one sponsored by a user's group—is the exchange of public domain

Teleconferencing with special microphones and video equipment brings geographically separated parties "face to face."

software. This is software that has not been copyrighted and so can be copied without violation of copyright laws. Exchanging software (or other information) involves **downloading** and saving the software. If software is being sent from the user's PC disk to the host computer, it is being **uploaded.**

Since the mainframe host computers of national services like CompuServe and Prodigy can serve multiple users simultaneously, conferences or other multiple-user sessions can take place on these services, ranging from informal "gab" sessions to formal, long-term conferences on a particular topic. For formal teleconferencing, it is possible to have a real-time conference or a delayed conference. In a **real-time conference,** all participants are actually logged onto the system at the time of the conference. In a **delayed conference,** the comments of the participants are stored sequentially as they are entered. In the latter case a conference can go on for months, with participants taking whatever time they need to formulate replies to comments already made by others. Normally, a real-time conference would be used to address a pressing topic that requires a quick resolution, while the delayed conference might be used for philosophical or policy questions that do not require immediate decisions. Teleconferencing has also become popular as a means of training employees in widely separated locations around the country.

Electronic Mail

Just as electronic mail is very useful within the organization and over wide area networks, it is also useful for communications on a PC. In fact, PC users often have access to the same wide area network mail services as are available to mainframe users. In addition, PC users can use the electronic mail services of such operations as CompuServe and Prodigy, which offer the facility to communicate with other subscribers through their electronic mail services. A subscriber can send a "letter" to another subscriber by "addressing" it to the recipient's account number.

A lot of people are able to talk at once without stepping on toes.

Robert E. Johnson, director of research and business development, Phelps Dodge

Quoted in "At These Shouting Matches, No One Says a Word," *Business Week,* June 11, 1990, p. 78.

Telecommuting

One of the very first forms of telecommunications involved using a portable terminal to call back to a mainframe in order to work on some project. The introduction of the personal computer made this approach easier by lessening the need for access to a mainframe. Now employees can use their personal computers at some location other than the office, store the results on disk, and then download them to a computer at work. These workers are said to be **telecommuting** to work, and in 1988, there were an estimated 27 million of them. In addition, there are now almost 15 million home-based businesses, and this number is expected to grow to almost 21 million by 1995.

Basically, there are three types of telecommuters: individuals who use their personal computers to access the office mainframe to avoid having to make a trip to the office, individuals who use their personal computers at home to continue or finish work begun at the office, and individuals who usually work on a personal computer at home full time. For the first two types of telecommuter, having a computer at home is a convenience that allows them to complete their work more quickly and easily. For the third type of telecommuter, work at home becomes a way of life.

Of course, there are problems with any of the three types of telecommuting. The mainframe user may have problems reaching a free line into the computer and may end up using the home telephone line for long periods of time. The individual who uses the personal computer at home to complete work begun at the office faces problems with accessing the data bases on the office mainframe: Often these mainframes are not set up for access from the outside, and the company's MIS department must be willing to change its policies toward outside access.

For the telecommuter who works at home the majority of the time, what may be perceived as the perfect work situation has its own set of problems involving time management and lack of interaction with co-workers and superiors in the office.

Videotex

When a new avenue of communication opens, businesses are always quick to take advantage of it for advertising and selling. The "opening" of the telecommunications avenue was no different. **Videotex** refers to a system that combines the computer, telephone, modem, and software to allow users to view and purchase various services and products. Although videotex is widely used in France, where it is supported by the telephone company, it is a relatively small industry in the United States. Several attempts have been made to start videotex companies here, with Prodigy the most recent example. It was introduced by IBM and Sears in 1988.

Prodigy's features are similar to those of CompuServe and GEnie, other information sources, but Prodigy brings colorful graphics to videotex. Currently, over 1 million people subscribe to Prodigy, but experts believe that 2.5 million individuals must subscribe to Prodigy before Sears and IBM can break even on their investment, which means that Prodigy must continue to grow if it is to become a financial success.

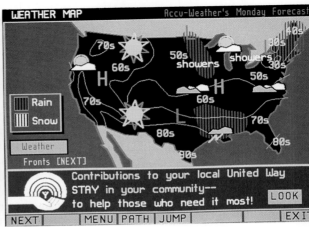

```
                                    WORLD STOCKS
▓▓▓MARKET UPDATE                Nov 12  3:54 pm ET

INDEX                 LAST    CHANGE  PCT CHG      TIME
Sydney All Ordinaries 1677.00  -  16.40  -  .97  Tue Close
Tokyo Nikkei Index   24667.73  + 434.74  + 1.79  Tue Close
Hong Kong Hang Seng   4253.02  +  22.11  +  .52  Tue Close
Singapore Straits     1482.20  -   9.22  -  .62  Tue Close
Frankfurt DAX         1621.22  +  12.20  +  .76  Tue Close
Paris CAC-40          1858.44  +    .89  +  .05  Tue Close
Zurich Swiss Index    1108.20  +   6.70  +  .61  Tue Close
London FTSE-100       2575.50  +  20.60  +  .81  Tue Close
New York DJ Indus     3055.68  +  13.42  +  .44   3:30 pm
Toronto Composite     3600.25  +  20.95  +  .59   3:09 pm
                                        World Gold [NEXT]
 Topics  Notes
        PLACE AN AD FOR TWO WEEKS
   FOR THE PRICE OF ONE WEEK!
   When you place an On-line Classified in
   selected BUSINESS CATEGORIES in November. LOOK
 NEXT      MENU PATH JUMP          HELP EXIT
```

With the Prodigy videotex system, users can carry on many different activities, including checking their stock portfolio.

Prodigy offers its subscribers a number of services; for example, they can purchase such things as clothing, sporting goods, airline tickets, and computer hardware and software. They can view news stories and weather, bank at home, use electronic mail, and play games. As previously noted, Prodigy is similar to CompuServe, but it uses a colorful graphic menu system, which makes it popular among first-time computer users. Its banking and shopping features also distinguish Prodigy from other online services or data bases.

THE FUTURE OF TELE-COMMUNICATIONS

Even as this is being written, telecommunications technology is evolving even further. In fact, telecommunications is the one area that may be changing faster than computer technology! In addition to increasing the use of fiber optics and satellites as communications media, technology is evolving by replacing analog transmissions with digital (binary) voice transmissions. The transition to a digital standard called **integrated services digital network (ISDN)** will make possible the transmission of all types of signals—voice, video, data, and so on—on the same lines. Many experts expect that as ISDN becomes a standard, there will

Two more features of Prodigy are bulletin boards (left) and nationwide weather information (right).

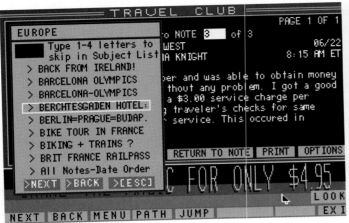

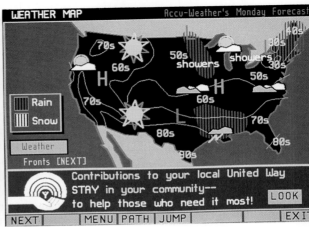

USING PRODIGY FOR TRIP PLANNING

As discussed in the text, Prodigy is now one of the most widely-used electronic information sources in the United States. It is also a videotex service on which members can purchase goods. And, as the author discovered, it can be very useful for planning an overseas trip.

Prodigy was used in several ways to plan a trip for four (the author's entire family) to Australia in the summer of 1991. It helped us find the least expensive airfare from the United States to Australia and between cities within Australia. We checked weather forecasts in Australia, and, through the Prodigy Travel Club bulletin board, we discussed travel options with members who had been to Australia.

For airfares, we accessed the Eaasy Sabre airline guide to find the lowest fares. Had we chosen, we also could have purchased the tickets through Eaasy Sabre. Even after we purchased the tickets, however, we were able to obtain a refund from the Australian airline, because a random check of the airline guide showed that the company had reduced its fare from Sydney to Cairns after we had purchased our tickets.

By tracking Australia's winter weather patterns on the Prodigy weather service, we were able to decide which types of clothes to pack. The weather service was especially important because it correctly predicted that an extended warm spell in Sydney would end before our arrival and that cold and wet conditions would prevail while we were in Sydney.

By leaving queries on the Prodigy Travel Club bulletin board, we obtained much useful information about hotels, restaurants, tours, and so on. These queries were answered by members who had been to Australia, or as it is known to Prodigy members, the "Land of Oz." In some cases, E-mail was used to carry on extended correspondence regarding specific questions.

be a tremendous increase in the use of home-related information services, resulting in turn in users having better access to the large institutional data bases discussed earlier in this chapter. Another direction of future growth is **wireless LANs,** that is, local area networks that use radio waves for transmission of data rather than wires.

REVIEW OF KEY POINTS

1. The electronic transmission of information is known as telecommunications.
2. Two or more computers tied together with communications links form a computer network.
3. A popular form of telecommunications that does not always involve computers is the use of the facsimile (fax) machine.
4. Local area network (LANs) are personal computer networks at a single location. They can facilitate the transfer of information and the sharing of secondary storage devices, peripherals, and data bases.
5. Popular types of LANs are ring, star, and bus.
6. When computer communications are required over long distances, wide area networks (WANs) are used. There are three types of WANs: specialized networks, private networks, and value-added networks (VANs).
7. Distributed data processing (DDP) uses small computers to handle local processing and to relieve the central mainframe of

some processing chores. Electronic data interchange (EDI) allows companies to electronically order and pay for raw materials and finished goods.

8. A computer can be combined with a telephone, a modem, and communications software to allow the user to communicate with other users and computers.

9. Important uses of telecommunications include finding information, interacting with other users, sending and receiving electronic mail, shopping and banking by computer, and working from home using a computer.

10. CompuServe, GEnie, and Prodigy are online services that offer the user many telecommunication functions.

11. Data base vendors provide access to a large number of data bases and are a wide-ranging source of information.

12. A user can interact with users at other locations through electronic bulletin boards and teleconferences.

13. Electronic mail enables a computer user to send messages and documents over long distances instantaneously and to communicate more efficiently with other users in the same office or local network.

14. The number of individuals working at home has increased with the availability of personal computers and communications packages.

15. Communications software and services enable people to use the computer for such everyday activities as buying goods and services, carrying out their banking, and managing their stock portfolio.

16. The future of telecommunications appears to be in the implementation of the integrated services digital network (ISDN), which will use an all-digital communications system.

KEY TERMS

analog equivalent
asynchronous communication
autoanswer modem
autodial modem
bit
bits per second (bps)
bridge
broadband transmission
bulletin board service
bus
bus network
client-server configuration
coaxial cable
communications software
compound document
computer network
data base vendor
data communication
delayed conference
diskless workstation

distributed data processing (DDP)
distributed data base
downloading
downsizing
dumb terminal
electronic data interchange (EDI)
electronic mail (E-mail)
external modem
facsimile machine
fax machine
fiber optic cable
file-server configuration
full-duplex mode
gateway
half-duplex mode
Hayes compatibility
host computer
integrated services digital network (ISDN)
internal modem

leased line
local area network (LAN)
microwave
modem
multiple access network
network operating system
node
online service
packet
packet switching
parallel form
parity bit
peer-to-peer configuration
port
protocol
real-time conference
ring network
serial form

serial port
simplex mode
star network
start bit
stop bit
synchronous communication
telecommunications
telecommuting
terminal emulation
token
token sharing network
twisted pairs
uploading
value-added network (VAN)
videotex
voice-grade transmission
wide area network (WAN)
wireless LANs

1. Define *telecommunications*. What is a compound document?

2. What is the difference between a "dumb" terminal and a "smart" terminal? What is "terminal emulation"?

3. Give an example of a computer network other than those listed in the text.

4. How is fax communication like PC communication? How is it different?

5. How are computer networks differentiated by size? Which type of network would normally be found in a college or university?

6. Give three reasons why a LAN is useful. What does a file server have to do with the use of a LAN?

7. Describe three commonly used types of LANs and give an example of each.

8. Describe the three types of wide area networks. Why is packet switching used in these networks?

9. What are the advantages and disadvantages of DDP?

10. List the five main categories of use of the PC for telecommunications.

11. List the steps necessary to send data and information between computers. Why are start and stop bits necessary in asynchronous communications?

12. Discuss the difference between simplex, half-duplex, and full-duplex modes of communication between computers. What is a protocol used for?

13. What is the difference between an online service and a data base vendor? Give an example of each.

14. List the advantages and disadvantages of telecommuting. Name three services that Prodigy can provide.

15. What does ISDN have to do with the future of telecommunications?

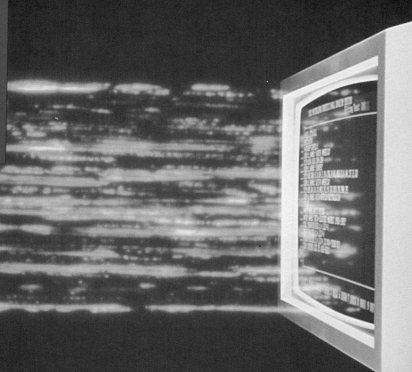

9

An Introduction to Information Systems

This chapter is an overview of information systems and their impact on organizations. We will define information systems, discuss them briefly, and then discuss each of the types of information systems that are used in organizations. The chapter next takes up the process known as systems analysis and design for assessing and solving problems within information systems. A seven-step procedure is outlined for systems analysis and design and an important type of problem that is addressed by systems analysis and design—software development—is discussed.

STUDY OBJECTIVES

After reading this chapter, you should be able to

- understand the importance of information systems to any organization;
- describe the various managerial levels in an organization;
- discuss various types of information systems and their relationship to managerial levels;
- understand the role of the office information system relative to the other types of information systems;
- describe the characteristics of an expert system and a strategic information system;
- understand the systems analysis and design process and the role of the systems analyst;
- list the seven steps in the systems life cycle and discuss the role each plays in the analysis and design of an information system;
- explain the relationship between software development and the process of systems analysis and design.

INFORMATION SYSTEMS AT WAL-MART

One of the reasons that Wal-Mart is the fastest-growing retailer in the United States is its emphasis on the use of information systems (IS) to support retail operations. Wal-Mart, which grew from 276 stores to over 1,400 by 1990, has always viewed information technology as a key part of its strategic thrust. As one industry analyst put it,

Wal-Mart stands out in the use of information technology because it was the first retailer to realize that IS was "integral to their success. They've been pursuing this for the last ten years." It is estimated that Wal-Mart has invested over $500 million in information technology over the last five years.

Wal-Mart has the industry's first private satellite network, which links almost 1,600 computers at stores, distribution centers, and central management in Arkansas. This satellite network gives Wal-Mart the capability to collect and distribute ordering and sales information quickly. It also allows for the constant flow of information between the operating, merchandising, and distributing functions. Wal-Mart also has information systems that monitor each store's daily sales and

inventory and send these data to Wal-Mart's 17 distribution centers around the country. This allows Wal-Mart to provide a "quick response" to sales trends without carrying large in-store inventories—the retail industry's equivalent to the use of just-in-time systems in the manufacturing industry.

In addition to these systems, online storage capacity is growing at the rate of 100 percent per year, and about 5,000 terminals are added each year, including point-of-sale devices, personal computers, and handheld radio units. There are also over 4,000 users of the company's office information system.

Source: Ellis Booker, "IS Trailblazing Puts Retailer on Top," *Computerworld*, February 12, 1990, pp. 69–70.

Wal-Mart's point-of-sale/IS system has helped to make it one of the nation's fastest-growing retail chains.

INFORMATION SYSTEMS IN ORGANIZATIONS

Recall from Chapter 1 that information systems are crucial to an organization's well-being because of the value of information. Multiple information systems are often required to facilitate the processing, storage, retrieval, and flow of information throughout the organization. This is clearly shown in the box that discusses the importance of information systems to the success of the retailing giant Wal-Mart. An **information system** may be defined as *a combination of support staff, hardware, and software that facilitates the processing, storage, retrieval, and flow of information to support decision making.* In this definition, information systems are more than just computer hardware and software; they also must include the all-important human support staff, and they must serve to support the managerial decision making that ultimately determines the future well-being of the organization.

At one time, information systems depended strictly on manual processing of raw data into information that managers used in making decisions. For the last 30 years, the computer has taken over more and more of this manual processing. Now the **computer-based information system (CBIS)** has become synonymous with the concept of the information system in general, and it would be virtually impossible for businesses to be competitive without computers. The term **data processing** has been closely tied to CBISs because of the need to process data into a meaningful form. However, data processing is only the purely mechanical function of processing raw data. For a CBIS to be truly useful to management, it must provide the information in a useful form, for example, as a report, as graphics, or as spreadsheet analysis. This requires a data base management system of the type discussed in Chapter 7 to store the processed data in a data base. Recall that a **data base** is a collection of information that is arranged for easy manipulation and retrieval. Once stored in the data base, the information can be retrieved as needed by the **data base management system (DBMS).** A conceptual CBIS is shown in Figure 9-1, which illustrates the relationship between raw data, information, the data base, and the DBMS.

> **At one time the computer was viewed as a service to handle the payroll or inventory. Now people are realizing that it is becoming the competitive edge that makes the company successful.**
>
> *John Imlay, chairman, Management Science America; past president, Association of Data Processing Service Organizations*
>
> From an interview with the author.

Systems in General

An information system is one of many *systems* that simultaneously coexist within an organization. A **system** is *a group of elements (people, machines, cells, etc.) organized for the purpose of achieving a particular goal.* Within the organization, there may also be a management system, a manufacturing system, a distribution system, and so forth. However, because the information system provides information to all of these other systems, and because it relies on computers, we provide an in-depth discussion of it in this chapter. While the discussion of systems analysis and design later in the chapter is aimed at developing information systems, the process can be used in developing any type of system.

Most systems have some attributes in common, including input, processing, output, feedback, an environment, and a boundary. The **input, processing, and output** elements have much the same relationships in a system generally as they do in a computer. Data enter the system as input, which is processed in some way and then output as information. **Feedback** is a form of output that, when sent back to the input or processing function of the system for review, indicates to the system whether a change in operation is necessary. Feedback can come from within the system or from the environment. In a sense, feedback acts as a monitor to ensure that the system is meeting its goal.

Surrounding and interacting with the input, processing, output, and processing elements of the system are the environment and the boundary. The **environment** includes everything not in the system, and the **boundary** separates the system from the environment. Figure 9-2 shows the relationships among these elements.

As we said earlier, CBISs are extremely important to the efficient management of any organization. Various types of information systems have been

FIGURE 9-1
Conceptual View of CBIS

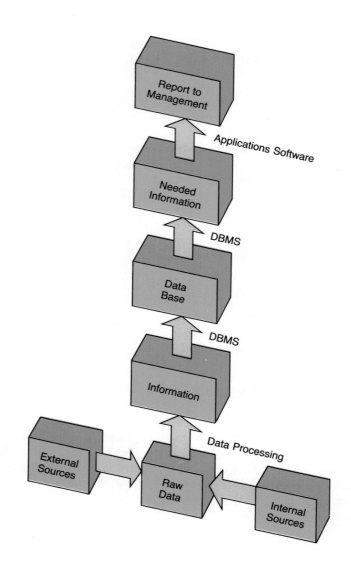

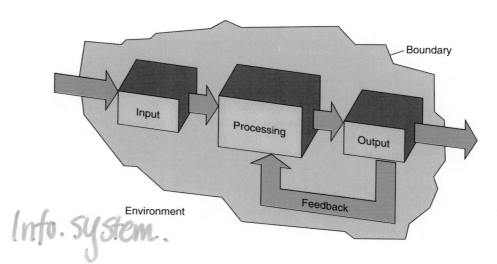

FIGURE 9-2
The Elements of a System

Info. system.

developed to meet the many needs of the decision makers for different types of information. These information systems may be classified according to the type of information they provide and the managerial level to which the information is provided. To help you understand how different types of information systems serve different managerial levels in the organization, we will first examine the managerial levels. Then we will discuss five different types of information systems—the transaction processing system, the management information system, the decision support system, the executive information system, and the office information system—and the ways in which they meet the information needs of the organization.

Managerial Levels

To understand the various types of information systems within an organization, we must look first at the various managerial levels in an organization. At the lowest, or *operational,* management level, the foremen and supervisors need detailed information on the day-to-day operation of the company's production process. These managers must make decisions about ordering parts, assigning jobs, checking shipments, and so on, and their decisions are made on the basis of rules and policies set at higher management levels. Because of the structure in the decisions at this level and because the decision maker can be given a list of rules to follow to make decisions, the decisions are said to be **programmable.**

At the next higher level in the organization are the middle-level managers, who need summary reports on the firm's operation to make **tactical decisions**

Operational managers like this factory supervisor often make programmed decisions based on the information they receive from various sources.

Middle-level managers often use decision support systems to help them make tactical decisions.

To make strategic decisions, top-level managers require the different types of information provided by an executive information system.

to implement the policy or **strategic decisions** made at the top level of the company. The decisions at these two upper levels are not as easily programmable as those at the lower level. The pyramid in Figure 9-3 demonstrates the relative number of people in the organization who make each type of decision.

From Figure 9-3 we can see that there is a broad base of day-to-day operational decision makers, fewer tactical decision makers, and only a few strategic decision makers. The flow of decision making is from the top down; each level depends on the level above for the policy to use in making its decisions. For the operational managers and some tactical managers, timely reports are very important to decision making. For the tactical and strategic managers, more long-term information about the financial health of the firm is needed. In addition, these managers must have the ability to make forecasts about the company's future. The various information systems in the organization must be designed to ensure that the appropriate information is available to each level of the managerial pyramid.

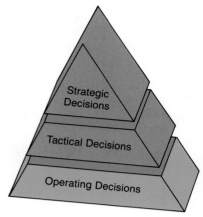

FIGURE 9-3
Levels of Management Decision Making

3 Levels of a
computer system

How Information Systems Support Management

There are five types of information systems that are commonly thought of as providing support for managerial decision making: the transaction processing system, the management information system, the decision support system, the executive information system, and the office information system. While some of these—notably the management information system—may be given a different name in some contexts, the function is generally the same, as we will describe shortly.

Figure 9-4 shows the three levels of management and their relationships to the various information systems. We see, at the bottom of the managerial pyramid, the **transaction processing system (TPS),** which supplies information to the operational manager about the many daily transactions that are the lifeblood of any organization. The TPS does this by performing the data processing function of converting raw data into a form that is stored in a data base and then accessed by the manager for the most up-to-date information. Once the information is in the data base, it is then possible to use a DBMS like those discussed

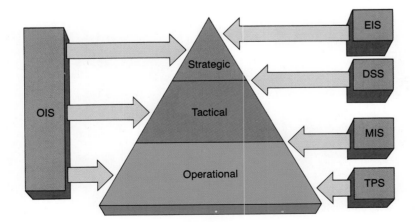

FIGURE 9-4
Relationship of Information Systems to Managerial Levels

> **Simply stated, a DSS is any system that can be used to increase the efficiency and effectiveness of the decision-making process.**
>
> *James Martin*
>
> From "DSS Applications Should Shed New Light on Problem," *PC Week*, May 1, 1989, p. 50.

in Chapter 7 on either a mainframe or a PC to retrieve the needed data. In addition to providing information directly to the operational managers, the data base is a source of information for the other types of information systems at the higher levels of management.

Transaction processing systems can be classified according to the manner in which the data are input, processed, and output; that is, the TPS can use batch, transactional, or real-time processing.

In a **batch processing system,** the data from multiple users or time periods are combined, input, and processed as a batch. Payroll systems are often batch systems. In **transactional processing,** each transaction is processed as it occurs. In a transactional processing system, the data are processed at the time of entry rather than being held for later processing. Grocery checkout systems are good examples of transactional processing systems. In **real-time processing,** the processing of the transaction can actually affect the transaction itself. Such processing may be necessary when several users are competing for the same resources, as with an airline reservation system.

At the level above the TPS in the managerial pyramid is the management information system. The **management information system (MIS)** is aimed at helping managers make decisions by providing them with reports that are timely and to the point. The MIS is very important to operational and lower-level tactical managers because they need the information from these reports to make their programmable decisions. While upper-level tactical and strategic managers also use the reports generated by the MIS, their decisions cannot be programmed and must depend on intuition and problem solving. For this reason, they use information from many other sources in addition to the MIS reports. An example of a report that would be provided by the MIS is one regarding the level of employee turnover in various departments. This report would be generated from attendance data provided by department managers and would aid the company personnel manager in making decisions about company personnel policies.

To further aid the upper levels of decision makers, a **decision support system (DSS)** combines data with mathematical models to provide alternative solutions to problems facing tactical and strategic managers. A DSS goes further than the MIS to help the decision maker with more complex problems. A DSS allows a decision maker to use mathematical models to determine the effect that different assumptions would have on the future of the company.

(Left) Modern batch systems can handle the huge volume of remittances that a large billing department must process. (Center) A transaction system such as this automated hotel checkout system processes data as they are entered. (Right) Airline reservation systems must use real-time transaction processing.

While both MIS and DSS help managers make decisions, there is a crucial difference between them that depends on the degree of structure in the decision. If a decision is highly structured—that is, if the decision can be made using set policies—then the reports that an MIS provides are sufficient to make the decision. For example, a decision on how many spare parts to keep on hand for production equipment can usually be made based on reports generated by an MIS. On the other hand, if the decision is unstructured and cannot be made using clearly defined policies, then a DSS must be used. For example, the decision on how to finance a company's debt might be based on forecasts on sales and future interest rates. This type of decision is very unstructured and must be made using the models supplied by a DSS.

At the top levels of management in many organizations, executives are just beginning to exploit the power of computers to provide them with the information needed to make decisions. In more and more cases, they are doing this through the use of an **executive information system (EIS).** An EIS differs from a DSS in that while the DSS uses models to find alternative solutions to problems, the EIS is a personalized means of presenting information to the top-level executive. Using an EIS, executives can monitor the daily operations of the organization using either a graphical or a report format to present the information. In many EISs a mouse or a touchscreen, rather than a keyboard, is used for input, allowing the executive to make selections quickly and easily by simply pointing to a picture. Also, the EIS depends on external data sources far more than either the MIS or the DSS since the top-level executive is often more interested in what is happening in national and global markets than are lower-level managers.

Note that in Figure 9-4, the **office information system (OIS)** is shown spanning the entire range of managerial levels, because the OIS provides a sup-

Managers frequently rely on decision support systems for help in solving complex problems.

port structure throughout the organization. For managers at all levels it provides printed reports through word processing and copying operations. It also provides quick communications between managers through electronic mail. The OIS facilitates managerial access to external information sources through facsimile transmission and other telecommunications operations. In general, OIS is the glue that holds the entire information system together by providing the needed support operations.

Table 9-1 summarizes the input, processing, output, and level of use for the five information systems discussed in this section.

Using Information Systems

As an example of the interaction of the various types of information systems, consider a company that has handwritten raw data on each of its transactions for the past month. Management wishes to find out which customers are purchasing the largest dollar volume from the company and which salespeople are doing the most business. The current handwritten data, because they are in the form of individual transactions and do not contain totals, is not useful to the company. Before these data on transactions can be used to answer management's questions, they must first be processed into an electronic form. This processing is handled by the transaction processing system and stored on a data base using the DBMS.

At this point, however, there is still only a large number of transactions, though now in an electronic rather than a paper form. The next step is for the

TABLE 9-1
Summary of Types of Information Systems

Information System	Input	Processing	Output	Level of Use
Transaction processing system (TPS)	Raw data	Conversion to information	Information in data base	Operational
Management information system (MIS)	Summary data from data base	Generation of reports	Reports on organizational activities	Operational and tactical
Decision support system (DSS)	Specific data from data base	Mathematical analyses; forecasts	Alternative solutions to problems	Tactical and strategic
Executive information system (EIS)	Internal and external data	Graphical presentations	Answers to questions	Strategic
Office information system (OIS)	Information to be transcribed, transmitted, or stored	Word processing; electronic mail; disk storage and retrieval	Paper and electronic documents; mail	All levels

MIS to retrieve specific information to generate reports that will answer some of management's questions. In this case, the specific information is the total sales for each customer, arranged in descending order of dollar volume, and the total sales for each salesperson, once again arranged in descending order by dollar volume. With a word processor, the OIS can then produce a printed report that will be forwarded to operational management and, if needed, to higher-level management.

At the same time, as in the process shown in Figure 9-5, the DSS may query the data base for specific information that can be used with a mathematical model to generate sales forecasts. These forecasts will go to middle management for use in preparing the next year's budget. The EIS can also use the data base to create a graphical presentation that upper management can then use to make long-range plans about the sales force and about various products.

Other Types of Information Systems

Two types of information systems that are becoming increasingly important to companies of all sizes are expert systems and strategic information systems. An **expert system (ES)** combines the knowledge and rules of several experts on a given subject and stores this information in the computer. The computer thus becomes an "expert" on the subject by synthesizing the knowledge and rules to aid humans in decision making. ESs have been successfully used in searching for oil, making medical diagnoses, finding problems with large machinery, and giving advice on business decisions. They were originally designed to run on mainframes or large minicomputers. However, with the increasing speed and size of PCs, they are now being used on many smaller computers.

While the traditional use of information systems is to automate basic operations such as payroll and to support managerial decision making, some forward-thinking companies are beginning to use their information systems as strategic weapons in the constant battle for market share. A **strategic information system (SIS)** is typically used to support or develop a company's competitive strategy.

> Strategic systems alone don't make a firm more competitive; they help people become more competitive.
>
> *Dean Meyer and Mary Boone, authors of* The Information Edge
>
> Quoted in "The End of the Rainbow," *Information Week,* July 23, 1990, p. 60.

FIGURE 9-5
Example Uses of Types of
Information Systems

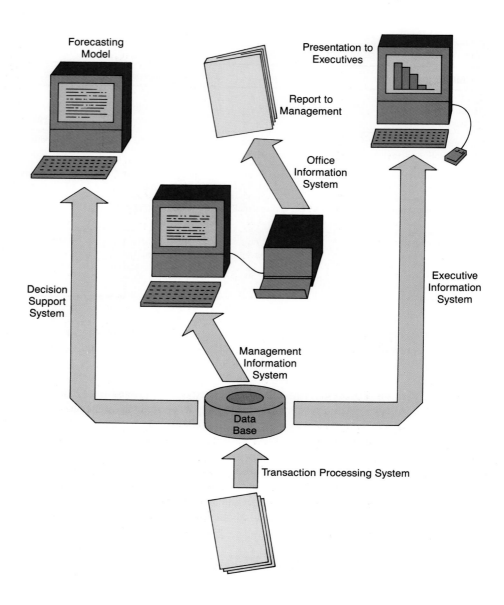

Forecasting Model

Presentation to Executives

Report to Management

Office Information System

Decision Support System

Management Information System

Data Base

Executive Information System

Transaction Processing System

Examples of the ways that an SIS can be used include increasing product differentiation, creating or distributing an innovative product, and reducing costs to increase the company's market penetration. As discussed in the box at the beginning of this chapter, Wal-Mart uses SISs to turn information to its competitive advantage.

SYSTEMS ANALYSIS AND DESIGN

As defined, all information systems are a combination of humans, hardware, and software. For an information system to carry out its purpose—that is, for it to support managerial decision making—it must be correctly designed and then

```
        The research is now complete, and Your Wine Advisor is selecting.

The bottlings that Anthony Dias Blue feels are most appropriate for your
selection criteria will now be listed sequentially, beginning with the best
selection.

Please wait. It will take a little more time to select your wines.

White wines are being selected to go with Shellfish and no sauce.




Hacienda Wine Cellar Chenin Blanc 1984  Dry Chenin Blanc.  Clarksburg.
Average dryness, Light 3 stars. 0.85% residual sugar.  Soft, fruity,
balanced, clean, extremely charming. Probably priced at $5 to $10.
 This is a good choice with your selected main course and sauce.
Anthony Dias Blue considers this wine to be a very good value.
Do you want the next wine (if there is one)?
YES                    NO

↑ ↓ →    Enter to go on    END to complete    ⁄Q to Quit   DEL to delete
```

There are innumerable, and perhaps unexpected, areas in which good advice would be appreciated. This expert system can tell you which wine would go well with a special meal you're planning.

programmed or purchased. This process is known as **systems analysis and design.** As the name implies, this process involves developing a system design to meet a new need or to solve a problem in an existing system. Unfortunately, the process is much more complex than this description. In fact, this process has spawned an entirely new occupation whose practitioners are known as systems analysts. The **systems analyst** carries out the problem-solving process to determine the cause of the current system's problem, suggests solutions to this problem, and then sees that one of these solutions is implemented. The new system may be one that must be programmed, or it may be a hardware or software system that can be purchased from an outside vendor. In the former case, the new system must be designed in such a way that the programmer can follow the design to create the software. In the latter case, the analyst must know enough about the various commercial systems to make a recommendation to management.

The Role of the Systems Analyst

In almost every systems analysis and design process, there are three groups of people to be considered: (1) the users of the system, (2) the information professionals or computer vendors who will actually implement the new system, and (3) the management who must oversee the transition from the old system to the new.

The complicating factor with these three groups is that each group views the problem in a different light. The users know they have a problem, but they don't know how to solve it. The information professionals or computer vendors can probably solve the problem, but they are not aware it exists and may not understand the terminology that the users use to describe the problem. Management may not know there is a problem or how to solve it but it does control the money needed to solve the problem. The individual who must work with all three groups to ensure that the problem is solved is the systems analyst. This person must be able to see the problem from the users' point of view, must

GEOGRAPHICAL INFORMATION SYSTEM MAY HELP DECIDE WHO RULES AMERICA IN THE 1990s

> It [redistricting] was a very tedious, error-prone, and laborious exercise that no one enjoyed.
>
> *Robert K. Bratt, executive director of the Civil Rights Division of the U.S. Justice Department*
>
> Quoted in "GIS Eases Redistricting Worry," *Computerworld,* October 7, 1991, p. 65.

Shortly after the 1990 U.S. census was completed, the reapportionment battle began, and for the first time in the process, computers are playing a prominent role. Every ten years, the House of Representatives must be reapportioned to take into account the new Census Bureau population tabulation. Depending on population gains and losses, this means that some some states may lose seats while others may gain seats. After it is determined which states gain and which lose, the state legislatures begin the actual reapportionment process for the seats in their state by redrawing their House districts. This is an extremely important process, because the new makeup of a House district could cause a political party to lose a seat. (Creating districts that are favorable to one party or the other is known as "gerrymandering," after a governor of Massachusetts, named Gerry, who created an oddly shaped district in 1812 that ensured victory for his party.)

As recently as 1980, districts were created with little or no involvement of computers. However, both political parties made extensive use of computers in the 1990 reapportionment process, using a **geographical information system (GIS)** to integrate the official census map of the United States with the 1990 census count. The census map—TIGER for Topographically Integrated Geographic Encoding and Referencing system—divides the country into 9 million census blocks, for each of which a population count is known. The GIS can then be used to create many different districting plans. For example, the state of Georgia, which gained a seat as a result of the 1990 census, used workstations to create approximately 2,300 plans as compared to around 100 plans considered in 1980. So, if in 1992, you wonder how your House district came to be shaped as it is, a computer was probably involved in the process.

Source: Tom Baxter, "Computers Are Latest Weapons in Reapportionment Wars," *The Atlanta Journal-Constitution,* April 2, 1989, p. A-6, as updated by the author in 1991.

Census maps on computer.

understand the solution methodology of the information professionals, and must have a feel for the budgetary constraints of management. In a sense, the systems analyst must act as an intermediary between the users and the information professional or vendors while also being responsible to management. This relationship is shown in Figure 9-6.

The Systems Life Cycle

The process of systems analysis and design can be thought of as a sequence of seven steps, with each step depending upon the successful completion of the previous steps. These seven steps are also referred to as the **systems life cycle** since they describe the conception, birth, and growth of the system. Figure 9-7 shows the seven steps as they appear in the systems life cycle.

We begin the seven-step systems life cycle at problem definition, when management becomes aware that either an existing system is not working correctly or a new system is needed. The process of management becoming aware that a problem exists depends on many environmental and behavioral situations. For the time being, we will just assume that management is aware of a problem. As we move from problem definition through the feasibility study all of the way to the final implementation and maintenance steps, we are moving from a broad,

A systems analyst must understand a client's needs before designing a system.

FIGURE 9-6
The Role of the Systems Analyst

Source: William S. Davies, *Systems Analysis
and Design,* © 1983 by Addison-Wesley
Publishing Co., Inc. Reprinted by permission
of Addison-Wesley Publishing Co., Inc.,
Reading, Mass.

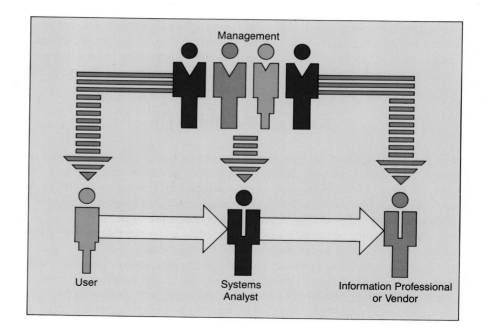

logical understanding of the problem to a detailed solution of the problem. The process of moving from the broad and logical to the narrow and physical is termed a **top-down,** or **structured, approach** to systems analysis and design. One way to think of this is as the process of constructing a building. The process goes from an idea to a set of preliminary sketches to preliminary plans to blueprints to the actual construction process. In both the construction of a building and the process of systems analysis, the movement is from a logical concept to a physical system.

In the first three steps—problem definition, feasibility study, and analysis—the systems analyst gathers data, decides what problem is to be solved, determines if solving the problem is feasible, and generates alternative solutions to the problem—moving closer and closer to a detailed understanding of the required system.

In the next step—systems design—users and management select one of the alternative logical solutions, and the systems analyst develops a physical design to match this alternative. Next—in the acquisition/programming step—any hardware specified in the systems design step is acquired. A decision is also made as to whether to use a software package or develop special software. If the decision is to acquire a software package, it too is acquired at this stage. If, on the other hand, the decision is to develop special software, it is programmed in this step.

Any hardware and/or software acquired in the acquisition/programming design step is installed in the implementation step. If any software was programmed in the previous step, in this step it is also installed. In either case, a great deal of work must be carried out to install and test the new system and to convert the existing data to a form that can be input into the new system.

In the last step—maintenance—the solution is in place and the job is to iron out any day-to-day problems and keep the system running. During the maintenance stage, if so much maintenance work is necessary to keep the system

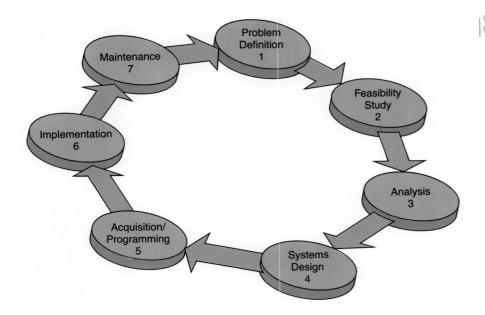

FIGURE 9-7
The Systems Life Cycle

running that it becomes obvious the current system is not adequate because of changing information requirements or business conditions or because of technological breakthroughs, we move back to the problem definition state and start the life cycle over again.

We will now consider the systems life cycle briefly.

Problem Definition

The systems analysis and design process begins with the determination that a problem exists in the current system. Complaints from users of a system may signal that a problem exists, management may find the current system too expensive even though it is working in an acceptable manner, or the output from the system may not match the system's objectives. Once an awareness of the problem exists, the problem definition stage begins.

The first step in problem definition is assigning a systems analyst to investigate the problem. The analyst meets with management and users to obtain a broad understanding of the problem. Based on these meetings, the analyst prepares a written declaration of his or her understanding of the user's objectives and the scope of the problem. When users and management, in the form of a steering committee, agree on the objectives and scope of the problem, the systems analyst moves to the next step.

Feasibility Study

Now the systems analyst can investigate the nature of the problem. A feasibility study is carried out to answer the following questions:

1. Is the problem worth solving?
2. Is a solution to the problem possible?

In the problem definition step of the systems life cycle, the systems analyst becomes very familiar with the client's problem.

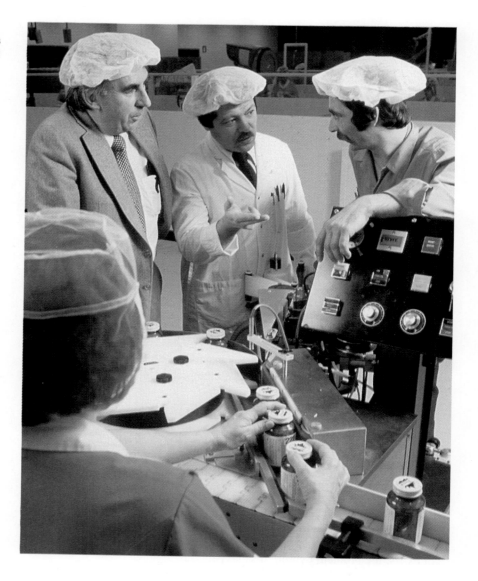

If the answer to either question is no, then the systems analysis and design process is terminated.

In a feasibility study, the analyst does not attempt actually to find a solution to the problem. Instead, the objective is to come to an initial understanding of the problem and to decide whether or not it is feasible to proceed with a full-scale study of the problem.

An important result of this stage of the systems life cycle is the cost/benefit analysis that the systems analyst prepares. This analysis should take into account both monetary and nonmonetary costs and benefits of solving the problem. If this cost/benefit analysis shows that the costs will outweigh the potential benefits, the systems analyst will recommend that the project be scrapped. Using the analyst's report, the steering committee will decide whether or not to continue the process.

Analysis

After the feasibility study has shown that the problem is worth solving and that there is a good chance that an acceptable solution exists, the analysis stage of the process begins. In this stage, the analyst works closely with the user to develop a logical model of the system. A **model** is *a simplified version of reality* and as such does not attempt to capture every detail of the system. Instead, the model is useful for conceptualizing the way the system works and for determining what must be done to solve the problem. It is important at this stage for the analyst and the user to work together, since it is the user who knows what must be done and the analyst who can figure out how to do it.

The development of the logical model is made easier if the analyst uses a tool known as a **data flow diagram.** A data flow diagram is simply a pictorial representation of the flow of data into and out of the system. At this stage the data flow diagram can be fairly elementary since we are not seeking to capture the detail of the model. Figure 9-8 shows the symbols used in data flow diagrams, and Figure 9-9 shows a simple data flow diagram for a situation in which various types of data are accumulated and tabulated before being stored in an inventory file for use later in the processing operation.

At each step of the systems analysis and design process, beginning with the problem definition step, the systems analyst collects and analyzes data. In the initial step, very general data are collected from interviews and written descriptions of the system. Then, as the process continues, more and more detailed data are collected from interviews with people close to the day-to-day operation of the system, from operational reports, and from actual data that are flowing through the system. At this, the analysis step, the data flow diagram is used to understand the flow of these data through the system. Data collection is

FIGURE 9-8
Data Flow Diagram Symbols

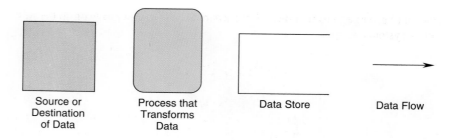

| Source or Destination of Data | Process that Transforms Data | Data Store | Data Flow |

not a one-time-only process but is an ongoing process in which the level of detail becomes greater at each step.

Once the analyst has developed a logical model of the system, he or she needs to develop a logical design that solves the problem defined earlier. This requires the analyst to use all of his or her experience, education, and creativity. Care must be taken to consider all factors, including the human and organizational ones. A logical solution will never be implemented if it runs counter to the objectives of the organization or if it requires people to act in a manner that they perceive as not being in their best interests.

Once the logical design has been developed, it must be validated against the problem definition to ensure that the design actually solves the problem. The analyst does this by discussing the logical design with the steering committee.

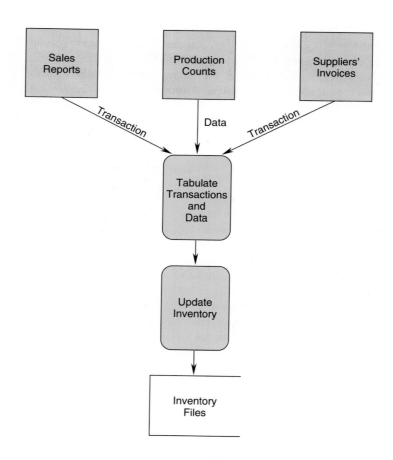

FIGURE 9-9
Data Flow Diagram

Once that group agrees to a design, the systems analyst can move on to the next step—systems design.

Systems Design

After the analysis step of the process, the analyst knows what must be done to solve the problem but has not yet worked out the best way to do it. The solution process requires that the systems analyst develop a number of plans for a new system and present each to the potential user for comments. It is at this stage that close contact between the analyst and the user is extremely important to ensure that the new system will solve the problems in the existing system without introducing any new ones. The process of developing a physical design to match the logical design developed in the analysis step requires that the analyst consider the problem from the output, input, and process points of view. That is, the analyst needs to determine what outputs are required from the information system being designed and what form these outputs should take, what inputs are going into the system and what form the data are in, and what process will be utilized to convert the specified inputs into the desired outputs. After considering the outputs, inputs, and process, the analyst develops alternative physical designs to give the steering committee a choice of ways to revise the system. A useful tool for describing the various alternatives to the committee is the **systems flowchart,** similar to the data flow diagram except that the emphasis is on the hardware devices involved in the design. Figure 9-10 shows the systems flowchart symbols, and Figure 9-11 shows one physical design corresponding to the data flow diagram shown in Figure 9-9.

Usually, the steering committee is given at least three alternatives. After considering these alternatives, the steering committee has a decision to make: It

In the systems design and acquisition/programming steps, the analyst develops a logical design and then a physical design of the final system.

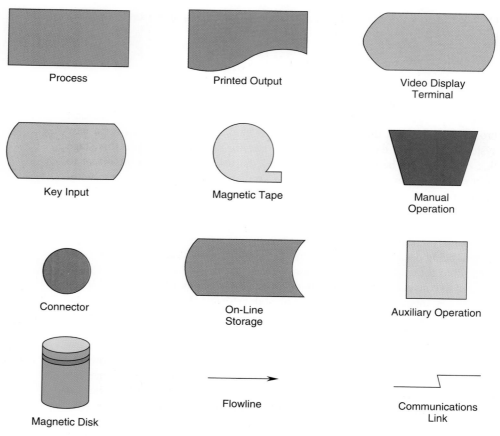

FIGURE 9-10
Systems Flowchart Diagrams

can decide that the overall cost is too great for any further development, or it can decide to use one of the alternatives the analyst offers, or it can ask the analyst to develop yet another design that contains characteristics not included in any of the previous alternatives.

Acquisition/Programming

If the user–management steering committee selects one of the analyst's physical designs, then the process of acquisition/programming can begin, using the chosen alternative as the general strategy. This process should answer the question of specifically which hardware and software systems should be purchased or, if software programs are to be developed, what the design of the software should be. This process will include the specifications on the computer hardware and software that will be needed to implement the alternative chosen by the user. If the software can be purchased from a commercial vendor, then the specifications should give all of the information necessary to choose the package. On the other hand, if the software is going to be developed by programmers, the specifications should be detailed enough for the programmers to understand what is required of their programs. These specifications are analogous to an engineer's blueprints in that they should show the user what the finished product will look like and they should guide the actions of the programmers.

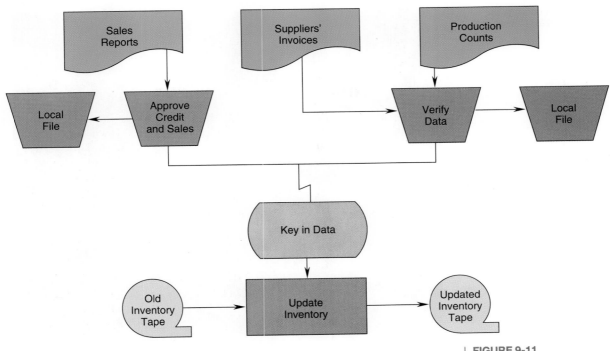

FIGURE 9-11
Systems Flowchart

If any hardware items or software packages are to be acquired, various vendors are given these detailed specifications and are asked to offer bids for the time and money involved in preparing the packages. Based on the resulting proposals, the hardware and software packages are purchased.

If software is to be developed, various tools are used to design the software to meet the specifications from the previous step, and the software is written.

Implementation

In this step, all of the detailed plans developed in the previous step are put into action, including actual installation of the previously purchased hardware and commercial software or installation of the programs that were written to make up the new software. Regardless of whether commercial software or specially developed software is used, this process involves testing the hardware and software in actual use situations, preparing documentation on the use of the new system, training personnel to use the new system, and evaluating the new system to determine whether or not it is performing satisfactorily. A commonly used approach to the implementation process is to have the old and new systems running side by side until it is clear that the new system is going to handle the required tasks. This is known as a **parallel conversion**—as compared to a **direct conversion,** in which the old system is discarded and the new system used immediately. Failure to test a new system adequately before doing away with the old one can have a profoundly negative effect on the organization if problems are found in the new system after the old system has been discarded.

Another problem in the implementation process for a new system involves resistance to change by the personnel of the organization. This problem can be avoided to a large extent if management sees to it that the personnel are involved

in all stages of the analysis, design, and implementation process and if a high priority is placed on training personnel on the new system.

If software has been specially written, testing is extremely important to ensure that the programs are error free and perform according to the user's needs. The systems analyst should be very involved in the development of test plans, the writing of operating and security procedures, and the formal testing of all components and procedures.

Once all systems have been installed and tested, the next step is to convert the data used in the old system to a form that can be input into the new information system. This can be time consuming, requiring careful validation of the data as they are moved to the new system. Only after the new system has been installed and tested, the personnel trained on the new system, the data converted to the new system, and the entire system validated as working correctly is the implementation step completed.

Maintenance

Any system, no matter how well designed, will need to be continually modified to handle changes in input, output, or logic requirements. This is done through maintenance, the ongoing process of keeping a system up to date by making necessary changes. While it may seem like a minor part of the analysis, design, and implementation process, maintenance of existing systems has been shown to take up about 70 percent of a professional programmer's work time.

Maintenance consists of two important steps: determining what needs to be changed and then making the change. Determining what needs to be changed is very similar to the problem definition step in that it requires the systems analyst to study a situation and to pinpoint the problem. Once the problem is defined, changing the existing system is a small-scale version of the systems life cycle that can involve all the steps shown in Figure 9-7. This is why we show the life cycle as a continuing process.

The ease with which an existing system can be maintained depends a great deal on the system documentation, made up of the descriptions and instructions that come with the hardware and commercial software or the documentation for programmed software that was written during the programming step. Without this documentation, changing the system may be virtually impossible and the existing system may have to be junked in favor of an entirely new system—a potentially expensive process.

MORE ON THE PROCESS OF DEVELOPING SOFTWARE

While we have encouraged the use of purchased software packages to solve problems using computers, there will always exist those situations in which it will be necessary to develop software by writing computer programs. These are usually cases in which problems exist that are not general enough to be addressed by a commercial software company or the user finds that the software does not suit his or her needs.

In the acquisition/programming step of the systems analysis and design process, we noted that if some or all of the software is to be written rather than purchased commercially, the programs are written in this step of the process.

In general, the process of creating software moves from a step-by-step statement of the solution to the problem, called an **algorithm,** to a program flowchart or to pseudocode. A **program flowchart,** a pictorial form of the logic needed to solve the problem, is similar to a systems flowchart except that it is directed at the more detailed logic of a computer program. **Pseudocode** is a structured form of English that allows the systems analyst to express the logic of the program in a form that the programmer easily understands. Once the logic of the program has been expressed as either a program flowchart or pseudocode, it is possible for a programmer who knows little about the original problem to write a computer program that will match the logic. This is where the systems analyst acts as an intermediary for the user and the programmer. In this case, the user understands the problem but does not know how to write a program to

All programs consist of a series of steps that must implement the logic needed to solve a stated problem or to carry out a given task.

solve it, and the programmer can write a program but does not know anything about the problem. The systems analyst has some knowledge of both sides.

The next step is for the programmer actually to write one or more programs that will give the computer the instructions it needs to solve the problem.

Programming Computers

To program a computer—that is, to give the computer a sequence of instructions—requires an ability to communicate with the computer. To understand how this communication can take place, we must realize that the computer does

SOFTWARE FROM J. P. MORGAN

Very few people would think of software development when they hear the name J. P. Morgan. Instead, they usually think of money. This is not surprising given that J. P. Morgan & Co. is the fifth largest bank in the United States and is possibly the most widely respected financial institution in the country. However, a reason for J. P. Morgan to be associated with software development and design is a unique product called MPI/PC Report that the institution introduced in 1986. MPI/PC Report seeks to exploit a niche in the issuing and paying agency services market that allows Morgan to offer reporting services that are superior to those of the competition, but at radically reduced prices. Specifically, companies use the product to generate sophisticated financial and analytical reports on their commercial paper programs.

Commercial paper is one of the largest financial debt securities in use by institutions today, with a total market size of over $500 billion. Commercial paper is short-term promissory notes that are sold by issuers to investors to handle cash flow needs. To monitor the amount of commercial paper outstanding, and to generate detailed analytical reports, issuers rely on issuing and paying agents (that is, the banks responsible for creating the debt security) to provide them with a reporting service. Most bank systems, however, limit issuers to relying on expensive mainframe computer resources to generate reports. These expenses can exceed $100,000 per year. With MPI/PC Report, however, issuers use a PC-based software package that allows issuers to generate reports using the processing powers of their own PCs. The Commercial Paper Management Group at Morgan made the decision to develop and write a PC-based product in 1985 to lower issuer costs and to enable Morgan's clients to use PCs, which were becoming more commonplace in the business environment. The system design, analysis, and programming effort was completed within nine months, and the product was launched in August 1986.

MPI/PC Report does two basic operations. First, it retrieves the commercial paper issuance data from Morgan's mainframe computer and downloads it to the issuer's PC.

Second, it uses this downloaded information to generate reports offline. Selling for $2,500 with a $250-per-month usage fee for the basic system, this package is substantially cheaper than the mainframe alternative. Currently, the product is used by over 100 *Fortune* 500 clients, some sovereign governments (e.g., Canada and New Zealand), and numerous foreign issuers. Since the product was introduced it has generated over $1 million in revenues for the Commercial Paper Management Group, while offering flexibility to Morgan's clients.

Morgan has not rested on its laurels, however. In the first quarter of 1990, the bank introduced the second release of MPI/PC Report, which was totally redesigned. The new version is written entirely in the C programming language and has several added features to enable issuers to take advantage of hardware and software developments (e.g., local area networks and pop-up window screens). Additionally, Morgan is already looking into expanding the product to include other debt securities, such as certificates of deposit and medium-term notes.

Source: Jeffrey Rothfeder, "Bank-Developed Software Transforms Lackluster Service into a Profit Leader," *PC Week,* November 24, 1987, pp. 66, 70; and Morgan Guaranty Trust Company of New York, a subsidiary of J. P. Morgan & Co., Incorporated, 1990.

not understand any human language without some form of translation. From our discussion on bits and binary numbers in Chapter 2 on hardware, you know that the computer "thinks" in terms of on/off switches that we know as bits. In other words, the language of the computer is in the binary number system. So, to be understood by the computer, human language must be translated into these binary numbers. The computer's binary language is referred to as **machine language,** a very specific language that details every operation of the computer as a series of 0s and 1s.

Because every type of computer is different, each has a different machine language. Programming in machine language would be very inefficient, however, because the programs would have to be changed whenever they were transferred to a new computer. For this reason, **high-level languages** were developed. These languages are English-like in that programmers use English words combined with a specific grammar. The languages have also been standardized to some degree, so that a program written in a high-level language on one type of computer *may* not have to be totally rewritten when used on a different type of computer. The most commonly used high-level languages have such names as BASIC, FORTRAN, COBOL, C, and Pascal. This wide diversity of high-level languages came about because no one language could satisfy every need. Some are business languages, some are teaching languages, and some are scientific languages. In addition to these traditional high-level languages, many data base management packages have a programming language associated with them that allows automization of the search and rearrangement of data bases. dBASE is a popular data base management package for PCs that comes equipped with a powerful programming language.

If the computer understands only machine language and we write in high-level languages, how does the computer ever understand our programs? The answer is that some type of translation between the two levels of languages is

```
   File    Edit    Run    Compile    Options    Debug    Break/watch
                                    ═══ Edit ═══
      Line 1      Col 17   Insert Indent          Unindent * C:EXAM2.Q1
Program Averages;
Uses crt;
type
     Stringtype = string[20];
var
   Inputfile: text;
   Name: Stringtype;
   Height: Integer;
   Ppg: Real;
   Count72,Count78,Count79,CountAll:Integer;
   Ppg72,Ppg78,Ppg79,PpgAll: real;
   SumH, AverageHt: real;
procedure Initialize;
     begin
     Count72:=0;Count78:=0;Count79:=0;CountAll:=0;SumHt:=0;
     Ppg72:=0;Ppg78:=0;Ppg79:=0;PpgAll:= 0;
     Clrscr;
     Assign(inputfile,'player.dat');
                              ─── Watch ───
 F1-Help  F5-Zoom  F6-Switch  F7-Trace  F8-Step  F9-Make  F10-Menu
```

High-level programming languages, such as Pascal, combine English words with specific grammar rules.

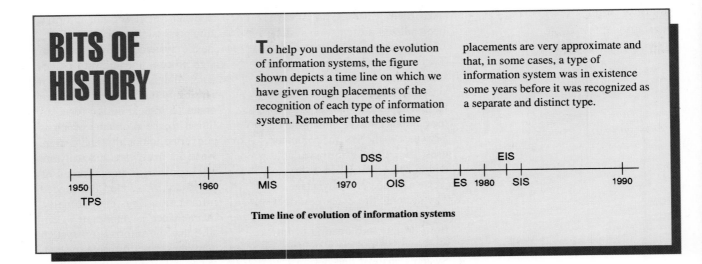

required. Utility software performs this task, converting the high-level language down to a corresponding machine-language program.

Regardless of the high-level language in which the program is written, the programmer must be able to translate correctly the logic developed in the design phase into a working program, first by learning the vocabulary and syntax (grammar) of the language and then by studying how various logical situations are handled in that particular language.

REVIEW OF KEY POINTS

1. An information system is a combination of user, hardware, and software that supports managerial decision making. A computer-based information system uses the computer to process data into a form usable by management.

2. A system is a group of elements organized for the purpose of achieving a particular goal. It is made up of input, processing, output, and feedback operations, with a boundary separating the system from its environment.

3. Five types of information systems are commonly found in all organizations—the transaction processing system (TPS), the management information system (MIS), the decision support system (DSS), the executive information system (EIS), and the office information system (OIS).

4. In any organization there are three levels of managerial decision making—operational, tactical, and strategic—with each needing a different type of information. Thus each type of information system is important to a different managerial level of the organization.

5. The TPS is usually associated with operational decisions, while the MIS is associated with both operational and tactical decisions.

6. The DSS is used by middle- and upper-level managers to help

make their decisions; the EIS is a personalized presentation system used by strategic managers.

7. Two other important types of information systems are expert systems (ES) and strategic information systems (SIS). In the ES, the computer serves in the role of an expert; in the SIS, the computer uses the information available within the organization to try to create a competitive advantage.

8. The systems life cycle describes the steps a system goes through from design and creation to implementation and maintenance.

9. Systems analysis and design is a seven-step process used to solve problems in a company's computer system by developing a new system or modifying an old system.

10. A systems analyst, the key figure in the systems analysis and design process, acts as a go-between for users and information professionals or vendors.

11. In the systems analysis and design process, the analyst first defines the problem and does a feasibility study. The analyst then creates a logical design for a solution to the problem, which is converted into a physical design. Next, the hardware and software are acquired or programmed as necessary to develop the needed information system. Finally, maintenance is important to ensure that the information system continues to perform as expected.

12. When software for the information system cannot be purchased, it must be designed and computer programs must be written to implement the design.

13. Computer languages are used to execute the instructions needed to accomplish a task or solve a problem on a computer.

KEY TERMS

algorithm
batch processing system
boundary
computer-based information system (CBIS)
data base
data base management system (DBMS)
data flow diagram
data processing
decision support system (DSS)
direct conversion
environment
executive information system (EIS)
expert system (ES)
feedback
geographical information system (GIS)
high-level language
information system

input
machine language
management information system (MIS)
model
office information system (OIS)
output
parallel conversion
processing
program flowchart
programmable decisions
pseudocode
real-time processing
strategic decisions
strategic information system (SIS)
structured approach
system
systems analysis and design
systems analyst
systems flowchart

systems life cycle
tactical decisions
top-down approach

transactional processing
transaction processing system (TPS)

1. Discuss how an information system is important to some club or organization to which you belong. How might this information system be converted into a computer-based information system?
2. Discuss the difference between a computer-based information system and data processing.
3. List the managerial levels of any organization.
4. List the five information systems commonly found in most organizations. Discuss how information systems are used in colleges or universities to support the managerial system.
5. Discuss the importance of the transaction processing system. Name the three types of transaction processing systems.
6. Discuss the importance of the management information system for any organization. What managerial level(s) would most likely use the output from this system?
7. What level(s) of management would most benefit from a decision support system?
8. Why is the executive information system referred to as a "personalized presentation system"?
9. How does an office information system support the various levels of management?
10. Discuss the rules and knowledge that might be incorporated in an expert system for a subject in which you are an "expert."
11. How are strategic information systems used in organizations?
12. List the seven steps of the systems analysis and design process. Why is this referred to as a systems life cycle?
13. Why is the systems analyst needed in this process?
14. In what step of the system analysis and design process is programming carried out?
15. What is the purpose of an algorithm in the programming process? What is pseudocode and how is it used?

10

An Introduction to Computers and Society

Having discussed computer hardware, software, and systems in earlier chapters, we will now address the interaction between people and computers. This discussion will examine the impact, both positive and negative, that computers have had on people. This will be followed by an introductory discussion of computer crime and data security, including the various types of crimes that involve computers. Next is a discussion of personal privacy and health issues in the use of computers. Then the various careers available to individuals with training or an interest in either mainframe or personal computers are noted and, finally, future trends in computer use are reviewed.

STUDY OBJECTIVES

After reading this chapter, you should be able to

- discuss the impact that the computer has had on various segments of our society;
- recognize the types of problems that occur when people interact with the computer in the workplace;
- describe health problems that have been reported by frequent computer users;
- discuss the various types of computer crime, including those that involve copying software for personal computers;
- discuss the depersonalization of society that can occur with the use of computers;
- describe the types of careers available in the computer industry;
- note some of the trends in computer use that have been predicted for the future.

SMART WORKERS FOR SMART MACHINES

A decade ago, many workers worried that they would be replaced by robots and computerized manufacturing equipment. However, in some cases exactly the opposite has occurred—workers not only have *not* been replaced by machines but many have found that their jobs have been made more meaningful by the introduction of smart machines. This has come about because workers are being given more responsibility and authority to deal with problems or to make production-line decisions that were once reserved for supervisory personnel. Workers do more than just run machines; they spend large parts of their time collecting and processing data on quality control, inventory, and shipments. The result of this change is an **informated factory,** where machines not only perform some operations, but they supply workers with information on processing operations.

As an example of this type of change, consider General Electric's Salisbury, North Carolina, factory. At this plant, which is highly automated, it was decided in 1984 to cut factory floor bottlenecks by giving workers the information and power to make decisions to keep the manufacturing process running. A machine operator with a problem, for example, now can talk directly to manufacturing engineers about solutions to the problem or can order parts for the machine without prior approval of management. Workers also serve on committees to hire new workers in the plant.

From 1985 through 1988, General Electric's pairing of smart workers with smart machines resulted in a tenfold decrease in delivery time, a reduction in employee turnover, a reduction by two-thirds in the number of hours per production unit, and an increase in General Electric's market share. Since 1988, concrete figures have not been available on the effect of these measures; however, plant management believes that the workers are continuing to assume more and more responsibility for running the plant. Each year, they have exceeded production goals and reduced production cost.

Source: Doron P. Levin, "Smart Machines, Smart Workers," *The New York Times,* October 17, 1988, pp. 25–29, as updated in interview with Rick Fior of General Electric, November 14, 1991.

Workers at this plant are often authorized to make production and scheduling decisions without checking with their supervisors.

While a great deal of attention is often paid to hardware and software, the human aspect of the "age of smart machines" is all too often ignored. However, as just discussed in the box, organizations that recognize the need for change in the way workers interact with computers are realizing tremendous increases in productivity and are making the workers' jobs more interesting and rewarding. Because the interaction between people and computers is such an important topic, this chapter is devoted to the many and varied ways that people react to and with computers.

This discussion of the interaction between people and computers will be divided into four sections:

1. the impact of the computer in the workplace, including health-related issues;
2. data security and computer crime;
3. the impact of computers on personal privacy;
4. computer careers now and in the future.

THE IMPACT OF THE COMPUTER IN THE WORKPLACE

In the workplace there are many situations in which people come into contact with computers. In situations like the one described at the beginning of this chapter, where "smart workers" are working with smart machines, this interaction has been positive. However, there are also negative interactions between workers and the computers that they use to carry out their work.

The use of computer terminals is fast becoming commonplace in offices of all types.

On the positive side of computers in the workplace is a reduction in many of the more boring or monotonous tasks. Office personnel who once took dictation with pencil and paper and transcribed the information on a typewriter have been transformed into **information specialists**—people who work with personal computers to perform such wide-ranging tasks as word processing, data base management, and spreadsheet analysis. As a second example, consider the automobile workers who once had to perform the dirtiest job in the automobile industry—arc welding. They have now been retrained to repair the robots that took their place. They, too, are information specialists, but of a different variety.

However, on the negative side is a group of workers who suffer from a malady known as **computerphobia**—the fear of computers. The malady (also known as *cyberphobia* or *terminal phobia*) is thought to occur in about 30 percent of students and workers forced to contend with the computer for the first time. The symptoms of computerphobia are nervousness, uneasiness, anxiety, and tension when the affected individual is confronted with a computer. The causes of computerphobia are described as fear of change, fear of machines (especially machines such as computers that are capable of highly sophisticated tasks), fear of breaking the computer, frustration with a machine that tends to stop for unknown reasons, fear of job loss, discomfort with the impersonal nature of computers, and an inability to use the keyboard. Several studies have revealed that some computerphobes even leave a company that is in the process of computerization and join a company that has not yet gone through the process. Some people even change professions to avoid using computers. This problem has been blamed on the fact that the current work force is the first to have to come to grips with computers. The problem is slowly disappearing as younger people who have grown up with computers and video games move into the work force.

Another potential problem with the computer in the work place is the **video display terminal (VDT).** This display can be either a personal computer or a terminal tied into a mainframe or minicomputer, and it has become a fixture in offices throughout the United States. These terminals allow the user to access and process data, display and print the results, and make decisions based on the results. As a result, the VDT is an important facet in the office of both today and the future. However, for the individual who uses a VDT over a long period of time, there may be health hazards associated with the radiation from the screen, the eye strain from watching the screen for long periods each day, and the muscular and joint problems resulting from the rigid posture associated with the use of the keyboard. In fact, a new job-oriented syndrome called "computeritis" has been associated with day-in/day-out use of the keyboard. **Computeritis** involves extremely painful musculoskeletal problems that can keep workers off their regular jobs for months at a time.

The study of work-related problems is known as human factors engineering or ergonomics. **Ergonomics** can be defined as the study of the relationship between the productivity of machines and the comfort of the people using them. When ergonomics are applied to the various body positions required in the use of a VDT, the types of keyboards used, and the other factors involved in the use of a VDT, a more healthful and productive working environment usually results.

For the organization and the individual, another problem involving the computer is unemployment due to automation of many tasks. Examples of this include the use of robots to replace workers in the automobile, electronics, and supply industries. These robots take over many of the dirtiest, most dangerous,

A wrist brace helps relieve this data entry operator of some of the musculoskeletal problems associated with computeritis.

and most boring jobs in these industries. While many of the individuals displaced by the robots do find other, more responsible positions in the same company, like those discussed at the beginning of this chapter, tens of thousands of workers may lose their jobs due to automation during the 1990s. This displacement has already occurred in the automobile industry, where the U.S. companies have responded to the Japanese competition by attempting to reduce labor costs through automation. The future holds additional opportunities for the application of automation to many industries, and the effect on the work force is yet to be determined.

DATA SECURITY AND COMPUTER CRIME

In the fall of 1988, over 6,000 computers at universities and military labs were "infected" with a "computer worm" sent over a network by a high-tech vandal. This so-called **computer worm** was a computer program that replicated itself over and over after being transmitted on a computer network. While this particular worm brought many computers to a grinding halt by taking up large amounts of internal memory, it did not destroy valuable records. However, another type of computer program called a **computer virus** has wiped out entire disk storage systems. Worms and viruses are just one type of computer crime. Sometimes money is stolen or data are stolen or the computer itself is attacked. The dramatic increase

Desktop forgers are using desktop publishing equipment to modify checks, credit card receipts, academic transcripts, and a variety of other documents for illicit purposes.

in the use of computers of all sizes now requires business and government to determine ways to provide security for their computers and data.

While the personal computer is often seen as the cause of many computer crimes, many of these same problems existed when individuals used terminals tied into institutional computers to steal funds or to destroy data. In fact, the 1988 worm attack was sent over a mainframe network. It is true, however, that the personal computer has made access to computers much easier. It has been suggested that any computer with a telephone connection is vulnerable to an incursion regardless of the type of security system devised to protect it. The annual cost of computer crime in the United States has been estimated to be in the range of $3 to $5 billion.

Computer crime can be defined as the theft of money, merchandise, data, or computer time using a computer or the unauthorized incursion into computer data files. As we have discussed, computer crime can take a number of forms, including the following:

- Manipulation of company financial records to steal funds from the company. This type of crime can involve employees of the firm or individuals from outside the firm.
- Theft of merchandise by manipulating the inventory records to hide the loss of the merchandise or by charging the merchandise to a fake account or to another customer's account.
- Theft of company data. Company consumer data, customer lists, and computer programs are common targets for data theft.
- Use of the company computer for personal purposes. This includes using the computer to develop computer programs of a personal nature or using the computer for "moonlighting" as a consultant.
- Damage to the computer or to data storage by an angry employee or ex-employee. This can include physical damage to the hardware, destruction of mass storage devices such as disks or tape, or damage to the programs that control the computer.
- Incursions into the computer programs or files or unauthorized use of the computer by individuals who are doing it for the "fun of it" or for the challenge of breaking into the computer.
- Unauthorized use of or destruction of voice mail systems.

Individuals who specialize in breaking into computers are often referred to as "hackers." The term **hacker** was originally applied to anyone who would spend many hours at the computer "hacking" programs, that is, learning how they work. In fact, many of today's leaders in the computer industry started out as hackers who wanted to make computers do more. Unfortunately, the term has recently taken on a negative connotation due to the harm many of these people have caused. For example, the individual who sent the worm across the country in 1988 was a hacker who was just trying to see if it could be done. Unfortunately, a bug in the program caused it to replicate itself throughout all available memory.

Examples of computer crimes show up almost every day in the national media, but in many other cases these crimes go undetected, unreported, or unpunished. Some cases of computer crime that have involved a great deal of money or have been well publicized include a computer-based currency fraud that cost a West German automobile company nearly $480 million, the theft of more than $20 million from a California bank through electronic funds transfer, the diversion of at least $2 million from bettors at a dog track in Florida by a group of employees using the track computers, and the incursion into NASA computers and U.S. military networks by a group of West German hackers using international phone links.

A problem in prosecution of computer crime is that until recently there were no laws appropriate to the crimes. It was a case of using outdated laws to prosecute high-tech crimes. This situation has been rectified to some extent by new laws at both state and federal levels. One sticky question remains regarding incursion into a computer when no harm is done. Is this a crime? Many state courts and legislatures have ruled that it is.

Some experts have blamed management for the lax security that enables these crimes to be carried out so easily. The most common security measure involves using special passwords to keep intruders from using the computer. Unfortunately, easy-to-remember (and easy-to-guess) passwords are often chosen, and as a result, computer security is easily breached.

Software Piracy

Most of the computer crime discussed so far involves incursions into or theft from institutional or business mainframe computers, since these are the computers that contain the large quantity of records and calculations usually needed for the crime to be profitable. Another type of computer crime that involves personal computers almost exclusively is **software piracy.** PC software is copied and used without payment to the company that developed it. Persons copying software that they did not purchase are probably violating *at least* one of various U.S. copyright laws. One survey indicated that software piracy results in lost sales of between $1.2 billion and $2 billion annually in the United States alone. Also, 40 percent of the software used on personal computers is believed to have been obtained illegally. The ease of theft comes from the need for users to be able to **backup** the software disks as protection against the primary disk being damaged by a power surge, power outage, or the like. If software companies make their disks so that they cannot be copied, then the disks also cannot be backed up. As a result, users may not buy them.

In the past, the solution to software piracy was **copy protection,** which kept products from being copied even for backup purposes. The companies would send backup disks to registered owners of their software or would limit the number of backups that could be made from the original or master disk. Another antipiracy measure required that the master disk be used at some point in the package startup process. While these measures worked in some cases, there was always someone who could devise a way around these protective measures. As a result of the many problems associated with copy protection, most PC software is sold today without any copy protection. Software companies hope that most of their users are honest and will not steal software by copying disks.

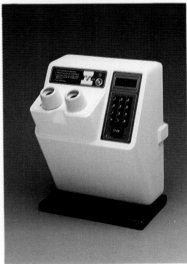

In one method of computer security, a computer compares the pattern in the potential user's retina with the patterns of valid users, which are stored in its memory.

COMPUTERS AND PERSONAL PRIVACY

In his well-known book *1984,* George Orwell describes how the society of Oceania can be totally controlled by the Party through the control of information. Although computers are never mentioned in the book, it has been assumed that it would be impossible for the Party to control the society unless it used computers to collect and store needed information. The year 1984 has passed, and it is obvious that America is far from becoming like Oceania. However, some of Orwell's ideas in *1984* about the collection and storage of data on citizens have indeed come to pass. We do not currently have a national **data bank** that contains the names of and records on every citizen of the United States, but recent surveys indicate that many people are concerned about the amount of information stored in many small, private data banks.

At the national level, there are numerous data banks: The Social Security Administration maintains data files on all individuals who pay taxes into or receive benefits from Social Security, the Internal Revenue Service keeps records on all taxpayers, the Department of Agriculture keeps track of farm incomes, and the Secret Service stores information on threats to the president. At last count in 1982, it was reported that the federal government maintained an average of 15 files on each American. Undoubtedly, other files have been added since that time. The Federal Bureau of Investigation is one of the largest holders of data, with records on over 25 million individuals who have been arrested, regardless of whether they were actually convicted of a crime.

At the state level, a 1982 study by New York State's Committee on Open Government determined that state agencies operated over 1,700 data banks on New York citizens. These data banks contain such things as voter registration

At FBI headquarters in Washington, D.C., employees use computers to sort and match over 184 million fingerprints on file there.

lists, driver's licenses, car registrations, state income and property tax records, and building permits. State and local police keep records on offenders within their jurisdiction and are quite willing to share this information with other law enforcement agencies.

In the private sector, a growing number of data banks contain data on most Americans alive today. This information may be as crucial as the credit bureau records that can affect your search for a car loan or a job or as seemingly innocent as a magazine mailing list. Private data banks also house your school records, your memberships in unions or other professional organizations, and your record of political contributions. Credit card companies keep track of your payment record, banks retain information on the checks you write, telephone companies record the numbers you have dialed, and insurance companies have a large amount of data on your driving record and medical care. In fact, the data collection industry is now a $1-billion-a-year industry.

The problem with all these data banks is that while they may be innocent enough individually, taken together they can be used to portray a fairly complete, though perhaps not altogether accurate, portrayal of each of us—our habits, our tastes, and possibly our religious and political beliefs. Before the age of computers, it was very difficult to search through all the data banks to collate all the information on a single individual, but now it is fairly easy using a single key identifier such as a Social Security number. The linking of two or more individual data banks to match information from separate data banks is more than a possibility; it is being done now. The Selective Service System performs matches to check student loan records against its registration records to ensure that the loan applicant has registered for the draft. The Internal Revenue Service attempts to detect tax fraud by comparing reported income against data maintained by various business information services to determine if an individual is living beyond his or her means. While both these matching programs are legal, there is concern about potential abuse through the interaction of data banks, especially when the right to confidentiality has not been guaranteed or has been waived.

Compounding this problem is the fear that much of the information included in these data banks is erroneous, either through errors in data collection or through improper entering of data into the data bank. Horror stories abound about people being declared dead by some agency while they are in fact very much alive. One attempt to remove fraudulent individuals from the rolls of disabled persons receiving Social Security benefits led to many cases of truly disabled people losing their only source of income.

While all these problems with data banks that include incorrect data or that are being used for purposes for which they were not intended are worrisome, what do they have to do with personal privacy? To see the relationship, let's define privacy as control over personal information. Under this definition, it is obvious that the inability of the individual to control what goes into these data banks and how this information is used is indeed an intrusion into personal privacy. Since 1970, numerous federal statutes have been enacted to give the individual more control over the information that goes into these data banks, and all 50 states now have laws that protect computer records. However, the continuing technological changes tend to make these laws outdated as soon as they are passed.

Computer Monitoring of Workers

With so many people using computer terminals and PCs in their jobs today, it is not surprising that employers are monitoring the workers' productivity on those computers. In this application of computers, workers are monitored to ensure that production is maintained at an acceptable rate. For example, a telephone operator may be monitored to determine that a set number of callers per hour is being served, or a data entry clerk may be monitored to quantify his or her production level. At one time, monitoring was strictly a mainframe concern since PCs were primarily stand-alone computers, but with the proliferation of PCs linked to networks, monitoring of work on the smaller computers has become more prevalent.

There are various estimates on the extent of monitoring. The Congressional Office of Technology Assessment estimates that between 25 and 35 percent of all service workers using computers are monitored, and a labor union representing many communications workers estimates that over 6 million workers are being monitored each year.

Numerous questions are unresolved about the constitutionality of this practice, since it may violate workers' Fourth Amendment rights to security of "their persons, houses, papers, and effects, against unreasonable search and seizure." In addition, many labor organizations feel that such practices fail to account for the many different situations a worker may encounter during the day. It is also believed that monitoring may actually be counterproductive because it may increase a worker's stress level, resulting in lower efficiency and increased turnover rates. Several bills have been submitted in Congress to restrict the use of monitoring, but, at this writing, no action had been taken on any of them.

Problems with the Computer Depersonalizing Society

One of the common complaints about computers is that they precipitate a depersonalization of society. This is the other side of the privacy question. It appears that instead of always invading our privacy, computers may also ignore our individuality or modify a user's personality. In the first case, the increased use of bar codes, banking machines, computerized billing, and the like may tend to ignore the "people" side of business. For example, the use of bar codes in grocery stores for pricing and inventory control has been shown to reduce checkout times and stocking costs, but it also can cause problems when the wrong price has been entered into the store computer. Many people are also uncomfortable with the bar code because they cannot determine the price by simply looking at the product; they must find the shelf sticker and perform a price comparison. There are even "self-serve" bar code readers that allow shoppers to check themselves out, totally bypassing the human aspects of shopping.

One of the most frustrating experiences is trying to straighten out an incorrect bill that was prepared by a computer. Numerous comedians have used this situation as material for their monologues, but when it happens to you, it is not funny. As we have said before, this problem is not usually the fault of the computer (which is often the reason given for the problem) but rather the people working with the computer. This problem can occur in the programming of the computer or in the data entry. Either way, to straighten out the problem, you

Computer monitoring of telephone operators is becoming more prevalent as companies seek to ensure that production is maintained at a predetermined level.

must contact the right person. Writing letters to the computer usually has no effect!

In the second case—computers modifying users' personalities—studies have shown that patterns of human interaction are modified by the way in which people use computers. Just as living with other humans teaches us certain ways of interacting with people, working with a computer tends to modify our behavior patterns. Apparently, the more a person works with a computer, the more he or she becomes intolerant of ambiguous, digressive, or tangential behavior and prefers simple yes–no answers. Some heavy computer users have been observed to put a high premium on efficient communication and to avoid people who talk slowly or in general terms.

Personal Computers and Information Flow

The data banks just discussed are all maintained by mainframe computers, as they require considerable internal and external storage. The personal computer is thought by some to be on the other side of the personal privacy coin; that is, personal computers are the individual's way of gaining access to information and communicating with other users via telecommunication systems like CompuServe and Prodigy. Without control of information, no government can hope to control its people, and wherever personal computers and telecommunications devices are sold freely, information becomes an uncontrollable entity. Recent examples include the 1989 demonstrations by Chinese students in Bejing, where fax machines were a primary source of information to the outside world,

> They [computer compulsives] prefer to communicate with people who are "system literate" so as to transfer information quickly.
>
> *Craig Bond, psychologist*
>
> Quoted in Jeremy Rifkin, *Time Wars* (New York: Henry Holt, 1987).

> The overwhelming impact of the PC is to empower individuals against large organizations.
>
> *George Gilder, author of* Microcosm *and senior fellow at the Hudson Institute*
>
> Quoted in "What the PC Means to Me," *Computer World*, August 5, 1991, p. 55.

ANOTHER VIEW

James E. Katz

James E. Katz is a sociologist with Bell Communications Research and is the author of such books as *People in Space*. The following discussion is quoted from an article by Mr. Katz and provides an opposing view of the effect of technology on privacy:

[A] technological development enhancing personal privacy is the public key-coding procedures. These allow ordinary citizens to communicate with one another in practically total secrecy. Anyone having access to a phone line, a modem, a personal computer, and some software can telecommunicate instantaneously via electronic mail with any other person in the world who has the same technology. Their communication can be so highly encrypted that it would take the most powerful computers in the world a century of computing time to break the code. That is a big step in personal privacy. In addition, a variety of protective systems are emerging that will prevent anyone but an authorized person from access to particular computer files. Unlike the paper records that historically have been used, and can be read by nearly anyone into whose possession they fall, files under these [computer] security systems will self-destruct rather than allow themselves to be compromised.

Source: James E. Katz, "Telecommunications and Computers: Whither Privacy Policy?" *Society*, November/December 1987, pp. 81–86.

PC HELPS THWART SOVIET COUP

One of the most dramatic stories of 1991 was the failure of the Soviet coup in August of that year. Russian president Boris Yeltsin, the leader of the anticoup group, was greatly aided in his efforts by an IBM PC and a Hewlett-Packard laser printer. The coup leaders had managed to deny Mr. Yeltsin access to newspapers and broadcast stations, but they failed to consider the impact of a ten-year-old PC, a laser printer, and a telephone.

The IBM PC was used to create newsletters that were printed on the laser printer and then distributed to thousands of Yeltsin supporters who surrounded the Russian parliament building. The same PC was also combined with the telephone to send electronic copies of the flyers all over the Soviet Union and to Western countries. It was also used to receive electronic messages from such supporters as British Prime Minister John Major. The messages were immediately interpreted and distributed to the supporters. The PC provided Yeltsin with a form of free press that the coup leaders forgot about!

Source: Bill Husted, "Comrade PC Saves the Day," *Atlanta Journal-Constitution,* August 21, 1991, p. C-2.

Boris Yeltsin used a PC and laser printer to create his own news source during the attempted coup.

and the 1991 Soviet coup attempt (see box), where use of a PC allowed Russian president Boris Yeltsin to communicate with both his supporters and with the outside world.

CAREERS IN COMPUTERS

So far in this chapter we have discussed some of the problems that arise from the interaction of computers and people. At one point we said that unemployment caused by automation could be one of these problems. However, there has also been a tremendous increase in computer-related occupations during the past decade. While many of these jobs have occurred in the more traditional main-

frame or minicomputer areas, a great number of jobs have opened up strictly in relation to the use of personal computers. Here we will simply provide an overview of the types of jobs open in the computer field.

In the mainframe/minicomputer area, the jobs that are available include (but are by no means limited to) such positions as information system manager, systems analyst, programmer/analyst, data base specialist or manager, telecommunications specialist, software engineer, network specialist, computer operator, and service technician. With the exception of the last two positions, all these positions require some degree of specialized training on the type of system being used in addition to a postsecondary education in the general area of computers or data processing. The last two positions usually require extensive knowledge of the computer system being used plus training in the specialized occupation.

Table 10-1 shows the starting salary ranges for experienced professionals in those positions just mentioned that require postsecondary education. In most surveys, managers state that the employment background and systems or technical background of the applicant are the most important criteria for hiring. Communication skills, education, and enthusiasm are also high-priority qualities.

In the personal computer field, with the increasing use of PCs in all types of organizations, there is a corresponding need for individuals to support and

TABLE 10-1
Starting Salary Ranges for Experienced Professionals

IS manager	$68,000–91,000
Systems analyst	37,000–48,000
Programmer/analyst	32,000–42,000
Data base analyst	38,000–50,000
Telecommunications specialist	40,000–55,000
Software engineer	38,000–53,000
Network specialist	38,000–51,000

Source: Adapted from Robert Half and Accountemps Salary Guide, 1991, Robert Half International, Inc., 1990.

maintain the smaller computers. This is in addition to the continuing need by the large personal computer hardware manufacturers and software companies for systems and applications programmers. In organizations with many PCs, three areas of particular need are end user support, network support, and maintenance. End user support includes all efforts that help end users do their job better using a PC. Network support includes installing and maintaining local area networks composed of PCs. Finally, all PCs will eventually need some type of maintenance, whether it is fixing a stuck key, installing a circuit board, or replacing a bad hard disk. Positions like these do not always require the level of formal education that might be required in a mainframe/minicomputer company since the important requirement is a knowledge of the specialized nature of the product.

Another source of employment in the personal computer field is with the growing number of dealers who sell computer hardware, software, and supplies. It is hard to find a town of any size that does not have at least one computer store. These stores need knowledgeable salespeople, service technicians, and sometimes, programmers to handle the demand for their products. This network

PERSON WITH CP "GOES TO WORK" USING COMPUTER

Even though she has had cerebral palsy since birth and has been unable to control the movements of her arms and legs, Barbara Clements has used her home computer to find a job. She works for the Regional Consortium for Education and Technology reading computer-related magazines and summarizing articles that may be of interest to members of the consortium.

Barbara controls her computer by pressing its keys with a foot-long pointer that is attached to the top of an aluminum head brace she wears. While she's not fast—seven to eight words a minute—she gets the job done. Barbara also manages the consortium's electronic bulletin board and transmits article summaries over it once they are completed.

She found her job the same way she does her work—by linking up with the consortium's office computer and telling it about herself. After a few weeks of corresponding with her prospective supervisor, Carl Hoagland, she asked him for a job. He hired her, and they worked out an arrangement where Barbara works from her home on a part-time basis. Now, after over six years on the job, she continues to draw rave reviews about the quality of her work. In the words of Hoagland, "Barb has more capabilities than just data entry. She can read as fast as you or I can. And she's an excellent writer."

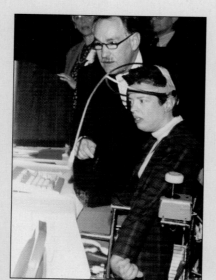

Barbara Clements, who has cerebral palsey, works from her home, thanks to her computer.

Source: Ellen Futterman, "Computers Give Jobs to Disabled," *St. Louis Post-Dispatch,* January 20, 1986, p. A-5, as updated by author in interview with Carl Hoagland, November 3, 1991.

of computer dealers has become such an important link in the personal computer market that a series of trade shows has come into existence to bring hardware and software companies together with dealers. COMputer Dealer EXchange (COMDEX) shows are held throughout the year in the United States, Europe, and Japan, and it is not uncommon to have over 50,000 exhibitors, dealers, and journalists attend.

Finally, the proliferation of PCs in business has resulted in an increasing need for consultants to advise potential users on merits of one system over another. In addition, for those persons interested in teaching, the training field (preparing users to get the most from their personal computer system) is wide open.

FUTURE TRENDS IN COMPUTER USE

In the fast-paced and rapidly changing computer world, it is difficult to predict exactly when various events will happen. But they usually come sooner, not later! One trend is the increasing number of machines that are being made smart. For example, experiments with "smart cars" that will guide their drivers are now underway. By the end of the century, we may all be driving cars with built-in intelligence, yet as recently as 40 years ago, while automobiles and telephones were commonplace, there were fewer than ten computers anywhere in the world. As late as 1981, when the original IBM PC was introduced, there were only 200,000 computers of any kind in the United States. Since then, however, over 70 million personal computers have been sold. Not only has the use of computers proliferated, but the speed and memory of computers has also increased, and they have become cheaper. For example, today an IBM PS/2 sells for much less than the original IBM PC of 1981, but it is ten times faster and has over

New computer hardware and software products are often unveiled at the annual COMDEX show.

1,000 times more memory. If you had asked a computer professional for an opinion on the potential growth of the personal computer in 1981, he or she probably would not have predicted the success for this machine that we see today. However, even with the unpredictability of future computer use, some trends seem well established in computer hardware and software.

Trends in Computer Hardware

The key trend in computer hardware has been "smaller, faster, and cheaper," and this trend is expected to continue and even accelerate. Mainframes are shrinking to the size once reserved for minicomputers, and personal computers are as fast as the mainframes of ten years ago. Much of this change is the result of the ongoing research in microchip technology, which has given us the ability to pack more and more electronic elements into less and less space. Today, research is progressing into manipulating molecules to reduce the size of computer elements even further. In addition, recent advances in the field of **superconductivity** (the capability for electricity at low temperatures to flow without any resistance) have increased the possibility of using it to dramatically increase the speed of computers.

At the supercomputer level, an industry is constantly seeking ways to build faster computers. Much of this research involves finding shorter wiring paths, which would reduce the amount of time needed for information to flow between the parts of the computer. A great deal of research is going into the development of **massively parallel computers** that are capable of performing many different operations at the same time and, thus, greatly speed up the processing of data into information. In addition, research is ongoing in the field of **neural networks**—computers that can learn how to solve a problem from examples rather than having to be specifically programmed.

In personal computers, the trend is toward using 32-bit processors such as the Intel i486 chip and the Motorola 68000 series of chips. These chips permit much faster processing and access to larger amounts of internal memory. Intel and other chip companies are working on 64-bit CPU chips that would give the PC supercomputerlike capabilities.

Trends in Computer Software

As discussed in Chapter 3, the trend in software is toward the use of graphical user interfaces (GUI) as a way of making software easier to use. This is true primarily at the PC level, but there is also research into using the same type of interfaces for minicomputers and mainframes. All popular PC packages are being rewritten to run with a graphical interface.

Another trend in mainframe software packages has been the emulation of personal computer packages (word processors, spreadsheets, and so on) on the mainframe. This has been done by writing packages that work like the PC packages but take advantage of the increased power and storage on the mainframe or by moving PC packages to the mainframe. For example, WordPerfect, the current best-selling PC word processor package for IBM compatible PCs, is now available for mainframe systems as well as for the Apple Macintosh series of computers. It is highly probable that this trend will continue as software com-

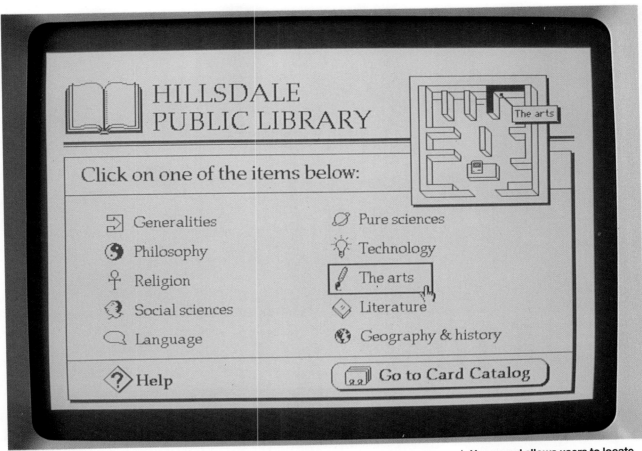

HILLSDALE PUBLIC LIBRARY

Click on one of the items below:

Generalities

Philosophy

Religion

Social sciences

Language

Pure sciences

Technology

The arts

Literature

Geography & history

? Help

Go to Card Catalog

The arts

Hypercard allows users to locate information through multiple access paths.

panies move to combine the ease of use often associated with PC packages with the power and storage capacity of a mainframe.

In the world of educational software, a great deal of work is ongoing in using authoring languages to create educational systems that are both easy to use and exciting. An **authoring language** is a computer package that enables the user to create a sequence of interactive learning activities where the user uses a mouse to click on a "hot button" on the screen to answer a question or seek additional information. An example of an authoring language is HyperCard for the Apple Macintosh. It has been used to develop many educational programs, including a system called KonjiMaster, which teaches students how to draw Japanese konji characters.

Artificial Intelligence

Probably the most exciting possibility in computers today and in the future is artificial intelligence. **Artificial intelligence (AI)** is produced when computer hardware and software systems are combined in such a way as to exhibit some level of human intelligence. Because the term *AI* has such a broad definition, it has been applied to many different types of computer systems. Among other things, AI has been applied to robotics; to expert systems (systems that help managers make decisions); and to systems that can listen and understand, read

Artificial intelligence was popularized in the movie *2001: A Space Odyssey* in the form of the talking computer HAL.

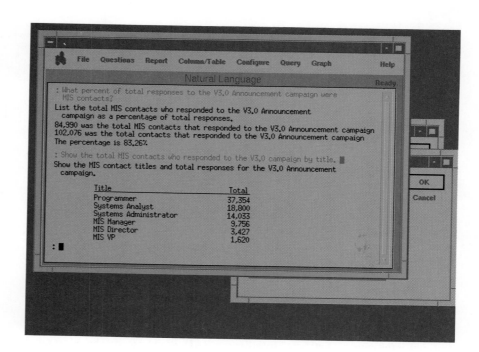

Natural Language

: What percent of total responses to the V3.0 Announcement campaign were
    MIS contacts?
List the total MIS contacts who responded to the V3.0 Announcement
    campaign as a percentage of total responses.
84,990 was the total MIS contacts that responded to the V3.0 Announcement campaign
102,076 was the total contacts that responded to the V3.0 Announcement campaign
The percentage is 83.26%

: Show the total MIS contacts who responded to the V3.0 campaign by title. ▮
Show the MIS contact titles and total responses for the V3.0 Announcement
    campaign.

Title	Total
Programmer	37,354
Systems Analyst	18,800
Systems Administrator	14,033
MIS Manager	9,756
MIS Director	3,427
MIS VP	1,620

: ▮

Users may request information using natural language instead of special codes, making software more user friendly.

printed material, generate speech, help solve problems, and so on. To many people, AI is the most important area of computer research today. However, other writers feel that there is no such thing as AI, since intelligence is a strictly human quality.

One application of AI that may have a more profound effect than other applications is "softer software"—software that is much easier to use than what is available today. One such area of research is determining the capability of a computer to understand **natural languages,** such as English rather than sometimes cryptic computer languages. Also dependent on AI are voice-input computers, pen-based computers, and **virtual reality,** which seeks to make computer and human interaction transparent. It is envisioned that virtual reality might be achieved through a high-tech bodysuit that senses its wearer's body movements and translates them to the computer. In many ways, AI is being used to make computers "people literate" rather than forcing people to become computer literate!

While still in its infancy, AI is one of the fastest-growing high-tech areas. Many companies are spending large amounts of money either to develop AI systems or to purchase systems developed by other companies. However, no one is close to developing a computer system like the fictional HAL from the movies *2001: A Space Odyssey* and *2010: The Year We Make Contact.*

> **HAL: Good afternoon, Gent-le-men. I am a HAL 9000 computer. I became operational at the H.A.L. labs in Urbana, Ill., on the 12th of January 1992. My instructor was Mr. Langley and he taught me to sing a song. If you'd like to hear it, I can sing it for you.**
> **Astronaut: Yes, I'd like to hear it, HAL. Sing it for me.**
> **HAL: It's called "Daisy"** . . .
>
> From Arthur C. Clarke, *2001: A Space Odyssey.* (New York: New American Library, 1968).

REVIEW OF KEY POINTS

1. The interaction of computers and society has brought many benefits but has also brought some problems.

2. The four main ways in which people and computers interact are (a) through computers in the workplace, (b) when computers are used to commit crimes, (c) when computers affect personal privacy, and (d) when computers create new career opportunities.

3. Computers in the workplace can affect workers by creating new jobs, causing unemployment, creating potential health hazards, and causing psychological problems for workers who fear computers.

4. Computer crime can involve theft of money, merchandise, time, or data; destruction of hardware, software, or data; or the incursion into a computer "for fun."

5. Personal computer software piracy occurs when software is copied illegally.

6. Computers threaten personal privacy because they are so efficient at searching out and matching elements from individual data banks. Computer monitoring of workers is another area that potentially invades personal privacy.

7. Computers have the potential to depersonalize society by removing the face-to-face human contact from many everyday actions or by modifying the personalities of users.

8. Personal computers act as safeguards to personal freedom by allowing us to communicate with other users and to exchange information freely.

9. Careers in computers are available for people who understand

and can work with mainframes, minicomputers, or personal computers. The many computer-oriented careers have varying educational requirements.

10. There are many openings for people with education or experience in working with personal computers.

11. Future trends in computer hardware are toward smaller, faster, and cheaper computers. Trends in computer software include moving personal computer software to mainframes, using authoring languages to create educational presentations, and developing the exciting field of artificial intelligence.

KEY TERMS

artificial intelligence (AI)
authoring language
backup
computer crime
computeritis
computerphobia
computer virus
computer worm
copy protection
data bank
ergonomics

hacker
informated factory
information specialist
massively parallel computers
natural languages
neural networks
software piracy
superconductivity
video display terminal (VDT)
virtual reality

REVIEW QUESTIONS

1. Name the four types of interface between society and computers.
2. Discuss possible health problems arising from the use of VDTs. What is computeritis?
3. What psychological problem can arise for workers who are uncomfortable working with computers?
4. How can computers create new jobs and at the same time create potential unemployment? How does the informated factory relate to this seeming contradiction?
5. What does the science of ergonomics have to do with computers?
6. Why is it sometimes very easy for a criminal to gain access to a mainframe computer? What is a computer virus?
7. Explain the term *software piracy.* Why is it a problem for both the software company and the personal computer user?
8. List as many data banks as you can that you think may have your name included in them.
9. In what ways could data from two or more of the data banks you named in the previous question be matched?
10. What is computer monitoring and what does it have to do with personal privacy? Why does it now include PCs as well as mainframe terminals?
11. Name two ways in which you have experienced the depersonalizing effect of computers. How can a computer modify a user's personality?
12. Discuss the ways in which a personal computer can be used to increase the information flow to individuals.

13. Check a local newspaper or your college or university employment service and determine what salaries are being paid for two of the positions listed in Table 10-1.

14. Visit a local computer store and determine which of the jobs mentioned in this textbook are actually being carried on there.

15. What is artificial intelligence? Discuss how it might be used to develop "softer software" or natural languages.

A Guide to Buying a Personal Computer

Since the early 1980s, personal computers have been a subject of great interest, and more and more individuals and businesses are entering the world of PCs by buying their first personal computer, while others are upgrading old computers or buying additional computers. It has been estimated that at the end of 1991, over 100 million PCs were in use in the United States alone.

Many of these PCs are used in business to help companies save money and increase profits, but the number of them used in homes is growing. Surveys show that over one-third of U.S. households (17 million) have a personal computer, and by the end of the century, statisticians believe that the average home will have more PCs (2.2) than children. Your reading this textbook indicates that you, too, may soon be in the market for a personal computer—if you do not already own one!

Because there are so many makes and models of personal computer to choose from, purchasing a computer tends to require more research on the part of the prospective owner than the comparable purchase of, say, an automobile or a television. Another complicating characteristic of personal computers is that they are not all equally effective in handling the different tasks for which computers are commonly used. For example, one machine might be great for running educational software but not have the speed or memory to handle business-related tasks such as working large spreadsheets or data bases. The computer you purchase should suit your computing needs in the same way that the type of vehicle (car, van, truck, sports car, etc.) you buy fits your transportation needs.

Because your needs are particular to you and the computer that suits your needs may not suit those of another person and vice versa, directing you to one brand of computer over another would not be a sound approach. Instead, we will describe a five-step process for selecting a personal computer. The brand of computer you actually choose will depend on the results of this procedure and the prices available to you.

STEP-BY-STEP PURCHASING PROCEDURE

The five steps for buying a computer system are these:

1. Define the tasks for which you will be using your personal computer.
2. Determine which software will accomplish these tasks.
3. Determine which hardware systems will support the software you selected in step 2.
4. Find suppliers that can provide the hardware and software selected in the previous steps.
5. Purchase the software and the hardware system.

> **Personal computers promise an incredibly positive impact on productivity, economy, and quality of life in corporate America, in small offices, homes, schools, and home offices.**
>
> *John Roach, chairman, Tandy Corp.*
>
> Quoted in "The Pace of Change in Corporate America," *Personal Computing,* October 1989, p. 240.

This procedure assumes that you have already learned enough about computers to know what they can and cannot do and that you are able to define the tasks for which a computer will be useful to you. These may include managing your finances, handling correspondence or writing papers, managing a business, or learning to program. Then, whatever your needs are, you can determine what software packages will meet your computing needs. There is such a wide variety of software available today that this step requires the most time and research; you will probably end up with a list of software from which you must make a subjective choice. Selecting the particular software package that meets your needs greatly narrows the choice of computers, since not all computers will run all software. With this reduced range of computers to choose from, you can select suppliers who carry both the software and the hardware you're considering. We will discuss each of these steps in detail.

An important concept to remember about buying a computer is that the original purchase of hardware and software is just the beginning; you can purchase additional software packages as you find additional uses for the computer, or you can add hardware devices to expand the capabilities of the computer system. For example, a buyer planning to use the computer for managing finances may decide to add a data base management package or a high-quality printer to enhance the use of the computer. Following the purchasing procedure just outlined will help ensure that you purchase an expandable computer system. By planning ahead, you avoid being locked out of the future.

STEP ONE: DEFINING YOUR NEEDS

All too often—perhaps because it is "the thing to do"—people purchase computers before they have clearly defined their needs. But as the personal computer is a tool, it is crucial to define what you will use it for before moving any further into the personal computer market. You would not normally buy an expensive woodworking tool, such as a lathe or a table saw, unless you needed it for your business or hobby. The same should be true of a computer.

Because the computer is such a versatile machine—capable of being used for word processing, financial management, publishing, education, and so on— most people find that they have multiple needs. To help in the decision process, you should rank these needs according to which computer application you use the most. This will help you determine the most appropriate computer and so avoid over- or underbuying.

(Top left) Personal computers are used at home for education and games. (Top right) Macintosh computers are becoming very popular for use in schools. (Bottom) Today it is almost impossible to find an office that does not have at least one personal computer.

Types of Computer Needs

Most people find that their computer needs fall into one of the following three broad categories:

1. personal
2. school related
3. work related

Personal uses of the computer include home budgeting, correspondence, tele-communications, and volunteer activities.

School-related computer use includes writing papers, doing research with electronic data bases, writing computer programs, and using computer software to complete assigned homework and projects. It may also include using packages that provide math drill, computer-aided instruction, and SAT/GRE review to prepare for college and graduate school entrance exams.

Finally, work-related computer use includes bringing work home from the office to complete on a personal computer, using the computer to carry out activities from a home office, and using the computer to manage a small business.

STEP TWO: SELECTING SOFTWARE

Once you have determined your computer needs, the next step is to look for software that will meet those needs. Remember that without software the computer is nothing but a collection of silicon chips and electronic components. For this reason, you should select the software first. In selecting software, you should try to match your needs and your level of computer experience with the software rather than just buying the most popular package on the market. For example, while there are several popular word processing packages that sell for close to $500, there are also numerous less expensive, less sophisticated word processing packages that may easily handle home correspondence or short papers. If you are going to use the software to prepare a senior or graduate thesis, then you will probably need a more sophisticated word processing package to handle the volume and complexity of the work.

Methods of Selecting Software

There are several ways to go about selecting software: You can read articles or reviews about the software, discuss software with members of a user's group, visit a computer store and explain your needs to a salesperson there, and—possibly the best of all—actually use the software at work or school. In many cases, your research into computer software may require you to take advantage of more than one of these research avenues.

Reading Articles and Reviews Some of the better-known computer magazines, listed in Table 5-1, often review individual packages, listing specific capabilities and drawbacks. Occasionally, a computer magazine will review an entire class of software, comparing the available packages on a feature-by-feature basis. Looking through back issues of these magazines, you will find reviews of software packages for almost every need imaginable. Often, general-purpose magazines and newspapers also have periodic columns discussing various software packages, usually at a less technical level than the discussions in computer magazines.

Visiting a User's Group   You may be able to find information on various packages by visiting a computer user's group meeting and asking questions of members. You can find out meeting times of user's groups by calling a computer store or watching for notices in the newspaper. At a user's group meeting, you can talk to experienced users about problems they have faced, look at the types of software they use, and, possibly, try out some software and hardware in a friendly environment. Most members of a user's group are very happy to show off their hardware, software, and computer expertise to a novice.

Visiting a Computer Store   Visiting a computer store can be very helpful if you can talk with someone who is knowledgeable about your specific computer need. To ensure that you will be able to talk to this person, call ahead and make an appointment. Once at the store, you should be able to have the salesperson walk you through the use of the packages that you think will fit your needs. To make this "test use" worthwhile, bring some data for the type of problem for which you will use the software. Ease of use and applicability to your problem are two important criteria for deciding whether a software package fits your needs. This demonstration should also include a review of the user's manual and any other documentation that comes with the software. If you have difficulty reading the user's manual and other documentation, then this package may not fit your needs.

> **Today's emphasis on the entrepreneur and the small business is due, in part, to the PC.**
>
> *Art Afshar, president,*
> *Micro Express*
>
> Quoted in "View from the Top,"
> *Personal Computing,* October 1989,
> p. 262.

A computer store is a good place to discover the great potential of a PC.

Actually Using the Software   Without a doubt, the best way to decide which software package to purchase is to experiment with several of them in a work or school environment.

Software Support

A crucial consideration in selecting software is the degree of support that is available from the vendor or software developer. At one end of the support spectrum are those companies that offer unlimited free technical support for their products over toll-free (800) telephone lines. At the other extreme are those companies that offer no support at all or require you to pay for the call as well as for each minute of help they provide. Obviously, software that comes with the first type of support is preferable to other types, but sometimes, if you must have particular software, you simply must pay for the support. Buying software that offers no telephone support at all is a risky proposition at best!

STEP THREE: SELECTING HARDWARE

After you have determined your software needs, the next step is to select the hardware that will run the software. Since not all computers will run all software, this is an important matching process. Computers differ in the number of bits that they can manipulate (16 or 32), the amount of memory they have (640K, 1 Mbyte, or more), and the operating system that directs the computer operations (MS-DOS, OS/2, Windows, or proprietary). Just as it is impossible to insert an Atari cartridge in a Nintendo game computer, it is also impossible to run MS-DOS software on an Apple Macintosh and vice versa. Some typical examples of each type of computer are shown in Table PC-1.

When discussing a personal computer, we need to recall its component parts. Shown originally as Figure 2-4, these include the central processing unit (CPU), the keyboard, the video screen, secondary storage, a printer, and, possibly, a mouse and modem. These are shown again as Figure PC-1.

Since the keyboard and the CPU come with the computer, the decisions facing the computer buyer usually involve the amount of internal and secondary storage, the type of video system, the type of modem, the type of printer, and the expandability of the system.

Selection of CPU, RAM, and Secondary Storage

As software has become more sophisticated and users have found more reasons to process and store data on a computer, requirements for CPUs, RAM, and disk storage have increased. Users today find that they need fast CPUs, large amounts

TABLE PC-1
Some Popular Computers

Type	Operating System	Bits	Examples
AT compatible	MS-DOS/OS/2	16/32	Compaq, Dell, ZEOS
PS/2	OS/2/MS-DOS	16/32	IBM PS/2 Model 80
Macintosh	Proprietary	32	Mac SE, Mac II

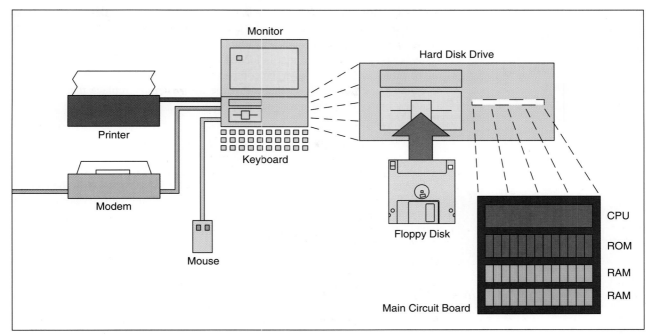

FIGURE PC-1
Personal Computer System

of RAM, at least one floppy drive, and a hard drive. In choosing a PC, you should consider the CPU's **clock speed.** Clock speed measures in **Megahertz (MHz)** the CPU's top processing speed. It is to a CPU what horsepower is to an engine; all other things being equal, the higher the clock speed, the faster the computer's processing capability.

The original IBM PC had a clock speed of 4.88 MHz, whereas the current i486-based computers, such as the IBM PS/2 Model 95, have clock speeds of up to 50 MHz. Still faster machines will soon be available. Macintosh computers are running at up to 33 MHz.

Intel 80386 and i486 CPU chips now come in two versions, SX and DX. The SX version transfers 16 bits of data to the CPU from RAM, whereas the DX transfers 32 bits. Although computers based on the 80386SX or i486SX chips run somewhat more slowly than those based on the DX version, they are significantly cheaper and have all the other advantages of using these chips. Given the choice between a computer based on the 80286 and one based on the 80386SX, you would be much better off, in general, with the SX version of the 80386 chip.

The amount of internal memory and secondary storage you will need depends on which software you plan to use and how you plan to use your computer. Today's PCs usually have at least 1 Mbyte of memory and often have 2 Mbytes or more. You should not consider buying a computer that does not have a hard disk drive. In choosing a hard drive, consider its **access speed,** which is the amount of time the disk requires to find and move data. Most hard disks today offer access speeds of less than 20 milliseconds—many are even faster. For many applications, a fast hard disk can make as much difference as a fast CPU. If you are using a large-capacity (60 Mbyte or more) hard drive, you should consider some form of tape backup as protection against loss of precious data and software.

> **For business applications, the Intel 80286 CPU, even at 12 MHz, just isn't fast enough.**
>
> *Paul Rubin, director of product marketing at Dell Computer Corporation*
>
> Quoted in ''Computer Technology: A Look to the Future,'' *WordPerfect: The Magazine,* January 1991, p. 59.

Expandability of the system is something else you should consider: How easy is it to add extra RAM to the system? Can the system be upgraded to a faster processor if one becomes available? Will the system run newer operating systems? Buying a system that is locked into its present condition may lock you out of future improvements in the computer field. Several companies are offering so-called "upgradable PCs" that allow the user to easily replace the CPU with a newer, more powerful one.

Hardware Required to Use Windows

A consideration in buying IBM compatible and PS/2 computers is their capability of running the Windows operating environment and the software rewritten for it. The absolute minimum configuration is a machine that runs the Intel 80286 CPU and has a hard disk, 2 Mbytes of memory, and VGA graphics. Even this configuration, however, is often too slow to run Windows adequately. Most experts recommend an 80386 or i486 machine with at least 4 Mbytes of RAM and "Super VGA" graphics to take full advantage of all Windows's features.

Choosing a Video System and Printer

Chapter 5 discussed video systems and printers, but let's review the options here. There are essentially three types of video systems to choose from: Hercules-compatible, VGA, and Super VGA (CGA and EGA systems are seldom available, if ever, for new PCs). Recall that the Hercules-compatible system provides high-quality text and graphics on a monochrome monitor. It is by far the least expensive of the three options. The VGA system provides high-resolution text and color graphics on either a VGA or multiscanning monitor, but the Super VGA system provides yet higher resolution. Most top-of-the-line desktop sys-

(Left) Dot matrix printers are an inexpensive device for producing printed output. (Right) Laser printers are now widely used for producing business-quality output.

tems sold today package the Super VGA system. (IBM PS/2 computers have this type of video system, but it is called XGA, which means eXtended Graphics Array.)

If you are considering a Super VGA system, make sure the monitor has a **dot pitch** of no more than 0.28 millimeters and that it is "noninterlaced." Dot pitch refers to the width of a dot on the screen; the smaller the dot pitch, the sharper the image. Interlacing is a technique that "paints" every other line on the monitor with each pass of the cathode ray tube; therefore, a **noninterlaced monitor** paints *each* line, which results in a sharper screen image.

Printers come in three categories: dot matrix, ink-jet, and laser. All three form characters with tiny dots, but each does so with a different mechanism. Dot matrix printers use a series of small rods that impress a ribbon to form letters on a page. Ink-jet printers, on the other hand, spray tiny droplets of ink onto the page. Finally, laser printers use a light-activated system (similar to that of photocopy machines) to create dots of ink on a page. Dot matrix printers are the least expensive of the three types and are usually fine for most school work; however, they are not usually suitable for printing formal correspondence. Laser printers are capable of producing very high-quality output, and they have become more popular since their price has dropped to below $800. Ink-jet printers are not as fast as laser printers, but they offer many of the same capabilities for less money.

Modems

Although the selection of a modem was discussed in detail in Chapter 8, we review it here. Most modems sold today are 1,200 bits per second (bps), 2,400 bps, or 9,600 bps and can be external or internal. While the 1,200-bps modems are the least expensive, many people are buying the 2,400-bps or 9,600-bps modems because of their higher speed. The choice between an internal modem and an external modem depends on the type of computer you are using and whether or not there is space for the internal modem inside the computer. In any case, remember that you will need communications software to implement the modem.

A Package Approach

With the exception of the modem and the mouse, all the components just listed are necessary to make full use of the computer and should be included when you purchase a computer. It is probably best to use a package approach to make your hardware purchase. Sometimes suppliers promise to "back order" some part of the hardware, meaning that they must order it from the factory since they do not have the item in stock. This is a somewhat risky process that can leave you unable to perform the operations for which you purchased the computer system in the first place. According to the step-by-step approach discussed here, you should view the computer system as a whole. Make every attempt to avoid having only part of it. Another problem that could arise with a new hardware model is that promised hardware devices might not be forthcoming when they are expected. If you purchase a new type of system that requires a special printer not yet available, the system will be virtually useless until the printer arrives.

Types of Computers

Besides classifying computers by operating system, number of bits, and memory size, we can also classify them by four major types:

1. IBM compatible PC
2. IBM PS/2
3. Apple Macintosh
4. Other (Amiga and NeXT machines)

IBM compatible computers are those that are compatible with IBM's original 8088-based XT and 80286 AT PCs in that they will run any software written for the XTs and ATs. IBM no longer markets the original PC, XT, or AT, but many companies, including IBM, market computers that are compatible to them and, therefore, can run the vast amount of software written for MS-DOS. Although you can still buy an 8088-based computer that is compatible with the IBM XT, most IBM compatible computers sold today use Intel 80286, 80386, or i486 chips and are compatible with the IBM 80286-based AT computer. These include the IBM PS/1 series, Compaq, Tandy, and Dell computers, as well as those manufactured by many other companies. Most of the IBM AT compatible computers cost between $750 and $4,000, depending on the type of CPU chip used and the types and number of peripherals. They are popular in business and industry, and many universities are buying them for computer labs. With sufficient RAM, all AT-class compatible computers will run Windows and the software written for it. XT compatible computers, however, will not run Windows.

IBM PS/2 computers were developed by IBM to replace the original PC, XT, and AT computers. Engineers aimed at creating a machine that other companies could not duplicate. The features of PS/2 computers vary from model to model. Some have a high-resolution video system, some are capable of running the OS/2 operating system, and they have differing internal communication systems. As with the AT compatible computers, all PS/2 machines can run software written for MS-DOS or the Windows operating environment. Many companies

(Left) The 486 Dell computer is a popular IBM compatible PC. (Right) IBM's 486 PS/2 is a popular new model.

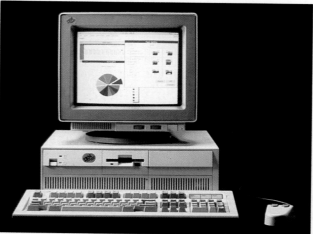

(Top left) The IBM PS/2 386 is purchased by many people to get started in computing. (Top right) The Model 55SX provides the computing power of the 80386 chip at a reduced cost. (Bottom) The Model 80 is a popular PC in many business and engineering offices.

The Macintosh Classic II (left) uses a high-quality black-and-white screen; the Mac II (right) offers the user the option of a color monitor.

and colleges and universities buy this type of computer. Popular models are Model 25, Model 30, Model 55SX, and Model 95.

The Apple Macintosh is an extremely innovative computer introduced in 1984. The first Mac combined text and graphics on a high-resolution white screen. Recent versions offer high-resolution color monitors as well as the original white screen. The Mac is without peer when it comes to creating newsletters, forms, greeting cards, and so forth. In fact, desktop publishing owes its origin to the Macintosh's unique abilities. Because of the Mac's increasing popularity, more and more software is being written for it for use in business, education, and home. In addition, it is now possible to convert some software from a Macintosh version to an MS-DOS version and vice versa with a special floppy disk drive called a "super drive." Popular lines of the Macintosh include the Mac Classic II, the Mac LC II, and the Mac II series.

The NeXT computer combines the UNIX operating system with powerful graphics and easy-to-use menuing systems.

THINGS TO CONSIDER WHEN BUYING A PORTABLE COMPUTER

It is true that all personal computers are portable, to some extent, but an entire class of extremely portable computers arose in the last half of the 1980s. While the overall market for PCs is becoming saturated, sales of easily transportable computers continue to grow at a rapid rate. There are four types of portable computers: luggable, laptop, notebook, and pocket. Size distinguishes the categories. **Luggable PCs** are at one extreme. They weigh over 10 pounds, require AC power, and are portable from desk to desk. Examples of luggable PCs are the Toshiba T5200 and the Zenith TurboSport. At the other extreme are **pocket PCs,** which are about the size of a large calculator and replace such things as traditional address books, calculators, and appointment calendars. They are battery powered and do not include a disk drive. Examples of pocket PCs are the Poquet PC, the Fujitsu System 29, and the Sharp Wizard.

Laptop PCs and **notebook PCs** fall between the two extremes. Both are full-power computers that can run on either AC power or rechargeable batteries. Laptops and notebooks are distinguishable by weight, options, and expandability. The distinction, however, is rapidly fading as computer companies steadily design portables to fit inside the average briefcase, which requires a size of approximately $8\frac{1}{2}$ by 11 inches.

Laptops and notebooks have a similar design, either "clamshell" or "lunch box," depending on the keyboard. With a clamshell design, the screen folds down over the keyboard; whereas, with the lunch-box design, the keyboard pulls out for positioning at various angles.

The Macintosh Portable, or "Mactop," and the three types of Power Book PCs from Apple Computer require special attention. The Mactop was designed to be completely "Mac-like" and will run any software designed for desktop Macintosh computers. Mactops come with a mouse, but a built-in trackball and mousebar make them truly portable. The Power Book computers are smaller than the Mactop and can run software created for either the Mac or MS-DOS.

Hints for Buying a Notebook

MS-DOS–based notebook computers are becoming the most popular portable computers among business persons and students. Tips for buying an MS-DOS–based notebook computer follow:

- Look for at least an 80286 CPU processor with as much memory as is available. If you plan to run Windows, you will need at least an 80386SX CPU and up to 4 megabytes of RAM. Make sure you can easily add an internal modem, so that you can communicate with other computers.
- Make sure the notebook PC has a hard drive and a 1.44-Mbyte, $3\frac{1}{2}$-inch floppy drive, and insist on a VGA display that will drive an external monitor. Check the visibility of the display from several angles and under different intensities of light to ensure that you can read it.
- Carefully check the keyboard to make sure it satisfies your needs. Test it by keying text and figures into documents and spreadsheets—this may prevent you from buying a keyboard that will frustrate you later.
- Look for a well-padded case and a handle on the PC. Make sure the purchase price includes a battery and charger and that the charger is small and lightweight. Do not buy a PC that does not have a low-battery light.
- Look for at least a one-year warranty and the availability of a "loaner" if the PC requires repair while under warranty.

Sources: "Buying: Making the Decision," *WordPerfect The Magazine,* July 1991, pp. 46–47; and Mary Jerome, "How to Buy a Notebook PC," *PC Computing,* June 1991, pp. 132–134.

Other computers include the Amiga and NeXT machines. The Commodore Amiga uses the same chip as the Apple Macintosh and competes with the Mac for sales in the graphics market. The NeXT computer is a Unix-based PC developed by Steve Jobs' NeXT company. Its hardware and software have many innovative features.

STEP FOUR: SELECTING A SUPPLIER

Once you have selected software and hardware, it then becomes important to choose a supplier from whom to make the purchases. Most people have three choices of where to buy computer hardware and software:

1. a local computer/software store
2. a discount computer/software outlet
3. through the mail

Each option has good points and bad points. A local computer store usually stocks a range of computer hardware and software and usually (but not always) has a staff knowledgeable about what they sell. Such a store can also offer the local touch you may need to help with problems, and for a novice in computers it can be a good place to learn about the various types of hardware and software.

On the other hand, a discount computer store is usually larger than the local computer store and may carry a wider variety of computer equipment and software at lower prices. Usually the salespeople are as knowledgeable as those at a local store about the various pieces of equipment and types of software they may have in stock and so can help you make your selection. There are even specialty discount stores for one particular type of equipment, say, printers, or just for software. On the negative side, a discount computer store, especially if it is not located in your hometown, may not offer the help you need when problems arise after the purchase.

Finally, often the least expensive way to buy computer software and hardware is through the mail. Computer magazines carry numerous advertisements for software and hardware at prices that are quite a bit lower than the list price. While it is possible to save a great deal of money by going through a mail order company, you must be well informed and experienced since you will get no help setting up the equipment or installing the software. Another point to consider about software purchased from a mail order house is that there is no way to test it before you buy it; once you have opened the package, it may be that the software cannot be returned to the company for a cash refund.

> For beginners, it's important to look for a store that will help, even if your problems have nothing to do with a flaw in the machine.
>
> *Ed Juge, director of marketing for Radio Shack*
>
> Quoted in "How to Buy a Computer," *Atlanta Journal/Constitution*, February 11, 1992, p. B2.

Service Factors

A key point to consider in selecting a hardware supplier is service. While a computer is usually a very trouble-free machine with few moving parts, there *will* come a time when service is needed. Perhaps a disk drive falls out of alignment or a key gets stuck; in any case, some type of repair will eventually be necessary. Most local and discount computer stores have repair services to handle such problems. Most equipment has anywhere from a 90-day to a two-year warranty that computer stores will honor on equipment purchased from them. If the equipment was purchased from another source, say, through a mail order house, you may need to return the equipment to the factory at your own expense.

It is also possible to purchase a service contract from either the seller or a third-party service company. Whether to purchase such a contract depends to a large degree on how much risk you are willing to accept and how important it is to you to know that the cost of repair is covered. In general, businesses

Discount computer stores in metropolitan areas often offer lower prices, combined with technical help.

with a large number of machines that are important to them are probably smart to purchase such an agreement.

Once you have selected the software, hardware, and supplier, making the purchase is the final step. But first it is worthwhile to go through a checklist to ensure that you are getting a "ready-to-use" system and will not have to return to the supplier for extra items. (This checklist includes questions the supplier must answer as well as items that need to be included in the purchase.)

1. Are all printer and monitor cables included in the system or will they have to be purchased separately?
2. Are any additional interface cards or boards needed to run the printer or the monitor?

TIPS FOR BUYING BY MAIL

Before you buy computer hardware or software by mail:

- Check on the company's payment policy and determine whether you will be charged extra for using a credit card. Also find out how long you will have to wait for a check to clear before the product is shipped.
- Make sure incidental costs such as shipping and handling don't raise the price above that offered by a local supplier.
- Check if the product is in stock and ask how long the company will take to deliver it to you. If it is not in stock, determine the back-order time.
- Get a clear idea of return policies— whether the company offers an unconditional 30-day money-back guarantee or replaces defective products only. Also determine if the company will accept the return of opened software for a refund, for credit toward another product, or not at all.
- If the price is a great deal lower than that found locally, check the description carefully to ensure that you are actually getting what you want. Check to see if a local store may be willing to meet or come close to the mail order price. Remember, however, that you may have to pay sales tax locally, but may not have to through mail order.
- Make sure that the company has a toll-free (800) number and is willing to answer questions about the product in addition to accepting orders.
- Keep all records of the transaction, including the salesperson's name and *all* correspondence, in case a problem arises.
- You are entitled to a full refund if the merchandise is not delivered within 30 days of payment. If there are problems, first call the company and then write, explaining your problem in a clear, logical, polite manner. If these steps fail and you have paid by credit card, the Fair Credit Billing Act allows you to contact your credit company and have them withhold payment until the problem is resolved.

Source: Ron Bel Bruno, "Tips for Buying by Mail," *Personal Computing,* February 1989, p. 83.

3. Are there sufficient connections to be able to hook up a modem and a printer at the same time? If not, what is the cost of these interfaces?
4. Is communications software included with the modem? If not, what is the cost of software that is compatible with the computer?
5. Can you expand the system in the future by adding additional memory or disk drives?
6. Have you included in your purchase price the cost of an initial purchase of blank floppy disks, printer paper, and, if you have a tape backup system, tape cartridges?
7. If you are buying a laser printer, is the toner cartridge included in the purchase price?

ALTERNATIVES TO BUYING A NEW PC

You do not have to buy a factory-fresh PC to have use of one. You can buy a used one, or you can rent one. One advantage of buying a used PC is that the original owner, rather than you, sustained the 40 percent loss in value that occurs when a computer is removed from its box. If you rent, you will not have to make a large outlay of capital.

As the power and speed of PCs increase, PC owners often upgrade to newer, more powerful machines; therefore, used PCs are widely available. In fact, the Boston Computer Society maintains a market price index on various types of used PCs. Used machines are not only cheaper but fully set up—the first owner has already invested the hours of time required to get the PC up and running. They may not be "state-of-the-art," but that does *not* mean they cannot serve the purpose for which they were built. A used computer is like an old pickup truck; it may not be shiny and new, but it still does the job. There are things you should remember, however, if you are considering buying a used PC.

■ Know what you want and thoroughly research the market prices before you shop. It is worthwhile to have the system appraised before you seal the deal.

■ Thoroughly test all the equipment before you buy it. You should check each key on the keyboard to make sure each works smoothly and that none cause extraneous letters to appear. Also, test the disk drives thoroughly to ensure that the computer will boot up and copy files without difficulty.

■ Unless you are somewhat of a computer expert, find a friend or hire a consultant to help you check the system.

■ Watch for "hot" machines if you are buying through a newspaper advertisement. Always ask to see the original sales receipt.

PC rentals total approximately $500 million annually, and analysts believe the figure will increase 30 to 40 percent annually. Most PC rental business is short term (30 days or less), and most businesses deliver the PC to you, set it up, provide free technical support for the term of the rental, and pick it up at the end of the rental period. Rates vary, depending on machine type and geographical location. In general, however, you can expect to pay at least $100 per week or $175 per month for an 80286 machine. This may seem expensive, but if your machine has died and you have four papers due in one week, a rental machine at even twice the price could seem cheap!

Sources: Alex Randall, "How to Buy Used PCs Without Getting Ripped Off," *Computerworld*, March 11, 1991, p. 84; and Jennifer Smith, "If You Can't Buy It, Rent It," *Lotus*, May 1991, p. 18.

Once the questions in this checklist have been answered satisfactorily, you can make the purchase knowing that the system will run just as soon as it is set up in the home or office. If any answers imply that additional equipment or purchases are required, then you might need to do more research before making the final purchase.

After the Purchase

Once you have purchased your personal computer, it is always wise to "burn in" the machine immediately by running it for several hours. In many cases, components in computers will fail during the first 50 to 100 hours of operation or not at all. Turning on the computer and running a repetitive program overnight improves the chance of catching a problem while the computer is still under warranty. It is also a good idea to test the software again to detect problems not found during the test-use phase. Once the hardware "burn-in" phase is over and the software has been tested, you are ready to enjoy the use of this wonderful mind tool.

BITS OF HISTORY

A Short History of the Personal Computer

The term *personal computer* was coined by a computer scientist, Alan Kay, in a 1972 paper titled "A Personal Computer for Children of All Ages." As a result of Kay's work in this area, Xerox built a personal computer called the Alto, though they never put it on the market. Other established computer companies also considered the concept of a personal computer but decided that there was no market for such a machine. As a result, it was not until 1975 that an Albuquerque, New Mexico, company called MITS released the first personal computer in kit form. This machine, named "Altair" after a planet in the "Star Trek" TV series,

had just 1K of memory and was very slow by today's standards. MITS had 5,000 orders for the Altair after it was pictured on the cover of *Popular Electronics.* A pioneer in the field, the current computer science publisher Rodney Zaks, remarked that "Never before had such a powerful tool been invented and so few people realized what it could do."

While MITS was the first to come out with a personal computer, it was up to Apple, Radio Shack, and Commodore to popularize its use. These were among almost 100 companies that rushed to put out personal computers in the years immediately after MITS offered the first one.

An amazing success story of this period is that of the Apple Company, formed by two young Californians, Steve Jobs and Steve Wozniak, when they built the first Apple computer in their garage.

With all these infant companies competing for the emerging computer

market, Apple made a real breakthrough in 1978 when it offered a disk drive to go along with the original Apple II. This was the key addition that, along with the VisiCalc software package offered only on the Apple, allowed Apple to leapfrog over Radio Shack and Commodore into first place among the pioneer companies.

The next breakthrough came when IBM offered its PC in 1981. While not an innovation technologically, the IBM PC almost immediately became an industry standard and legitimized the concept of a personal computer. It was followed by the Apple Macintosh in 1984, the IBM PS/2 line in 1987, and the NeXT computer in 1988. These introductions have divided the industry roughly into five types of computers: IBM PS/2, IBM PC AT compatibles, Apple II series, Apple Macintosh series, and others (Commodore, Atari, NeXT, and so on).

Source: John Hillkirk, "Computer Whiz Kids Recall Magic," *USA Today,* June 18, 1984, p. B3. Updated by the author.

The original IBM PC quickly became an industry standard and made IBM a force in PC manufacturing.

American Standard Code for Information Interchange (ASCII) Ordering of Symbols

ASCII Order	HEX Symbol	Control	Character	ASCII Order	HEX Symbol	Character
000	00H	NUL	(null)	032	20H	(space)
001	01H	SOH		033	21H	!
002	02H	STX		034	22H	,,
003	03H	ETX	♥	035	23H	#
004	04H	EOT	♦	036	24H	$
005	05H	ENQ	♣	037	25H	%
006	06H	ACK	♠	038	26H	&
007	07H	BEL	(beep)	039	27H	'
008	08H	BS	(backspace)	040	28H	(
009	09H	HT	(tab)	041	29H	)
010	0AH	LF	(line feed)	042	2AH	*
011	0BH	VT	(home)	043	2BH	+
012	0CH	FF	(form feed)	044	2CH	,
013	0DH	CR	(carriage return)	045	2DH	−
014	0EH	SO		046	2EH	.
015	0FH	SI		047	2FH	/
016	10H	DLE	►	048	30H	0
017	11H	DC1	◄	049	31H	1
018	12H	DC2		050	32H	2
019	13H	DC3	!!	051	33H	3
020	14H	DC4	¶	052	34H	4
021	15H	NAK	§	053	35H	5
022	16H	SYN	■	054	36H	6
023	17H	ETB		055	37H	7
024	18H	CAN		056	38H	8
025	19H	EM		057	39H	9
026	1AH	SUB	→	058	3AH	:
027	1BH	ESC	←	059	3BH	;
028	1CH	FS	(cursor right)	060	3CH	<
029	1DH	GS	(cursor left)	061	3DH	=
030	1EH	RS	(cursor up)	062	2EH	>
031	1FH	US	(cursor down)	063	3FH	?

ASCII Order	HEX Symbol	Character	ASCII Order	HEX Symbol	Character
064	40H	@	096	60H	'
065	41H	A	097	61H	a
066	42H	B	098	62H	b
067	43H	C	099	63H	c
068	44H	D	100	64H	d
069	45H	E	101	65H	e
070	46H	F	102	66H	f
071	47H	G	103	67H	g
072	48H	H	104	68H	h
073	49H	I	105	69H	i
074	4AH	J	106	6AH	j
075	4BH	K	107	6BH	k
076	4CH	L	108	6CH	l
077	4DH	M	109	6DH	m
078	4EH	N	110	6EH	n
079	4FH	O	111	6FH	o
080	50H	P	112	70H	p
081	51H	Q	113	71H	q
082	52H	R	114	72H	r
083	53H	S	115	73H	s
084	54H	T	116	74H	t
085	55H	U	117	75H	u
086	56H	V	118	76H	v
087	57H	W	119	77H	w
088	58H	X	120	78H	x
089	59H	Y	121	79H	y
090	5AH	Z	122	7AH	z
091	5BH	[	123	7BH	{
092	5CH	/	124	7CH	|
093	5DH	]	125	7DH	}
094	5EH	^	126	7EH	~
095	5FH	—	127	7FH	

GLOSSARY

access speed The amount of time required for a disk to find and move data. (PC Guide)

accounting A process that tracks the financial health of a company or an individual. (Chapter 6)

accounting software Software that is used to handle the accounting function of a business. (Chapter 3)

accounts payable A module of a business accounting software package that monitors the money the firm owes its suppliers. (Chapter 6)

accounts receivable A module of a business accounting software package that keeps track of money owed to a firm and when payments are due. (Chapter 6)

algorithm A step-by-step procedure used to solve a problem. (Chapter 4)

analog computer A machine that uses physical relationships to make its calculations; a measuring machine. (Chapter 1)

analog equivalent Data converted from serial form to analog form so that the telecommunications link can carry it. (Chapter 8)

analysis graphics A graphics software package that allows analysis of data to determine if patterns exist or to gain a better understanding of the data. (Chapter 5)

Analytical Engine The computer designed but not built by Charles Babbage in the mid-nineteenth century. (Chapter 1)

applications software Software that constitutes the greatest proportion of software used on computers and performs specialized tasks. (Chapter 3)

arithmetic-logic unit (ALU) The part of the CPU that handles the actual manipulation of the data. (Chapter 2)

artificial intelligence (AI) Hardware and software systems that exhibit the same type of intelligence-related activities as humans—listening, reading, speaking, solving problems, and making inferences. (Chapter 5)

ASCII An acronym for American Standard Code for Information Interchange—a code for the binary representation of characters within the computer. (Chapter 2)

asynchronous communication A form of communication between computers that does not require that the computers be synchronized in the rate at which they process data. (Chapter 8)

authoring languages A computer package that enables the user to create a sequence of interactive learning activities by using the mouse to select a "hot button" to answer a question or seek additional information. (Chapter 10)

auto-answer modem A modem that receives outside calls under the direction of the computer. (Chapter 8)

auto-dial modem A modem that dials a number under the direction of a computer. (Chapter 8)

automatic pagination A word processing operation that allows the user to include a page number automatically on each page of text. (Chapter 5)

backspace key Key used to delete text to the left of the cursor. (Chapter 5)

backup A copy of software or data that is made by the user to guard against accidental loss of software or data. (Chapters 2 and 10)

bar graph A type of analysis graphics that uses vertical or horizontal bars to show relative differences between categories of data. (Chapter 5)

batch commands Especially in MS-DOS-based personal computers, commands that cause batch files to execute. (Chapter 4)

batch mode A job entry mode in which the entire job is entered at one time from a disk drive or tape drive. (Chapter 4)

batch processing system Combining data from multiple users or time periods and submitting them to the computer for processing in a batch. (Chapter 9)

binary number system Base 2 number system based on zero and one. (Chapter 2)

bit The basic unit of measure in a computer; contraction of BInary and digiT. (Chapters 2 and 8)

bit-mapped graphics A type of graphics in which each pixel on the screen can be controlled individually. (Chapter 5)

bits per second (bps) A measure of the speed at which modems can send and receive information. (Chapter 8)

block-action command In word processing, the definition and subsequent movement, deletion, or other action on a block of text. (Chapter 5)

boiler plate material In word processing, a block of text that has been defined and copied to different points in a document or to different documents. (Chapter 5)

boldface Word processing operation that gives a heavier version of type. (Chapter 5)

booting process The process of starting up a computer. (Chapters 2 and 4)

boundary The delineation between the system and its environment. (Chapter 9)

bridge A combination of hardware and software that connects two similar networks. (Chapter 8)

broadband transmissions High-speed transmission requiring media that can transmit large amounts of data. (Chapter 8)

bulletin board service A telecommunications service that enables users to interact with each other. (Chapter 8)

bus The main cable in a bus network that links the central computers with all other computers in the network. (Chapter 8)

bus network A computer network in which computers are tied into a main cable, or bus, without a central computer. (Chapter 8)

business accounting package Computer software package designed to handle accounting for businesses. (Chapter 6)

business graphics Analysis graphics. (Chapter 5)

byte A group of eight bits—equivalent to a single character. (Chapter 2)

cartridge A form of magnetic tape, stored in a cartridge, that stores data using a magnetic bit pattern. (Chapter 2)

cell The intersection of a row and a column. (Chapters 3 and 6)

cell identifier A letter (for the column) and a number (for the row) that together indicate which cell is being referred to in a formula, such as A10 or B2. (Chapter 6)

cell pointer A special cursor used to designate the spreadsheet cell into which the information is being entered. (Chapter 6)

centering The word processing function that centers material between the margins. (Chapter 5)

central processing unit (CPU) The part of the computer that handles the actual processing of data into information. (Chapter 2)

character field A data base field that will contain any sequence of letters and numbers. (Appendix A)

character graphics Symbols that result when the dots on a screen can be controlled as a group, not individually. (Chapter 5)

charting package A presentation graphics package that shows the relationship between sets of numerical information. (Chapter 5)

children In a hierarchical data model, the lower-level elements. (Chapter 7)

chip A tiny piece of silicon that can consist of over a million electronic elements. (Chapters 1 and 2)

client-server configuration A LAN in which the processing burden is on the central computer. (Chapter 8)

clip art Desktop publishing element that imports previously created art images into a document. (Chapter 5)

clock speed A machine's top CPU processing speed, measured in megaHertz. (PC Guide)

coaxial cable A type of LAN cable similar to that used to transmit cable television signals into your home. (Chapter 8)

Color Graphics Adapter (CGA) A graphics board that allows an IBM PC or compatible to show four-color graphics as well as text. (Chapter 5)

color monitor A multicolor monitor. (Chapter 2)

column A series of values placed vertically. (Chapter 6)

command Instruction to the computer to carry out a specified operation; in BASIC, commands input by the user for immediate execution. (Chapter 3)

command driven Requiring the user to know and enter the needed commands and data. (Chapter 3)

command files Files that will execute a program in which a file name is entered. (Chapter 12)

command interpreter A part of the operating system that interprets the user's keystrokes and sends a message to the appropriate utility or applications program to carry out the command. (Chapter 4)

communications software A type of software package that enables the computer and the modem to communicate with the other computers, including uploading and downloading files. (Chapter 8)

completion screen A screen that requests information and data from the user. (Chapter 6 and Appendix A)

compound document A form of telecommunications combining written, voice, and computer communications to express an idea clearly. (Chapter 8)

computer An electronic, automatic machine that manipulates and stores symbols based on instructions from the user. (Chapter 1)

computer-aided design (CAD) A graphics software package that assists the user in developing engineering and architectural designs. (Chapter 5)

computer-based information system (CBIS) A system that uses computers to provide information needed by management. (Chapter 9)

computer chip *See* chip.

computer competence The level of computer knowledge reached by an individual who can use a computer to solve sophisticated problems in his or her field of expertise. (Chapter 1)

computer crime The unauthorized invasion of a computer data file, or theft of money, merchandise, data, or computer time, using a computer. (Chapter 5)

computer disk *See* disk.

computer error A misnomer—actually a human error. (Chapter 1)

computer language A language used by humans to give instructions to computers. (Chapters 2 and 3)

computer literacy An understanding of what a computer can and cannot do and an ability to make the computer do what is desired. (Chapter 1)

computer mastery The level of knowledge required of an individual who wants to be a success in the computer field. (Chapter 1)

computer network A combination of two or more computers with a communications system that allows exchange of information between the computers. (Chapters 1, 3, and 8)

computer package Commercially available software. (Chapters 1 and 3)

computeritis Painful musculo-skeletal problems associated with day-in/day-out use of the keyboard. (Chapter 10)

computerphobia A fear of the computer, especially among first-time users. (Chapter 10)

computer program A set of specific instructions for controlling the computer. (Chapter 3)

computer terminal A keyboard and monitor without a CPU or any secondary storage devices. (Chapter 1)

computer virus A self-replicating, potentially damaging computer program sent over a computer network by mischievous or malicious persons. (Chapter 10)

computer worm A stand alone computer program that replicates itself over and over after gaining access to a computer network. (Chapter 10)

conceptual computer A simplified computer that can demonstrate the major functions of a computer without involving the operational details of the machine. (Chapter 2)

control unit Part of the CPU that handles the management of the symbol manipulation process. (Chapter 2)

conventional memory The first 640 Kbytes of RAM recognized by MS-DOS for executing programs. (Chapter 2)

copy protection The process whereby software manufacturers guard against software piracy by making it impossible to make copies of personal computer software. (Chapter 10)

credit An accounting term used in double-entry bookkeeping. (Chapter 6)

cursor A blinking rectangle of light on the screen that designates the current position. (Chapters 2 and 5)

cursor control keys Keys on a personal computer keyboard that control the movement of the cursor on the screen. (Chapter 5)

cut-and-paste In word processing, a block-action command that defines a block of text and then moves it to another part of the document or to another document. (Chapter 5)

cyberphobia *See* computerphobia.

data The raw facts that are fed into the computer for processing. (Chapter 1)

data bank A store of information on people or organizations. (Chapter 10)

data base A collection of information that is arranged for easy manipulation and retrieval. (Chapters 3, 7, and 9)

data base management software Software that manages an electronic data base in such a way that it is possible to find elements that fit some criteria. (Chapters 3 and 7)

data base structure The data base fields defined in terms of their names, widths, and types. (Chapter 7)

data base vendors Companies that offer subscribers extensive, often full-text, data bases on specialized topics. (Chapter 8)

data communications Any communication between two computers that involves a transfer of data. (Chapter 8)

data dependence The dependency between data and data storage. (Chapter 7)

data dictionary A list of data elements, along with information regarding name, source, description, and use. (Chapter 7)

data entry screen A set of requests for data, displayed on the screen of a monitor. (Chapter 7 and ASCII Symbols)

data flow diagram A pictorial representation of the flow of data into and out of the system. (Chapter 9)

data hierarchy The order in which data or information is organized in the computer. (Chapter 7)

data integrity The correctness of data in a data base. (Chapter 7)

data models One of several models of the way data will be represented in a data base management system. (Chapter 7)

data processing The mechanical process of converting raw data into meaningful information; usually refers to the processing of numeric data. (Chapters 1 and 9)

data redundancy The repetition of data on multiple files. (Chapter 7)

date field A numeric field that can store only the date in dd/mm/yy format. (Chapter 7)

debit An accounting term used in double-entry bookkeeping. (Chapter 6)

decision support system (DSS) A subsystem of the MIS that combines data with models and graphics to answer a decision maker's questions about the data. (Chapter 9)

default answer The answer to a prompt that will be accepted if the user presses the Enter key without changing any information. (ASCII Symbols)

delayed conference A form of teleconferencing in which the participant's comments are stored sequentially as they are entered; these comments are read and replied to by other participants over a long period of time. (Chapter 8)

desktop computers See personal computers.

desktop publishing Combining word processing, graphics, and special page-definition software to create documents. (Chapters 3 and 5)

diagramming package A presentation graphics package that works with shapes to display a set of facts graphically in the form of organizational charts, flowcharts, schedules, office layouts, and so on. (Chapter 5)

digital computer A machine that uses numbers to make its calculations; a counting machine. (Chapter 1)

digitizer board A piece of computer hardware that will convert a blueprint or photographic image into a digital form. (Chapter 7)

direct-access storage Secondary storage on which information may be accessed in any desired order. (Chapter 2)

direct-access storage device (DASD) A secondary storage device on which information can be accessed in any desired order. (Chapter 2)

direct conversion A conversion from one system to another in which the old system is discarded at the time that the new system is installed. (Chapter 9)

disk A thin, recordlike piece of metal or plastic, covered with iron oxide particles whose magnetic direction can be arranged to represent symbols. (Chapter 2)

disk directory A list of the files that are stored on a disk. (Chapter 4)

disk drive A device that writes information onto or reads information from magnetic disk. (Chapter 2)

disk operating system (DOS) An operating system for a personal computer that depends on disks for secondary storage. (Chapters 2, 3, and 4)

disk packs Collections of magnetic disks, each about the size of a record album, used on mainframes. (Chapter 2)

diskette See floppy disk.

diskless workstation In a LAN, a personal computer that does not have a disk drive and is dependent on the file server for disk access. (Chapter 8)

distributed data bases Small, specialized data bases that are separate from a primary data base; usually associated with minicomputers in a distributed data processing arrangement. (Chapter 8)

distributed data processing (DDP) A processing system that uses a mainframe computer for storage or data bases and for large-scale processing; combined with minicomputers or personal computers for local processing. (Chapter 8)

document translation A word processor function to convert documents from one word processing package to another. (Chapter 5)

documentation A written description of a software package and the tasks it can perform; in a program, the explanation of the logic and program statements. (Chapter 3)

dot matrix printer A personal computer printer that uses a matrix of wires to form symbols on paper. (Chapter 2)

dot pitch The width of a dot on the monitor screen; the smaller the dot pitch, the sharper the image. (PC Guide)

double-entry bookkeeping An accounting system that enters each transaction as an increase to one account and a decrease to another account. (Chapter 6)

downloading The process of shifting software or data from a central computer to a personal computer and saving it on disk. (Chapter 8)

downsizing The process of replacing a mainframe or a minicomputer system with a LAN. (Chapter 8)

drawing package A presentation graphics package that allows the user to add lines to library shapes or create onscreen animation, usually using a mouse as an input device. (Chapter 5)

dumb terminal A computer with no CPU or secondary storage. Its sole purpose is as an input/output device for a mainframe. (Chapters 2 and 8)

EBCDIC An acronym for Extended Binary Coded Decimal Interchange Code and a code for the binary representation of characters within the computer. (Chapter 2)

edited to check computer data for reasonableness or discrepancies; also, the process of changing a statement without having to reenter it entirely. (ASCII Symbols)

edit line The line above or below a spreadsheet, on which the information being entered actually shows up. (Chapter 6)

electronic data interchange (EDI) Allows computers to exchange electronic transmissions of data and information thus automating routine business between retail stores, distributors, and manufacturers. (Chapter 8)

electronic funds transfer (EFT) The payment of bills and other forms of funds transfer via computer. (Chapter 1)

electronic mail The process of sending letters, documents, and messages between computers. (Chapter 8)

electronic spreadsheet On a computer, a spreadsheet that allows for easy recalculation of values based on changes within the spreadsheet. (Chapter 6)

End key A key on the IBM compatible PC keyboard often used with word processing packages to place the cursor. (Chapters 2 and 5)

end user A non-data processing professional who uses the computer to solve problems associated with his or her job and may be quite sophisticated in the use of the computer. (Chapter 1)

Enhanced Graphics Adapter (EGA) A digital computer graphic board that displays 16-color graphics in 640 × 360 resolution as well as displaying high-quality text. (Chapter 5)

environment All elements outside of a system that have some effect on the system. (Chapter 9)

ergonomics The study of the relationship between efficiency and comfort in a worker's use of machines. (Chapter 10)

error trapping A mechanism in a software package that keeps a user from entering the incorrect type of data. (Chapter 6)

Executive Information System (EIS) A personalized, easy-to-use system for executives, providing data on the daily operations of an organization. (Chapter 4)

expanded memory Includes conventional memory plus any RAM up to 8 Mbytes that has been modified to work with MS-DOS-based software. (Chapter 2)

expert system A computer system that makes the collective knowledge of various experts in a field available to the user. (Chapters 1 and 9)

extended memory All RAM between 1 and 32 Mbytes. MS-DOS-based software programs cannot use extended memory because they were written to another type of memory called **expanded memory.** (Chapter 2)

external commands Operating system commands that require that the system disk be in the active drive to be implemented. (Chapter 4)

external modem A modem that is outside the computer but is connected to the computer through the serial port. (Chapter 8)

facsimile (fax) machine A telecommunications machine used to send a reproduction of any document over phone lines to any place in the world. (Chapter 8)

feedback A form of output that is sent back to a system's input or processing function, enabling a system to change its operation if necessary. (Chapter 9)

fiber optic cable The newest type of media that consists of thousands of glass fiber strands that transmit information over networks. (Chapter 8)

field A single piece of information—such as a name, a Social Security number, or a profit value. (Chapter 7)

field name An identifier given to a field in a data base file. (Chapter 7)

field type The type of information—that is, character, numeric, date, or logical—that will be stored in a field. (Chapter 7)

field width The number of positions set aside for data in a particular field. (Chapter 12)

file A collection of records all having the same fields, to which the user can attach a name. (Chapters 3 and 7)

file allocation table (FAT) A list of the diskette's contents, used to locate programs and files. (Chapters 2 and 4)

file manager A part of a data base management package that controls the actual creation of the file and various utility functions associated with the use of the file. (Chapter 7)

file processing system (FPS) Data base management software that can work with only one file at a time. (Chapter 7)

file processor *See* file processing system.

file server A hard disk that provides users of a network access to files. (Chapter 8)

financial analysis software *See* spreadsheet.

firmware Instructions on a ROM chip. (Chapter 1)

fixed expenses Expenses that do not change from month to month. (Chapter 6)

flat file Another name for a table in a relational data model. (Chapter 7)

floppy disk Disk made of Mylar plastic and covered with iron oxide particles for use with the personal computer. (Chapter 2)

flowchart A pictorial form of an algorithm that can easily be converted into a computer program. (Chapter 9)

footers A text entry operation that allows the display of special information at the bottom of each page. (Chapter 5)

footnotes A word processing operation that allocates spacing at the bottom of a page for cited references. (Chapter 5)

formal documentation For the systems analysis and design process, the data dictionary and list of data elements; for a software package, the user's manual and other written descriptions. (Chapter 3)

formatting The process of organizing the sectors and tracks of a floppy disk; in word processing, the process of setting up a document in a particular form. (Chapters 2 and 5)

formula Values in the spreadsheet combined with other constants to define the relationships among the spreadsheet values. (Chapter 6)

frames In desktop publishing packages, holes left in the text for graphics, drawings, and photographs. (Chapter 5)

freeware Software packages that can be obtained for free or for a small fee. (Chapter 3)

full-duplex mode A mode of communication between computers in which both computers can send at the same time. (Chapter 8)

function In a spreadsheet, a specific operation; in programming, a short program stored in computer memory that can be accessed by the program as needed. (Chapter 6)

gateway A combination of hardware and software that connects two dissimilar computer networks. It allows a LAN user to access a mainframe network without leaving his or her PC. (Chapter 8)

general ledger Record that contains all the firm's financial transactions. (Chapter 6)

general-purpose computer A computer that can be used for many purposes. (Chapter 1)

generic operating system Personal computer operating system that runs on many different makes of computers. (Chapters 3 and 4)

geographical information system (GIS) A computer system used to work with geographical entities, such as states, counties, or census blocks. (Chapter 9)

gigabyte (GByte) The largest commonly used measure of computer storage, equal to 1 billion (2^{30}) bytes of storage. (Chapter 2)

global change In a spreadsheet, a change made by the user to change all cell widths. (Chapter 6)

graphics adapter board Computer hardware that supports color and graphics. (Chapter 5)

graphics software A group of programs for visual presentation of information or for creation of new and different art forms. (Chapter 3)

hackers Individuals who gain unauthorized access to a computer for fun or challenge. (Chapter 10)

half-duplex mode Communications between two computers during which both computers can send and receive information but only one computer can send at a time. (Chapter 8)

handheld portable A battery-powered, pocket-sized personal computer. (PC Guide)

hard copy A printed version of what appears on the video screen. (Chapter 2)

hard disk A scaled-down version of a mainframe disk pack with metal disks that is used for storing information from a personal computer. (Chapter 2)

hardware The electronic part of the computer that stores and manipulates symbols under the direction of the computer software. (Chapters 1 and 2)

Hayes compatibility Whether a modem uses the same commands as a Hayes modem, which has become the industry standard. (Chapter 8)

head window The area of a floppy disk that is in contact with the read/write head. (Chapter 2)

headers A text entry operation that allows the display of special information at the top of each page. (Chapter 5)

Hercules Graphics Card The add-in board necessary to display high-resolution (720 × 348) monochrome graphics on the monochrome monitor. (Chapter 5)

hierarchical data model A data model in which each element has only one parent or owner—similar to an organization chart. (Chapter 7)

hierarchical structure Division of long lists of files into subdirectories that are easier to keep track of. Also called a tree structure. (Chapter 4)

high-level languages Languages combining English words with a specific grammar to give the computer instructions. (Chapter 6)

Home key A key on the numeric keypad that is often used in word processing packages. (Chapter 5)

horizontal scrolling In a spreadsheet, the horizontal movement of the columns across the screen. (Chapter 6)

host computer In a star network configuration, the central computer to which all other computers are linked. (Chapter 8)

hub ring The part of a floppy disk where the disk drive clamps onto the disk and rotates it. (Chapter 2)

human-factors engineering *See* ergonomics.

hypertext Information retrieval software that stores information in discrete nodes that can be reached from any other node, allowing users to move about within the data base according to whatever mental connections they make. (Chapter 7)

IBM compatible PC A computer with the ability to run software written for the original IBM PC or one of its successors. (Chapters 2 and 3)

icons Pictures that represent various operations on the computer. (Chapters 3 and 4)

image scanner A device often used in desktop publishing that allows images to be scanned and converted into a digital form that can be included in a document. (Chapter 5)

index hole A hole in the vinyl cover of a floppy disk that indicates to the computer the current position of the disk in its rotation. (Chapter 2)

indexing A system of keeping track of records in a data base using record numbers. (Chapter 7)

informated factory A workplace where computers perform operations and supply workers with information on the processing operations. (Chapter 10)

information Data that has been processed into a form that is useful to the user. (Chapter 1)

information society A society in which the majority of the workers are involved in the transmittal of information. (Chapter 1)

information specialist A person who works with a personal computer to perform such wide-ranging tasks as word processing, data base management, and spreadsheet analysis. (Chapter 10)

information system Within an organization, a system that converts raw data into information that is useful to managers and other interested parties. (Chapters 1 and 9)

information technology The use of computers for information and productivity. (Chapter 1)

ink-jet printer A nonimpact printer that forms symbols by spraying dots of ink on the paper. (Chapter 2)

input Receiving the data to be manipulated and the instructions for performing that manipulation. (Chapters 2 and 9)

insert mode A word processing mode in which new symbols that are entered are inserted to the left of the existing symbols, pushing the existing material to the right. (Chapter 5)

integer field A data base field that will contain a number without a decimal. (Chapter 7 and ASCII Symbols)

integrated circuit (IC) The combination of transistors and circuits on a chip. (Chapter 2)

Integrated Service Digital Network (ISDN) Digital network of the future that will dramatically increase telecommunications transmission capabilities. (Chapter 8).

integrated package Software that contains some or all of the most commonly used packages and a procedure to access the various packages. (Chapters 3 and 6)

internal commands Operating system commands that do not require that the system disk be in the active drive. (Chapter 4)

internal memory The part of the computer used to store instructions and data internally. (Chapter 2)

internal modem A modem that is located in a slot inside the computer in the back. (Chapter 8)

inventory control A process that keeps track of raw materials, goods in process, finished goods, and other supplies for a company. (Chapter 6)

investment analysis package Packages to keep track of investments and help choose the best way to invest money. (Chapter 6)

Kbyte 1 Kbyte equals 1,024 bytes. (Chapter 2)

keyboard An input device made up of keys that allow input of alphanumeric and punctuation characters. (Chapter 2)

label For a spreadsheet, a combination of letters and numbers that defines a cell; in programming, a number that allows reference to a statement in the program; in BASIC, any string constant enclosed in quotation marks. (Chapter 6)

LAN operating systems Systems that operate at a level above the basic operating system to allow users access to software and files on the file server. (Chapter 4)

laptop computer A portable computer designed to fit on one's lap or some other nonpermanent surface where no AC power is available. (PC Guide)

laser printer A nonimpact printer that uses a laser beam to write dots on a drum coated with light-sensitive material that transfers ink to the paper. (Chapter 2)

leased lines Special high-speed telephone lines that are leased from the telephone company for the express purpose of carrying data between computers. (Chapter 8)

light pen An input device that allows the user to select a command by pointing it at a portion of the screen. (Chapter 2)

line graph A type of analysis graphics that shows relationships by connecting points on the screen. (Chapter 5)

local area network (LAN) A network of personal computers within one building. (Chapters 3 and 8)

local change A change made by the user in a spreadsheet to change the width of only a designated group of cells. (Chapter 6)

logical field A field whose format can only be true or false (yes or no). (Chapter 7)

luggable PCs Portable personal computers that weigh over 10 pounds, require AC power, and are portable from desk to desk. (PC Guide)

machine language A computer's binary language, which is a very specific language that details every computer operation as a series of zeroes and ones. (Chapter 9)

macro A facility in a spreadsheet that allows the user to do an operation once and then to save that series of keystrokes by assigning a name to them. (Chapter 6)

magnetic disk A metal or plastic disk coated with ferrous oxide particles, on which information can be stored via a magnetic bit pattern. (Chapter 2)

magnetic (mag) tape A form of secondary storage composed on thin Mylar tape coated with ferrous oxide particles, on which information is recorded in binary form by selective magnetization of spots on the tape. (Chapter 2)

mail-merge A function of word processing that prepares form letters by combining a letter with different names and addresses. (Chapter 5)

mainframe A very large and fast computer that requires a special support staff and a special physical environment. (Chapter 1)

main memory *See* internal memory.

management information system (MIS) An integrated user-machine system for providing information to support operations, management, and decision-making functions in an organization. (Chapter 9)

many-to-many relationship In a data model, the situation in which multiple fields are related to one another. (Chapter 7)

massively parallel computers Computers that speed up data processing by performing many different operations at one time. (Chapter 10)

megabyte (Mbyte) Measure of computer memory equal to 1 million (2^{30}) bytes of storage. (Chapter 2)

megaHertz Unit of measurement or the clock speed of a CPU. (PC Guide)

memory manager A type of utility software that causes the extended memory to emulate expanded memory. (Chapter 2)

menu A list of commands or requests for data. (Chapter 3)

menu driven A software package that uses a menu to allow the user to make selections of commands or to enter data. (Chapter 3)

microchip *See* chip.

microcomputers *See* personal computers.

microfloppy disk A floppy disk that is less than 4 inches in diameter and is usually contained within a hard plastic cartridge. (Chapter 2)

microprocessor A computer chip that is programmed to control a machine's actions; also, a CPU on a chip. (Chapters 1 and 2)

microwaves High-frequency radio transmissions that can be transmitted between two earth stations or between earth stations and communications satellites, which are commonly used to transmit such things as television signals. (Chapter 8)

mind tool Another name for a computer. (Chapter 1)

minicomputer Computer size between a mainframe and a personal computer. (Chapter 1)

model A simplified version of the system that allows the analyst to understand the system's important parts. (Chapter 9)

modem A communications device that modulates computer signals into outgoing audio signals and demodulates incoming audio signals into computer signals. (Chapters 2 and 8)

module A separate program that performs a specific task and shares data with the other modules to lead to an integrated system. (Chapter 6)

monitor A cathode ray tube output device that shows the output on a video screen. (Chapter 2)

monochrome monitor A one-color monitor. (Chapter 2)

mouse An input device—about the size of a mouse and connected to the computer by a long cord—that allows input through movement over a flat surface. (Chapter 2)

MS-DOS A single-user, single-task generic operating system for use on IBM compatible PCs; currently the most popular disk operating system. (Chapters 3 and 4)

multiple-access network A local area network in which all users can transmit at any time, but collision-detecting software is necessary to control transmissions. (Chapter 8)

multimedia The traditional PC along with a VCR, optical storage disk, compact disks, and high-fidelity stereo that will provide interactive, full-motion video. (Chapter 1)

multiscanning monitor A computer monitor that can display the output from analog VGA or from any digital graphics adapter. (Chapter 5)

natural languages Languages that use everyday terminology and grammar to communicate with the computer. (Chapters 7 and 10)

network A combination of two or more computers with a communications system that allows exchange of information between the computers. (Chapters 1, 3, and 8)

network data model A data model in which each element may have more than one parent or owner. (Chapter 7)

neural network Computer processing using multiple processors that are "trained," through repetition, to handle some task without an extensive, highly specific program. (Chapter 10)

node The location of a computer or terminal in a network or electronic mail system. (Chapter 8)

noninterlaced monitor A monitor that paints each line during each pass, which results in a sharper screen image. (PC Guide)

nonprocedural language A computer language that does not require the user to develop a logical procedure but only to answer questions or make choices from a menu. (Chapter 7)

notebook PCs Portable, full-power personal computers that can run on either AC power or rechargeable batteries and are similar to **laptops** but are generally lighter. (PC Guide)

numeric field A field with the ability to store numeric information and make calculations. (Chapter 7)

office automation *See* office information system.

office information system (OIS) A machine or machines combined with a communications system and users to effi-

ciently handle the job of obtaining, organizing, storing, retrieving, and preparing needed information; also called **office automation.** (Chapter 9)

one-to-many In a data model, the situation in which one field is related to multiple other fields. (Chapter 7)

one-to-one In a data model, the situation in which one field is related to only one other field. (Chapter 7)

online services Companies that provide a wide range of computerized information to their subscribers. (Chapter 3)

operating environment A program that overlays the operating system to allow a menu-driven operating system, multitasking, or the use of windows. (Chapters 3 and 4)

operating system The primary component of systems software; manages the many tasks that are going on concurrently within a computer. (Chapters 3 and 4)

optical disk A form of secondary storage that uses lasers and pits in a reflective surface to store information. (Chapter 2)

order processing A module that a retail or wholesale operation uses to make sure that customers' orders are filled in a timely manner. (Chapter 6)

OS/2 A single-user, multitasking generic operating system for use on some IBM compatible PCs. (Chapter 3)

outline processor An operation that aids the user by automatically numbering the various levels of an outline. (Chapter 5)

output The result of the processing as displayed or printed for the user. (Chapters 2 and 9)

packet switching In a wide area network, dividing long messages into smaller data units to be transmitted more easily through a network. (Chapter 8)

packets The smaller data units that long messages are divided into for packet switching. (Chapter 8)

page description language (PDL) In a desktop publishing package, the operation that combines the user's text and graphics into a final page format. (Chapter 5)

page printer A laser printer capable of printing an entire page at a time. (Chapter 2)

paint packages Graphics packages that are used to develop artistic creations on the computer screen. (Chapter 5)

paragraph indention A function of a word processing package that allows an entire paragraph to be indented. (Chapter 5)

parallel conversion The conversion of one system to another in which both systems run in parallel before the conversion is completed. (Chapter 9)

parallel form The processing of data 8, 16, 32 bits at a time. (Chapter 8)

parent In a hierarchical data base, the data element that is linked in a superior fashion to other elements called children. (Chapter 7)

parity bit On magnetic storage devices and in communications, an extra bit that is used for error-checking. (Chapter 8)

payroll A list of employees to be paid and the amount each is paid by the organization. (Chapter 6)

peer-to-peer configuration A LAN configuration in smaller networks in which the emphasis is on users sharing files. Each computer can function as both a server and a workstation instead of as a single dedicated file server. (Chapter 8)

pen-based computing A form of input in which the user writes directly to the screen. (Chapter 2)

personal accounting packages Software designed to help keep track of an individual's or even a small business's finances. (Chapter 6)

personal budgeting package A group of programs that includes checkbook accounting and home budget planning. (Chapters 3 and 6)

personal computer Small, one-user computers that are relatively inexpensive to own and do not require a special environment or special knowledge to use them. (Chapter 1)

personal financial management package Software designed to help the individual monitor his or her finances. (Chapter 6)

personal productivity software PC applications software, so-called because it allows individuals to increase their productivity. (Chapter 3)

PgDn key A key on the IBM compatible PC keyboard that facilitates large downward movements of the cursor. (Chapters 2 and 5)

PgUp key A key on the IBM compatible PC keyboard that facilitates large upward movements of the cursor. (Chapters 2 and 5)

pie graph A type of analysis graphics that demonstrates the manner in which some quantity is proportionally divided by showing those divisions as pieces of a pie. (Chapter 5)

piping The ability to send output from one program to another program, where it becomes input. (Chapter 4)

pixel A picture element made up of a dot of light on the screen. (Chapter 5)

pocket PCs Portable personal computers are about the size of a large calculator and replace traditional address books, calculators, and appointment calendars. They are battery powered and do not usually include a disk drive. (PC Guide)

pointer system An indexing system in which the value associated with each element in a list points to the next element in the list. (Chapter 7)

port An entry line to the computer. (Chapter 8)

portable computer A computer that can be transported. (PC Guide)

presentation graphics Graphics software packages that allow the presentation of data and information in a more understandable or dramatic form. (Chapter 5)

Presentation Manager A graphical interface incorporated into OS/2. (Chapter 4)

primary storage *See* internal memory.

primitives Basic graphic objects such as points, lines, and circles used in designs. (Chapter 5)

print spooler A word processing function that allows text to be printed while other text is being entered or edited. (Chapter 5)

printer An output device that places words and symbols on paper. (Chapter 2)

printer codes Instructions that the printer uses to convert the special characters for underlining, boldface, and subscripts. (Chapter 5)

printer driver In word processing, a software package that handles the conversion of special characters in the document to symbols the printer can use. (Chapter 5)

procedural language A computer language that requires the programmer to use a logical procedure to perform some task. (Chapter 7)

processing The conversion of data into information. (Chapter 9)

processing/internal memory unit The part of the computer of the computer where data are stored and manipulated. (Chapter 2)

program A series of instructions to the computer. (Chapter 1)

program flowchart A pictorial form of the logic needed to solve a problem. (Chapter 9)

programmable decisions Day-to-day operational decisions based on basic rules and policies set at higher management levels. (Chapter 9)

programming The process of writing a series of instructions for the computer to follow in performing some specific task. (Chapters 1 and 3)

prompt A signal on the screen, indicating that the computer is waiting for a command or data. (Chapter 3)

proportional spacing A text print that creates different amounts of space between different letters. (Chapter 5)

proprietary operating system Personal computer operating systems that run on only one type of computer. (Chapters 3 and 4)

protocol The set of rules two computers follow when communicating with each other. (Chapter 8)

pseudocode A written form of an algorithm that can easily be converted into a computer program. (Chapter 9)

puck A stylus on a digitizer tablet used in computer-aided design. (Chapter 5)

pull-down menu A menu that uses icons to represent various commands or operations and appears as needed. (Chapter 3)

pushover mode *See* insert mode.

query language A computer language associated with the use of data base management packages that allows a user to request information. (Chapter 7)

queue The use of a waiting line by operating systems to execute jobs according to their level of priority. (Chapter 4)

RAM-resident program A program that, once run, remains resident in RAM and can be called up during the operation of another program. (Chapter 4)

random-access memory (RAM) The section of memory that is available for storing the instructions to the computer and the symbols to be manipulated. (Chapter 2)

range In a spreadsheet, a part of a row, a part of a column, or a rectangle of cells. (Chapter 6 and ASCII Symbols)

read-only memory (ROM) The section of memory that is placed in the computer during the manufacturing process and remains there even after the computer is turned off. (Chapter 2)

read/write head The part of a disk or tape drive that handles the actual transfer of information to or from the disk or tape. (Chapter 2)

real field A data base field that will contain a number containing a decimal. (Chapter 7 and Appendix A)

real-time conference A form of teleconferencing in which all participants are logged onto the system at the same time. (Chapter 8)

real-time processing Used when several users are competing for the same resource—e.g., an airline reservation system. (Chapter 9)

record A collection of fields with information that usually pertains to only one subject (person, place, event, and so on). (Chapter 7)

record number The physical position of a record in a list. (Chapter 7)

reformatted The realignment of a paragraph's margins after material has been deleted. (Chapter 5)

relational data model A data model in which elements are represented as being parts of tables, which are then related through common elements. (Chapter 7)

relative copy A copy of a formula being moved that retains the original formula structure but changes that formula to match the location of the new cell. (Chapter 6)

remote job entry (RJE) site A batch job entry site that is separate from the CPU. (Chapter 4)

replace mode The word processing mode in which current symbols are replaced by new symbols. (Chapter 5)

report generator The part of a data base management package that handles the reporting of information in whatever order the user desires. (Chapter 7)

resolution The quality of the picture on a monitor as defined by the number of pixels on the screen. (Chapter 5)

reverse video On a computer screen, dark letters appearing on a light background instead of vice versa. (Chapter 1)

right justification The addition of extra space in a line to make the right margins line up. (Chapter 5)

ring network A computer network that links multiple computers in a circle or ring with no host computer. (Chapter 8)

robots Automated machines. (*Also see* robotics). (Chapter 1)

row A series of values placed horizontally. (Chapter 6)

scatter diagram A type of analysis graphics that uses a symbol such as the asterisk to plot the relationships between values on the horizontal and vertical axes. (Chapter 5)

scrolling For word processing, spreadsheets, or telecommunications, the up and down or left and right movements of the text or cells on the screen so that additional material can be seen. (Chapter 5 and Appendix A)

search and replace In word processing, the operation of searching for and replacing a particular character string with another string. (Chapter 5)

secondary storage Storage area outside of the computer, used to hold an overflow of information or to save information when the computer is turned off. (Chapter 2)

sector A pie-shaped section of a floppy disk that is used to divide the tracks on a floppy disk. (Chapter 2)

sequential access A form of access in which the records are accessed in the same order in which they are physically stored. (Chapter 2)

serial form The processing of data one bit at a time. (Chapter 8)

serial port The connection between the computer and the modem cable. (Chapter 8)

shareware Software that is made available to users for a nominal fee or donation. (Chapter 3)

shell A software application working with MS-DOS to allow a graphical interface, multitasking, and the use of windows. (Chapter 4)

simplex mode Communications between computers, in which the communication can be in only one direction. (Chapter 8)

smart machine Computer-based machine that can make decisions and provide information. (Chapter 1)

soft sectoring A sectoring plan that depends on the personal computer in use and on the disk operating system. (Chapter 2)

software The programs that direct the activity of the computer. (Chapters 1 and 3)

software package A combination of one or more computer programs and documentation describing the programs and their use. (Chapter 3)

software piracy The unauthorized copying of software for either personal use or financial gain. (Chapter 10)

sorting The process of arranging records in ascending or descending order. (Chapters 3 and 7 and ASCII Symbols)

special-purpose computer A computer designed for only one purpose. (Chapter 1)

speller A function of a word processor that checks the spelling of words in a document. (Chapter 5)

spreadsheet A table having rows and columns of values, labels, and formulas that can be used to make calculations, plan budgets, make forecasts, and ask "What if?" questions about the data. (Chapters 3 and 6)

spreadsheet linking The capacity to link data and formulas in multiple spreadsheets so that a change in one spreadsheet is transferred to other spreadsheets using the same value or formula. (Chapter 6)

stacked bar graphs A type of analysis graphics that places multiple quantities on the same bar. (Chapter 5)

star network A computer network with one host computer, to which many smaller computers or terminals are linked. (Chapter 8)

start bit A bit at the beginning of a character in asynchronous communication that signals the computer that a character is beginning to be sent. (Chapter 8)

status line A line at the top or bottom of the screen that provides information regarding the current status of the screen. (Chapter 5)

stop bit A bit at the end of a character in asynchronous communication that signals the computer that the transmission of a character is ended. (Chapter 8)

strategic decisions Top-level decisions that are not easily programmable. (Chapter 9)

strategic information system (SIS) An information system used to support or develop a company's competitive strategy. (Chapter 9)

structured approach The movement from a logical design to a physical design following a set pattern of steps. Also called **top-down approach.** (Chapter 9)

stylesheet An operation of the desktop publishing package that specifies the format of a document. (Chapter 5)

subdirectories Subgroups of files, each of which is assigned a name. (Chapter 4)

supercomputer The biggest, fastest computers used today. (Chapter 1)

superconductivity The ability of certain materials at low temperatures to conduct electricity without resistance. (Chapter 10)

symbol processor A computer that can manipulate symbols as well as numbers; another name for a computer. (Chapter 5)

synchronous communications A form of communication between computers that does not require the computers to be synchronized and allows large numbers of characters to be sent as a block. (Chapter 8)

system A group of elements organized for the purpose of achieving a particular goal. (Chapters 2 and 9)

systems analysis and design process The process of developing a system design to meet a new need or to solve a problem in an existing system. (Chapter 9)

systems analyst The person who carries out the systems analysis and design process. (Chapter 9)

systems development life cycle *See* systems analysis and design.

systems flowchart A special type of flowchart that demonstrates the flows of information and control in the existing system. (Chapter 9)

systems life cycle *See* systems analysis and design.

systems programmers Programmers that maintain mainframe operating systems. (Chapter 4)

systems software The programming that controls the operations of utility software and applications software. (Chapter 3)

tactical decisions Decisions made by middle-level managers using summary reports. These are not easily programmable. (Chapter 9)

tape *See* magnetic tape.

tape cartridge Storage medium used by personal or mainframe computers to back up hard disks. (Chapter 2)

tape drive An electronic device that uses a read/write head to transfer information to and from magnetic tape. (Chapter 2)

tax planning and preparation package A package used to keep track of tax records throughout the year and to determine the effects of financial decisions. (Chapter 6)

telecommunications The combining of a computer with a communications link, a modem, and appropriate communications software to become a communications tool. (Chapter 8)

telecommunications software A group of programs allowing a personal computer user to communicate with other people, computers, and data bases. (Chapters 3 and 8)

telecommuting The process of working at home using either a personal computer or a terminal tied into a mainframe. (Chapter 8)

template A skeleton spreadsheet that matches a particular application but does not include the data. (Chapter 6)

terminal A keyboard and a monitor connected to a computer. (*Also see* computer terminal) (Chapters 1 and 2)

terminal emulation A hardware/software combination that allows a personal computer to work like a dedicated mainframe terminal. (Chapter 8)

text editing The word processing function that allows material to be changed, inserted, or deleted from existing text. (Chapter 5)

thesaurus An editing tool that provides synonyms and antonyms for specified words. (Chapter 5)

time slice A small fraction of the total execution time that is allocated to a terminal in a time-sharing system. (Chapter 4)

token A special bit pattern used in a token-sharing local area network to determine which user can transmit information. (Chapter 8)

token/sharing network A local area network in which a bit pattern called a token is used to determine which user on the network can send information. (Chapter 8)

top-down approach *See* structured approach.

touchscreen An input device wherein the user simply touches a part of the screen to enter information. (Chapter 2)

transaction processing system (TPS) Converting raw data into a usable, electronic form. (Chapter 9)

transaction screen A screen on which the user enters actual income and expenses. (Chapter 6)

transactional processing Data are processed as they occur at the time of entry— e.g., grocery checkout systems. (Chapter 9)

transistors Solid-state elements on a chip that carry out the control and logic operations. (Chapter 2)

tree structure *See* hierarchical structure.

typeover mode *See* replace mode.

UNIX Originally developed for use on minicomputers, a multiple-machine, multitasking generic operating system converted to work on PCs. (Chapter 4)

uploaded The process of shifting software or data from a personal computer to a central computer. (Chapter 8)

upper memory The 384 bytes above conventional memory up to 1 Mbyte. Upper memory is normally reserved for software that is required for hardware devices, such as monitors or network linkages. (Chapter 2)

user friendly A software package that is easy to use. (Chapter 3)

user interface Allows the software user to enter data and commands. The three most common are menu driven, command driven, and graphical. (Chapter 3)

user's manual A set of directions for the use of software packages. (Chapter 3)

utility software Software that controls the computer's day-to-day housekeeping operations. (Chapter 3)

value A number, either positive or negative, with or without a decimal. (Chapter 6)

value-added network (VAN) Public networks available by subscription to provide clients with data communications facilities. (Chapter 8)

variable expense Expense that tend to fluctuate from month to month. (Chapter 6)

video disk A read-only form of secondary storage using a laser or an optical disk. (Chapter 2)

video display terminal (VDT) Any personal computer or terminal tied into a mainframe that uses a cathode ray tube (CRT) to echo input and display output. (Chapters 2 and 10)

Video Graphics Array (VGA) An analog graphics adaptor that will display 256 colors in 640 × 480 resolution as well as displaying high-quality text. (Chapter 5)

video page The amount of word processing text that can actually be seen on the screen. (Chapter 5)

videotex The process of shopping, banking, or managing stocks and bonds from the home using a computer and a communications link. (Chapter 8)

virtual reality Input devices dependent on artificial intelligence that seek to make computer and human interaction transparent in order to create a custom universe within a computer. (Chapter 10)

voice-grade transmissions A slow type of information transmission that generally uses twisted pairs as a media device. (Chapter 8)

voice recognition systems A form of input to computers that uses the spoken word to enter data and instructions; also called **voice input.** (Chapter 2)

volatile Computer memory that exists only while there is power to the computer or while the user is connected to a mainframe. (Chapter 2)

wide area network (WAN) A network covering more than a single building. (Chapters 3 and 8)

wildcard search In word processing, a search for a word when only part of the word is known. (Chapter 5)

window A section of the monitor screen that is set aside by the software package to display a specific portion of output. (Chapters 3 and 6)

wireless LANs Local area networks that use radio waves rather than wires for transmission of data. (Chapter 8)

word processing software Software designed to manipulate letters, digits, and punctuation marks to compose letters, papers, and documents. (Chapters 3 and 5)

word wrap The word processing function that causes words that fall outside the right margin to be moved to the next line. (Chapter 5 and ASCII Symbols)

worksheet A computer spreadsheet. (Chapter 6)

workstation A terminal tied into a mainframe or minicomputer or a personal computer that allows a worker to process information. (Chapter 1)

WYSIWYG (What You See Is What You Get) A function of word processing that allows the user to see on the screen exactly what will be printed. (Chapter 5)

x-terminal A special type of workstation which uses high-resolution graphics to display subscripts and special symbols on the screen. (Chapter 3)

INDEX

Numbers in italics indicate boxed inserts.

R

RAM-resident program, 118–119
random-access memory (RAM), 43, 52, 55,
    58, 314–316
    definition of, 43
    information storage, 55, 58
read-only memory (ROM), 43, 52, 55, 58
    in booting process, 43, 103
    definition of, 43
read/write head, 45, 56
real field, 200
real time conference, 247
real-time processing, 264
record(s),
    defined, 194
    listing, 198–200
    sorting of, 202–204
reel-to-reel magnetic tape, 45
Regional Consortium for Education and
    Technology, *300*
relational data model, 209–212
    data dictionary, 211
    example of, 210–212
    flat files, 209
    operations with, 211–212
report generator, 198, 201
resolution, 140, 143, 145
reverse video, 170
RGB monitor. *See* red, green, blue monitor
right justification, 128–129
ring network, 231
robotics, 22–23, 290–291
    future of, 291
robots. *See* robotics
ROM. *See* read-only memory

S

San Mateo County, *175*
scanner, 155
scatter diagrams, 146, 332
secondary storage, 40, 45, 47, 58
    backups for, 47
    cartridge tape, 47
    disk, 45, 56–60, 64
    disk packs, 45
    floppy disks, 45, 52, 58, 56–60
    hard disks, 45, 52
    as input device, 49–51
    microfloppy disks, 45, 56–60
    optical media, 45–56, 58
    reel-to-reel magnetic tape, 45, 47
    selecting, 156–161
    tape, 45, 58
    terminology, 45–47
    video disk, 45
    sectors, 57, 58
    See also crime, computer privacy
semiconductor. *See* integrated circuits
sequential access file organization, 230
sequential access storage device, 47, 230
serial form, 239
serial port, 239
shareware, 93
silicon chip. *See* Chips
simplex mode, 243
smart machines, 7–8, 20, *288*, 289
soft sectoring, 57
software, 13, *70*, 71–94
    agricultural applications, *70*, 71

applications, 72, 76–92
    command driven, 78, 81
    data base management, 80, 88–89, 197,
        200
    defined, 13, 71
    development process, 281–285
    downloading, 247
    future of, 302
    graphical user interface (GUI) for, 80–81
    graphics, 138, 140, 145–150
    history of, *94*
    importance of, 71
    inexpensive, 93
    integrated, 90–91, 178–237
    menu driven, 78–82, 106
    operating system and, 72–75, *100*, 103
    personal computer and, 82–93
    personal productivity, 82
    piracy, 293
    public domain, 93
    selecting, 312–316
    shareware, 93
    softer, 305
    support, 156
    systems, 72–75
    telecommunications and, 90, 93, 239,
        248
    types of, 72
    uploading of, 147
    utility, 75–76
    word processing, 82, 84, 127–196
software packages,
    business accounting, 82, 88, 164, 183–245
    data base management, 80, 82, 88,
        192–218, *200*
    desktop publishing, 92, *126*, 150–156
    financial analysis, 86–87, 162–164
    graphics, 84–86, 138, 140, 142–150,
        151
    integrated, 90–91, 178–180
    personal budgeting, 88, 180–241
    purchasing guide, 93
    spreadsheet, 86–87, *163*, *175*, 165–241,
        186
    telecommunications, 82, 90, 244
    terminology, 77
    user friendly, 78
    word processing, 82–84, *132*, 127–137
sorting procedures, 89, 202–203
    example of, 202–203
    indexing, 202
    pointer system, 202–203
special purpose computer, 19
spreadsheet, 86–87, *163*, *175*, 165–241,
    186
    analysis, 86–87, 171, 172
    cell, 86, 168
    cell identifier, 170
    cell pointer, 168
    column, 86, 168
    copy command, 172
    edit line, 168–169
    electronic, 171
    as electronic gradebook, *175*
    formatting, 174
    formula, 86, 169
    functions, 172, 175
    global change, 169

    graphics, 146–147, 174
    and health costs, *175*
    history of, 165, *186*
    horizontal scrolling, 175
    in Kuwait, *162*
    label, 168
    local change, 327
    Lotus 1-2-3, 82, 87, 146, 162, 165, *171*,
        173–232, 176, 186
macro, 176
    Quattro Pro, 87
    range, 172
    relative copy, 173
    row, 86, 168
    template, 332
    uses of, 86–87, *163*, 164, 173, *175*
    value, 168
    VisiCalc, 165, 169, *186*
    What If? questions, 167–226
    windows in, 172, 175
Starlight Express, 33
start bit, 241–242
stop bit, 242
strategic decisions, 263
strategic information system (SIS),
    267–268
structured approach, 272
Structured Query Language (SQL),
    214
subdirectories, 108
SuperCalc, 165
super VGA video system, 145
supercomputer, 14, 18, 25, 138
superconductivity, 302
symbol processors, 127
system,
    boundary, 259
    computer, 256
    defined, 259
    environment, 259
    feedback, 259
    input, 259
    output, 259
    processing, 259
system design, 277
systems analysis and design, 268–281
acquisition/programming, 278–279
    data flow diagrams, 275–276
    design and, 277
    direct conversion, 279
    feasibility study, 273–274
    implementation, 279–280
    life cycle analysis, 272
    logical definition, 275–276
    maintenance, 280–281
    parallel conversion, 279
    problem definition, 273
    process of, 268–269
    program development and, 281–285
    steps in, 272–273
    systems flowchart, 277–278
    See also specific systems
systems analyst, 269–270
systems development life cycle. *See* systems
    analysis and design
systems flowchart, 277–278
    symbols, 278
systems life cycle. *See* systems analysis and
    design
systems software, 73–75